THE CAMBRIDGE COMPANION TO LITERATURE AND ECONOMICS

In recent years, money, finance, and the economy have emerged as central topics in literary studies. *The Cambridge Companion to Literature and Economics* explains the innovative critical methods that scholars have developed to explore the economic concerns of texts ranging from the medieval period to the present. Across seventeen chapters by leading experts in various fields, the book highlights how, throughout literary history, economic matters have intersected with crucial topics including race, gender, sexuality, nation, empire, and the environment. It also explores how researchers in other disciplines are turning to literature and literary theory for insights into economic questions. Combining thorough historical coverage with attention to emerging issues and approaches, this book will appeal to literary scholars and to historians and social scientists interested in the literary and cultural dimensions of economics.

Paul Crosthwaite is a senior lecturer in the Department of English Literature at the University of Edinburgh.

Peter Knight is Professor of American Studies at the University of Manchester.

Nicky Marsh is a professor of twentieth-century literary studies at the University of Southampton and Director of the Southampton Institute for Arts and Humanities (SIAH).

T0381626

THE CAMBRIDGE COMPANION TO LITERATURE AND ECONOMICS

EDITED BY

PAUL CROSTHWAITE

University of Edinburgh

PETER KNIGHT

University of Manchester

NICKY MARSH

University of Southampton

CAMBRIDGE
UNIVERSITY PRESS

CAMBRIDGE
UNIVERSITY PRESS

University Printing House, Cambridge CB2 8BS, United Kingdom

One Liberty Plaza, 20th Floor, New York, NY 10006, USA

477 Williamstown Road, Port Melbourne, VIC 3207, Australia

314–321, 3rd Floor, Plot 3, Splendor Forum, Jasola District Centre, New Delhi – 110025, India

103 Penang Road, #05–06/07, Visioncrest Commercial, Singapore 238467

Cambridge University Press is part of the University of Cambridge.

It furthers the University's mission by disseminating knowledge in the pursuit of education, learning, and research at the highest international levels of excellence.

www.cambridge.org
Information on this title: www.cambridge.org/9781316515754
DOI: 10.1017/9781009026550

First published 2022

A catalogue record for this publication is available from the British Library.

ISBN 978-1-316-51575-4 Hardback
ISBN 978-1-009-01299-7 Paperback

Contents

Contributors

David Alderson is Professor of Literary and Cultural Studies at the University of Manchester and has written extensively on gender, sexuality, and the neoliberal transition. He is the author of *Sex, Needs, and Queer Culture* (2016), and coeditor of *For Humanism: Explorations in Theory and Politics* (2017). He is currently working on a project on culture and the political economy of the family.

Jens Beckert is Professor of Sociology and a director of the Max Planck Institute for the Study of Societies in Cologne. He is the author, most recently, of *Imagined Futures: Fictional Expectations and Capitalist Dynamics* (2016) and coeditor, with Richard Bronk, of *Uncertain Futures: Imaginaries, Narratives, and Calculation in the Economy* (2018).

Craig E. Bertolet is Professor of English at Auburn University. He is the author of *Chaucer, Gower, Hoccleve, and the Commercial Practices of Late Fourteenth-Century London* (2013). He has coedited, with Robert Epstein, *Money, Commerce, and Economics in Late Medieval English Literature* (2018). His articles have appeared in *Studies in the Age of Chaucer*, *Chaucer Review*, and *Studies in Philology*, among others. He is at present working on a book on money in late medieval English literature.

Richard Bronk is author of *The Romantic Economist: Imagination in Economics* (2009) and coeditor, with Jens Beckert, of *Uncertain Futures: Imaginaries, Narratives, and Calculation in the Economy* (2018). He worked for seventeen years in the City of London – as a European equity fund manager and an adviser at the Bank of England. From 2000, he taught political economy in the European Institute at the London School of Economics, where he was a Visiting Senior Fellow until 2020.

E. J. Clery is Professor of English Literature at Uppsala University. Her publications include *The Rise of Supernatural Fiction, 1762–1800* (1995); *Women's Gothic from Clara Reeve to Mary Shelley* (2000); *The Feminization Debate in Eighteenth-Century England: Literature, Commerce, and Luxury* (2004); *Jane Austen: The Banker's Sister* (2017); and *Eighteen Hundred and Eleven: Poetry, Protest, and Economic Crisis* (2017), awarded the British Academy Rose Mary Crawshay Prize. She teaches and researches eighteenth-century and Romantic-era literature, book history, and the cultural history of economics.

Sarah Comyn is a Lecturer and Ad Astra Fellow in the School of English, Drama, and Film at University College Dublin. Recent publications include *Political Economy and the Novel: A Literary History of "Homo Economicus"* (2018), *Early Public Libraries and Colonial Citizenship in the British Southern Hemisphere* (with Lara Atkin, Porscha Fermanis, and Nathan Garvey; 2019), and *Worlding the South: Nineteenth-Century Literary Culture and the Southern Settler Colonies* (coedited with Porscha Fermanis; 2021).

Liam Connell is Principal Lecturer in Literature at the University of Brighton. He is the author of *Precarious Labour and the Contemporary Novel* (2017). His research interests include the representations of gender and the global divisions of labor within contemporary culture.

Paul Crosthwaite is a senior lecturer in the Department of English Literature at the University of Edinburgh. He is the author of *The Market Logics of Contemporary Fiction* (2019) and *Trauma, Postmodernism, and the Aftermath of World War II* (2009); coauthor of *Invested: How Three Centuries of Stock Market Advice Reshaped Our Money, Markets, and Minds* (2022); editor of *Criticism, Crisis, and Contemporary Narrative: Textual Horizons in an Age of Global Risk* (2010); and coeditor, with Peter Knight and Nicky Marsh, of *Show Me the Money: The Image of Finance, 1700 to the Present* (2014) and the book series Palgrave Studies in Literature, Culture, and Economics.

Laura Finch is an Assistant Professor in the Literature Section at the Massachusetts Institute of Technology, and her research focuses on twenty-first-century novels and finance. Her work has appeared in *American Literary History, Comparative Literature Studies*, the *Journal of American Studies*, the *Journal of Cultural Economy*, and *boundary2*.

Michael Germana is Professor of English at West Virginia University. His research examines how technologies of racialization are inseparable from prevailing ideas about money and time. He is the author of

Standards of Value: Money, Race, and Literature in America (2009) and *Ralph Ellison, Temporal Technologist* (2018).

Peter Knight is Professor of American Studies at the University of Manchester. He researches conspiracy theories and the cultural studies of finance, and is the author of *Reading the Market: Genres of Financial Capitalism in Gilded Age America* (2019) and coauthor of *Invested: How Three Centuries of Stock Market Advice Reshaped Our Money, Markets, and Minds* (2022). Together with Paul Crosthwaite and Nicky Marsh, he curated the "Show Me the Money" exhibition, and edits the book series Palgrave Studies in Literature, Culture, and Economics.

David Landreth is Associate Professor of English at the University of California, Berkeley. He is the author of *The Face of Mammon: The Matter of Money in English Renaissance Literature* (2012), and of several articles and chapters addressing the changing conditions of material value in early modern literature and culture. His new work considers less material forms of value, such as glory and charity, which early modern writers draw from the medieval and classical past.

Nicky Marsh is a professor of twentieth-century literary studies at the University of Southampton and Director of the Southampton Institute for Arts and Humanities (SIAH). She is the author of *Credit Culture: The Politics of Money in the American Novel of the 1970s* (2020), *Money, Speculation, and Finance in Contemporary British Fiction* (2007), and *Democracy in Contemporary US Women's Poetry* (2007). She is coauthor of *Invested: How Three Centuries of Stock Market Advice Reshaped Our Money, Markets, and Minds* (2022). She is also coeditor, with Paul Crosthwaite and Peter Knight, of *Show Me the Money: The Image of Finance, 1700 to the Present* (2014) and the book series Palgrave Studies in Literature, Culture, and Economics.

Gary Saul Morson is the Lawrence B. Dumas Professor of the Arts and Humanities and a Professor in the Slavic Languages and Literatures Department at Northwestern University. His books include *The Long and the Short of It: From Aphorism to Novel* (2012) and *Narrative and Freedom: The Shadows of Time* (1994). He and Morton Schapiro are the authors of *Minds Wide Shut: How the New Fundamentalisms Divide Us* (2021) and *Cents and Sensibility: What Economics Can Learn from the Humanities* (2017).

Cheryl Narumi Naruse is Assistant Professor of English and the Mellon Assistant Professor in the Humanities at Tulane University. Her research and teaching interests include Anglophone literatures from Asia and the Pacific, diasporic Asian literature, post-colonial theory, and genre studies. She is completing a book manuscript on the literary/cultural production of Singapore as global Asia as it relates to the history of postcolonial capitalism.

Morton Schapiro has been Professor of Economics and President of Northwestern University since 2009, after serving in similar roles at Williams College. He and Gary Saul Morson are the authors of *Minds Wide Shut: How the New Fundamentalisms Divide Us* (2021) and *Cents and Sensibility: What Economics Can Learn from the Humanities* (2017). In 2010 he was elected a fellow of the American Academy of Arts and Sciences, and in 2017 he was elected to the National Academy of Education.

Matt Seybold is Associate Professor of American Literature and Mark Twain Studies at Elmira College, as well as scholar-in-residence at the Center for Mark Twain Studies, editor of MarkTwainStudies.org, and host of *The American Vandal Podcast*. He coedited *The Routledge Companion to Literature and Economics* (2018) and a 2019 special issue of *American Literary History* on "Economics and American Literary Studies in the New Gilded Age." Recent publications can be found in *Aeon, American Studies, Mark Twain Annual, Leviathan, The Los Angeles Review of Books*, and *The Johns Hopkins Guide to Critical and Cultural Theory*.

Stephen Shapiro teaches in the Department of English and Comparative Literary Studies at the University of Warwick. Recent work includes *Pentecostal Modernism: Lovecraft, Los Angeles, and World-Systems Culture* (with Philip Barnard; 2017); *Neoliberalism and Contemporary American Literature* (edited with Liam Kennedy; 2019); and *World Literature, Neoliberalism, and the Culture of Discontent* (edited with Sharae Deckard; 2019). Work-in-progress includes *The Cultural Fix: Capital, Social Labor-Power, and the Long Spiral* and *Neoliberalism, Data Capitalism, and Cultures of the Intersectional Left*.

Jo Lindsay Walton is a Research Fellow in Critical and Cultural Theory at the Sussex Humanities Lab. His other writing about SFF and economics includes "Computing Utopia: The Horizons of Computational Economies in History and Science Fiction," coauthored with Elizabeth Stainforth, in *Science Fiction Studies* (2019), and "Estranged Entrepreneurs and the Meaning of Money in Cory Doctorow's *Down and Out in the Magic Kingdom*" in *Foundation*

(2020). He is the also the author of the fantasy novel *Invocation* (2013) and the coauthor, with Polina Levontin and Jana Kleinberg, of *Visualizing Uncertainty: An Introduction* (2020). Currently, he is editing *Utopia on the Tabletop*, a collection about tabletop roleplaying games.

Introduction
The Interwovenness of Literature and Economics
Paul Crosthwaite, Peter Knight, and Nicky Marsh

On the face of it, literature and economics might seem remote from – even antithetical to – one another. Literature is conventionally thought of as the realm of imagination and introspection, of alternate worlds and psychological and spiritual insights – a space apart from workaday life, one in which aesthetic values of beauty, truth, and expressive power hold sway. Economics, meanwhile, is typically viewed as confining itself to the brute facts of scarce resources and basic human wants, to measurement and quantification, and to hard-headed, rational calculation of means and ends. A huge body of scholarship, however, has established the extent to which literature and economics are in fact mutually constitutive phenomena. Scholars have shown that what now look like the separate domains of "the literary" and "the economic" emerged from a shared nexus of discourses and practices and intertwined systems of inscription and value. And they have highlighted how, even as literature and economics have taken on the appearance of discrete categories, the two fields of study have continued to shape one another's language and rhetoric and habits of thought and behavior in myriad ways. Indeed, the very incongruity of the two fields as they are conventionally conceived today is a product of their imbricated histories, and speaks to the extent to which their mutually constitutive relationship has been a relationship of mutual disavowal: historically (and especially in the wake of literary Romanticism), many poets, playwrights, novelists, and critics – as well as economists and businesspeople – have been inclined to define the literary precisely as that which is most sharply distinct from the economic, even as such a definition has been belied by the multiple points of contact across this ostensible "divide."[1]

Long an important subject of scholarly interest, the relationship between literature and economics has, since the global financial crisis of 2007–2008, emerged as one of the key areas of critical inquiry not only in literary studies, but also in the wider humanities, and indeed various

I

branches of the social sciences, including economics itself. The "credit crunch" not only prompted an outpouring of novels, plays, and poems concerned with the relations between household debt, precarious work, real estate transactions, and derivatives markets (a corpus of "crunch lit" examined in several prominent critical studies);[2] it also made starkly apparent the disastrous simplifications and distortions inherent to the theories and models developed by mainstream economists and operationalized by banks, hedge funds, regulators, and other financial institutions and actors. In a manner that could hardly have been more spectacular, the crisis demonstrated that the study of economic processes cannot be the exclusive purview of the economics profession and must instead be brought (back) into contact with other disciplines. Given the crucial roles of representational models, ideological narratives, and multiple forms of rhetoric, discourse, and mediation in normalizing the exploitative and risk-laden practices that led to the crash, the analytical tools of literary studies (and the wider humanities) have vitally important contributions to make to this interdisciplinary project. The devastating effects on livelihoods due to the Coronavirus pandemic that began in early 2020 have further highlighted the need to reconceive the fundamental bases on which key economic categories – labor, value, markets, risk, security – are premised.

Across seventeen chapters by leading scholars in various fields, this book offers an authoritative guide to the interrelations of literature and economics from the medieval period to the present. It explores the various critical and theoretical paradigms via which these interrelations have been analyzed, and engages with the historical, conceptual, and methodological questions that have been at the forefront of the field in recent years. If literary critics are increasingly fascinated by economic questions, then they are in many ways merely catching up with a central and abiding concern of imaginative writing itself across the centuries. As the following chapters make clear, at the core of many of literary history's most significant works are deep and complex engagements with economic systems – from early medieval gift exchange codes to the monetary regimes of the early modern period to the eighteenth- and nineteenth-century financial and industrial revolutions; and from the shopping emporia of the modern metropolis to the migrant labor routes, corporate structures, and financial trading platforms that define the economic conditions of the present. Literary representations of these major economic phenomena (as well as many others) figure prominently in this collection volume. Such representations display what Christopher Newfield calls "literary knowledge of economy": a mode of understanding, analysis, and (often) critique of the relations between

economic systems and structures and subjective experiences and perceptions that is peculiar to fiction, drama, poetry, and other strands of
imaginative writing.[3] Such knowledge is manifest in literary texts' variously
thematic, stylistic, formal, and generic features, and can be extrapolated by
literary and cultural critics in turning their attention to economic texts,
discourses, representations, and practices that are not – obviously or
narrowly – "literary" but have crucial rhetorical, semiotic, narrative, and
imaginative dimensions.

In this Introduction, we identify the key ways in which literature and
literary criticism offer singularly insightful cognizance of economic forms
and processes. We first consider how literary texts encode economic
knowledge in metaphorical – and more broadly figurative or tropological –
uses of economic vocabulary, and via styles and forms that stand in a
"homological" relation to monetary and financial systems. We then explain
how critics have understood the ongoing overlaps between literature and
economics as "genres" of writing, which have continued to borrow conventions from one another, even as the discipline of economics has become
increasingly technical and mathematical. We next address the ways in
which literary texts register the economic pressures to which they are most
directly exposed: namely, the pressures of literary consumption and the
literary marketplace. And we close by showing how social scientists are
increasingly turning to literature and literary studies for economic insights,
and by highlighting the emergence of the economic humanities as an
interdisciplinary research field to which the approaches covered in this
book have made defining contributions.

Language and Form

A significant body of scholarship has detailed the ways in which literary
texts register economic conditions in their figurative use of rhetorics of
money, commerce, and exchange, or in their adoption of formal patterns
structurally homologous to economic phenomena of multiple kinds and
scales. "Money," Marc Shell has asserted, "talks in and through discourse"
and the "monetary information of thought" cannot be "eradicated" without "changing thought itself, within whose tropes and processes the
language of wares ... is an ineradicable participant."[4] Shell's emphasis
on the relationship between money and language/thought can be read
back into the move within literary theory from structuralism to poststructuralism. A recognition of parallels between money and language was
evident in some of structuralism's most important early works, including

both Georg Simmel's writing about money and Ferdinand de Saussure's writing about language. When Simmel described money as "colourless" and Saussure described language as "unmotivated," for example, both were pointing to a process by which monetary or linguistic meaning – which each tellingly termed "value" – was given through processes of selection and substitution.[5] Saussure compared language and money because both were symbols of relational value without fixed or inherent meaning: "it is not the metal in a piece of money that fixes its value," Saussure noted, because its "value varies according to the effigy it bears." Such considerations were "even more pertinent to linguistic signals," which were "constituted solely by the differences which distinguish one sound pattern from another."[6] Saussure's formulation of how we arrive at meaning was echoed by his contemporary Simmel, for whom money was like language, an abstract and relational form, which possessed a "relativity [that] creates the value of objects in an objective sense, because only through relativity are things placed at a distance from the subject."[7] Money and language were thus both general equivalents, involving a move from content (the particular note or word) to form and structure (the relational structure through which the note or word was given its abstracted meaning). Simmel, in particular, confirmed Karl Marx's analysis of the reification that this phenomenon implies when he suggested that money was "nothing but the pure form of exchangeability."[8]

The implications of this apparently homologous relationship between money and language for literary theory received their fullest exploration in poststructuralist and postmodernist criticism.[9] One of the first forays into the field was Jacques Derrida's essay "White Mythology," published in French in 1971 and in English in 1974, which connected the "truth" effaced by Friedrich Nietzsche's coin in a famous metaphor to the structural "value" realized by Saussure's coin in order to suggest a theory of difference that could deconstruct the metaphysical opposition of the material and the immaterial.[10] The reiteration of the shared emptiness of money and language, universal signifiers unmoored from any material referent, was frequently repeated through the 1980s and 1990s, although the political implications and historical specificity of the homology did not remain static. For Marxist critics such as David Harvey, Fredric Jameson, and Brian Rotman, for example, the key historical moment was the ending of the gold standard in the early 1970s that allowed for the ascendancy of the postmodern floating signifier. The "breakdown of money as a secure means of representing value has itself created a crisis of representation in advanced capitalism," Harvey wrote, and this shift in turn signaled a crisis of political strategy and action because it is "hard to tell exactly what space we are in when it comes to assessing causes and effects, meanings or values."[11] For literary critics such as Jean-Joseph Goux, however, the crisis had already occurred some half a century earlier. Goux's focus was the coincidence of literary modernism and the World War I-era suspension of the gold standard in Europe: for him, the two breaks collectively signaled the loss of a psychodynamic paternal, rather than political, order. When money and language "come under attack," Goux suggests, then "all other values that regulate exchanges are questioned." "Gold, father, language, phallus" – these "structurally homologous general equivalents" – undergo a "fundamental crisis that is also the crisis of the novel as a genre."[12] The assigning of a sweeping meaning to the homologies between money and language, as Michael Tratner, Anna Tsing, and Joshua Clover have now variously suggested, risks confirming, rather than engaging with, the processes of financialization that are often their ostensible objects of critique.[13]

This homological analysis was also important for allowing a recognition of the role that language and the imagination played in both fictional and financial worlds. J. G. A. Pocock's recognition that the emergence of credit in eighteenth-century Britain was dependent upon the "investor's imagination" – as property itself, "the material foundation of both personality and government," had "ceased to be real and ... become not merely mobile but imaginary" – shaped the field of eighteenth-century literary studies, as E. J. Clery's chapter in this book comprehensively maps.[14] Yet this phenomenon is not restricted to the past. Joseph Vogl's *The Specter of Capital* (2010/2015), for example, gives an overview of the continued role that the spectral and phantasmatic have played in the material construction of an immaterial money, tracing a process that extends from the eighteenth century to the present. Vogl finds the "primal scene" for the "disquiet" surrounding money's relinquishment of the material in the inconvertibility of paper to gold occasioned by the British Bank Restriction Act of 1797, which formally announced the "equilibrium between signs and riches" and laid bare the "complex deal between the public and private, the economic and the legal" that money relied upon.[15] For Vogl, finance is dependent on a "paradoxical structure" in which paper money comes to represent "both the promise of a certain sum of money and the failure of that sum to materialize," and the financial culture that results is "focused less on acts of exchange" than on fantasies, projections, and predictions: "irritating factors of uncertainty, potential outlooks, and future expectations."[16]

Analysis of the Bank of England, as the robustly physical institution that presides over an immaterial and phantasmatic sector, has formed a fascinating subgenre of its own. In its most direct form, such as Martin Parker and Valerie Hamilton's *Daniel Defoe and the Bank of England: The Dark Arts of Projectors* (2016), the fiction of Defoe is read in parallel to the founding of the Bank because both "reflect and create a transformative shift in the operation of the imagination," which is able to conjure up new worlds, rather than merely replicate what already exists.[17] The Bank has also been used to explore the parallels between financial and aesthetic modes of exchange and value, a set of debates about speculation, worth, provenance, and utility that has often drawn more on fine art than literature. Neil Cummings and Marysia Lewandowska's *Capital* (2001), for example, places the Bank in conversation with the Tate. They suggest that the former regulates and underwrites our monetary and commodity markets and that the latter does the same with a "parallel 'symbolic economy' underwriting the integrity and value of the artworks in which it deals and thus ensuring the stability and health of a network of inter-connected relationships which constitute the art world."[18] The project is characteristic of the ways in which literary and cultural critics and theo-rists – as well as practitioners – have drawn parallels between the func-tioning of meaning and value in economic and aesthetic fields.

Genre and Rhetoric

Where some critics have identified convergence between literary and economic registers, others have focused on divergence. Mary Poovey's account of the emergence of the credit economy in Britain, for example, suggests that the genres of literary and economic writing separated from one another in the late eighteenth century, as writers from different traditions sought to manage the "troubling effects" of credit – the ability to "turn paper into gold and vice versa" – in very different ways. According to Poovey, the "genres associated with economic writing" established themselves as factual through recourse to the language of natural philoso-phy that made "market transactions seem as regular and as harmonious as nature." Fiction, conversely, sought to manage the same anxieties by "creating a non-factual form of representation that was nevertheless not a lie" and provided "safe forms in which writers could explore the troubling and exciting possibility that representation could always float free of its ground."[19]

Other economic historians have given a different emphasis to the distinction between factual and fictional writing. In key essays such as

"The Consequences of Rhetoric" (1988), Deirdre McCloskey, for example, pays close attention to the significance of the generic distinction between economic and literary registers of authority. For McCloskey, economics' disavowal of its own rhetorical tropes represents a failure because it blunts the ability of economists to fully register, and even stand to one side of, their own rhetorical dependencies: "to the sneer that learning rhetoric 'isn't economics' one can only point out that most of what economists do is reading. It would be like saying learning mathematics 'isn't economics' and then expect[ing] the economist denied mathematical sophistication to read and write well in mathematical theory."[20] For McCloskey, an analysis of rhetoric will make better economists, not only because they will be enriched by the humanist traditions of philosophy, literature, and the "better life," but also because those in the profession "cannot be honest about their arguments if they cannot see what they are."[21]

Yet where McCloskey sought to keep the economist "honest," and saw no tension between her embrace of a Chicago School neoclassical position and her embrace of literary theory, Philip Mirowski provided a more acerbically political critique of how the language of the natural sciences has shored up, rather than merely illustrated, the authority of conservative economics. For Mirowski, neoclassical economic theory depends upon a mathematical metaphor that "equates 'utility' with the potential energy of mid-nineteenth century physics. From Walras to Pareto to McCloskey the tendency has been to admit the metaphor in a coy and indirect manner, hedged about with the qualification that it is merely a matter of words, and therefore of no consequence to the evaluations of the content and significance of the theory."[22] For Mirowski, the physics metaphor gives economics the legitimacy of a natural science. It presents the economy itself as an entity that possesses the character of a "natural stable process" and bestows "differential ontological validity upon sets of social phenomena: the 'individual' is taken to be more real than any other social formation, be it the family, the firm, the nation-state, and so on."[23] Mirowski goes further than Poovey and McCloskey, then, in identifying economic writing's use of the natural sciences not only as a means of grounding its authority and casting off the suspicion to which its reliance on the imaginary has made it susceptible, but as also carrying a specific and marked political freight. Attending to the rhetoric of economics, that is, provides crucial insights into its politics.

Literary Production, Circulation, and Consumption

We have so far focused primarily on how imaginative writing shares generic, figurative, and discursive – that is, broadly textual – features with economic discourses and practices. But literature is also "economic" in more overtly material ways. Any work of literature – no matter how ostensibly far removed from worldly concerns – is tightly bound up with material conditions of production, circulation, and consumption. How do authors accrue the resources necessary to pursue their work? By what channels and in what physical forms are finished texts disseminated to their readership? And what kinds of economic transactions do readers enter into in order to access works of literature? Over the past few decades, scholars in literary studies – and allied fields, such as book history – have attended closely to such questions. They have argued persuasively that we cannot properly understand literary texts' forms, meanings, and functions outside of the economic relations in which they are enmeshed.

Scholars have paid particular attention to the phenomenon of literary patronage: both its historical prevalence and its distinctive twentieth- and twenty-first-century revivals. In medieval and early modern Europe, writers often relied on royal or aristocratic patrons for protection from legal censure and the award of stipends or administrative appointments, while their works might be confined to private performances at court or in noble households, or circulation in manuscript form among small groups of ecclesiastical or gentry readers.[24] Historians of literary modernism have highlighted the resurgence of a culture of patronage in the early twentieth century, as wealthy benefactors (typically female) supported avant-garde writers (typically male) in the sometimes protracted production of works whose formal and linguistic difficulty made them unpromising commercial propositions.[25] And in his influential study *The Program Era* (2009), Mark McGurl has argued that the rise of university-based creative writing pro-grams in the United States and elsewhere since the mid-twentieth century has created a literary patronage system of unprecedented scale.[26]

Much critical and historical research has addressed the emergence, through the eighteenth and nineteenth centuries, of the figure of the "professional" author, writing not in the service of an influential patron, but rather for an expanding literary marketplace populated by anonymous readers whose tastes demanded to be variously anticipated, satisfied, and reshaped.[27] As Nicky Marsh and Paul Crosthwaite explore in detail in their chapters for this volume, the question of literature's constitutive relation to the publishing industry and book trade has become particularly central to the study of modern and contemporary literature. Scholars have examined how modernist writers negotiated complex relationships not only with patrons, but also with publishers, editors, booksellers, and the media, and how they cultivated niche audiences of elite readers in order to differentiate their deliberately challenging or experimental writing from the "middle brow" and "mass market" segments of an increasingly stratified literary culture. Critics of contemporary literature are likewise seeking to reckon with the effects of the seismic economic and technological shifts – from publishing industry consolidation to the advent of e-books to the rise of Amazon to the "self-publishing revolution" – that have transformed how literature is written, sold, and read over recent decades.

Underlying much of this scholarship are concepts derived from the work of the French sociologist of culture Pierre Bourdieu. In his hugely influential study of French literary culture around the turn of the twentieth century, *The Rules of Art: Genesis and Structure of the Literary Field* (1992), Bourdieu argues that the "literary field" as a whole is divided into "subfields," dominant among them being the subfield of "large-scale production" – the sphere of "commercial" literature "oriented towards the satisfaction of the demands of a wide audience" and "dedicated and devoted to the market and profit." This sector coexists, however, with the "subfield of restricted production," which Bourdieu associates with the Aestheticists, Decadents, Symbolists, and other avant-garde groups. While "large-scale" literary producers simply fixate on accumulating material or economic capital – monetary profit – by selling books to the largest possible readership, those working in the "restricted" subfield draw on their "cultural capital" (erudition, knowledge, education) in order to accrue the "symbolic capital" of prestige or respect by pursuing an uncompromising artistic vision in defiance of prevailing market tastes.[28] As Marsh's and Crosthwaite's chapters suggest, the relations between such "sub-fields" – and the extent to which their dominant forms of capital are fungible or exchangeable – are central questions for the study of modern and contemporary literature.

Toward the Economic Humanities

In this Introduction we have seen how literature and literary critics have a long history of exploring economic ideas, narratives, and rhetoric, as well as the impact of market forces on literary production. From the other direction, however, a growing number of economists and other social scientists have begun to discover in literature's inherently imaginative and counterfactual qualities a crucial resource for theorizing the speculative, projective logics of capitalism.

As we have seen, although once closely related, the genres of economics and imaginative writing began to pull apart in the late eighteenth century and increasingly diverged through the nineteenth century. Economics turned to the language and logic of mathematics to make its arguments, but the two modes of knowledge have continued to shadow one another. The subfield of rhetorical economics, as discussed above, has revealed the often unacknowledged literary nature of economic writing. But even when the connections are more literal, they are still rarely acknowledged. While there are well-known examples of literary writers who maintained a day job in the world of finance (most notably T. S. Eliot in banking, and Wallace Stevens in insurance), less familiar is the fact that a number of prominent economists and economic forecasters also dabbled in literature. As Dominic Walker's research has demonstrated, "literary writing has often been a proving ground for new economic ideas."[29] For example, Stanley Jevons, the nineteenth-century economist whose work on marginalism paved the way for a more mathematical form of economics, wrote "endless novels with [himself] as the constant hero."[30] Similarly, his French contemporary Léon Walras sketched out the principles of his general equilibrium theory in a short story long before he became an economist. John Maynard Keynes, one of the towering figures of economics in the twentieth century, was a prolific writer of literary criticism and producer of plays, and was closely connected to the Bloomsbury Set of writers and artists.[31] Or, most recently, the economist Thomas Piketty's bestselling book *Capital in the Twenty-First Century* (2013) repeatedly turns to Jane Austen and Honoré de Balzac to help explain the idea of inherited wealth.

Even though the discipline of economics has increasingly relied on mathematics and physics, it has a long and continuing tradition of using parables and stories – and even works of literature – to explain some of its basic principles. Economists have returned repeatedly to Daniel Defoe's novel *Robinson Crusoe* (1719), for example, to naturalize the myth that money was invented as an improvement on barter exchange. Business schools sometimes draw examples from literary classics in their teaching. One book in this vein, for example, asserts that "literary works often describe human behavior and motivations more eloquently, powerfully, or humorously than economists typically do, even when dealing with economic subjects."[32] These studies of what might be called the "What Literature Can Teach Us about Capitalism" approach tend to be written by free market apologists with no training in literary studies, who merely mine literature for the character traits, plots, and morals that fit their pre-existing conclusions, with little concern for the political and historical context or aesthetic complexities of the literary works. Taken to the extreme, there is the fantasy that literature can even provide investment advice, with one financial advice blog, for example, explaining to readers "How Charles Dickens Changed My Investment Life."[33]

Some economists and business studies scholars have engaged more thoughtfully with literature. Mihir Desai's *The Wisdom of Finance: How the Humanities Can Illuminate and Improve Finance* (2017), uses insights from across the humanities – not only literature, but religion, classics, philosophy, critical theory, history, and popular culture – to explain the intellectual underpinnings of contemporary finance. Desai explains, for example, how an episode in Dashiell Hammett's *The Maltese Falcon* (1929) affords an insight into the nature of risk and probability in an uncertain world. Although Desai's readings of a wide variety of cultural texts are fascinating, ultimately his use of the humanities is instrumental. Literature and other arts are useful because they help show how finance involves not merely unthinking acquisitiveness, but a complex engagement with profound issues. Other scholars, however, have made a more conscious effort to avoid merely placing literature in the service of economics. The chapter by Gary Saul Morson and Morton Schapiro in the present volume (as well as their two book-length studies on which it draws) is the result of a collaboration between an economist and a literary scholar. As they explain, their aim was to resist the idea that either economics or the humanities should lay claim imperialistically to the other's core domain of knowledge. In their view, although economists are very good at providing rigorous, evidence-based analysis that avoids politicized grandstanding, they often fail to acknowledge that life is unpredictable and complicated. In contrast, great writers (especially the classic realist novelists of the nineteenth century) can show how a life is actually lived, making sense of their characters' motivations and moral choices, especially the tensions between rationality and emotion. Morson and Schapiro conclude that "learning from literature, philosophy, and the other humanities, along with history, sociology, anthropology, psychology, and political science, may lead economists to develop more realistic models of human behavior." This is an important rallying cry for the value of the humanities, but it raises two issues. First, it still suggests that the role of these other disciplines is merely to improve economics, rather than to challenge it fundamentally. And second, is it only the classic realist novel that can provide an insight into economic ideas and behaviors? As several critics have argued (see, for example, Laura Finch's, Liam Connell's, and Jo Lindsay Walton's chapters in this volume), nonrealist writing – including speculative fiction and poetry – can help to defamiliarize the ideological assumptions of economics that have come to seem natural.

Instead of reading individual works of literature for the insights that they give into behavioral psychology, some economists have proposed alternative ways that the discipline can learn from the humanities. Robert Shiller (the Nobel-prize-winning economist) and Mervyn King (the former governor of the Bank of England) have each recommended what they term "narrative economics" as a way to improve economics in the wake of its catastrophic failure to predict the global financial crash of 2007–2008.[34] Shiller insists that "ideas from other disciplines need to be added to economics. High on this list of disciplines are the humanities, like history and literature."[35] Although Shiller does point to narratology, his version of narrative economics ultimately has little to do with the kind of knowledge that literature and literary analysis might provide. His focus is, rather, on the way that stories go viral. For Shiller, "narrative" is a capacious category that includes rumors, memes, speculative bubbles, and advertising hype, as well as economic ideas and larger cultural narratives. Despite suggesting that literature and history are the disciplines that have the most to offer economics, it is in fact epidemiology that Shiller draws on most often, because, he claims, narratives spread in the same way as epidemic diseases. Whereas few scholars in the humanities today subscribe to what has long been dismissed as the "hypodermic needle" theory of mass communication, in which ideas infect an individual's mind with little chance for resistance, Shiller takes the metaphor of the viral spread of ideas quite literally. The appeal by a prominent economist for a more interdisciplinary approach to economics is, though, welcome – as Morson and Schapiro point out, fewer than half of academic economists believe they can learn from other fields. Yet interdisciplinarity engagement is not a one-way street: the ideas and the methods of the humanities need to be taken seriously in their own right.

A more promising approach to bridging the gap between literature and economics is represented by the chapter by Jens Beckert and Richard Bronk in this book, which involves a collaboration between an economic sociologist and an intellectual and literary historian (and former financial analyst). Beckert and Bronk note that capitalist markets are "dynamic, socially embedded, and indeterminate systems characterized by relentless innovation and novelty." Given that the future is radically uncertain, we all rely on imaginative projections and persuasive narratives as much as calculation in making our economic decisions. These "fictional expectations" (in contrast to the "rational expectations" more usually assumed in economics) operate in a similar way to the *as if* construction of a literary text and the reader's willing suspension of disbelief. Literature and literary theory are therefore necessary to help make sense of the fictional expectations of future-oriented finance. Like fiction, speculative economic projects manage to create unreal worlds that nevertheless can become self-fulfilling prophecies, helping bring into being the world they imagine. Beckert and Bronk also argue that narratives and imaginaries underpin not only the individual financial projections that we find in, say, a corporate prospectus, but also the broader narratives that structure beliefs and behavior about markets in different societies and historical periods. To understand how these kinds of narratives work, Beckert and Bronk advocate turning to ideas from literary studies, such as theories of affect, imagination, deconstruction, and performativity. This kind of work is already beginning to happen. For example, the economic sociologist Donald Mackenzie has persuasively demonstrated in *An Engine, Not a Camera* (2006) that the detailed models of financial theory, such as the Black-Scholes-Merton option pricing theory, *performatively* create the market that they claim objectively to model.[36] However, as Judith Butler has noted, it is important to remember that the "performance" created by those financial models is not inevitable and final (as some of the studies of the "black box of finance" suggest), but is open to wider political contestation.[37]

   In this Introduction we have outlined key ways in which scholars have thought about the relationship between literature and economics. In concluding, we want to propose the Economic Humanities as a productive way forward. The Economic Humanities involves an expansive mode of research that is needed to tackle the complex, global challenges that beset us, in a similar vein to the Medical Humanities, the Digital Humanities, and, most recently, the Environmental Humanities. The latter is the most useful comparison, because the Economic Humanities, like the Environmental Humanities, challenges the assumption that the world's problems are best left to scientific and technical experts. The economy, like the environment, involves a complex interweaving of material processes, political struggles, conceptual paradigms, and emotional narratives. The Environmental Humanities is also a useful model for the Economic Humanities because it has shown the necessity of the creative arts in helping us not merely to defamiliarize the world we think we know, but also to imagine a world otherwise. The aim of the Economic Humanities, then, is to shed light on the stories, images, ideas, and technologies that actively constitute what we call "the economy." Literature and literary studies will play important parts in this project, which also needs to involve other humanities and related disciplines, from history to anthropology, and philosophy to musicology. We hope that this book will help readers to grasp the shape and significance of this developing field, and to envision its future directions.

Notes

1 On these patterns of affiliation and disavowal in the Romantic era, see Philip Connell, *Romanticism, Economics, and the Question of "Culture"* (Oxford: Oxford University Press, 2005).

2 See Liam Connell, *Precarious Labour and the Contemporary Novel* (London: Palgrave Macmillan, 2017); Paul Crosthwaite, *The Market Logics of Contemporary Fiction* (Cambridge: Cambridge University Press, 2019); Arne De Boever, *Finance Fictions: Realism and Psychosis in a Time of Economic Crisis* (New York: Fordham University Press, 2018); Annie McClanahan, *Dead Pledges: Debt, Crisis, and Twenty-First-Century Culture* (Stanford: Stanford University Press, 2016); Katy Shaw, *Crunch Lit* (London: Bloomsbury, 2015); Alison Shonkwiler, *The Financial Imaginary: Economic Mystification and the Limits of Realist Fiction* (Minneapolis: University of Minnesota Press, 2017).

3 See Christopher Newfield, "What Is Literary Knowledge of Economy?" in *The Routledge Companion to Literature and Economics*, edited by Matt Seybold and Michelle Chihara (New York: Routledge, 2019), 15–26.

4 Marc Shell, *Money, Language, and Thought: Literary and Philosophic Economies from the Medieval to the Modern Era* (Baltimore: Johns Hopkins University Press, 1982), 180–181.

5 Ferdinand de Saussure, *Course in General Linguistics*, translated by Roy Harris (1916; Chicago: Open Court, 2001), 132; Georg Simmel, *The Philosophy of Money*, translated by Tom Bottomore and David Frisby (1900; London: Routledge & Kegan Paul, 1978), 238.

6 Saussure, *Course in General Linguistics*, 117.

7 Simmel, *Philosophy of Money*, 78.

8 Ibid., 138.

9 Such approaches were central to Martha Woodmansee and Mark Osteen's landmark collection *The New Economic Criticism: Studies at the Interface of Literature and Economics* (London: Routledge, 1999).

10 Jacques Derrida, "White Mythology: Metaphor in the Text of Philosophy," translated by F. C. T. Moore, *New Literary History* 6.1 (1974), 5–74.

11 David Harvey, *The Condition of Postmodernity: An Enquiry into the Origins of Cultural Change* (Oxford: Blackwell, 1989), 298.

12 Jean-Joseph Goux, *The Coiners of Language*, translated by Jennifer Curtiss Gage (1984; Norman: University of Oklahoma Press, 1994), 4.

13 Anna Tsing, "The Global Situation," *Cultural Anthropology* 15.3(2000), 327–360; Michael Tratner, "Derrida's Debt to Milton Friedman," *New Literary History* 34.4 (2004), 791–806; Joshua Clover, *"Value | Theory | Crisis,"* *PMLA* 127.1 (2012), 107–114.

14 J. G. A. Pocock, *Virtue, Commerce, and History: Essays on Political Thought and History, Chiefly in the Eighteenth Century* (Cambridge: Cambridge University Press, 1985), 112.

15 Joseph Vogl, *The Specter of Capital*, translated by Joachim Redner and Robert Savage (2010; Stanford: Stanford University Press, 2014), 51.

16 Ibid.

17 Martin Parker and Valerie Hamilton, *Daniel Defoe and the Bank of England: The Dark Arts of Projectors* (London: Zero Books, 2016), 29.

18 Frances Morris, "Gift, Economy, Trust," in *Capital: A Project*, ed. Neil Cummings and Marysia Lewandowska (London: Tate Publishing, 2001), 11–12.

19 Mary Poovey, *Genres of the Credit Economy: Mediating Value in Eighteenth- and Nineteenth-Century Britain* (Chicago: University of Chicago Press, 2008), 6.

20 Deirdre McCloskey, "The Consequences of Rhetoric," *Fundamenta Scientiae* 9.2–3(1988), 269–284; 274.

21 Ibid., 275.

22 Philip Mirowski, "Shall I Compare Thee to a Monkowski – Ricardo – Leontief – Metzler Matrix of the Mosak-Hicks Type? Or, Rhetoric, Mathematics, and the Nature of Neoclassical Economic Theory," in *The Consequences of Economic Rhetoric*, edited by Arjo Klamer, Deirdre McCloskey, and Robert M. Solow (Cambridge: Cambridge University Press, 1988), 117–145; 136.

23 Ibid., 141.

24 See e.g. Elizabeth Salter, *English and International: Studies in the Literature, Art, and Patronage of Medieval England*, edited by Derek Pearsall and Nicolette Zeeman (Cambridge: Cambridge University Press, 1988); Richard A. McCabe, *"Ungainefull Arte:" Poetry, Patronage, and Print in the Early Modern Era* (Oxford: Oxford University Press, 2016); Graham Parry, "Literary Patronage," in *The Cambridge History of Early Modern English Literature*, edited by David Loewenstein and Janel Mueller (Cambridge: Cambridge University Press, 2002), 117–140; Dustin Griffin, *Literary Patronage in England, 1650–1800* (Cambridge: Cambridge University Press, 1996).

25 See Paul Delany, "Who Paid for Modernism?" in *The New Economic Criticism*, edited by Woodmansee and Osteen, 335–351; Joyce Piell Wexler, *Who Paid for Modernism? Art, Money, and the Fiction of Conrad, Joyce, and Lawrence* (Fayetteville: University of Arkansas Press, 1997).

26 Mark McGurl, *The Program Era: Postwar Fiction and the Rise of Creative Writing* (Cambridge, MA: Harvard University Press, 2009).

27 See Dustin Griffin, "The Rise of the Professional Author?" in *The Cambridge History of the Book in Britain, Vol. 5: 1695–1830*, edited by Michael F. Suarez,

S. J. and Michael L. Turner (Cambridge: Cambridge University Press, 2009), 132–145; George Justice, *The Manufacturers of Literature: Writing and the Literary Marketplace in Eighteenth-Century England* (Newark: University of Delaware Press, 2002); John O. Jordan and Robert L. Patten, eds., *Literature in the Marketplace: Nineteenth-Century British Publishing and Reading Practices* (Cambridge: Cambridge University Press, 1995).

28 Pierre Bourdieu, *The Rules of Art: Genesis and Structure of the Literary Field*, translated by Susan Emanuel (1992; Cambridge: Polity, 1996), 121, 220.

29 Dominic Walker, "Underwriting the Market: A Literary Genealogy of Modern Economic Thought," Leverhulme Early Career Research Fellowship, CRASSH, University of Cambridge, www.crassh.cam.ac.uk/peo ple/profile/dominic-walker.

30 W. S. Jevons, *Papers and Correspondence of William Stanley Jevons*, Vol. 1, edited by R. D. Collinson Black and Rosamond Koenekamp (London: Macmillan, 1972), 16.

31 Gilles Dostaler, *Keynes and His Battles*, translated by Niall B. Mann (Cheltenham: Edward Elgar, 2005), 229–241.

32 Michael Watts, ed., *The Literary Book of Economics: Literary Passages on Economic Concepts, Issues, and Themes* (Wilmington, DE: ISI Books), xxi.

33 Tim McAleenan, "How Charles Dickens Changed My Investment Life," http://theconservativeincomeinvestor.com/2013/10/12/how-charles-dickens-changed-my-investing-life/.

34 Robert J. Shiller, *Narrative Economics*, rev. ed. (Princeton: Princeton University Press, 2020); Mervyn King, *The End of Alchemy: Money, Banking, and the Future of the Global Economy* (New York: W. W. Norton, 2016).

35 Shiller, *Narrative Economics*, 16.

36 Donald MacKenzie, *An Engine Not a Camera: How Financial Models Shape Markets* (Cambridge, MA: Massachusetts Institute of Technology Press, 2006).

37 Judith Butler, "Performative Agency," *Journal of Cultural Economy* 3.2 (2010), 147–161.

PART I

Histories and Critical Traditions

CHAPTER I

Medieval Literature's Economic Imagination

Craig E. Bertolet

The changing structures of what we would now think of as "the economy" during the Middle Ages left deep and extensive marks on the period's cultures of writing and storytelling. And yet, surveying the economic imagination in medieval English literature encounters two challenges: one in supply and one in interpretation. In the case of supply, literary texts in English do not survive in continuous production from the first appearances of the language in written form in the seventh century to the establishment of the first printing press in England in the 1470s. The Norman Conquest imposed continental political models on native English systems and the Anglo-Norman dialect of French on the royal and judicial courts. English ceased to be a language of power in England until the fourteenth century. Some literary productions in English do survive from roughly 1100 to 1350, but not enough to provide consistent literary witnesses to changes in England's economy. Therefore, any examination of economic issues in English literature prior to the first visitation of the Black Death in 1348–1349 can provide only sporadic and idiosyncratic evidence.

The problem of interpretation is more complicated. Historically, economics in the Middle Ages has been read as a transition from feudalism to capitalism, with the focus on how capitalism evolved from different practices that coalesced over time into a coherent system.[1] This approach ignores the process for the result, which is unfortunate for two reasons: (1) Humans are not naturally clairvoyant – no one alive in any period of time is particularly certain how their practices will form a system in place 200 years after they are dead; and (2) it deemphasizes the necessity to understand those systems that were in place during the latter part of the medieval period when feudalism and manorialism were in operation.[2] The focus of this chapter will be on how English writers of the period roughly between 800 and 1500 imagined economic issues and not what these practices would become.

One last point of clarification is that economics takes many forms in these texts beyond simply the exchange of money for goods and services, the establishment of credit and banking, and the development of complex and varied trade networks. Economics appears in how a household is run, gift-exchange, and even the language of reckoning of sins with punishment or penance. This chapter will trace the ways in which canonical and noncanonical medieval writers used epic, satire, complaint, allegory, dream vision, mystery play, and other generic modes to explore the economic shifts that shaped the period. What we see in medieval English literature is that the language and practice of economics appear in more ways than any one system governs.

Texts in English, 800–1100

Following the withdrawal of the Roman legions in 410 in the face of invasions by Germanic tribes through to the incursions of the Vikings and Danes in the eleventh century, the island of Britain suffered long periods of instability. What historians refer to as the time of the Heptarchy – or seven kingdoms south of the Scottish marches – was a period when one kingdom had a brief period of preeminence until it was eclipsed by another or annihilated by an invasion. During this period, travel was hazardous, and any trading was local out of necessity. Most economic production was agricultural or pastoral, and much of it was on a subsistence level. Petty kings controlled coinage, and gift exchange tended to be the basis of political alliances.

The Old English epic *Beowulf*, the manuscript of which dates from around 1000, provides one of the earliest examples of a domestic economy in a medieval text. The action of the poem does not take place in England. Therefore, the practices of household economics the poem reveals could just as easily reflect common behaviors across northern Europe before the arrival of the Normans in England. Of course, taking a single literary text as the basis for analyzing an entire civilization is dangerous. My brief focus here will be on how the text shows a pre-Conquest domestic manorial economy. In the poem, the Danish King Hrothgar must maintain peace in the kingdom outside of Heorot, his manorial building. Wealtheow, his queen, governs the interior space of Heorot. The poet implies that, while Hrothgar is failing in his duty, she governs her space successfully. Wealtheow ensures that all their guests have accommodation, food, and drink. Though the text is unclear on this, she must also govern the servants. The result is what the poet calls "bencsweg" ("bench-music"; 1.

1161), the validating noise that comes from eating, drinking, and conversation by people sitting together inside the building.[3] Hospitality is, of course, basic economics. Literary texts addressing the running of a household do appear after the Norman Conquest, as do literary versions of great households themselves. Much of the work of this domestic economy in these texts is still done by female characters, like Wealtheow.

Wealtheow appears first bearing a cup for Hrothgar to drink from, reminding him in her subsequent speech of his duty to be a "goldwine gumena" ("gold-giving king"; 1. 1171). Gift-exchange is central to the poem's economy. Beowulf couches his offer to defeat Grendel as a gift that repays Hrothgar's service to Beowulf's father years earlier. Hrothgar gives Beowulf gifts upon the defeat of Grendel and his mother. All of these exchanges are intended to create an endless reciprocity, as the recipient of the gift must provide something to repay the gift as opposed to a commercial transaction in which any relationship between two parties ends when a good or service is exchanged for cash or items of equal value agreed upon by both parties.

Similarly, in the elegy known as *The Wanderer*, dating also from the early eleventh century, the speaker recalls the generosity of his long-dead lord who was his ring-giver. The lord gave treasure as a gift; it was not a payment or salary. As Robert Epstein explains, "commodity exchange objectifies people; gift exchange personifies objects." Items exchanged as gifts retain the memory of the donor, as many given items become narrative devices for recounting to an audience the reason for the donation. Items that are merely bought do not have this significance.[4] Wealtheow is a gift to the Danes to remind them of peace with her people. Beowulf's destruction of Grendel and his mother are gifts to Hrothgar. When Beowulf slays the Dragon, he only wants to look at its horde, give a necklace from it to Wiglaf for his service, and then seal the horde into the dragon's former lair. Treasure is only good for gifts; it is not for commerce or personal enrichment.

Texts in England, 1100–1500

The Manorial System

When Athelstan (r. 927–939) and his nephew Edgar (r. 959–975) unified England in the mid-tenth century, they established a kingdom with unified laws, a reasonably efficient tax system for the period, and recognized boundaries in order to protect the free exchange of people and goods.

England did not, however, have uniformity in weights and measures.[5] Part of the reason that William of Normandy (r. 1066–1087) wanted to take over England was that it had become one of the richest and most stable kingdoms in Western Europe. It had two basic advantages over its neighbors: its king exercised effective economic control over his kingdom, and it maintained "a common and reliable currency."[6] Other kings debased the coinage as a way to get a quick shot of cash for themselves. Parliamentary action opposed royal attempts to debase the coinage in England because, as J. L. Bolton concludes, "it was seen as the king's duty to maintain both the quantity and the quality of money put into circulation by his mints."[7]

But land in this period was the principal guarantor of wealth and status. The *Domesday Book* itemizes not just who held what lands in England from the king, but also every barn, animal, and person. It is a testament to the manorial system, which had been put in place before the Norman period as the economic structure of the shires. Its basic elements consisted of the lord (lay or secular) at the top and the peasants, who owed their labor to him, at the bottom. Lords tended to derive their income from rents paid by their peasant tenants, mills, and agricultural products.[8] Christopher Dyer explains that "continued investment in mills in the later middle ages rewarded many lords with substantial revenues, whether directly in the form of toll corn taken from the grain as it was being processed, or in rent paid by millers in exchange for the lease of the mill."[9] The mill required a miller who would devote his entire energies to running it rather than laboring in the field. Geoffrey Chaucer describes in his late fourteenth-century *Reeve's Tale* how two Cambridge scholars believe they can learn the milling trade just by watching the miller work. They fail, and the miller cheats them because milling was too complicated to learn from mere observation.

As with any system, the manor created its own bureaucracy of individuals specially charged with discrete tasks to maximize the efficiency of the system while at the same time requiring compensation for their offices. One such official was the reeve. Though the role originated before the Conquest as merely an "agent," the late medieval reeve oversaw the labor of the peasants attached to an estate in order to ensure that the necessary work was accomplished and (more importantly) that he would get the taxes and produce to which he was entitled.[10] Chaucer's Reeve, like his millers, is also a cheat because he skillfully defrauds his young master by managing not to pay him what he is owed in rents from his tenants, skimming some of these profits for himself.

But the manorial system developed other bureaucratic officials. For instance, the poem known as the *Song of the Husbandman* from the Harley MS 2253 is an early fourteenth-century critique of the rural economic system that victimizes the peasant at the expense of this growing manorial bureaucracy.[11] The poem's speaker complains that the king gets "ever the furthe peni" ("every fourth penny"; l. 8) of all his produce collected by the king's "budeles" ("beadles" or tax collectors; l. 37). The speaker also needs to pay the hayward, bailiff, and woodward. The tasks that these three offices supervise are necessary for the orderly running of the manor: the bailiff, among other things, collects rents for the lord of the manor; the hayward is responsible for fences and enclosures in the parish, ensuring that cattle do not run free and cause damage; and the woodward is in charge of managing the local timber. Dyer claims that a "manor would not have worked without the peasants who served as reeves, haywards, and grangers."[12] Richard Newhauser writes that the "beadle, bailiff, and hayward are familiar figures from other writings and complaints, though the woodward is, in English poetry of this time, a figure not altogether common."[13] All of these offices ruin the speaker in the poem, so that he must sell his livestock and his grain while it is still green to pay his taxes (ll. 46, 65), paradoxically reducing the value of the work that these offices were allegedly supporting.

In addition to the fiscal obligations imposed by the manor and the king, the Church increasingly required money rather than labor. The early fourteenth-century anonymous poem called *The Simony* indicts the Church for its rapacity. In addition to the poem's claims that the Church expects anyone who wants a benefice to pay for it (the definition of simony), it also claims that archdeacons will take bribes to allow priests to marry and that priests use parish funds to buy goods for themselves rather than for the people (ll. 51–52).[14] The poet complains that a person can be granted a divorce just by hiring two liars to witness to the priest that a man should be separated from his wife and people can buy political offices to cheat the king (ll. 201–204, 331–333). Throughout the fourteenth and fifteenth centuries, the rapacity of the Church became a frequent topic of moralist wrath. William Langland, in his *Piers Plowman*, written in the second half of the fourteenth century, examines the corruption of the Church by money. He catalogues many religious figures who cheat the faithful. For instance, he comments that the friars dress richly "for here money and merchandise marchen togideres" ("for their money and merchandise work together"; C Prol. 62–63).[15]

The Commercial System

In the decades just before the Black Death, England experienced significant population growth with the concomitant shrinkage in the size of estates divided among surviving heirs. Additionally, an increase of bad weather and plagues on livestock lasting roughly from the 1280s to the 1330s strained an already stressed rural economy.[16] Conversely, immigration from the shires to the cities and towns increased. London had succeeded Winchester as the capital of the kingdom by the early twelfth century because of its easier access to the king's continental holdings. It became the largest city on the island. Bristol, Hull, and Great Yarmouth also grew thanks to their ports.

Increasingly, the chief commodity produced in England sent out through these ports was wool. Flemish and Italian merchants had been actively engaged in trading for wool since the late eleventh century, meeting in fairs throughout France, principally in Champagne. However, by 1314, the French king Philip IV (r. 1285–1314) barred the Flemish from the Champagne fairs and subjected the Italian traders to, as Jonathan Sumption describes, "persecution, forced loans, and discriminatory taxation."[17] As a result, the Flemish and Italian traders ceased crossing French territory to trade together. Instead, they turned to the sea route that, while longer, was now more cost-effective because of a "new and larger form of Italian ship that permitted navigation on the Atlantic."[18] Because these ships needed to put into ports frequently, Flemish and Italian merchants came into England in larger numbers to trade for wool, bringing in many other goods, such as spices, silk, and textiles. England did have a robust trade with Byzantium but lost it with the Norman Conquest. Trade with the Flemings and Italians rebuilt England's trade networks over the course of the next centuries, but trading was not in English hands until the 1300s.[19] The English were trading directly again with Constantinople by 1500.[20]

England also began trading with the cities along the North and Baltic Seas that eventually formed what was known as the Hanseatic League. While no English city was a member of the League, Hanseatic merchants had offices in major English ports, such as in London (where their enclave was known as the Steelyard) and in Lynn in Lincolnshire. Margery Kempe, daughter of the mayor of Lynn, relates in her book how her son had been trading in the Hanseatic port of Danzig where he married a "Dewche" (German-speaking) woman.[21] While she does not say what commodities he traded there, the Hanseatic network brought to England timber, grain, wax, and furs while it primarily exported wool and finished cloth.[22] After she spends six weeks in Danzig with her daughter-in-law and granddaughter following the death of her son, Kempe returns to England by foot because, after traveling by ship to Danzig, she decided she had a pronounced fear of the sea. Instead, she travels as a pilgrim, and her trip home is a clear reaction against any association with commercial exchange. For example, the only places she mentions on her journey home are religious shrines, and she makes no reference to markets.

Postpandemic England saw comparatively rapid and significant change to the English economy. Tenurial rents in the manorial system stayed pretty much flat while the profits from trade rose. This rise caused the shopkeepers and merchants to be able to diversify and become rich. Conversely, many lords had to sell their property to rich merchants or marry into a merchant's family in order to survive. The de la Poles, a merchant family from Hull in the early fourteenth century who became earls of Suffolk by the late fourteenth century, are an example of a family who were able to buy their way into the nobility. Parliaments, alarmed by these changes, passed laws intending to roll back the clock to prepandemic society. One such act was the Statute of Laborers (1351), which dictated that everyone in the kingdom needed to work for their hire. Langland cites the Statute of Laborers when the Dreamer of his poem is interrogated to find out whether he is a healthy beggar who should be working or an infirm one who needs parish charity to survive (C.5. 1–104).[23] Another parliamentary act was the set of Sumptuary Laws (1363), which dictated how people should dress and what they should eat so that, even if a carpenter could now afford to dress as well as a lord, he must not.

The Man of Law and the Physician from Chaucer's *The Canterbury Tales* each wear expensive clothes to advertise their wealth as a way of attracting clients. These two individuals are part of a rising group of professionals who, with Chaucer's Merchant, gain money by what they know rather than what they make, harvest, or produce. By dressing the way they do, they hope to convince a potential client that, because they dress well, they must make a lot of money. They make a lot of money because they are successful. They are successful because they are much sought after by clients. In a period when advertising one's skills can only be done at a personal level, dressing well is advertising. But advertising could also be false. Chaucer's Cook also advertises his skills. Virtually his entire description in the *General Prologue* is a list of all the foods he can prepare. The only aspect of his material physicality is the weeping sore on his shin, which may reveal he is not as successful as he claims he is.

Another great advertiser among Chaucer's Canterbury pilgrims is the Wife of Bath. She says she has had five husbands and is looking for the sixth. She is dressed to attract such attention. In addition to the fine kerchiefs on her head, she wears red stockings (I. 456).[24] Red is, of course, an eye-catching color. However, Chaucer is specific that these stockings are made out of scarlet, which is the most expensive fabric. Red dyes could be cheap, yielding more of a dull or brownish red. The Wife's stockings are of expensive material and very likely a rich dye, yielding a vivid red. While drawing attention to her legs certainly emphasizes the sexual aspect of her advertising, she is also showing off her wealth. Rich red socks on the legs of a lascivious older woman might catch the attention of any poor young man quite possibly hoping to inherit her wealth when she dies. She admits that her fifth husband married her for that reason, while she married him for the sex. Throughout her own Prologue, she explains how she barters with her husbands for control in the marriage, arguing that "al is for to selle" (III. 414). She also explains that her corn is gone, so she will sell the chaff, meaning that she may not draw suitors by her looks, so she sells what she can (III. 478). Equating marriage with sales and spousal agreements with business negotiations shows how economic language influenced (in albeit comical fashion) dealings between husbands and wives.

Chaucer's Shipman is a member of the carrying trade, moving people and goods from the continent to England and back, and is a figure of the growing international trade in which English cities are participating. The Shipman knows "alle the havenes ... / Fro Gootland to the cape of Fynystere, / And every cryke in Britaigne and in Spayne" (I. 407–409). While the Shipman does not appear to go west into the Irish Sea, he knows all the ports between Sweden and Spain together with the inlets and coves in the rough coastlines of Brittany and Spain. We are told that he often carries wine traders. Bordeaux produced most of the wine sold in London. The vintage fleet came into England by Christmas, and the *reek* wines made from the lees arrived in the spring.[25] By the late fourteenth century, Gascon wines had been joined by Spanish, French, Rhenish, Italian, and other wines in London shops. Chaucer's Pardoner digresses in his Prologue to mention the Spanish wine of Lepe for its "fumositee" ("vapors"; VI. 567). He says that this wine is sold in London on "Fysshstrete or in Chepe" (VI. 564). John Gower, in his French poem *Mirour de L'Omme*, lists several wines also available in London: Greek, Malmsey, Candy, Ribole, Romanian, Provençal, Montross, Rivere, and Muscatel (ll. 26089–26100).[26]

In contrast to the wide range of the Shipman's scope, Chaucer's Pilgrim Merchant's interest is comparatively narrow, extending just to the part of the English Channel between "Middelburgh and Orewelle" (I. 277). Edward III (r. 1327–1377) had argued in Parliament that his authority as king extended through the Channel. He was also probably the first English king to realize the financial importance of international trade to the kingdom. Partly, Edward needed to assert control over the Channel and its islands in order to deny the French an opportunity to get a toehold in Britain. At the same time, he maintained a bridgehead into the continent when he conquered the port town of Calais. But his concern to maintain this sovereignty was also economic. He realized significant profit from the wool trade to finance his wars with France. To encourage this trade and also fund the expensive garrisoning of Calais, he wanted to locate the Wool Staple, the continental town where English, Flemish, and Dutch merchants could sell wool, at Calais. He also struck the first English gold coin – the noble – with his royal image on a ship. Up until the striking of this coin, English kings had always appeared on horseback on their coins, underscoring their land-based power. Appearing in a ship emphasized that Edward's power extended to the sea. The early fifteenth-century anonymous *Libelle of Englyshe Polycye* makes a similar argument that, because the English king's authority extends to the English Channel, he needs to keep it secure so that English trade can thrive.

Coins make an important figurative appearance in the mid-fourteenth century anonymous poem, *Wynnere and Wastoure*, where two allegorical figures debate before Edward III the best use of money. Wynnere, whose name means "to gain," argues that it is better to gather money and property and not spend it. Wastoure, whose name means "to deplete one's property," argues that spending one's wealth is important to keep everyone working. While it may seem that attributing the accumulation of money to winning seems positive and equating spending with wasting negative, the surviving poem breaks off before a victor in this debate is declared, making the conclusion ambiguous.

But it is the pavilion in the dream where the king receives the two debaters and their armies that has the conspicuous appearance of coins. The pavilion has as its principal decorations "ynglysse besantes full brighte, betyn of golde" ("very bright English besants of beaten gold," l. 61).[27] The besant is a gold coin originating from Byzantium. While its position here is decorative, it is also a coin. The pavilion is rich and literally covered in money. The point of the debate is to explore how getting and spending are two important practices for a national economy.

Money in Chaucer's *Shipman's Tale* circulates among the merchant, his wife, and a monk who is their friend.[28] It is considered a loan from one of the characters to another, not a gift, because it is intended to be repaid and this repayment does not guarantee enduring reciprocity between the lender and the debtor. Different from a gift, a loan also has the expectation of interest. But the question of the morality of interest on a loan was perennial in the Middle Ages, especially as mercantile activity increased. Merchants had initially been considered incapable of salvation because they dealt in money and potentially usury. That changed by the twelfth century when theologians argued that a merchant could sell an item for more than he bought it for, thereby collecting profit on goods sold. This was compensation for his labor bringing the goods to market. The problem, though, was in determining what a "just price" was on a saleable item.[29] The City of London and its guilds established prices in the fourteenth century for their goods so that no one should charge more than what anyone else in the guild did.

If there was growing consensus that a merchant could make money from selling a good, there was complete agreement that charging interest on a loan was usury, and usury was sinful. In medieval Europe, only the Jews were allowed to charge interest. Later, the popes allowed the "Lombards" (or any Italian) to charge interest. Gower rails against usury in his *Mirour* and in his English poem, *Confessio Amantis*. Usury, he argues, is a fraud because the usurer has not done any labor when he loans money but wants more when the loan is paid back.

Usury was not the only immorality feared in the commercial system. Fraud was a significant problem too, especially since the average person might not be able to distinguish shoddy goods or tainted food from a quick (and unprofessional) observation. In the *Mirour*, Gower catalogues many examples of shopkeepers committing fraud, from drapers selling inferior green cloth for a more expensive one, to cooks selling bad food, to old wine marketed as good. He begins this catalogue with the claim that God has divided goods unevenly across the world so that no one nation has everything it needs. If a nation did have everything, Gower argues, then it would be too proud and would not need any other (l. 25191). Merchants who betray their vocation by committing fraud go against God's law (ll. 25198–25200). Gower's catalogue shows both the extensive markets of London and how little protection a consumer had against a wily shopkeeper. London guilds were charged with policing their own members, but when a member defrauded a customer and the guild did nothing, that customer, according to Gower, was powerless or, if he ate bad food, possibly dead.

Of course, having a large market requires the money to spend on the commodities sold therein. For the poor person, this may be impossible. A poem from around 1400 known as *London Lickpenny* describes how a person comes to London, has his hood stolen, and is unable to recover it due to his lack of money. Throughout the course of the poem, the speaker encounters cooks who want to sell him bread with wine and ale together with "rybbes of befe, bothe fat and fine" (ll. 61–63); others who sell "hot pescods ... strabery rype" and "chery in the ryse" ("hot peapods, ripe strawberries, and cherries on the branch"; ll. 67–68); and yet others who try to sell him pepper and saffron (l. 70).[30] In the Cheapside neighborhood, he encounters sellers of cotton, lawn, and expensive thread (ll. 75–76). He finds pewter pots in Eastcheap (l. 91) and dyed cloth sold by drapers in Candlewick Street (ll. 83–84). None of these are affordable to him since he has no money. While he does come across his hood for sale, he cannot buy it.

The problem of not having money is a common theme in some of the poetry of Thomas Hoccleve, a chancery clerk from the early fifteenth century who appears to have been perennially short of cash. The function of the Office of Chancery was to record the transfer of property. With the court of the Exchequer supervising the income from taxation, Chancery is part of the growing national bureaucracy that developed to provide written records of transactions and the wealth of the nation. Part of Hoccleve's problem as a government clerk was that, when Henry Bolingbroke usurped the English throne from Richard II (r. 1377–1399) in 1399 to reign as Henry IV (r. 1399–1413), people thought that he would live within his substantial means and not raise taxes. This was impossible.[31] For years, Henry's government functioned in deficit with government officials, like Hoccleve, going unpaid for months.

Hoccleve wrote a poem, *La Male Regle* (1408), ostensibly to Thomas Nevill, Lord Furnival, Treasurer of England, to show that he used to be wasteful in his youth, but now is reformed and frugal. He hopes implicitly that Lord Furnival will manage money as well and pay him. Hoccleve's later poem, *Regiment of Princes* (1410–1411), begins with the speaker having insomnia. Many medieval dream visions begin with a sleepless poet pondering some philosophical question that a subsequent dream may help him solve. What keeps Hoccleve awake is a less philosophical and more mundane concern; he worries about money. Going for a walk, he meets an Old Man who suggests that he write something in order to be compensated for his labor. The subsequent *Regiment* is to be a gift, but one expecting a reward that should solve his financial problems. In other words, he wants his recipient, Prince Henry, the future Henry V (r. 1413–1422), to pay him for a labor the prince has not asked Hoccleve to provide.

A final example of economics in a literary text, where we end this survey, is the play of the *Remorse of Judas* from the later fifteenth-century *York Corpus Christi Plays*. In this play, Judas wants to return the thirty pieces of silver that Kayphas (Caiaphas) and Anna (Annas), two members of the Sanhedrin instrumental in condemning Christ, gave him for betraying Jesus. Pilate is also present in this scene. While the episode is an elaboration on the conversation from the Gospels of Judas repenting of his deed and then throwing the silver on the ground, what the poet does here is emphasize that the betrayal of Jesus was a commercial transaction. Judas sold Christ to Kayphas and Anna. Now, he wants to buy Christ back, but they will not resell him. Moreover, Kayphas argues that Christ is their property to do with as they like. Kayphas says, "We bought hym for he schulde be slayne" (32, l. 176) and "We bought hym for he schulde be spilte" (l. 248).[32] The point here is that Judas knew their purpose in paying for Christ, and their "bargayne" was that they planned to kill him (l. 168). Now that Judas has sold Christ to them, they intend to carry out their intent. Judas argues that his repentance should cancel the bargain. But Kayphas does not see it as a transaction that can be reversed. Biblical scholars have always read Judas's betrayal as based in greed. To this is added, according to the playwright, renegotiating a settled sale after the fact.

The York Cycle itself is a text dedicated to the importance of commerce. The surviving manuscript identifies each play with its sponsoring guild. These plays were evidently examples of a guild's wealth as well as their civic pride. They could showcase their goods or services in the play they produced. For instance, the cooks and waterdrawers, who sponsored the production of *The Remorse of Judas*, would have needed to fit out a pageant wagon, provide costumes and props, and perhaps even pay the actors.

By the end of the fifteenth century, the manorial system was still in place, although the fluidity in the landed nobility and gentry brought more mercantile wealth into this estate. William Caxton, who set up the first printing press in England in 1476, printed books he knew he could sell. These included romances that were especially popular for city readers who wanted to learn behavioral practices of the nobility from them in order to be more easily accepted into their society. Caxton himself saw the importance of selling literature, and consequently created an English identity marketed in its literature and based on its economic principles. As such, some might consider him an early capitalist. Instead, he is that dynamic late medieval individual who works at the same time in both the manorial and the commercial systems.

Notes

1 See, for instance, Immanuel Wallerstein, *Capitalist Agriculture and the Origins of the European World-Economy in the Sixteenth Century* (Berkeley: University of California Press, 1974); R. H. Hilton, ed., *The Transition from Feudalism to Capitalism* (London: Verso, 1976); R. J. Holton, *The Transition from Feudalism to Capitalism* (New York: St. Martin's Press, 1985).

2 For an examination of the parallel economic systems in a late fourteenth-century literary text, see my "Tales of Two Transactions: The Franklin, the Shipman, Feudalism, and the Fourteenth-Century World System," in *Later Middle English Literature, Materiality, and Culture: Essays in Honor of James M. Dean*, edited by Brian Gastle and Erick Keleman (Newark: University of Delaware Press, 2018), 167–188.

3 *Beowulf*, ed. Frederick Klaeber (Boston: Heath, 1922).

4 Robert Epstein, *Chaucer's Gifts: Exchange and Value in the* Canterbury Tales (Cardiff: University of Wales Press, 2018), 7.

5 Christopher Dyer, *An Age of Transition? Economy and Society in England in the Later Middle Ages* (Oxford: Oxford University Press, 2005), 111.

6 Robert S. Lopez, *The Commercial Revolution of the Middle Ages, 950–1350* (Englewood Cliffs, NJ: Prentice-Hall, 1971), 121; Steven A. Epstein, *An Economic and Social History of Later Medieval Europe, 1000–1500* (Cambridge: Cambridge University Press, 2009), 106.

7 J. L. Bolton, *Money in the Medieval English Economy: 973–1489* (Manchester: Manchester University Press, 2012), 37.

8 Dyer, *Age of Transition*, 87; J. L. Bolton, *The Medieval English Economy, 1150–1500* (London: Dent, 1980), 40.

9 Dyer, *Age of Transition*, 92.

10 Rosamond Faith, *The Moral Economy of the Countryside: Anglo-Saxon to Anglo-Norman England* (Cambridge: Cambridge University Press, 2020), 109–110.

11 Susanna Fein, ed., *The Complete Harley 2253 Manuscript*, 3 vols. (Kalamazoo, MI: Medieval Institute Publications, 2014–2015), vol. 2, 128–131.

12 Dyer, *Age of Transition*, 94.

13 Richard Newhauser, "Historicity and Complaint in *Song of the Husbandman*," in *Studies in the Harley Manuscript: The Scribes, Contents, and Social Contexts of British Library MS Harley 2253*, edited by Susanna Fein (Kalamazoo, MI: Medieval Institute Publications, 2000), 215.

14 Dan Embree and Elizabeth Urquhart, eds., *The Simonie: A Parallel-Text Edition*, Middle English Texts 24 (Heidelberg: Carl Winter, 1991).

15 William Langland, *C-Text of Piers Plowman*, edited by Derek Pearsall (Exeter: University of Exeter Press, 1994).

16 Bruce M. S. Campbell, *The Great Transition: Climate, Disease, and Society in the Late-Medieval World* (Cambridge: Cambridge University Press, 2016), 253–261.

17 Jonathan Sumption, *The Hundred Years War, Vol. I: Trial by Battle* (Philadelphia: University of Pennsylvania Press, 1991), 13.

18 Janet Abu-Lughod, *Before European Hegemony: The World System A. D. 1250–1350* (Oxford: Oxford University Press, 1989), 70.

19 Bolton, *Medieval English Economy*, 178–179.

20 Pamela Nightingale, *A Medieval Mercantile Community: The Grocers' Company and the Politics and Trade of London, 1000–1485* (New Haven: Yale University Press, 1995), 9–16.

21 Margery Kempe, *The Book of Margery Kempe*, edited by Lynn Staley (Kalamazoo, MI: Medieval Institute Publications, 1996), 210.

22 Johannes Schildhauer, *The Hansa: History and Culture*, translated by Katherine Vanovitch (Dorset: Dorset Press, 1988), 42.

23 See Robert Epstein, "Summoning Hunger: Polanyi, *Piers Plowman*, and the Labor Market," in *Money, Commerce, and Economics in Late Medieval English Literature*, edited by Craig E. Bertolet and Robert Epstein (New York: Palgrave, 2018), 59–76.

24 All Chaucer references are to Larry D. Benson, gen. ed., *The Riverside Chaucer*, 3rd ed. (Boston: Houghton Mifflin, 1987).

25 Margery K. James, *Studies in the Medieval Wine Trade*, edited by Elspeth M. Veale (Oxford: Oxford University Press, 1971), 124–127.

26 All Gower references are to G. C. Macaulay, ed., *Complete Works of John Gower*, 4 vols. (Oxford: Oxford University Press, 1899–1901). All translations, unless otherwise indicated, are my own.

27 Stephanie Trigg, ed., *Wynnere and Wastoure* (Oxford: Early English Text Society, 1990).

28 See my discussion of this tale in *Chaucer, Gower, Hoccleve, and the Commercial Practices of Late Fourteenth-Century London* (Farnham: Ashgate, 2013), 81–104.

29 See John W. Baldwin, "The Medieval Theories of the Just Price: Romanists, Canonists, and Theologians in the Twelfth and Thirteenth Centuries," *Transactions of the American Philosophical Society*, n. s. 49.4 (1959), 5–92; Joel Kaye, *Economy and Nature in the Fourteenth Century: Money, Market Exchange, and the Emergence of Scientific Thought* (Cambridge: Cambridge University Press, 1998), 87–101.

30 James Dean, ed., *Medieval English Political Writings* (Kalamazoo, MI: Medieval Institute Publications, 1996), 222–225.

31 Chris Given-Wilson, *Henry IV* (New Haven: Yale University Press, 2016), 174–180.

32 *York Corpus Christi Plays*, edited by Clifford Davidson (Kalamazoo, MI: Medieval Institute Publications, 2011).

CHAPTER 2

Early Modern Literature and Monetary Debate

David Landreth

This chapter considers English writing about market values from the sixteenth and earlier seventeenth centuries – taking as its termini the dissolution of the monasteries, which began in 1536, and the trade depression of the early 1620s. It is anachronistic to speak very directly of either "literature" or "economics" in this period: the discursive field of writing was still divided mainly according to genres rather than according to disciplines, so the self-conscious autonomy that defines those two disciplinary objects for us wasn't yet realized.[1] Of course contemporary readers differentiated between writing that was openly fabulous and writing that aimed to represent present practices of trade. But in positing "writing about market values" as a continuum linking those two poles, I mean to underline how much protoliterary writing and protoeconomic writing have in common in this early modern moment – both with respect to premises and with respect to techniques. The fabulous was not fully separable from the didactically allegorical in this period: the representation of fictive worlds tended to map back onto the world of lived experience, systematizing material conditions according to moral terms. At the other end of the continuum, writing about money and trade relied on existing genres, such as the dialogue and the complaint, for its precedent form, and relied for its techniques of persuasion on the ancient rhetorical legacy of tropes and tactics it shared with imaginative writing.

But it is also true that a "protoliterature" and a "protoeconomics" are coming into focus in English writing of this era, if we do view it retrospectively. The terms according to which we define those objects in modernity are emerging into visibility as we look at early modern writing, and are beginning to constellate themselves into forms we recognize. It is in this moment that concepts such as "commodity," "consumption," "demand," and "investment" acquire their modern, economic meanings.[2] This chapter portrays some of the give and take between protoliterary and protoeconomic writing in this moment by focusing on the emergent concept of productivity. The emergence of productivity endows with value a whole range of worldly activities beyond the scope of the money form (in saving and exchange), but still tends to define that value in monetary terms. Pursuits such as imaginative writing acquire new legitimacy by claiming to be productive, but must thereby interact with the expansion of market values. I'll begin by outlining the changing material and ideological conditions that prompted writerly attention to money and trade from merchants, statesmen, and imaginative writers. I'll show how apparently limited topics of monetary debate in the period – debasement, usury, and the export of bullion – were amplified into far-reaching critiques of value by imaginative writers. And I'll show how these value critiques tended in turn to support an emergent arena of autonomous value in what we might recognize as literary production.

Transformation and Transvaluation

As the fifteenth century drew toward its end, a rough theoretical consensus regarding the nature and proper uses of money held sway across western Europe. Money should exclusively be a measure, never a commodity. It was made of precious metal, though it could be represented as money of account to measure barter or credit transactions. The overt taking of interest was not only illegal, but sinful. The measurement that money provided should not be determined only by what a given buyer would pay or a given market would bear, but should refer itself to a communal standard, "the just price," that would attend to the utility of the commodity, to the cost of its production, and to established precedent, as much as to the local conditions of present exchange. The theory of the just price sought to situate the volatile contingency of particular transactions within a field of consistent, normative social expectations, and so to enlist money as a bulwark against change. In keeping with these principles, many prices and wage rates were directly regulated by local officials, and long leases tended to keep rents stable over multiple generations.[3]

This relative complacency regarding money's activity and character was shattered over the course of the sixteenth century. In the disruption of value systems in the period, three large-scale factors stand out. One was population growth, as Europe's peoples finally recovered to the numbers they had enjoyed before the Black Death of 1347–1350, and in short order shot past them. Internal migration drove huge new populations into cities, and significant numbers of the most desperate into permanent vagabondage. New growth, mobility, and urbanization together bring us to the next factor, the expansion and deepening of trade and market relations. The conquest of the Aztec and Inca empires by Spain brought unprecedented amounts of precious metals into Europe – followed shortly by the European discovery of monetary inflation.[4] But trade with Asia also intensified greatly in the period, and so did trade between and within European nations. Market exchange penetrated rapidly into particular transactions and whole social spheres to which it had previously been marginal: values that, to established moralities, ought to be unquantifiable were now seen to be scandalously "for sale." And, as the new demand for money outstripped even the metal supply afforded by the spoils of the New World, credit instruments grew more ubiquitous, more sophisticated, and more fungible.

Although it may seem less properly "economic" to our minds than population statistics and trade relations, the third of these large-scale disruptions is the Reformation. Luther's Wittenberg theses took as their immediate target the economy of penance by charitable works, and the system of Church property and distribution it maintained. Countries that, like England, dissolved Church property released vast amounts of land and treasure onto the market – and ruptured the lives of the thousands, lay and religious alike, who had depended upon those properties.[5] And the Reformation helped to motivate civil and international wars across Europe, culminating in the appalling conflagration of the Thirty Years' War. But it had subtler, ideological ramifications upon the concept of value as well. Although every claim of Weber's *The Protestant Ethic and the Spirit of Capitalism* (1904–1905) has by now been contested, his basic insight remains vital: the transition to capitalism entailed complex interactions between changing spiritual values and changing material values, through which ethical "profit" came to be identified with material productivity.[6]

For the Middle Ages, the great sin of material life was avarice, and the remedy for it was charity. To the extent that medieval thinkers recognized scarcity as a human problem, rather than a given characteristic of a fallen world, it was a problem of distribution. If some did not have enough, it was because others were claiming too much: when the burden of want was great upon the bodies of the poor, a burden of sin lay upon the souls of the wealthy, and both might be relieved at once through the material works of charity. Over the course of the sixteenth century in England, the wealthy unshouldered much of that burden. Charitable giving became a sign of predestined election, not an ongoing means to redemption. This change encouraged giving to become more discriminating, focusing on the "deserving poor" – orphans, the incapacitated, the elderly – and rejecting the "undeserving," defined as those judged able to work who were nevertheless not earning their own living.[7] Idleness was now becoming the great sin of material life, and its remedy was "industry" – which was to be enforced upon the "idle" poor through privation, and sometimes by compulsion. Rather than anticipating God's judgment of his greed, the wealthy man was now entitled to exercise his own judgment on the idleness of the poor. Their want became a sign of their own slothful depravity, not of their betters' avaricious grasping. Rather than a morally charged problem of distribution, scarcity was becoming a problem of productivity, with an equal but opposite moral charge.[8]

The responsibility of productivity was not only the province of the poor; though this ideological shift would prove the ground of industrialization, there was as yet little expectation that the "industry" of the poor would offer profit to the commonwealth beyond the benefits of stability imagined in making them occupied, located, and content.[9] It was from the lettered classes that early modern English social theorists demanded new profits for the commonwealth. Elizabethan educational texts and treatises manifest a positive horror of idleness, a vice equally associated with the lower classes and with the monastic past of education in letters as training for the contemplative life in the old religion. Instead, the Protestant liberal arts scholar should become "studied for action": learning was to afford direct, transactional benefits to the activity of the commonwealth in "the profitable discourse of the Elizabethans."[10]

In the face of such expectations for the public good of the liberal arts, the employment of wit and learning in imaginative writing would seem not only idle but actively wasteful. Richard Helgerson has described the self-conscious posture of prodigality among Elizabethan poets:

> [George] Whetstone gives the name "The Garden of Unthriftiness" to a section of his book that has nothing to do with money, a collection of "wanton" sonnets. He is unthrifty in the pursuit of beauty and in the celebration of love; he wastes not money, but time, wit, and learning, goods that should be spent in some way "beneficial to the commonweal" and "profitable to himself."
>
> This ideal of thrift, which recurs in the mercantile metaphors of Elizabethan love poetry – the audits and accounts which always prove the lover a bankrupt, the "expense of spirit in a waste of shame" – is very much the product of an educational system so intent on using every hour and so convinced that it knew how to use the hours profitably.

Helgerson goes on to trace the emergence of a model of national poetic industry over the next generations, which engages and finally repudiates the characterization of poetic activity as a wasteful, atomizing, selfish and self-destructive idleness.[11] In the second edition of *The Faerie Queene* (1596), Spenser introduces his new material with a remarkably impolitic attack on Lord Burghley, Elizabeth's *de facto* prime minister, as an over-literal, worldly reader who fails to recognize the value of imaginative writing. Aiming over Burghley's head, he addresses England's Queen as both the incarnation and the judge of "love," "honor," "virtue," and "bounty." These are the national values of a body politic that, Spenser says, Elizabeth shares with the sprawling poem he has written her, values that exceed Burghley's instrumental calculus of learning's worldly goods.[12]

The English had a voracious appetite for economic writing that pro-fessed to deliver such worldly goods – though, again, we would not recognize most of it as economic by modern lights. Household manage-ment guides, husbandry manuals and almanacs, recipe books: all these pertained to "economy" as the early modern English would define it, in their emphasis on domestic "thrift."[13] The subset of that writing that seems protoeconomic in our sense is limited, and focuses on debating the scope and character of the money form. Three central topics of monetary debate came to the fore successively: price inflation and the debasement of the coinage, which became a crisis in the 1540s; the expansion of credit and usury, most debated around and after the Usury Bill of 1571; and the export of bullion and the balance of foreign trade, culminating in the "mercantilist" tracts addressing the trade depression of the early 1620s.

Imaginative writing is a site in which value may be debated, and often debated more expansively than is possible in directly economic writing. I'll present below some instances in which fictive treatments enact the larger-scale clashes of value implicated in the apparently narrow terms of monetary debate – metallic purity, the proliferation of credit, the dis-placed rewards of foreign investment. But, as Spenser insists, imaginative writing is also a site in which value is produced. Should authors of fictions understand their own productivity in terms of substance, credit, or profitable exchange? Are poets like gods, creating their matter *ex nihilo* – or are they more like minters, usurers, or merchants? In what follows, I'll sketch the scope and course of these three monetary debates, and suggest how their expressions of value interact with the value of (proto) literary production.

Price and Purity

Between 1500 and 1550, prices rose roughly fourfold in England. Historians have dubbed the episode "the price revolution": the phrase conveys not only the material hardship of the inflation, but also its epistemic shock.[14] In preceding generations, prices had risen very little over the long term, while short-term variations in price had been traceable to immediate causes, most obviously to poor harvests and the disruptions of war; once those conditions returned to their presumed norm, so too should prices. The persistence of that baseline across the later fifteenth century sustained the theory of the just price. But once prices began to rise independently of such visible causes – in good harvests as well as in bad, in peacetime as well as in war – it became harder and harder to identify any political mechanism that might exert influence over price. The localized mediation that sought to ground the just price in a network of stable and consensual values was clearly no longer up to the task. That failure opened up two lines of inquiry. One, was there some larger-scale factor in play that obviated local conditions and solutions? Two, what did the failure of the just price mean for the vision of social cohesion and stability in which it had been anchored?

The former question is a recognizably economic one, and the latter question – that of the caustic effects upon other social relations of changes in the money form – has been a preeminent literary one. In mid-sixteenth-century writing, the two are closely integrated. Both lines of inquiry come to focus on the relationship of value to precious metal: on how the discrepancy between intrinsic value and face value in a minted coin inflected the whole set of social values that had been implicated in the structure of the just price.

In England, the price revolution was simultaneous with two large-scale expansions of royal power into the domains of property, labor, and price. The first was the dissolution of monasteries, friaries, and chantries after 1536, through which the Crown seized not only a huge stock of treasure, but also vast holdings of real estate, disrupting and reshaping the many lives – lay and religious alike – that had depended on those properties. The second expansion was the debasement of the silver coinage, which began in 1541 and by 1551 had reduced the coins from sterling (92.5 percent silver) to up to 75 percent dross. The dissolutions proclaimed that the medieval system of charitable distribution, whose nexus was these church properties, was both a material failure and a doctrinal fraud; and they implied a newly centralized and national context for distribution, through which Crown

policy would promote the mutual prosperity of the "common wealth."[15]
The debasements undermined this new potential of commonwealth-
minded governance, positioning the expanding reach of sovereign power
firmly on the side of fraudulence and failure.

"These testons look red: how like you the same?/'Tis a token of grace:
they blush for shame," wrote the epigrammatist John Heywood of some
drossy shillings around 1547, slyly moralizing the duple brazenness of the
debasement – its default of mineral purity and its default of shame.[16] The
most comprehensive treatise by an advocate of "commonwealth,"
A Discourse of the Commonweal of This Realm of England (1549), demonstrated the new autonomy of prices from agricultural cycles, and argued
that debasement was propelling inflation by reducing English purchasing
power in foreign exchange.[17] For Protestant "commonwealths-men"
addressing the reformed regimes of Henry VIII and Edward VI, debasement was a betrayal of the good governance embodied in the dissolutions;
for Catholics, the two interventions were cut from the same despicable
cloth. Upon her brother Edward's death, Mary Tudor set out to restore
both the monasteries and the sterling. The allegorical court play *Republica*
(1553), written to celebrate Mary's accession, deftly integrates the dissolution and debasement into the work of a single Vice figure. He calls
himself "Reformation," but his true name is "Oppression," and he is at
length forced to justify himself to "Respublica," the personification of
commonwealth, and her rustic subject "People":

> *Oppression.* First your priests and bishops have not as they have had.
> *Respublica.* When they had their livings men were both fed and clad ...
> *Oppression.* The coin eke is changed.
> *People.* Yea, from silver to dross.
> 'Twas told us, for the best: but poor we bare the loss.[18]

In this allegorical rendering, the theological agenda of the Reformation is a
mere cloak for worldly abuses. The posture of nationalized reform is a new
venue for the perennial vice of the material world, the greedy exploitation
of the poor by Oppression, who has attacked at once the distributive
mechanisms of charity and of just exchange, the Church and the coin.

Mary died in 1558, before her counter-reformations could reach fru-
ition. Her sister Elizabeth took on many of Edward's reformist councilors
as her own, and undertook a massive recoinage to restore the sterling
standard. Prices did become more stable, but continued to rise; inflation
began to be normalized, and by 1615 John Donne could quip in a sermon
that "however the ordinary murmuring may be true, in other things, that

all things are grown dearer, our souls are still cheap enough" – the clamorous scandal of the 1540s having quieted to an "ordinary murmur," or commonplace gripe.[19] But the deracination of exchange value from material purity and just price continued to fascinate early modern writers. Was the value generated by imaginative writing itself merely imaginary or formal, like the discrepancy between intrinsic and exchange values in a debased coin – and if so, did that make it necessarily delusional or exploitative? Or might the "matter" of imagination supply integrity and value in the material world? Philip Sidney's *Defence of Poesy* (1595) takes up these questions, rebuffing the charge of fraudulence by expressing poetic work as a minter's assay of metallic purity:

> ... [the poet] goeth hand in hand with nature, not enclosed within the narrow warrant of her gifts [as are writers who profess to describe the world as it is], but freely ranging only within the zodiac of his own wit. Nature never set forth the earth in so rich tapestry as poets have done; neither with so pleasant rivers, fruitful trees, sweet-smelling flowers, nor whatsoever else may make the too much loved earth more lovely. Her world is brazen, the poets only deliver a golden.[20]

The "golden" world that poets deliver is not merely idealized, like the pastoral fable of Ovid's "golden age": it is ideational, actively corrective within the world we know, refining away the debased temptations of the "too much loved earth" and leaving in their place an exalting loveliness that is to be admired rather than greedily desired. Poetic representation purges the dross of historical contingency to show the material truths of the human world in their real, supernatural purity.

Credit, Use, and Bond

The scope of monetized transactions expanded much more rapidly in the period than did the circulating medium itself. Cash was particularly sparse in the smallest denominations, and most small-scale transactions were local ones, between parties who shared at least a neighborhood, and perhaps further social bonds as well. Rather than resolving every transaction in cash at the moment of exchange, the parties would often let their accounts accumulate up to periodic reckonings, or address a credit owed from one neighbor to a debt owed to another. That network of mutual trust and accommodation supplied the want of ready coin, and each successful transaction reinforced it: "credit" was synonymous with "trust" and with "reputation" in the period. The value of credit as social and moral capital opposed its potential value as fiscal, interest-bearing capital. "Lend, hoping for no return," said the Gospel (Luke 6:35). A loan with no interest was a deed of charity, a way to promote the prosperity of a neighbor and of the whole neighborhood, and an investment in the soundness of the lender's credit network and so in their personal creditworthiness, against which they might expect to borrow in turn.[21] An interest-bearing loan was usury.

But, as the early modern market expanded, so did the utility of money, as did the demand to put a direct price upon the convenience of its "use" through usury. Contemporaries hotly debated whether usury was a necessary evil in their expanding market; in what forms or under what constraints it might be tolerable; and whether a sincere interest in each other's prosperity might clear the conscience of the two parties – but that usury was an evil remained given.[22] Usury was atomizing and antisocial, exploiting individuals rather than affirming communities. It endowed a sign system based in metallic tokens with an unnatural simulation of animate, organic life, the capacity not only to move but to breed. And it detached credit from its ground in an individual's material-ethical synthesis of "worth" and referred it instead to the expansion of this self-propagating sign system – not only parodying the professed order of human values rooted in living bodies and their social and familial relations, but also threatening to supersede it.[23] One of Donne's libertine speakers proclaims that "our new nature, use" has made gold "the soul of trade": the phrase is transgressive enough if we take "soul" in the sense of "essence," but even more disturbing if we apply its Aristotelian meaning of "animating principle" or "life force."[24] In "use," the practice of usury, the formerly "natur[al]" relation between agent and instrument in "trade" becomes transposed: money becomes the agent, people the instruments.

Between the informal reckoning of neighborly debits and loans and the problematically intraformal systems of usury lay the formal instrument of the bond, whose use expanded exponentially in the period.[25] A bond specified a debt and a term for its repayment, but did not exact any interest over the course of its term. Instead, it gave the lender a claim not only upon the estate of the borrower, but also upon the borrower's body: a defaulted bond authorized the lender to imprison the borrower, who would need to find some way of paying off the debt before he could regain freedom. The expectation was that imprisonment would force the debtor to draw upon resources he might otherwise be protecting from the creditor, by liquidating assets, calling up credits of his own, or pleading for the generosity of friends. Bonds allowed credit relations to move beyond their ground in direct expressions of local, interpersonal trust by affording a mechanism for credit that did not depend either on the borrower's position to impress the lender with his worthiness, or on the lender's position to shame the borrower into repayment. But the potential costs of doing business this way were savage; Francis Bacon pointed out that, despite the uncharitable nature of usury, the "easy borrowing upon interest" was a more generous provision than "the most sudden undoing" of liquidations or "forfeitures of mortgages and bonds."[26] Many playwrights, poets, and pamphleteers had personal experience of debt imprisonment, including Ben Jonson, John Lyly, Thomas Middleton, George Chapman, and Thomas Dekker.[27] But on stage, the struggle between the bankrupt sons of learning and their worldly-wise creditors went the other way. Their comedy glories in the triumph of wit over debt.

The contest between the witty young gentleman prodigal and the cunning old citizen usurer is a staple of comic plotting in the period. In plays such as Middleton's *A Trick to Catch the Old One* (1605), the usurer is cunning and spider-like, sitting at the center of a conspiratorial network of gallants and prostitutes in his pay, an antisociety. These human instruments lure the prodigal to partake of glamorous and expensive trifles, and steer him to the usurer for money to pay for them, so that he may snare the youth in bonds and make away with his land. But the prodigal proves to have a resource of his own to pit against the entrapments of financial instruments, the resource of his wits: an ingenious capacity for deception, for evasion, for the formulation of unlikely alliances and outlandish counterplots. Where the usurer's plotting is diabolical and apparently inescapable in its mastery of the ways of the material world, the prodigal's plotting is metafictively comic. The prodigal's eventual achievement of mastery not only identifies his witty ingenuity with the author's, but demonstrates, reassuringly, that his world is a comic one, in which events are ultimately determined by the proliferative forms of genre rather than by those of credit instruments.

As this isometric opposition suggests, wit is commensurate to credit in this comic world. But, where the credit instrument seems destructively autonomous – a former projection of personal value that has come to consume personal value – wit is normatively subordinate and serviceable: wit steps out of place only in order to solidify the proper regime of place, to reestablish the relation of person to property that the credit instrument is positioned to violate.[28] In this comic wish-fulfillment, we see the new productivity of sign systems enlisted to affirm the ancient system of feudal values that, in the lived experience of the market, they seem poised to eclipse.

Treasure and Trade

By the first decade of the seventeenth century, a number of late-Elizabethan innovations in national commercial development – the sponsoring of overseas trade through joint-stock companies, the cultivation of new commodity production through "projects" – had overcome early distrust and scandal and begun to thrive.[29] The range of luxuries and fashions offered for virtual consumption on the Jacobean stage amply testifies to the allure, as well as to the real practices, of cosmopolitan consumerism in London; these in turn testify to the expanding extent of trade relations and to the growing prosperity they yielded.[30] But in 1620 growth shuddered to a halt. The Thirty Years' War had begun to engulf trading partners on the continent; a blundering royal intervention into cloth manufacture, the Cockayne Project, had hamstrung England's principal export industry; the velocity of money had visibly slowed, and coin was perceived to be in short supply. The causes and the potential cures for the depression were hotly debated within and around government. The writers who supplied the terms of that debate have come to be known as "the mercantilists."

These writers shared the expectations that international trade followed consistent, observable patterns, from which regular "laws" should be abstracted; that international trade defined national prosperity; that a prosperous nation was one that exported more than it imported; and that the measure of such a happy balance of trade was a net influx of precious metals into the kingdom.[31] They differed sharply about the causal relations among these factors, and therefore about the best policies for reviving prosperity. For Gerard de Malynes, the key policies were monetary interventions – mandating foreign exchange rates, adjusting the mint par between gold and silver, forbidding usury. Where good money was, trade would follow. The exportation of bullion was therefore anathema, and those who profited from it did so at the commonwealth's expense. It was plain to Malynes that the shortage of coin was the cause of the depression, and that the shortage was itself caused by the malfeasance of exporters and exchangers who treated money as a commodity.

To Edward Misselden and Thomas Mun, the measures demanded by Malynes were delusive. The national and international money markets were not to be wished away by royal fiat; and the fact that so many states had again and again attempted to restrain the export of bullion showed that the task was futile. While the "laws" of mercantile trade were to Malynes continuous with ethical rectitude and political allegiance to the sovereign, to Misselden and Mun they were homologous to the laws of nature in their autonomy from ethical judgment and political will – "a necessity beyond all resistance," as Mun concludes.[32] Mun was a director of the East India Company, whose trade relied on exporting bullion to buy Indian goods for reexport in Europe. He argues that the export of money in this trade is only the appearance of loss to those who do not properly account for the full scope of its circuit: "thus take the voyages altogether in their medium [mean], the moneys exported will be returned to us more than trebled." Moreover, he argues, tradesmen don't make money by saving it, but by exchanging it for wares and selling those wares in turn; "they that have wares can never want money." And the same, Mun says, is true of the common wealth: "it is in the stock of the Kingdom as in the states of private men."[33] Rather than regulate the commercial practices of "private men," the state should emulate them – indeed, cannot *but* emulate them, as any attempt to differentiate the scalar congruence Mun posits between national and private "states" will bow to the "necessity beyond resistance" of the laws of commerce. This homology between the propertied individual and the state is the basis of political economy: it transposes "economy," previously a subset of pragmatic ethics regarding the management of household property and dependents, into the realm of politics.

Misselden and Mun adopted a tone of hard-headed matter-of-factness that professed to ground their theories in the world of experience, implying that their opponents were merely engaged in wishful thinking. Yet, as Valerie Forman has demonstrated, their discourse bears remarkable affinities to romance, the imaginative genre most invested in exotic fantasy and wish fulfillment.[34] For Forman, the give and take between mercantile and imaginative forms is crucial to Mun's formulation of investment. Not only do dramatic romances directly represent and valorize foreign travels and interactions; the tragi-comic plot of dramatic romance descends into apparently absolute loss as its first movement, and then, once all seems lost, it transforms that experience of loss into one of spectacular, unlooked-for bounty. This generic plot, she explains, mediates between Christian redemption and mercantile profit. It renders the exportation of bullion as a kind of prudential prodigality: a necessary loss, a wise waste, a sacrifice of present value that will reward the faithful many times over for their trust in destruction and their imagination of reward. This discursive interaction between trade and drama, argues Forman, is the genesis of the modern concept of productive investment.

For Forman, Shakespeare's *The Merchant of Venice* (printed 1600) falls short of this model: the play is too bound by a comic model of restitution, the conservative return to a *status quo ante*, to consider the commercial production of new value as tragicomic investment does.[35] Nevertheless I'd like to close by considering *Merchant*, as the play draws together all the particular terms of the period's debates around money, trade, writing, and fiction into an uneasy synthesis. In coupling Bassanio, the resourceful prodigal, with Portia, the poor little rich girl and disguised legal scholar, the play eroticizes the value and the prodigality of the liberal arts. In the competition among the silver, gold, and lead caskets to enclose Portia's image and fortune, it rehearses the ontological problematics between metallic purity and market price laid bare in the price revolution and debasement. In Antonio's far-flung and fragile trade relations, it considers the risks and rewards of globalized commerce. And in the terrifying "bond" between Antonio and Shylock, it stages credit relations as the means of potentially tragic extremity. Of *Merchant*'s manifold experiments with value, I'll discuss the last: the prolongation of the play after the defeat of Shylock.

Disappointed of his pound of flesh by Portia's legalistic chicanery, abjected before the unveiled power of the state, broken of his ancestral faith, and dispossessed of his wealth and trade in moneylending, Shylock retreats from the stage near the end of Act 4 and does not return. But the play continues for another act despite the early resolution of its harrowing central conflict. It finds new conflict in strife among its newlywed couples – first a war of words between Lorenzo and Jessica, then the strange quarrel over the ring Portia gave Bassanio and that Bassanio gave to Antonio's judge, who was (as Bassanio does not yet know) Portia in disguise. Yet this move to relocate the play's resolution among amatory and aesthetic values – rather than worldly concerns of commerce, law, and race – still produces its meaning in dialogue with the absent presence of the banished usurer.

The initial discord of Lorenzo and Jessica is resolved harmonically, as the two are drawn to listen to a starlit concert by Portia's musicians. In this celebrated passage Lorenzo seems well to be practicing the integrative theory of beauty that he preaches, until he turns to a negative example:

> *Lorenzo.* Sit, Jessica. Look how the floor of heaven
> Is thick inlaid with pattens of bright gold;
> There's not the smallest orb which thou behold'st
> But in his motion like an angel sings,
> Still quiring to the young-eyed cherubims.
> Such harmony is in immortal souls,
> But whilst this muddy vesture of decay [i.e. our body, or our world]
> Doth grossly close us in, we cannot hear it. . .

The man that hath no music in himself
Is fit for treasons, stratagems, and spoils;
The motions of his spirits are dull as night,
And his affections dark as Erebus.
Let no such man be trusted! Mark the music.[36]

"The man that hath no music in himself" must be Shylock, who had earlier in the play ordered Jessica to "stop my house's ears, I mean my casements" to prevent the sounds of street music entering within. Lorenzo seems to invoke Shylock as the scapegoat whose aesthetic failure justifies his exclusion from an otherwise-universal harmony. But, however easily excluded, the thought of Shylock cannot easily be dismissed from a passage that says the stars themselves are made of gold.

Though "pattens" here seem to be operating as tiles, in the other-worldly inversion that turns the roof of our sky into "the floor of heaven," the word denotes the plate on which a priest places the consecrated host. The material specificity of this golden disc seems as crucial as its sacramental status in connecting heavenly purity to base embodiment through aesthetic experience. It recalls the refining work of Sidney's poet, drawing golden values out of a world of brass. But the Eucharist calls for only one patten; it's strange to encounter "pattens" as a plural noun, much less in a multitude, from which their sacramental uniqueness necessarily recedes. How different is a skyful of "pattens of bright gold" from the chestful of ducats that Bassanio presented to Shylock at the trial?

Conversely, Portia's elaborate ruses around her ring would have it be both irreplaceable and inescapable: a fetter by which both Bassanio and Antonio may be "bound" to her satisfaction as once they were to Shylock's. Yet how can "a hoop of gold, a paltry ring" sustain such an all-encompassing burden of singularity in a material world of relational values?[37] In both cases the lovers' intent seems to be to find a way to think about value that could take the place of how Shylock would think: the harmony of the spheres beyond the muddy reach of the market, the compulsory exclusivity of wedded bliss. But every time the lovers insist that these things are as good as "gold," we are bound to wonder what Shylock would think about their material value. In this way Shylock's arbitration of worldly value undergirds their accounts of unworldly values, romantic and aesthetic alike. He remains their silent partner in the complexity of early modern monetary debate.

Notes

1 For the different claims of genre and discipline on the field of writing, see Mary Poovey, *Genres of the Credit Economy: Mediating Value in Eighteenth- and Nineteenth-Century Britain* (Chicago: University of Chicago Press, 2008).

2 Judith Anderson, *Translating Investments: Metaphor and the Dynamics of Cultural Change in Tudor-Stuart England* (New York: Fordham University Press, 2005); Jonathan Gil Harris, *Sick Economies: Drama, Mercantilism, and Disease in Shakespeare's England* (Philadelphia: University of Pennsylvania Press, 2004); David J. Baker, *On Demand: Writing for the Market in Early Modern England* (Stanford, CA: Stanford University Press, 2010); Valerie Forman, *Tragicomic Redemptions: Global Economics and the Early Modern English Stage* (Philadelphia: University of Pennsylvania Press, 2011).

3 Henry William Spiegel, *The Growth of Economic Thought*, 3rd ed. (Durham, NC: Duke University Press, 1991), 47–74; Keith Wrightson, *Earthly Necessities: Economic Lives in Early Modern Britain* (New Haven, CT: Yale University Press, 2000), 108–131.

4 For Spanish literature and culture in this economic moment, see Elvira Vilches, *New World Gold: Cultural Anxiety and Monetary Disorder in Early Modern Spain* (Chicago: University of Chicago Press, 2010).

5 Alec Ryrie, "Reformations," in *A Social History of England: 1500–1750*, edited by Keith Wrightson (Cambridge: Cambridge University Press, 2017), 107–128.

6 Max Weber, *The Protestant Ethic and the Spirit of Capitalism*, translated by Talcott Parsons (1904–1905; London: Routledge, 2001); Andrea Finkelstein, *The Grammar of Profit: The Price Revolution in Intellectual Context* (Leiden: Brill, 2006); Kasey Evans, *Colonial Virtue: The Mobility of Temperance in Renaissance England* (Toronto: University of Toronto Press, 2012).

7 Steve Hindle, *On the Parish? The Micro-Politics of Poor Relief in Rural England, c. 1550–1750* (Oxford: Clarendon Press, 2004).

8 Joyce Oldham Appleby, *Economic Thought and Ideology in Seventeenth-Century England* (Princeton, NJ: Princeton University Press, 1978), 52–72.

9 Ibid., 129–157.

10 Lisa Jardine and Anthony Grafton, "'Studied for Action': How Gabriel Harvey Read His Livy," *Past & Present* 129.1 (1990), 30–78; Lorna Hutson, *Thomas Nashe in Context* (Oxford: Clarendon Press, 1989).

11 Richard Helgerson, *The Elizabethan Prodigals* (Berkeley: University of California Press, 1976), 27; Richard Helgerson, *Self-Crowned Laureates: Spenser, Jonson, Milton, and the Literary System* (Berkeley: University of California Press, 1983).

12 Spenser, *The Faerie Queene*, edited by Thomas P. Roche, Jr. (New York: Penguin, 1978): 4.proem.i-v.

13 Wendy Wall, *Staging Domesticity: Household Work and English Identity in Early Modern Drama* (Cambridge: Cambridge University Press, 2002); Natasha

Korda, *Shakespeare's Domestic Economies: Gender and Property in Early Modern England* (Philadelphia: University of Pennsylvania Press, 2002).

14 Finkelstein, *Grammar of Profit*, 1–2.

15 Whitney R. D. Jones, *The Tudor Commonwealth 1529–1559* (London: Athlone, 1970).

16 Cited in R. H. Tawney and Eileen Power, eds., *Tudor Economic Documents* (London: Longmans, Green, and Co., 1924), vol. 2, 179. This paragraph condenses an argument I made in "Crisis Before Economy: Dearth and Reformation in the Tudor Commonwealth, 1541–1562," *Journal of Cultural Economy* 5.2 (2012), 147–163.

17 *A Discourse of the Commonweal of This Realm of England*, attributed to Sir Thomas Smith, edited by Mary Dewar (Charlottesville: University Press of Virginia, 1969).

18 *Respublica, an Interlude for Christmas 1553, Attributed to Nicholas Udall*, edited by W. W. Greg (London: Oxford University Press, 1952), 4.4.1069–1076.

19 John Donne, "A Sermon Preached at Greenwich, April 30, 1615," in *The Sermons of John Donne, Vol. 1*, edited by Evelyn M. Simpson and George R. Potter (Berkeley: University of California Press, 1953), 9.

20 Philip Sidney, *The Major Works*, edited by Katherine Duncan-Jones (Oxford: Oxford University Press, 2002), 216; and see Catherine Bates, *On Not Defending Poetry: Defence and Indefensibility in Sidney's* Defence of Poesy (Oxford: Oxford University Press, 2017).

21 Craig Muldrew, *The Economy of Obligation: The Culture of Credit and Social Relations in Early Modern England* (New York: Palgrave, 1998).

22 Norman Jones, *God and the Moneylenders: Usury and Law in Early Modern England* (Oxford: Basil Blackwell, 1989).

23 David Hawkes, *The Culture of Usury in Renaissance England* (New York: Palgrave Macmillan, 2010).

24 John Donne, "Elegy 13: Love's Progress," l. 16, in *The Major Works*, edited by John Carey (Oxford: Oxford University Press, 1990), 60.

25 Amanda Bailey, *Of Bondage: Debt, Property, and Personhood in Early Modern England* (Philadelphia: University of Pennsylvania Press, 2013).

26 Francis Bacon, "Of Usury," in *Francis Bacon: A Selection of His Works*, edited by Sidney Warhaft (New York: Macmillan, 1965), 153.

27 Bailey, *Of Bondage*, 4.

28 Michel de Certeau demonstrates how *le propre* integrates the normative regimes of propriety and property in *The Practice of Everyday Life*, translated by Steven Rendall (1980; Berkeley: University of California Press, 1984).

29 Joan Thirsk, *Economic Policy and Projects: The Development of a Consumer Society in Early Modern England* (Oxford: Clarendon Press, 1978).

30 Linda Levy Peck, *Consuming Splendor: Society and Culture in Seventeenth-Century England* (Cambridge: Cambridge University Press, 2005).

31 Appleby, *Economic Thought*, 24–51; Harris, *Sick Economies*, 1–28.

32 Gerard de Malynes, *Lex Mercatoria* (London, 1622); Thomas Mun, *England's Treasure by Forraign Trade* (Fairfield, NJ: Augustus M. Kelley, 1986), 87.

33 Mun, *England's Treasure*, 14–19.
34 Forman, *Tragicomic Redemptions*.
35 Ibid., 27–63.
36 William Shakespeare, *The Merchant of Venice*, edited by Leah Marcus (New York: W. W. Norton, 2006), 5.1.65–95.
37 Ibid., 5.1.267, 5.1.158.

CHAPTER 3

Literary and Economic Exchanges in the Long Eighteenth Century

E. J. Clery

Britain in the "long eighteenth century" was the stage for some of the most momentous phases in the emergence of modern capitalism, from the founding of key financial institutions to stock market crashes, rapid urbanization, the beginnings of industrialization, and the expansion of empire. This chapter will trace the often formative role of imaginative writing in conceptualizing monetary and socioeconomic transformation. Prior to the division of disciplines, figures such as Daniel Defoe and Bernard Mandeville moved between modes now differentiated as "literary" and "economic," while, at the end of the period, even exponents of emergent political economy – such as Thomas Malthus and Jane Marcet – felt called to answer the representations of a poet, and a verse satire helped to shift government economic policy. The following sections will examine by turn the place of literature in framing and contesting the new centrality of credit, the defining metaphors that marked the route to a "de-moralized" economic science, and how the focus on landed property and wealth inequality in the work of realist and Gothic novelists relates to heterodox traditions, outside neoclassical economics.

Debt Nation

In 1694 a private joint-stock company was founded, with the specific aim of raising loans to allow the government to rebuild a navy devastated by war with France. A syndicate of subscribers paid bullion and in return received generous interest payments of 8 percent per year. Government debt was itself then monetized in the form of "securities." The company, named the Bank of England, was at first seen as an emergency measure and, by opponents of the Whig government, as a temporary evil.

Writers now designated "literary," Daniel Defoe and Joseph Addison chief among them, began to translate fiscal innovation into politically and

culturally meaningful language, arguably contributing to the Bank's permanence by rendering it intelligible. The historian J. G. A. Pocock has
remarked: "[M]en cannot do what they have no means of saying they have
done; and what they do must in part be what they say and conceive that it
is."[1] Pocock's influential work on genealogies of eighteenth-century political thought draws substantially from periodicals such as *The Review* and
The Spectator in order to identify and explicate the conceptual vocabularies
attached to the paradigm shift from landed to mobile property, from "real"
ownership to the "unreal."[2] His own interdisciplinary method and rhetoric
encompassing commerce and virtue, money, passion, and fantasy, have
served as an invitation to investigate the engagement of "literary" authors
in public debate on economics. In addition, Pocock's attentiveness to the
troping of commerce and credit as permutations of the goddess *Fortuna*
has informed feminist work on the gendering of the economic. Civic
humanist denunciation of the effeminacy of the capitalist economic
"personality" overdetermines debate in this period, creating a discursive
field distinct from nineteenth-century political economy centered on men
and the masculine.[3]

The use of personification and analogy to represent economic ideas is a
striking feature of the new journalism of the Augustan era. Laura Brown
notes, "the female figure is the imaginative touchstone of the encounter
with the material transformations of the modern world."[4] Defoe introduced Credit in *The Review* (1706) as capricious and hypersensitive yet
highly desirable, reliant on regular support from her older sister Money in
order to continue in service to Trade. She shuns ardent suitors and favors
instead those indifferent to her charms. He revived the conceit during the
Sacheverell Riots of 1710–1711, when violent crowds targeted the businesses of Dissenters, a group increasingly prominent among the "monied
interest." Defoe, himself a Dissenter, dramatized the sad case of Lady
Credit, preparing to leave England in response to the upheavals. Addison
advocated the cause of moderation with his famous allegory in number
3 of *The Spectator* (1711), in which "Publick Credit" is presented as a
beautiful Virgin, withered to a skeleton by the cancellation of government
debts threatened by the opposition Tories. "Great is the Power of
Imagination!" Defoe declared; Colin Nicholson remarks, "We are made aware
that the power of the imaginary was becoming a moving force in secular and
material transformations of human relationship and circumstance."[5]

The realization that the nation had been reconfigured around a National
Debt "misrecognized . . . as wealth" was a sporadic process heightened at

times of national crisis.[6] Champions of the financial revolution adhered to
the fetish of Public Credit, construed as the power to borrow and therefore
a cause for political and commercial confidence. Conversely at critical
moments – such as the collapse of South Sea Bubble in 1720 or the
faltering start of the Seven Years' War with France in the late 1750s –
debt, corruption, and effeminacy became the watchwords in pamphlets,
periodicals, and poetry. Satirists such as Alexander Pope and Jonathan
Swift, later succeeded by Henry Fielding and Tobias Smollett, received
patronage from opponents of Whig oligarchy and excoriated a state riddled
with the speculators who dealt in stocks, banknotes, and government
bonds, labelled "stock-jobbers." "Blest paper-credit! last and best supply!
/ That lends Corruption lighter wings to fly," Pope wrote in mock-
obeisance in his "Moral Essay" in verse "On Riches," *Epistle to Bathurst*
(1733).[7]

Although Pope, Swift, and John Gay aimed Juvenalian darts at the
finance-friendly Walpole regime and articulated what Isaac Kramnick
influentially defined as a politics and poetics of nostalgia, they themselves
had dabbled in South Sea Company shares. When considering the
relationship of literature to economics, the marketization of print culture
should be taken into account. Pope's innovative subscription publishing,
which partially liberated him from the constraints of aristocratic patronage, has been compared in method to a joint-stock company.[8]
Unresolved contradictions are manifested in the *Epistle to Bathurst*,
which while deploying antifinance rhetoric also propounds what John
Barrell and Harriet Guest have called a "discourse of economic theodicy," a hybrid idiom that knots together "economic amoralism and
theodicy."[9]

Critical interest in the credit economy of eighteenth-century England
has been driven by the acceleration of stock market crashes through the
1990s and into the twenty-first century. A wide array of works have been
identified as parables of credit, from the novels of Defoe (Sherman,
Thompson) to Pope's *The Dunciad* (Nicholson, Ingrassia, Brown),
Swift's *Gulliver's Travels* (Brantlinger), Richardson's *Pamela* (Ingrassia),
Burney's *Camilla* (Lynch), and Austen's *Pride and Prejudice* (Poovey), to
name but a few. Beyond attending to references to money or promissory
notes or explicit economic argument, critics aim to decode narratives as
allegories or fables of finance, or to posit a shared structure between the
aesthetic and the economic. Peter de Bolla argues for a direct correlation
between treatises on the National Debt and theories of the sublime in the
1750s, both articulating visions of overwhelming excess. James Thompson

in *Models of Value* (1996) posits the kinship between novels and political economy as concurrent and mutually defining discourses, and Mary Poovey similarly privileges narrative fiction in *Genres of the Credit Economy* (2008). However, at one end of the century the first literary genre to grapple with the financial revolution is the journalistic essay, and at the other, a poet offers the clearest instance of an attempt to sway public opinion by troping Public Credit and manipulating the emotions most closely associated with it: hope and fear.[10]

The Bullion Report (1810) criticized the government's decision to impose the Bank Restriction Act (1797), suspending cash payments. The abrupt transition to a paper money regime brought to the fore the Bank of England and an elite of international financiers providing government loans. It also stimulated a mushrooming of banknote- and credit-issuing country banks throughout the country. At a low point in British military and commercial fortunes (1809–1812), the price of gold bullion escalated, banks and businesses collapsed, and public confidence plunged. In the resulting pamphlet war, David Ricardo, a retired stockbroker, debuted as an economic pundit arguing against the inflationary expansion of credit and for a return to convertibility.[11] Prophecies of economic doom were rife, and one of the most arresting and controversial was Anna Letitia Barbauld's vision of the nation in ruins, *Eighteen Hundred and Eleven*, described by its chief detractor as "a [political] pamphlet in verse."[12] Barbauld and her Dissenting circle were critics of the war against Napoleon and at this point strategically exploited the credit crisis in order to bring about a shift in policy. Of the line, "Thy baseless wealth dissolves in air away" the *Anti-Jacobin Review* remarked: "We presume that when Mrs. Barbauld wrote [this] line. . .she had just arisen from a perusal of the *alarming* report of the *Bullion Committee*."[13] Reviewers mocked, but the campaign gained traction and demonstrated the potential of public credit to engage popular opinion and serve as leverage for extra-Parliamentary democratic change.

While national debt fetishized as public credit came to be regarded either as a necessary evil or a foundation of sound government and national security, the laws on personal debt remained highly punitive. "Why," David Hume asked in his essay "Of Public Credit" (1752), "should the case be so different between the public and an individual, as to make us establish different maxims of conduct for each?"[14] He was a sceptic – both on government borrowing and the legitimacy of a legal code that condemned substantial numbers of private debtors to jail.

Personal experience of debt, and in some cases debtors' prison, informs the works of many of the most prominent writers of the period. Eliza Haywood's *The City Jilt* (1726) situates characters with the flowery names of romance in the London square mile, where an elaborate protofeminist revenge fantasy plays out through ruthless application of the laws on credit and debt.[15] In Henry Fielding's *Amelia* (1751) the feckless husband of the longsuffering heroine is imprisoned not once but twice for debt, as if to supply a test-case for the possibility of redemption in a society driven by economic passions. The discovery of a hapless heroine in a sponging-house plays a similarly symbolic role in *Clarissa* (1747–1748) by Samuel Richardson, signifying on the one hand her bankruptcy within a coercive marital economy, and on the other her ability to transcend the dictum of her persecutor Lovelace that "[n]othing sooner brings down a proud spirit, than a sense of lying under pecuniary obligations."[16]

Frances Burney wrote a series of novels in which the credit economy lies in wait for generous-spirited heroines, subjecting them to extremes of suffering that shatter reason and identity. In *Cecilia* (1782), an heiress understands her inheritance to be a "debt contracted to the poor," but her philanthropy drives her into the hands of money-lenders, and she witnesses the nightmare literalization of an "execution" by creditors before enduring her own losses, which leave her at the climax abandoned, without funds or wits, in the backroom of a pawnbroker's shop.[17] *Camilla* (1796) delves even more deeply into the consequences of usury, while in *The Wanderer* (1814) Burney offers immersive insight into the cruelties of the "client economy," "a hidden subsidy to aristocratic wealth" whereby tradespeople assume the debts of defaulting patricians, through the history of a dispossessed gentlewoman forced to enter the workforce.[18] In the 1810s, the grossly corpulent Prince Regent perfectly embodied this class inequity, uniting in his person the themes of public and private debt. Versions can be found in the works of Maria Edgeworth (notably *The Absentee* [1812]) and Jane Austen (*Mansfield Park* [1814]).

The "money-centric fictions" of the eighteenth century, a subset of the subgenre of "it-narratives" or "novels of circulation" in which nonhumans operate as protagonists, are at once witness to the prominence of the Bank of England in public consciousness and "the immediate intensity of credit ... in a way directly comparable to our own."[19] Joseph Addison's "Adventures of a Shilling" (*Tatler* 249, 11 Nov 1710) pays tribute to the Great Recoinage of 1696, an attempt to restore to face value a currency undermined by forgery. The appeal of Charles Johnstone's *Chrysal, or The*

Adventures of a Guinea (1760–1765) was in part due to the shortage of gold during the Seven Years' War, when coin-clipping was rife. Thomas Bridges' *Adventures of a Bank-Note* (1770–1771) has been described by Mary Poovey as a hybrid of economic and imaginative writing, first designed by its author, a former banker, to familiarize readers with the characteristics of paper money.[20] Although these tales typically employed the comic tone of the picaresque, the humanizing of money and its central agency involved a reciprocal decentering and even dehumanizing of people in a way that hinted at a menacing shift in values. Financial innovation came at a price. Percy Bysshe Shelley addressed the casualties of the wartime paper money regime, including those hung for passing forged banknotes, in *The Mask of Anarchy* (1819): "Paper Coin," the "Ghost of Gold," represented a new stage in the history of oppression and dispossession.

De-Moralizing the Economic

The metaphorics of national prosperity in the eighteenth century ended with an Invisible Hand, and began with a beehive. In 1705 *The Grumbling Hive: Or, Knaves turn'd Honest*, an anonymous 26-page doggerel poem, was published, to all appearances a satire on human foibles in the tradition of Aesop and La Fontaine, illustrating the clever paradox that national greatness depends on unruly selfish individualism and strict virtue will lead to economic and political decline. In 1714 the poem was reissued as *The Fable of the Bees: or, Private Vices, Publick Benefits*, supplemented by a prose commentary and an essay cynically locating the "Origin of Moral Virtue" in competitive pride. Only in 1723, in the aftermath of the South Sea Bubble, did Bernard Mandeville, a physician of Dutch origins, come forward as author, further expanding the work with explanatory "Remarks" and two new essays. At this moment of soul-searching over the economic direction of the nation, his outrageously irreligious arguments gained extensive publicity.

A long succession of commentators (today divided into disciplinary silos), including Samuel Johnson, Francis Hutcheson, Alexander Pope, Eliza Haywood, Voltaire, David Hume, Henry Fielding, and Adam Smith, felt compelled to contest Mandeville's central doctrine that shameless pursuit of personal gain will of itself ultimately yield public benefits. In doing so, they sometimes found their own stances altering. Adam Smith placed *Fable of the Bees* under the heading "licentious systems" in *The*

Theory of Moral Sentiments (1759) before embracing the idea of cohesion accidentally arising from self-interest in less tendentious form in *The Wealth of Nations* (1776).[21] Antagonists and disciples rarely mention the original poem, yet the distillation of socioeconomic theory into popular jingles enhanced the axiomatic quality of the claims: "Then leave Complaints: Fools only strive / To make a Great an Honest Hive"; "Fraud, Luxury and Pride must live, / While we the Benefits receive."[22]

Mandeville's insidious success relates to the aggressive expansion of British colonialism and overseas trade in the era of the financial revolution. The Bank of England, like the Scottish East India Company and the ill-fated Darien Scheme, was a project of the merchant adventurer and slave trader William Paterson. The South Sea Company was founded on the *Asiento*, the contract extracted from the Treaty of Utrecht (1712) for delivery of 148,000 Africans into slavery in Spanish America over a thirty year period. The collapse of the Darien Scheme and later the South Sea Bubble generated acute moral panic, but the evil of slavery itself was obfuscated in imperialist panegyrics such as Pope's *Windsor Forest* (1713) with its anticipation of nineteenth-century *pax britannica* as it was in James Thomson's more nakedly hypocritical "Rule, Britannia!" (1740).[23]

Robinson Crusoe (1719), the tale of a colonial adventurer marooned for twenty-eight years on an uninhabited Caribbean island, became the most popular and enduring instance of a mode that might be termed the imperialist *picaresque*, counting Aphra Behn, Penelope Aubin, Eliza Haywood, and Ambrose Evans, as well as Jonathan Swift (satirically) and later Olaudah Equiano (oppositionally), among its practitioners. The position of Defoe's novel at the intersection of literature and economics is, however, unique. Stripped of imperialist context and narrative complexity, the central episode in which Crusoe systematically achieves self-sufficiency and even prosperity in his solitary state came to operate metaphorically as a fable of *Homo economicus* and, from the 1870s onwards, as an illustration of the marginal theory of value, a textbook example of neoclassical economics that continues to be applied to this day.

If Defoe had arranged breadcrumb trails to lead economists and literary critics in opposite directions, the results after two centuries could not have been starker. Scholars of literary Crusoe discussed spiritual biography, seizing on sparse allusions to Original Sin, penitence, and redemption. Economists were transfixed by Crusoe, the amoral rational man intent on maximizing his resources. Evidence for both versions can be found in the work's most frequently quoted passage, in which the castaway apostrophizes coins salvaged from the shipwreck: "O Drug! said I aloud, what art thou good for... However, upon Second Thoughts, I took it away."[24] What begins as high-flown moral sermon ends with prudential *bathos*. The abrupt shift in register led Coleridge to make a comparison with Shakespeare. Irony or *aporia*?

The late twentieth century saw the start of a convergence. Literary critics shifted the focus of their ethical concerns from the state of Crusoe's soul to his dealings with colonized and enslaved subjects, while economists commenced a critique of the centrality of the Crusoe myth within their discipline. Deirdre McCloskey led the rhetorical turn of the 1980s, inspiring curiosity about the process by which Defoe's literary scenario metamorphosed into the favorite illustration of microeconomic principles of marginal utility, underpinning the claims of neoclassical economics to the status of science. During the 1990s, Ulla Grapard interrogated the myth from a feminist perspective, but it was only in the 2010s, with the spur of the wholesale failure of mainstream economics to prevent or account for the Global Financial Crisis, that the questioning of Crusoe as pedagogic model became urgent.[25]

In addition to occupying a singular position at the bifurcation of disciplines, *Robinson Crusoe* has also figured prominently in the development of the interdisciplinary field of economic criticism. Maximillian E. Novak in 1962 sought to demonstrate that "Defoe transmuted his economic theories into fiction in much the same manner as he fictionalized his economic tracts."[26] Studies by Bram Dijkstra (1987) and Mona Scheuermann (1993) explored *Roxana: The Fortunate Mistress* (1724), in which Defoe configures sexual exchange and women's economic agency with the bonus of a cameo appearance by the real-life banker Sir Robert Clayton (1629–1707). Through its portrayal of the Anglo-Dutch merchant class, it offers rich evidence of Defoe's mercantilist worldview.

Yet, in the day, it was a deserted village rather than a desert island that gained purchase as a metaphorical provocation to economic ideas. Oliver Goldsmith's *The Deserted Village* (1770) went through multiple editions by the end of the century before becoming both a radical touchstone and an anthology favorite during the nineteenth century. The poem was the product of the author's observation of rural depopulation during his upbringing in Ireland and field research in the hinterland of the imperial metropolis as he attempted to make his way as an impecunious author in London. One influence was John Brown's pamphlet *Estimate of the Manners and Principles of the Times* (1757–1758), inspired by humiliating military defeat, a blistering attack on Mandeville's argument that commerce promotes national greatness. Brown's prognosis revived the classical cyclical theory linking trade and luxury as a threat to the integrity of the social body.

Unease over Britain's territorial expansion following the Seven Years' War informs Goldsmith's vision, as he recasts the narrative of decline in seductively sentimental mode. The speaker laments "Sweet Auburn," a village reduced to ruin. The landlord is enriched by imperial trade and, indifferent to the welfare of the local peasantry, neglects agriculture and domestic manufacture while indulging his private pleasures. Landscape gardening, rampant consumerism, urbanization, and emigration driven by unemployment are among the poem's targets, all mediated by heart-wrenching vignettes contrasting then and now. A single couplet developed, meme-like, an independent afterlife as a vehicle of protest: "Ill fares the land, to hastening ills a prey, / Where wealth accumulates, and men decay" (ll. 51–52).

There is a hint that Adam Smith had *The Deserted Village* in mind when he formulated the counter-metaphor of the Invisible Hand, to illustrate the hidden workings of capital (whatever its source) as economic stimulus. Smith complains that "five years have seldom passed" without a publication "pretending to demonstrate that the wealth of the nation was fast declining, that the country was depopulated."[27] Goldsmith's poem had appeared exactly five years before Smith completed *The Wealth of Nations* for the press. It subsequently nettled Smith's disciples, not least due to its adoption by such champions of the working poor as Thomas Spence and John Thelwall, and its metamorphosis from quarto volume to penny pamphlet.[28]

Robert Malthus was prompted to publish *An Essay on the Principle of Population* (1798) as a rebuke to the socioeconomic argument associated with Goldsmith by demonstrating mathematically that excess population relative to subsistence, rather than depopulation, was the true danger. Still, the emotive power of the depiction of a lost village, combined with the moral stand against the "bloated mass" of empire and "the rage of gain" (ll. 389, 424), made it the case that apologists for political economy needed to answer when facing the general public. Malthus, in the second edition in 1803, utilized the explanatory fable of "Nature's Feast," from which paupers are excluded for the greater good. It caused an outcry and was removed from later editions. Jane Marcet, in her *Conversations on Political Economy* (1816; seven editions by 1827), was more successful, making a special point of demolishing the intellectual credentials of *The Deserted Village*.

As the "Industrious Revolution" fed into the Industrial Revolution and workers were reduced metonymically to "hands" and metaphorically or legally to slaves, literary writers continued to address economic dislocation, if rarely to analyze it. The Georgic tradition in English poetry, including John Dyer's *The Fleece* (1757) and James Grainger's *The Sugar Cane* (1764), was to some extent complicit in the reification of labor; a later poet objected, "The Muse thinks it disgraceful of a Briton to sing of the Sugar-cane, since it is owing the Slavery of the Negroes."[29] Laboring-class writers such as Stephen Duck, Mary Collier, and Robert Burns turned the genre's tropes to subversive ends. William Cowper and a host of other poets were instrumental in the slow shift of public opinion from utility to morality on the question of the slave trade in the period from the late 1780s to abolition in 1807. The Lake Poets William Wordsworth and Robert Southey championed the English rural poor in opposition to the growing influence of political economy on government policy.

"Economy" was itself adopted as metaphor by the pioneering Swedish scientist Carl Linnaeus, along with English poet-proselytizers Cowper, Erasmus Darwin, and Samuel Taylor Coleridge, when evoking the autonomy of nature as system. On the one hand Enlightenment, a secularized theodicy, granted human beings preeminence and justified their exploitation of other life-forms; on the other, the period saw the dawn of an anticapitalist ecological consciousness, found in the poetry of Charlotte Smith, William Blake, and, above all, John Clare. Clare condemned the "vile enclosure" of wild spaces in "The Lament of Swordy Wells" (c. 1821–1824): the limestone heath protests at being turned "inside out / For sand and grit and stones" while wildlife perishes from loss of habitat.[30] This rare attempt to lend a voice to nature was equally an attempt to articulate the value of the "noneconomic."

Maintaining Plutocracy?

Literary writers gave imaginative shape to aggressive capital accumulation. Novelists in the period compulsively explored the concentration of capital in landownership and the employment of new legal devices to erode the claims of wives, daughters, and younger sons to a share in property. The eighteenth century was the era of the "Bloody Code" during which the number of capital statutes quadrupled, and a thief could be hung for goods worth as little as twelve pence.[31] The French Revolution encouraged a generation of "Jacobin" writers to challenge the order of things as adumbrated by Adam Smith: "Civil government, so far as it is instituted for the security of property is in reality instituted for the defense of the rich against the poor, or those who have some property against those who have none at all."[32]

Cultural materialism has had a defining role in the field of eighteenth-century studies, and with it the Marxist doctrine that class struggle is the motor of history. Ian Watt in *The Rise of the Novel* (1957) linked the ascent of the bourgeoisie and the stylistic conventions of "classic realist" fiction, tacitly drawing on Lucien Goldmann's principle of homology: cultural forms as the expression of an economically determined worldview. Raymond Williams, attempting to describe Jane Austen's fictional world, attributed to literary representation a more nuanced yet still secondary relation to the "interlocking" of old and new class interests within agrarian capitalism: an "openly acquisitive [high bourgeois] society, which is concerned also with the transmission of wealth, is trying to judge itself at once by an inherited code and by the morality of improvement."[33] The prospect poem constructed a civic humanist version of social cohesion, John Barrell has argued, consolidating the perspective of the male landowner while figuring the rural laborer as a diminutive picturesque detail.[34]

A lineage has often been traced between the novel and criminal biography.[35] Sometimes the ties between literary form and the legal apparatus surrounding property could be direct. Defoe's *Moll Flanders* and *Colonel Jack* (both 1722) were outright propaganda for "secondary sentencing," the transportation of penitent convicts to labor in the American colonies as an alternative to the noose, a practice in which Defoe himself invested. Every year, as an entertainment for holidaying apprentices, George Lillo's "bourgeois tragedy" *The London Merchant* (1731) was performed to instill due reverence for the moral claims of property and the doctrine of *doux commerce*. Henry Fielding's patrician view of crime as the outgrowth of luxury and finance was backed by his position as London's chief magistrate and communicated simultaneously through his wildly popular novels, political journalism, and pamphlets such as *An Enquiry into the Causes of the late Increase of Robbers* (1750) and *Proposals for Making an Effectual Provision for the Poor* (1753).

Sentimental literature served to mediate the transition from the old Poor Laws, based on locality and statutory and religious duty, to an increasingly privatized conception of charity. At mid-century, grand philanthropic schemes such as Coram's Foundling Hospital and the Magdalen Hospital for Penitent Prostitutes enlisted the talents of artists, musicians, and writers to open the pockets of the rich. Sarah Fielding's *David Simple* (1744, 1753), Oliver Goldsmith's *The Vicar of Wakefield* (1766), Henry

Brooke's *The Fool of Quality* (1765–1770), Henry Mackenzie's *The Man of Feeling* (1771), and above all the works of Laurence Sterne, evolved an ornate language of disinterested sympathy and charitable disbursement that, many have argued, represents the reverse side of capitalist self-interest through its shared engagement in a calculus of "worthy" poverty.[36]

Edmund Burke's comparison of the state to an entailed inheritance launched the revolution debate in England; property safeguarded in perpetuity would form a natural bulwark against French radicalism, which he associated with financial speculation. The critique offered by the so-called Jacobin writers was economic as well as political. "Security of Property!" Mary Wollstonecraft wrote, disclaiming charity in favor of rights: "Behold in a few words the definition English liberty... But softly, it is only the property of the rich that is secure, the man who lives by the sweat of his brow has no asylum from oppression."[37] In her unfinished novel *The Wrongs of Woman* (1798), she gave voice to Jemima, a social outcast: "I began to consider the rich and poor as natural enemies, and became a thief from principle."[38] Redistribution of wealth became an increasingly prominent theme in the writings of Thomas Paine, while William Godwin supplemented his *Enquiry Concerning Political Justice* (1793) with a best-selling novel *Caleb Williams* (1794), in which a robber-chief tells the hero, a servant prosecuted on false charges by a feudalistic master (often described in criticism as an avatar of Burke), that his banditry aims "to counteract the partiality and iniquity of public institutions."[39] Establishment figures countered by commissioning Hannah More, dramatist and Evangelical abolitionist, to write short tales for working class readers justifying socioeconomic hierarchy that later served as a model for Harriet Martineau.

The political fictions of the 1790s coincided with the craze for "Gothic" and shared some of its conventions. The jurist William Blackstone compared the legal system to "an old Gothic castle" only partially modernized, and romance writers from Horace Walpole onwards were drawn to the current "hotspot" of landed property ownership.[40] Walpole's *The Castle of Otranto* (1764) inspired a host of imitations, and Ann Radcliffe's celebrated works many more, typically hinging on mysteries surrounding inheritance and usurpation that give rise to vengeful phantoms or more subtly nightmarish affects. Although generally set in a version of the distant past, *mortmain* or strict settlement, the inalienable possession of lands, a "dead hand" on the lives of future generations, was a device increasingly employed to counter the danger posed to great estates by the culture of credit. Walter Scott, well-versed in the stadial theory of the

Scottish school, took inspiration from Gothic for his more programmatic fictional explorations of "the opposition between a customary feudal authority and a competitive market economy, the worlds of fixed and fluid wealth."[41]

Female readers of fiction were the frequent target of moral denunciation or mockery. Not coincidentally, novels provided "a safe space for exploring economic reality for women."[42] It was here they could find copious illustrations of their commodity nature in the marriage market, and the hazard of their devaluation as property through seduction or rape. Ruth Perry describes Richardson's *Clarissa* as "an economic morality play" demonstrating "the combined effects of primogeniture and capital accumulation for female offspring in landowning families," and has shown that Richardson was not alone in chronicling the "Great Disinheritance," the systematic undermining of women's claims to property in the form of dowries, pin money, jointures, and annuities.[43] A work such as Eliza Haywood's *Betsy Thoughtless* (1751) was a primer in the economic and legal powerlessness of the wife in a marriage gone wrong. The 1753 Marriage Act, like the Game Laws, was designed primarily for the protection of property; specifically, the prevention of clandestine "love matches," which endangered patriarchal economic interests and legitimate succession. Many a female novelist prior to Wollstonecraft made the point that a *feme covert* was in effect the property of her husband, and therefore a slave. Divorce was unobtainable by female claimants; the best a beleaguered heroine could hope for was poetic justice, through the fortuitous death of the domestic despot. Fiction also broadcast women's limited options for subsistence outside wedlock; paid work from prostitution to the unreliable business of novel-writing itself.

Sense and Sensibility (1811), Jane Austen's debut, begins with the disinheritance of a bereaved family of women and proceeds to a meticulous account of property relations and the acquisitive spirit in British society, as we follow the Dashwood sisters from the provinces to the metropolis. The economist Thomas Piketty cites the novel in his celebrated long view of wealth distribution and the dominance of the rentier class. Austen is among those who "depicted the effects of inequality with a verisimilitude and evocative power that no statistical or theoretical analysis can match."[44] Joanna Rostek has gone much further, positioning Austen as an economic thinker whose fiction, alongside works by Mary Hays, Wollstonecraft, and others, represents an alternative mode of knowledge production remedying the androcentric bias of political economy.[45] Austen's command of economic questions is apparent in her final unfinished work *Sanditon* (1817), where she stages conversations (comparably to her contemporary Jane Marcet, but with laughs) suggesting an acquaintance with Hume, Smith, and Malthus, and insight gained from the career of her banker brother, who went under in the crash of 1816.[46]

Feminist, postcolonial, and ecocritical approaches conceive the literature of the period as a forum for debating the ethics of economics, with the capacity to articulate dissent, resistance, or outright opposition to emerging doctrines. Scholars have examined gift exchange – "a political economy not written from the perspective of capital and markets" – in the work of William Blake and other Romantic poets.[47] Sarah Fielding's *David Simple* (1744) has been described as "proto-communist"; *Millenium Hall* (1762) by Sarah Scott represents a utopia of noncommodified labor organized along nonpatriarchal lines.[48] They offer glimpses of a long history of economic heterodoxy. Meanwhile, the enduring preoccupation with landed property in eighteenth-century literature, alongside the new wealth of speculative capital, challenges the agenda set for economic criticism by neoclassical economics.

Notes

1 J. G. A. Pocock, "Virtue and Commerce in the Eighteenth Century," *Journal of Interdisciplinary History* 3.1 (1972), 119–134; 122.
2 J. G. A. Pocock, *The Machiavellian Moment: Florentine Political Thought and the Atlantic Republican Tradition* (Princeton, NJ: Princeton University Press, 1975), 451 and *passim*.
3 J. G. A. Pocock, *Virtue, Commerce, and History: Essays on Political Thought and History, Chiefly in the Eighteenth Century* (Cambridge: Cambridge University Press, 1985), 114.
4 Laura Brown, *Fables of Modernity: Literature and Culture in the English Eighteenth Century* (Ithaca, NY: Cornell University Press, 2001), 11.
5 *Daniel Defoe's Review*, edited by John McVeagh (London, 2009), vol. 3, 644–645; Colin Nicholson, *Writing and the Rise of Finance: Capital Satires of the Early Eighteenth Century* (Cambridge: Cambridge University Press, 1994), 46.
6 Patrick Brantlinger, *Fictions of State: Culture and Credit in Britain, 1684–1994* (Ithaca, NY: Cornell University Press, 1996), 3.
7 Alexander Pope, *Selected Poetry*, edited by Pat Rogers (Oxford: Oxford University Press, 2008), 76, ll. 39–40.
8 Nicholson, *Writing and the Rise of Finance*, citing Leslie Stephen, 9.
9 John Barrell and Harriet Guest, "The Uses of Contradiction: Pope's *Epistle to Bathurst*," in *Poetry, Language, and Politics* (Manchester: Manchester University Press, 1988), 79–99; 82–83.

10 On the economic application of the term "hopes and fears" from Davenant to Coleridge, see E .J. Clery, *Eighteen Hundred and Eleven: Poetry, Protest, and Economic Crisis* (Cambridge: Cambridge University Press, 2017), 141.

11 David Ricardo, *The High Price of Bullion, A Proof of the Depreciation of Bank Notes* (London, 1810).

12 John Wilson Croker, review of *Eighteen Hundred and Eleven*, *Quarterly Review* 7 (June 1812), 309.

13 *Anti-Jacobin Review* 42 (June 1812), 205.

14 David Hume, *Essays Moral, Political, and Literary*, edited by Eugene F. Miller, rev. ed. (Indianapolis, IN: Liberty Fund, 1985), 351.

15 See Catherine Ingrassia, *Authorship, Commerce, and Gender in Early Eighteenth-Century England: A Culture of Paper Credit* (Cambridge: Cambridge University Press, 1998), 89–95.

16 Samuel Richardson, *Clarissa*, edited by Angus Ross (1747–1748; Harmondsworth: Penguin, 1985), 449 (III, xxvi).

17 Frances Burney, *Cecilia*, edited by Peter Sabor and Margaret Anne Doody (1782; Oxford: Oxford University Press, 1988), 55.

18 John Brewer, "Commercialization and Politics," in Neil McKendrick, John Brewer, and J. H. Plumb, *The Birth of a Consumer Society: The Commercialization of Eighteenth-Century England* (London: Hutchinson, 1983), 197–262; 198.

19 Brown, *Fables of Modernity*, 97; see also Deidre Lynch, *The Economy of Character: Novels, Market Culture, and the Business of Inner Meaning* (Chicago: University of Chicago Press, 1998), 94–102.

20 Mary Poovey, *Genres of the Credit Economy: Mediating Value in Eighteenth- and Nineteenth-Century Britain* (Chicago: University of Chicago Press, 2008), 144–152.

21 Donald Winch, *Riches and Poverty: An Intellectual History of Political Economy in Britain, 1750–1834* (Cambridge: Cambridge University Press, 1996), 2.

22 Bernard Mandeville, *The Fable of the Bees: Or, Private Vices, Publick Benefits*, edited by F. B. Kaye, (Oxford: Clarendon Press, 1924), vol. 1, 36.

23 See for instance Laura Brown, *Fables of Modernity*, 74–77, and Suvir Kaul, *Poems of Nation, Anthems of Empire: English Verse in the Long Eighteenth Century* (Charlottesville: University Press of Virginia, 2000), 1–8.

24 Daniel Defoe, *Robinson Crusoe*, edited by Thomas Keymer (1719; Oxford: Oxford University Press, 2008), 50.

25 Notably Ulla Grapard and Gillian Hewitson, eds., *Robinson Crusoe's Economic Man: A Construction and Deconstruction* (London: Routledge, 2011); Ufuk Karagöz, "The Neoclassical Robinson: Antecedents and Implications," *History of Economic Ideas* 22.2 (2014), 1–22; Matthew Watson, "Crusoe, Friday and the Raced Market Frame of Orthodox Economics Textbooks," *New Political Economy* 23.5 (2018), 544–559, and other articles by the same author.

26 Maximillian E. Novak, *Economics and the Fiction of Daniel Defoe* (Berkeley: University of California Press, 1962), 102; See subsequent readings of Defoe by Thompson (1996), Poovey (2008), and Sandra Sherman, *Finance and*

Fictionality in the Early Eighteenth Century: Accounting for Defoe (Cambridge: Cambridge University Press, 1996).

27 Adam Smith, *The Wealth of Nations*, edited by R. A. Campbell and A. S. Skinner (1776; Oxford: Oxford University Press, 1976), vol. 1, 344 (II.iii.33).

28 Alfred Lutz, "The Politics of Reception: The Case of Goldsmith's 'The Deserted Village,'" *Studies in Philology* 95.2 (1998), 174–196; Matthew Clarke, "The 'Luxury of Woe': *The Deserted Village* and the Politics of Publication," *European Romantic Review* 26.2(2015), 165–182.

29 Anon, "Argument," *Jamaica* (1777).

30 John Clare, *Major Works*, edited by Eric Robinson, David Powell, and Tom Paulin (Oxford: Oxford University Press, 2008), 148.

31 Douglas Hay, *Albion's Fatal Tree* (London: Penguin, 1975), 18.

32 Smith, *Wealth of Nations*, vol. 2, 715 (V.i.b.12).

33 Raymond Williams, *The Country and the City* (Oxford: Oxford University Press, 1973), 115.

34 John Barrell, *English Literature in History, 1730–80: An Equal, Wide Survey* (London: Hutchinson, 1983).

35 See notably Lennard J. Davis, *Factual Fictions: The Origins of the English Novel* (New York: Columbia University Press, 1983), 126–131

36 See for instance studies by Markman Ellis (1996), Liz Bellamy (1998), and Gillian Skinner (1999).

37 Mary Wollstonecraft, *"A Vindication of the Rights of Men" and "A Vindication of the Rights of Woman,"* edited by Sylvana Tomaselli (Cambridge: Cambridge University Press, 1995), 13.

38 Mary Wollstonecraft, *"Mary" and "The Wrongs of Woman,"* edited by Gary Kelly (Oxford: Oxford University Press, 2007), 105.

39 William Godwin, *Caleb Williams*, edited by Pamela Clemit (1794; Oxford: Oxford University Press, 2009), 209.

40 E. J. Clery, *The Rise of Supernatural Fiction* (Cambridge: Cambridge University Press, 1995), 124.

41 Kathryn Sutherland, "Fictional Economies: Adam Smith, Walter Scott, and the Nineteenth-Century Novel," *ELH* 54.1 (1987), 97–127.

42 Edward Copeland, *Women Writing about Money: Women's Fiction in England, 1790–1820* (Cambridge: Cambridge University Press, 1995), 161.

43 Ruth Perry, *Novel Relations: The Transformation of Kinship in English Literature and Culture, 1748–1818* (Cambridge: Cambridge University Press, 2004), 65.

44 Thomas Piketty, *Capital in the Twenty-First Century*, translated by Arthur Goldhammer (Cambridge, MA: Belknap Presss of Harvard University Press, 2014), 2.

45 Joanna Rostek, *Women's Economic Thought in the Romantic Age: Towards a Transdisciplinary Herstory of Economic Thought* (Abingdon Routledge, 2021).

46 E. J. Clery, "Conversations on Political Economy in *Sanditon*," *Persuasions Online* 38.2 (2018), www.jasna.org/publications-2/persuasions-online/volume-38-no-2/clery.

47 Jack Amariglio and David F. Ruccio, "Literary/Cultural 'Economies,' Economic Discourse, and the Question of Marxism," in *The New Economic Criticism: Studies at the Intersection of Literature and Economics*, edited by Martha Woodmansee and Mark Osteen (London: Routledge, 1999), 381–400; 389.

48 See Donna Landry, "Picturing Benevolence against the Commercial Cry, 1750–98: Or, Sarah Fielding and the Secret Causes of Romanticism," in *The History of British Women's Writing, 1750–1830*, edited by Jacqueline M. Labbe (Houndmills: Palgrave Macmillan, 2010), 150–171; Jennie Batchelor, *Women's Work: Labour, Gender, Authorship, 1750–1830* (Manchester: Manchester University Press, 2010), 29–66.

CHAPTER 4

Economic Literature and Economic Thought in the Nineteenth Century

Sarah Comyn

Sitting in her library, struggling to contain the restlessness brought on by her encounters with Rosamond Lydgate and Will Ladislaw, Dorothea Casaubon tries to steady her mind by "throw[ing] herself energetically into the gravest [subject] of all": political economy. "Here was a weighty subject," she thinks, one that would indicate the "best ways of spending money so as not to injure one's neighbours, or – what comes to the same thing – so as to do them the most good." With her ideas for land management quickly dismissed by her uncle at the beginning of *Middlemarch* (1871–1872) – "[y]oung ladies don't understand political economy, you know" – Dorothea categorizes political economy as "that never-explained science," and yet the impetus to understand the "weighty subject" remains.[1] Despite the ironic undertones of George Eliot's appeal to the explanatory potential and necessity of political economy – Dorothea ultimately dismisses her study as "hopeless" – Dorothea's desire to grasp the gravest subject of all nonetheless points to the significance of political economy as an emergent science that required better explanation, as well as hinting at its social influence, its popularity, and its fascination for literary writers throughout the nineteenth century.

The development of a scientific economic discourse and the expansion of the financial system and markets across the nineteenth century and through the British Empire proved to be rich sources of inspiration for novelists and poets. Fictional writers not only explored the themes of stock market crashes, imperial investments, industrial expansion, gambling and risk taking, fraudulent currencies, and bank failures, but also the failure of political economy to account properly for the inadequacies of the economic system and the people who fell victim to those failures. By 1854, Charles Dickens was criticizing political economy's abstraction from real human experience and concerns, accusing the theory of being a "mere skeleton unless it has a little human covering and filling out, a little human bloom upon it, and a little human warmth in it."[2]

The interplay, interaction, and co-constitution of literary and economic discourses has received significant attention from literary scholars such as Patrick Brantlinger, Gordon Bigelow, Margot Finn, Regenia Gagnier, Catherine Gallagher, Gail Turley Houston, Claudia Klaver, and Mary Poovey, among others, who have examined the aesthetic, generic, and ethical developments and differentiations of these crucial discourses in consort.[3] Producing "a lively new subfield of nineteenth-century British studies," this scholarship has been instrumental in revealing the parallel concerns of literature and economics, investigating, for example, their shared anxieties about the relationship between representation and value, their occupation with the limits and costs of productive labor, and their fascination with the calculations attached to human desire.[4] Reading nineteenth-century literature and economics through this scholarship, this chapter will begin by demonstrating how reading the history of economic thought through the history of literature can offer new ways of exploring the divergences and convergences of these discourses as they became distinctive schools of thought while continuing to draw on each other for explanatory, thematic, and stylistic purposes. Despite literary and economic writers both drawing and developing their boundaries across the nineteenth century, this methodological approach therefore shows how these borders always remain porous and subject to collapse.

Building on this comparative analysis, the subsequent sections provide two case studies of how this methodology can be applied to key shared sites of analysis: the human body, and the economic systems and agents of the nineteenth century. Beginning at the microlevel, "Bodies of Value" considers the economic and ethical relationship of the human body to concepts of value in literary and economic writing. "Systems and Agents" broadens the view of literary and economic interaction, exploring some of the dominant economic systems and agents plotting and populating nineteenth-century literature, from the speculators operating in systems of credit to the commodities circulating around the British Empire and the increased interest of political economists in imperial expansion. Tracking the development of economic thought through the century – from David Ricardo and Thomas Malthus, through John Stuart Mill, to William Stanley Jevons – this chapter will explore the celebratory and critical ways economic writers, essayists, novelists, and poets represented and responded to political economy's evolution.

Literary and Economic Methodologies: Separating Fact from Fiction

One of the key areas of focus for scholars analyzing the relationship between literary and economic discourses has been investigating their demarcation as distinct fields of thought that eventually hardened into separate academic disciplines in a process of what Mary Poovey describes as "generic differentiation": how they came to be perceived as distinct fields not only in their content and subject matter, but also in their genre, form, and stylistic approach.[5] While the extent of this disciplinary separation and specialization as science versus the arts, humanities, and aesthetics continues to be debated, the correspondence between two important political economists of the early nineteenth century points to the unfolding of this delineation.

In response to Malthus's claim that his writings of political economy were "too theoretical," Ricardo famously replied: "If I am too theoretical (which I really believe is the case), you I think are too practical." In their thirteen years-long correspondence, Ricardo and Malthus were fierce intellectual combatants debating the remits, limits, purpose, and foundations of political economy. Ricardo disagreed with Malthus's emphasis on the practical application of his theories, seeing a "great danger in appealing to experience" when there are "so many combinations – so many operating causes in Political Economy."[6] Ricardo's approach as explicated in *On the Principles of Political Economy* (1817) marked a key moment in the development of political economy as a *science*. In contrast to the descriptive and metaphoric language used by Adam Smith in *The Wealth of Nations* (1776) to explain the division of labor in a pin factory or the creation of a woolen coat, for instance, Ricardo sought to assert the scientific and theoretical rigor of political economy, appealing to the "facts," "laws," and "operations" that defined it.[7]

The theoretical abstraction that defined Ricardo's work and irked Malthus managed, according to Poovey, to separate political economy from a "nonspecialist readership" and thereby confirm its disciplinary status as a science – or in Dorothea's words "that never-explained science."[8] Ricardo's turn away from eighteenth-century political economy's – and in particular Smith's – use of narrative and storytelling as an explanatory device in favor of "stylistic and methodological abstraction" saw the move of political economy toward the domain of *facts*.[9] Literary writing, in contrast, emphasized its *fictional* characteristics. Ricardo's abstractions separated, moreover, the economic individual from Smith's social model of human nature defined by "conflicting passions." Instead, an "autonomous" character marked by the "rational pursuit of self-interest emerged."[10]

Yet in separating itself from a common readership, nineteenth-century political economy relied on writers who used literary devices and narratives to explain this new science. Frequently dismissed as "popularizers" of political economy with their scientific contribution questioned, writers like Maria Edgeworth, Jane Marcet, and, later in the century, Harriet Martineau played a crucial role in explaining the theories of political economy.[11] Edgeworth's collection of educational short stories, *The Parent's Assistant* (1796), for instance, is situated in a "Smithean environment" that provides economic instruction to children and their parents, as the "protagonists struggle with issues of consumerism, poverty, competition for resources, and the responsible use of money."[12] Marcet's *Conversations on Political Economy* (1816) adopts a "colloquial form," presenting dialogues between a Mrs. B and her student Caroline that introduce the foundations of political economy.[13] Despite frequently deploying a semi-veiled attack against literature during the education of Caroline, Marcet relies on figurative language and story-telling techniques to advance and explain the theories of political economy. Unlike Ricardo's pursuit of the *scientification* of political economy through abstraction that separated his work from a general audience, Marcet's *Conversations* was praised and sought after precisely because of its popularization of political economy *as a science*. Inspired by Marcet's efforts and "the group of personages that rose up from [her] pages," Martineau would similarly turn to literature to "illustrate" political economy's *"picture"* in her *Illustrations of Political Economy* (1832). Martineau's approach of "exhibit[ing]" the tenets of political economy "in their natural workings in selected passages of social life" emphasized the "signs of increasing stability and prosperity" that lay "just beneath" the seemingly "troubled surface" of Britain's new and evolving economy.[14] Literature could therefore lend political economy its stabilizing explanatory power in ways that promoted the theories of this evolving science.

"Divided by common premises" and mobilizing a language of "switch-points" – "sites of overlap" between the two discourses where the lexical valences of terms such as credit and value were maintained – literature and political economy's "orientations" towards one another shifted over the nineteenth century.[15] Even some of political economy's most trenchant literary critics, such as Charles Dickens, often ironically returned to political economy's "own logic" in order to mount an attack on the theory they viewed as so detrimental to society, registering the mutual imbrication of literary and economic discourses even when they were intent on distinguishing their intellectual pursuits.[16]

John Stuart Mill, the key political economist of the mid-nineteenth century, is a crucial example of this complex relationship. Accused by his critics of creating *Homo economicus* (economic man) – the rational economic individual driven by self-interest – Mill appeared to further delimit political economy's definition, making an "entire abstraction of every other human passion or motive; except those as antagonizing to the desire of wealth."[17] The negative consequences of this limited economic concept of human nature are manifest in the arguments between Margaret Hale and John Thornton about the impending strike in Elizabeth Gaskell's novel *North and South* (1854). Thornton's insistence that "the owners of capital, have a right to choose what we will do with it" despite the costs for their workers, such as the suicide of John Boucher, demonstrates the deadly implications of Thornton's adoption of political economy's abstractions in his pursuit of wealth.[18] Yet in spite of Mill's moves to abstraction, as Claudia Klaver brilliantly shows, he also "return[s] to Smith" by combining scientific "abstract theory with practical application" through his "structural and methodological approach." Mill's distinction between the scientific laws of production and the institutionally-dependent laws of distribution that vary across different societies allows him to reconcile the "scientific aspects of political economy with human elements of social philosophy" and in doing so incorporate ethical concerns into his theory of political economy.[19] Through this intricate negotiation between the pursuit of abstraction and the concern for human nature and social welfare – a negotiation that saw Mill revise his *Principles of Political Economy* (first published in 1848) multiple times – Mill's work becomes emblematic of the economic and social tensions that defined the mid-nineteenth century. The same tensions enliven the work of novelists, poets, and essayists such as Dickens, Gaskell, Eliot, Benjamin Disraeli, Elizabeth Barrett Browning, Thomas Hood, and Henry Mayhew, among others.

In the final quarter of the nineteenth century, political economy underwent a profound change in its focus through the work of the neoclassical economists Jevons, Alfred Marshall, Carl Menger, and Léon Walrus: a shift from a focus on the "laws" of production to those governing consumption. The marginal revolution in economics saw a new theory of value that was not determined by the value of labor (as was the case in the works of Smith, Ricardo, and Mill, for example) but rather by human desires. "Pleasure and pain," Jevons emphatically states, "are undoubtedly the ultimate objects of the Calculus of Economics." Arguing that "*value depends entirely upon utility*," Jevons's *Theory of Political Economy* (1871) located and calculated value in the marginal utility of commodities in satisfying human desires, crucially arguing that the utility (value) of commodities was dependent on their quantity. This shift to a "calculus" of human wants and the ratio of satisfaction provided by various commodities – the relative value of consumer choices – instigated an increasing reliance on mathematics: what Jevons referred to as the "mathematical character of [economic] science." In doing so, Jevons separated his "economics" from the socially and ethically adjectival complexity – political – that determined many of the preceding works on political economy. Assigning economics the "lowest rank of feelings," Jevons delimited the boundaries of economics from the "higher calculus of moral right and wrong."[20]

While the revolution in economic thought undertaken by the neoclassical economists and their heightened emphasis on an economic calculus might suggest a distinct departure from the concerns of literature in the nineteenth century, Regenia Gagnier has made a compelling argument for considering this period as marking a convergence between the two discourses' interests in human desire. The rejection of the labor theory of value and political economy's preoccupation with production by the neoclassical economists was, according to Gagnier, equally prevalent in the "aesthetic rejection of the values of the producer or creator in favor of the consumers of the artwork" and the desires that dictated the purchasing choice.[21] The correspondence between literature and economics and their parallel histories in the emergence of desire are evident, for example, in Dorian Gray's developing "passions for sensations."[22] Gray's "mad hungers" that "grew more ravenous as he fed them" may, at first glance, suggest a counterpoint to the theory of diminishing utility, but instead embody the "insatiable" desire of the modern consumer.[23]

Value in both economics and literature became, therefore, more "subjective" and "psychological."[24] To conceptualize this transformation in the literature of the nineteenth century consider, for example, the difference in focus of the industrial and social problem novels like Dickens's *Hard Times* (1854), Gaskell's *Mary Barton* (1848) and *North and South*, Disraeli's *Sybil* (1845), or Charles Kingsley's *Alton Locke* (1850) – where attention and emphasis is turned towards production – and the economics of aestheticism, consumption, and desire that animate Oscar Wilde's *The Picture of Dorian Gray* (1890), Henry James's *The Spoils of Poynton* (1896–1897), or Walter Pater's *Marius the Epicurean* (1885).[25] The Aesthetic, Decadent, and New Woman "movements" that came to define *fin de siècle* literature were by no means monolithic and instead present a "plurality" and "multiplicity" in their push against cultural norms and their approach to the intersection of economics and aesthetics, ethics and taste, the practical and the psychological. Yet despite this diversity in method, *Homo economicus* and "Aesthetic man" remain kin, with "aesthetic agendas . . . related to economic agendas" through the changing concepts of art (autonomous or commodified?), artist ("creative or alienated producer"?), and consumer (critic, reader, or "man of taste"?).[26] This further interplay between literary and economic discourses in the latter half of the nineteenth century reveals how generative a combined analysis of the evolution of these discourses can be.

Bodies of Value

Labor, as already noted, was crucial to political economy's theory of value for at least the first seventy years of the nineteenth century. "Possessing utility, commodities derive their exchangeable value from two sources" argued Ricardo: "their scarcity ... and the quantity of labour required to obtain them."[27] In his extensive study of "labour as an agent of production," Mill is at pains to catalogue all the labor employed in the production of a staple produce, but it is exactly this aggregation and abstraction of labor that literary writers frequently resist through a humanistic counter discourse.[28] In his 1843 poem, "The Song of the Shirt," Thomas Hood explicitly details, for example, the labor involved and the conditions of "poverty, hunger, and dirt" in which the shirt is made, exclaiming: "It is not linen you're wearing out, / But human creatures' lives!" (ll. 6, 27–28). Playing with and against the abstraction of political economy, literary writers frequently contrasted the metonymic "hands" of industrial labor with characters that gave fuller accounts of their hopes and desires, their suffering, and, frequently, their death.

The bodily cost of labor is poignantly explored through the character of Bessy in Gaskell's *North and South*, who is dying from her work in the cotton factory and her lungs' exposure to the cotton "fluff." So dire are the conditions and remuneration that, Bessy claims, some of the workers rely on these unsafe environments to provide their sustenance, as the factory's waste – the "fluff" – becomes their food. Gaskell does not, however, limit her critique of the conditions of labor in Britain to the industrial cities or classes. Having had her idyllic concepts of the south challenged by the industrial north, Margaret advises Nicholas Higgins not to "go to the South" and become an agricultural laborer as the "mere bodily work would break you":

> You would not bear the dulness of the life; you don't know what it is; it would eat you away like rust ... The hard spade-work robs their brain of life; the sameness of their toil deadens their imagination; they don't care to meet to talk over thoughts and speculations ... You could not stir them up into any companionship, which you get in a town as plentiful as the air you breathe.[29]

As Margaret's observation about the deadening of the imagination and the impact on companionship suggests, nineteenth-century literature was not only concerned with the physical toll of labor, but also explored the mental and interpersonal impact of systems of capital, market relations, industrial modernization, and the commodification of value. One of the characters most demonstrative of the psychological, relational, and physical impacts of a rapidly modernizing and economizing society is the clerk Wemmick in Dickens' *Great Expectations* (1860–1861). Forced to compartmentalize his life – "the office is one thing, and private life is another thing" – Wemmick gets "harder and drier" the closer he gets to work, his smile transformed into a "post-office slit."[30] Wemmick's transformation corresponds to Karl Marx's concept of the commodity fetish that traces the transposition of human qualities onto commodities as the labor that produces them becomes increasingly invisible.[31] While Marx's famous table transforms from wood into a commodity and in doing so "transcends sensuousness," Wemmick's mechanical conversion enacts the opposite movement: from human being to abstracted object, thereby separating Wemmick from the personal relations and feelings that define his homelife in Walworth.[32]

The body and its exchange can, however, also form a site of resistance to market relations. Christina Rossetti's *Goblin Market* (1862) demonstrates the dangers for women entering the market (sexually and economically) through the character of Laura who, though she has "no coin," buys from the goblin men with a lock of her hair and thereby becomes herself a commodity of exchange. In contrast to Laura's exchange, her sister Lizzie refuses to participate in the forms of exchange dictated by the goblin men, standing "[l]ike a lily in a flood" and "a beacon left alone" in resistance to their temptation and physical abuse.[33] Lizzie's defiance of the goblin men's terms of engagement ultimately frees Laura from her debt and presents a case both for Lizzie's "power as a consumer" in navigating the male-dominated market, and the complex subversion of this market by the "shared bodily economies" that operate between the sisters and eventually exile the goblin men.[34] *Goblin Market* thereby illustrates not only the potential dangers of the commodification of the female "body in circulation," but also the female body's potential power to subvert gendered market relations and operations, and the "possibilities of a poetics of expenditure" in which "women need not sacrifice their desires in order to go to the market."[35]

The conjunction of gendered bodily economies and value in literature and economics is ironically embodied in the moniker of the Bank of England as the "Old Lady in Threadneedle Street."[36] While the metaphor of a healthy body as representative of a healthy body politic and nation has long been in operation, the dramatization of the Bank of England as an old lady in need of sustenance and protection in the nineteenth century provided impetus for the critique of the nation's economic health to be centered on the (female) body.[37] An 1850 essay by Dickens and W. H. Wills in *Household Words* portrays, for instance, the financial "Panic of 1825" as a grave bodily attack on the "old lady" when "the outflow of her circulating medium was so violent that she was in danger of bleeding to death."[38] Through the literary critiques and economic accounts of the bodily circulations and demands of capitalism, the body emerges as a clear site and sign of value for *both* political economy and literature, and further demonstrates how the concerns of literature and economics frequently intersect, even when their approaches and conclusions differ.[39]

Systems and Agents

Nineteenth-century British literature is populated with a variety of economic agents – bankers, debtors, speculators, laborers, industrial capitalists, imperial businessmen, to name but a few – interacting with a multitude of financial systems that frequently shape their choices, prospects, and relations. The "still-startling caesura" that interrupts the narrative focus on Dorothea's interiority in *Middlemarch* – "but why always Dorothea?" – and begins, instead, to reveal the multiple plots of the novel also shows, for example, how the increasingly modernizing economic system can connect seemingly disparate characters through its widening economic network.[40] Arguing that *Middlemarch* "represents a society that is at once highly fragmented *and* highly organised" and that draws on Smith's economic and "sociological insights," Imraan Coovadia shows how the realist multi-plot novel, where coincidence and connections between characters frequently drive the plot forward, is illustrative of "the mass of connections, some visible and some invisible, between all persons of a modern society."[41] The developing railway line of *Middlemarch* and the one that ends Captain Brown's life in Gaskell's *Cranford* (1851–1853) equally show, however, the disruptive potential of these economically modernizing connections.

As the century progressed, systems of credit multiplied, speculative manias were rampant, paper money flourished, and the British financial system was defined by its turbulence and instability.[42] Patrick Brantlinger, Margot Finn, and Gail Turley Houston have analyzed how systems of credit, the rapid increase of banks and the processes of banking, and the

panics that accompanied these changing financial structures and schemes
influenced and were managed by nineteenth-century literature and the
novel in particular.[43] Speculators from Mr. Merdle in Dickens's *Little
Dorrit* (1855–1857) to Mr. Melmotte in Trollope's *The Way We Live
Now* (1875), bankers like Mr. Bulstrode in *Middlemarch*, and debtors like
Mr. William Dorrit, demonstrate how systems of credit shape the characters populating novels.

In the response of novels and political economy to the banking panic
and "bankerization" that came to define the nineteenth century, Houston
traces a Gothic aesthetic of haunting.[44] Through an inspired gothic
reading of Marx's formula of the capitalist system, M-C-Ḿ, Houston
argues that "the diacritical accent mark above the M visually exhibits the
ghost in Marx's representation of circulation" where, as we have already
seen, commodities become divorced from the labor that produces them,
and money in turn no longer represents "the relations of commodities" but
"enters … into private relations with itself."[45] The ambiguous diacritical
mark over the representative of money carries for Houston all the Gothic
ambiguities that haunt Marx's formulation of capitalism: "the apostrophe
(indicating possession, lack, elision, fragmentation); an accent (indicating
distortion or emphasis); or, the mathematical symbol of the small prime
(indicating increase, return, repetition)." The diacritical mark that hangs over
and haunts circulating capital for Marx is, according to Houston, equally a
spectral presence marking Charlotte Brontë's *Villette* (1853), Dickens's *Little
Dorrit*, and even Robert Louis Stevenson's *Strange Case of Dr. Jekyll and
Mr. Hyde* (1886), where subjects by necessity "bank on panic."[46]

Though not Gothic in its mood or genre, Trollope's novel *The Way We
Live Now* equally dramatizes the effects of the nonreferential circulation of
money as it draws comparisons between Lady Carbury's novel and letter
writing, the angrily debated and ever circulating IOU's that operate in Sir
Felix's gambling circle, the fraudulent stock that accompanies the rise of
the South Central Pacific and Mexican Railway, and the tickets for the
Emperor's dinner that plummet in value as Melmotte's reputation takes a
dive.[47] Lady Carbury's title for her final novel, "The Wheel of Fortune,"
captures the constant speculative circulation of credit and debt in the novel
defined by "dealings in unsecured paper."[48] As "representational systems
relying on credit," fiction and money become "interchangeable: money as
the fiction of gold or of absolute value; fiction as commodity, exchangeable
for money."[49] This commodification of the joint enterprises of paper and
fiction and the complex relationship to pecuniary interest take center stage
in George Gissing's *New Grub Street* (1891).

Melmotte's infamous dinner for the Emperor of China, and the imperial reach of the imagined railway project, register the colonial and imperial substructures to the (fictional) capital circulating in London. The attempts of Lady Carbury's friends to manage Felix's numerous financial and social disgraces, moreover, draw upon a common trope in the Victorian novel of exiling characters to "one of the Colonies" and point to the embedded imperial economic system within which these literary worlds and nineteenth-century Britain operates.[50] Dickens's novels, for instance, are "littered with characters who disappear to the empire," while objects of colonial and imperial trade circulate, stimulate, decorate, and accumulate: from Lady Bertram's repeated request for a shawl from the "East Indies" in *Mansfield Park* (1814) to the Indian shawls draped over Margaret Hale at the start of *North and South*; from the furniture of *Jane Eyre* (1847) to the "Native-Hindoo chair" in *Bleak House* (1852–1853); from the exotic fruits that tempt Laura in *Goblin Market* to the tobacco that Magwitch smokes in *Great Expectations*.[51]

Like the diacritical mark that haunts Marx's formula, Dickens's convict returnee, Magwitch, haunts the novel's narrator, Pip, through his secret role as benefactor. Magwitch's colonial labor in Australia, however, also enables Pip, as Edward Said argues, to become not only a gentleman but finally a "colonial businessman."[52] While the figure of Magwitch demonstrates the uneasy and haunting potential of the colonial presence in nineteenth-century British literature, the enabling economic exchange created through colonial settlement and labor forms an important feature of Mill's political economy. Signaling a shift from Smith's and Ricardo's ambivalence toward the economic promise of the colonies, Mill's *Principles* presents a positive view of the British colonies as potentially providing important solutions to the metropole's social and financial problems. Inspired by Edward Gibbon Wakefield's theories of systematic colonization, Mill saw emigration to the colonies as a means of alleviating the poverty and "suffering among the British working classes" and addressing the "shortage of land" and the "excess of capital and labour" while creating new markets for British trade.[53] Wakefield's theory was famously critiqued and summarized by Marx as not being a new discovery about the colonies, but instead a discovery "*in* the Colonies [of] the truth as to the conditions of capitalist production in the mother country."[54]

Using various British colonies as the backdrops to some of the tales featured in her *Illustrations of Political Economy*, Martineau presents the "global scope" of this new science while also illustrating the "racist and genocidal implications" of settler colonialism.[55] Thus, in *Life in the Wilds* (1845) and *Homes Abroad* (1832), Martineau applies a racialist stadial theory of development in order to explore the division of labor and the economic promise of emigration, respectively, while depicting the murderous clashes caused by settler colonialism. In doing so, Martineau's colonial stories register the entanglement of literature, economics, and the British Empire in the nineteenth century.

While the colonial setting is emphatically dramatized in and frequently celebrated through the imperial jingoism of later novels by Joseph Conrad, H. Rider Haggard, G. A. Henty, Rudyard Kipling, and Stevenson, imperial economics nonetheless code literature across the nineteenth century and demonstrate the interleaving of British economic and imperial desires.[56] Even when only animating the margins of texts, the colonies provide dramatic exits and mysterious entries for characters, with imperial agents and objects circulating and speculative opportunities multiplying across the vast economic networks of the British Empire.

* * *

Imperial trade, consumer impulses, industrial production and waste, fraudulent stock markets, credit-worthy characters, and dubious investors: nineteenth-century British literature is brimming with economic subjects, questions, and consequences. Studying economic and literary discourses together enlivens the economic debates that shaped literary interventions in form, genre, and topic, while also demonstrating the concomitant significance of imaginative storytelling to the development of economics as a science in the nineteenth century. That "never-explained science," political economy, forms a crucial touchstone and simultaneously a counternarrative to nineteenth-century literature as literary texts work to shade in the economic abstractions calculating the costs and benefits of human relations. Reading the history of economic thought alongside the literary texts of the nineteenth century reveals their shared investments in value, representation, and human desires. Just as Margaret Hale learns to read the industrial setting of Milton, with the black clouds coming to signal pollution rather than storm clouds promising rain, literary texts allow readers to enter the world of economic relations and systems, to learn to read the defining characteristics of economic environments, and to consider the debates that surround production and consumption as they begin to make their own evaluative judgments.

Notes

1 George Eliot, *Middlemarch* (1871–1872; London: Vintage, 2007), 855, 12–13.
2 Charles Dickens, "On Strike," *Household Words*, February 11, 1854; 553–558.
3 See, for example, Patrick Brantlinger, *Fictions of State: Culture and Credit in Britain, 1694–1994* (Ithaca, NY: Cornell University Press, 1996); Gordon Bigelow, *Fiction, Famine, and the Rise of Economics in Victorian Britain and Ireland* (Cambridge: Cambridge University Press, 2003); Margot C. Finn, *The Character of Credit: Personal Debt in English Culture, 1740–1914* (Cambridge: Cambridge University Press, 2003); Regenia Gagnier, *The Insatiability of Human Wants: Economics and Aesthetics in Market Society* (Chicago: University of Chicago Press, 2000); Catherine Gallagher, *The Body Economic: Life, Death, and Sensation in Political Economy and the Victorian Novel* (Princeton, NJ: Princeton University Press, 2006); Gail Turley Houston, *From Dickens to* Dracula: *Gothic, Economics, and Victorian Fiction* (Cambridge: Cambridge University Press, 2005); Claudia C. Klaver, *A/Moral Economics: Classical Political Economy and Cultural Authority in Nineteenth-Century England* (Columbus: Ohio State University Press, 2003); Mary Poovey, *Genres of the Credit Economy: Mediating Value in Eighteenth- and Nineteenth-Century Britain* (Chicago: University of Chicago Press, 2008).
4 Gallagher, *Body Economic*, 6.
5 Poovey, *Genres of the Credit Economy*, 12.
6 David Ricardo to Thomas Malthus, October 7, 1815, letter 127 in *The Works and Correspondence of David Ricardo, Vol. 6: Letters 1810–1815*, edited by Piero Sraffa with the Collaboration of M. H. Dobb (Indianapolis, IN: Liberty Fund, 2005), https://oll.libertyfund.org/title/sraffa-the-works-and-correspon dence-of-david-ricardo-vol-6-letters-1810-1815.
7 David Ricardo, *The Works and Correspondence of David Ricardo, Vol. 1: Principles of Political Economy and Taxation* edited by Piero Sraffa with the Collaboration of M. H. Dobb (1817; Indianapolis: Liberty Fund, 2005), 6, https://oll.libertyfund.org/title/ricardo-the-works-and-correspondence-of-david-ricardo-vol-1-principles-of-political-economy-and-taxation.
8 Poovey, *Genres of the Credit Economy*, 224–225. See also Sarah Comyn, *Political Economy and the Novel: A Literary History of "Homo Economicus"* (Basingstoke: Palgrave Macmillan, 2018), 53–54; Klaver, *A/Moral Economics*, 1–32.
9 Poovey, *Genres of the Credit Economy*, 224.
10 Ibid.
11 For the significance of "popularizers" to economics, see Bette Polkinghorn, "Popularizers as Contributors to Economics: The Unappreciated Tribe," in *Joseph A. Schumpeter: Historian of Economics: Perspectives on the History of Economic Thought*, edited by Laurence S. Moss (London and New York: Routledge, 1996), 39–43.

12 Deborah Weiss, "Maria Edgeworth's Infant Economics: Capitalist Culture, Good-Will Networks, and 'Lazy Lawrence,'" *Journal for Eighteenth-Century Studies* 37.3 (2014), 395–408; 396, 398.

13 Jane Marcet, *Conversations on Political Economy; In Which the Elements of that Science are Familiarly Explained*, 6th ed. (London: Longman, Rees, Orme, Brown & Green, 1827), vi.

14 Harriet Martineau, *Illustrations of Political Economy*, 3rd ed., 9 vols. (London: Charles Fox, 1832; Online Library of Liberty), vol. 1, xii, https://oll .libertyfund.org/titles/1686; *Harriet Martineau's Autobiography*, edited by Maria Weston Chapman, 2 vols. (Boston: James R. Osgood & Co., 1877; Online Library of Liberty), vol. 1, 105, https://oll.libertyfund.org/titles/2011; Elaine Freedgood, "Banishing Panic: Harriet Martineau and the Popularization of Political Economy," *Victorian Studies* 39.1 (1995), 33–53; 33.

15 Gallagher, *Body Economic*, 4; Poovey, *Genres of the Credit Economy*, 7.

16 Gallagher, *Body Economic*, 4.

17 John Stuart Mill, *The Collected Works of John Stuart Mill, Vol. IV: Essays on Economics and Society Part I*, edited by John M. Robson (Toronto: University of Toronto Press; London: Routledge and Kegan Paul, 1967; Online Library of Liberty), 321, https://oll.libertyfund.org/titles/244#lf0223-04_head_055. For a discussion of Mill and the creation of *Homo economicus*, see Joseph Persky, "Retrospectives: The Ethology of *Homo Economicus*," *Journal of Economic Perspectives* 9.2 (1995), 221–231; 222.

18 Elizabeth Gaskell, *North and South*, edited by Angus Eason (1854; Oxford: Oxford University Press, 1992), 117.

19 Klaver, *A/Moral Economics*, 137.

20 William Stanley Jevons, *The Theory of Political Economy*, 3rd ed. (London: Macmillan, 1888; Online Library of Liberty), 37, 53, 3, 27; emphasis in original, https://oll.libertyfund.org/titles/625. For a discussion of the significance of Jevons's emphasis on mathematics, see Bigelow, *Fiction, Famine*, 69–72.

21 Regenia Gagnier, *Insatiability of Human Wants*, 48.

22 Oscar Wilde, *The Picture of Dorian Gray* edited by Robert Mighall (1891; London: Penguin, 2003), 48.

23 Ibid., 124; Gagnier, *Insatiability of Human Wants*, 14.

24 Gagnier, *Insatiability of Human Wants*, 4.

25 For an excellent analysis of the impact of industrialization on nineteenth-century literature, see, for example, Catherine Gallagher, *The Industrial Reformation of English Fiction: Social Discourse and Narrative Form* (Chicago: University of Chicago Press, 1980). On Wilde and Pater, see Gagnier, *Insatiability of Human Wants*. On *The Spoils of Poynton*, see, for example, Fotios Sarris, "Fetishism in *The Spoils of Poynton*," *Nineteenth-Century Literature* 51.1 (1996), 53–83; and Deborah Wynne, "The New Woman, Portable Property, and *The Spoils of Poynton*," *Henry James Review* 31.2 (2010), 142–153.

26 Gagnier, *Insatiability of Human Wants*, 145.

27 Ricardo, *Principles of Political Economy*, 12.

28 John Stuart Mill, *Principles of Political Economy with some of their Applications to Social Philosophy*, edited by William James Ashley, 7th ed. (London: Longmans, Green, and Co., 1909; Online Library of Liberty), 29, https://oll.libertyfund.org/titles/101.

29 Gaskell, *North and South*, 102, 306.

30 Charles Dickens, *Great Expectations*, edited by Margaret Cardwell (1861; Oxford: Oxford University Press, 1994), 206–207.

31 Karl Marx, *Capital: A Critique of Political Economy, Vol. 1*, edited by Ben Fowkes (1867; London: Penguin, 1990), 163–177.

32 Ibid., 163.

33 Christina Rossetti, *Poems and Prose*, edited by Simon Humphries (Oxford: Oxford University Press, 2008), 105–118, ll. 116, 409, 412.

34 Elizabeth K. Helsinger, "Consumer Power and the Utopia of Desire: Christina Rossetti's 'Goblin Market,'" *ELH* 58.4 (1991), 903–933; 903, 925; Krista Lysack, *Come Buy, Come Buy: Shopping and the Culture of Consumption in Victorian Women's Writing* (Athens: Ohio University Press, 2008), 41.

35 Lysack, *Come Buy, Come Buy*, 43.

36 So renowned is this nickname that it features in a number of contemporary dictionaries of economics, including the *Routledge Dictionary of Economics* (2003) and the *Oxford Dictionary of Finance and Banking* (2014).

37 For a close study of the emergence of the "social body" in the nineteenth century, see Mary Poovey, *Making a Social Body: British Cultural Formation, 1830–1864* (Chicago: University of Chicago Press, 1995).

38 Charles Dickens and W. H. Wills, "The Old Lady in Threadneedle Street," *Household Words*, July 6, 1850, 337–342; 341.

39 See, for example, Gallagher's discussion of the distinction between "bioeconomics" and "somaeconomics" in *The Body Economic*.

40 Nathan K. Hensley and Philip Steer, "Introduction: Ecological Formalism; or, Love among the Ruins," in *Ecological Form: System and Aesthetics in the Age of Empire*, edited by Nathan K. Hensley and Philip Steer (New York: Fordham University Press, 2019), 1–20; 9; Eliot, *Middlemarch*, 292.

41 Imraan Coovadia, "George Eliot's Realism and Adam Smith," *Studies in English Literature, 1500–1900* 42.4 (2002), 819–835; 821, 828; emphasis in original.

42 Houston, *From Dickens to* Dracula, 14.

43 Brantlinger, *Fictions of State*, 136–184; Finn, *The Character of Credit*; Houston, *From Dickens to* Dracula.

44 Houston, *From Dickens to* Dracula, 11.

45 Ibid., 38; Marx, *Capital*, 258.

46 Houston, *From Dickens to* Dracula, 38, 48.

47 For a detailed analysis of these connections see, Brantlinger, *Fictions of State*, 165–168; and Denise Lovett, "The Socially-Embedded Market and the Future of English Capitalism in Anthony Trollope's *The Way We Live Now*," *Victorian Literature and Culture* 42.4 (2014), 691–707.

48 Anthony Trollope, *The Way We Live Now*, edited by John Sutherland (1875; Oxford: Oxford University Press, 1999), 366, 91.

49 Brantlinger, *Fictions of State*, 144.

50 Trollope, *The Way We Live Now*, 210.

51 Grace Moore, "Turkish Robbers, Lumps of Delights, and the Detritus of Empire: The East Revisited in Dickens's Late Novels," *Critical Survey* 21.1 (2009), 74–87; 75; Jane Austen, *Mansfield Park*, edited by John Wiltshire (1814; Cambridge: Cambridge University Press, 2005), 353; Charles Dickens, *Bleak House*, edited by Stephen Gill (1853; Oxford: Oxford University Press, 2008), 78. For an excellent study of the importance of objects in Victorian novels and their imperial and colonial connections, see Elaine Freedgood, *The Ideas in Things: Fugitive Meaning in the Victorian Novel* (Chicago: University of Chicago Press, 2006).

52 Edward W. Said, *Culture and Imperialism* (London: Vintage, 1994), xvii.

53 Duncan Bell, "John Stuart Mill on Colonies," *Political Theory* 38.1 (2010), 34–64; 38, 39.

54 Marx, *Capital*, 932; emphasis in original.

55 Claudia C. Klaver, "Imperial Economics: Harriet Martineau's *Illustrations of Political Economy* and the Narration of Empire," *Victorian Literature and Culture* 35.1(2007), 21–40; 21, 28.

56 For a discussion of imperial economics and the adventure romance, see, for example, Nicholas Daly, *Modernism, Romance, and the Fin de Siècle: Popular Fiction and British Culture* (Cambridge: Cambridge University Press, 2004); and Cara Murray, "Catastrophe and Development in the Adventure Romance," *English Literature in Transition, 1880–1920* 53.2 (2010), 150–169.

Women, Money, and Modernism

Nicky Marsh

Money mattered, deeply, to literary modernists. The idea of their disinterest, that they were able to hold themselves at a distance from the prosaically grubby world of finance that compelled both the realism of their predecessors and the postmodernism of their successors, has been comprehensively overturned. Three decades of modernist scholarship have revealed modernist writers to be keenly attentive not only to the financial conditions in which they worked, but also to the wider, radical economic upheavals taking place at the start of the twentieth century. And these changes were clearly momentous. The shape of the nation state, the form of international order, the availability of mass consumption, the character and organization of labor, and the very currencies of money itself, were all being actively recast, reimagined, and debated. Modernist writers regarded these changes with a close, if often profoundly ambivalent, attention.

The first half of this chapter delineates three ways in which modernism engaged with economics, and the ordering broadly reflects the chronological development of scholarship in the field. The first approach involves a focus on modernism's own economic positioning, the movement's often reflexive engagement with the economic horizons that both enabled and constrained its self-realization. This research has drawn attention to the complex webs of modernism's cultural, social, and political institutions, the very specific costs and contradictions that its assumed distance from popular and mass culture involved. The second approach involves an exploration of modernism's intellectual engagements with the changes in economic thought that were taking place in this period. These were the changes that now seem dominated by the revolutions that John Maynard Keynes's thinking brought about, and Keynesian approaches to credit, debt, work, and the state clearly played through the work of many of the Bloomsbury modernists, in particular. However, Keynes was not the only economic thinker who shaped writers in the opening decades of the century, and his work can be usefully placed alongside that of more heterodox thinkers, such as Marcel Mauss, Georg Simmel, and Georges Bataille, who were radically expanding the ways in which credit, exchange, and consumption could be understood. The final approach of the chapter engages with literary modernism's response to the shifts that were occurring in the money form itself, specifically writing's ability to imaginatively speculate alternatives to the gold standard that was both hegemonic, and yet in frequent crisis, throughout much of this period.

The second half of the chapter explores the ways in which these issues were navigated in the work of modernist women writers. It explores how writers as varied as Jean Rhys, Zora Neale Hurston, Katherine Mansfield, Edith Wharton, and Virginia Woolf engaged with economics, particularly the centrality of the exchange of women that underpins both real and symbolic economies. In revealing and rewriting the relationship between metaphors of femininity and metaphors of money, these writers were able to explore and reimagine the relationship between their own sexual identities and consumer culture; the meanings of race, paternity and inheritance; and the possibilities of exchange, translation, and a new international order.

Modernist Economics

Materialist approaches to modernism have come to shape the field in the past three decades. The querying of the "great divide" between modernism and mass culture, which New Criticism had insisted upon as its legitimizing rationale, gave way in the 1990s to scholarship that scrutinized the institutional and economic structures through which modernism had been created, sustained, defended, and disseminated.[1] This attention to the role of agents, patrons, publishers, journals, reviewers, editors, bookshops, and university syllabi shaped the field for well over a decade. It complicated the idea of the modernist movement as a phenomenon able to hold itself aloof from the vagaries of the financial, reputational and cultural marketplaces, and instead revealed the dynamic and close investments of modernists in the production, consumption, and legacies of their own work. The approach of critics such as John Guillory and Lawrence Rainey revealed modernism to be less a "series of texts" than a "configuration of agents and practices that converge in their production, marketing, and publicization of an idiom."[2] Studies of the assumptions, investments, and decisions of individual writers, movements, and reading practices have appeared with regularity since the mid-1990s. The approach demonstrated that a writer's attentiveness to a text's economic status influenced not only presentation and publication, but also stylistic and aesthetic choices. Joyce Wexler's relatively early contribution to the field, for example, explored the papers of J. B. Pinker (the literary agent who represented Joseph Conrad, James Joyce, and D. H. Lawrence) in order to demonstrate the different ways in which the three negotiated the tension between their desire for experimentation and their desire for the privileges that a wider readership would bring: Conrad, most bluntly, was willing to accept the rewrites that his editors suggested because he refused to "live in an attic."[3]

This critique of the economic institutions and practices of modernism, and the division between high and low culture often baked into them, was unsurprisingly revealed to be driven by the hierarchies of class, race, and gender. The gendered accounts of journalism, editing, and authorship provided in the revisionist histories and archives of Bonnie Kime Scott's now classic work revealed something of the very specific circumstances surrounding women's position, and particular dependencies, within the experimental and often radical communities of the modernist era.[4] Nathan Huggins's and Ralph D. Story's work on the Harlem Renaissance reveals the insidiously toxic combination of patronage and exoticism at play in the literary cultures of New York in the 1920s that celebrated, and then only briefly, a very specifically constrained version of African American literary culture.[5]

A second approach to exploring the significance of modernists' engagement with contemporary economics focused on the new models for production and consumption that were being both theorized and practiced in these opening decades of the century. Piero V. Mini's *Keynes, Bloomsbury, and* The General Theory (1991) established the formative links between the thought of Keynes and that of his close literary friends, demonstrating that the latter's attention to the irrational, libidinous nature of the human mind found a perhaps unlikely corollary in the former's understanding of the entrepreneur who, infamously, "follows his animal spirits, nerves, and emotions rather than the calculus of money."[6] It was a seam of thinking that was to be richly mined in the following two decades by research that took the relationship between Keynes and modernism in a variety of directions, exploring its implications for representation, nationalism, and consumer culture.

For critics such as Jennifer Wicke and, later, Bill Maurer, Keynes presented modernists with a world defined by uncertainty and subjectivity, which matched their new postrealist aesthetic. Wicke suggested that Virginia Woolf's fiction lent itself "precisely to the economic gestures Keynes was trying to make" in rendering the market "comprehensively, dynamically, chaotically" and as a form that could "be a battlefield, or a minefield, or a liquid terrain of experience, choice, agency, and desire."[7] Maurer suggested that Duncan Grant's art "was a process of discovery through movement" that matched Keynes's economic reliance on "contingency" and that the latter's emphasis on probability "introduced a particular notion of time-space" that was "reminiscent" of the former's "play with enframing devices in interior design."[8] Jed Esty and Patrick Brantlinger focused on the parallels between Keynes's and modernism's ambivalent relationship to nationalism. Brantlinger compared Woolf, Conrad, and the younger Keynes, suggesting that they shared a "critical recognition of what is fetishistic about the very construction of national identity," whereas Esty offered a more ambivalent reading of the relationship between the mature Keynes and the modernism of the 1930s when he asserted that Keynes's grasp of economic aggregates in this decade occurred "within an intellectual culture that was rapidly confronting its own particularity and gaining a fresh sense of its nation as a limited but significant totality."[9] The final strand of this reading of Keynes among the modernists focuses on the ways in which Keynes's newly permissive attitudes to both credit and consumerism were interpreted by his literary peers. Michael Tratner reads libidinal and consumer economies as mutually reinforcing one another, and as emancipatory, in the work of writers such as Joyce, Ezra Pound, and William Carlos Williams, while Alissa Karl offers a more cautionary note of the profound ambivalence of commodity capitalism for "lay[ing] bare the contradictions of the regimes of capital, empire, and patriarchy" in the work of writers including Jean Rhys and Nella Larsen.[10] This emphasis on modernist fiction, however, was not exclusive. Matt Seybold reads the eight years that T. S. Eliot spent working in Lloyds bank in the interwar years as a period in which he was "occupied with testing macroeconomic theories," especially those Keynes had articulated in *The Economic Consequences of the Peace* (1919), against "the microeconomic evidence of Lloyds's ledgers," and suggestively finds the aesthetics of *The Waste Land* (1922) in a process in which Eliot read "every transcription and transaction as part of a global macroeconomic narrative in which Lloyds was a somewhat unreliable protagonist whom Eliot might ultimately badger into greater omniscience."[11]

Although Keynes's influence loomed large in this period, he was not the only economic thinker with whom writers engaged in the first half of the twentieth century. The period witnessed the publication of some key countereconomic texts, including Georg Simmel's *The Philosophy of Money* (1900), Marcel Mauss's *The Gift* (1925), and Georges Bataille's

The Accursed Share (1949). Subsequent modernist scholarship has made clear the influence of all three. Rebecca Colesworthy has explored the importance of Mauss's ideas of reciprocity and community to the work of writers including Woolf, Stein, and H. D.[12] The influence of Simmel's writing, particularly about the experience of the city and the cosmopolitanism it promised, has been traced through the experimentation of writers such as Nella Larsen.[13] Janet Lyon reads modernism through Simmel's notion of cosmopolitanism in an approach later extended further by Rebecca Walkowitz's notion of a cosmopolitan "style."[14] Bataille was integral to late modernism and active in developing the "impossible politics" of surrealism in the 1930s that called for a "revolt against anything that pretends to be completed, full, transparent, and necessary."[15] In *The Accursed Share*, for example, Bataille recasts the "mysteries of Keynes's bottles" – Keynes's suggestion that the Treasury could stimulate the economy by burying bottles filled with banknotes and allowing private enterprise to pay workers to find them – as an account consistent with the "detours of exuberance through eating, death, and sexual reproduction" which he posits as alternatives to the conventional metrics of economics, or what he termed the restricted economy.[16]

The third area of enquiry concerns the ways in which modernist writers were active in broader political discussions around what money itself was and could achieve. This focus on both the symbolic and literal meanings of the gold standard revolved around an anxiety about the distinction between money's real (gold) and abstract (paper or credit) forms. It was a debate that extends back to at least the eighteenth century and took a variety of forms in early twentieth-century Anglo-American modernist culture. In Britain, the gold standard was often a synecdoche for the hegemony of British imperialism and its extractive model of value found literary corollaries in the mining fantasies of Edwardian fiction, from H. Rider Haggard's *King Solomon's Mines* (1885) to Joseph Conrad's *Nostromo* (1904) to H. G. Wells's *Tono-Bungay* (1909). In the United States, conversely, the gold standard was associated with the class interests of the established East Coast banking elite, which was placed against the populist movement's desire for the expansion of a credit-based paper economy. The fictional text now synonymous with these debates, upon which successive American elections were won and lost, is, perhaps surprisingly, Frank L. Baum's *The Wonderful Wizard of Oz* (1900).[17] In modernist scholarship, the symbolically overdetermined gold standard has been subjected to its most sustained critique in the work associated with the New Economic Criticism, exemplified by theorists such as Jean-

Joseph Goux and Walter Benn Michaels.[18] Yet even in this narrowed ambit, these debates took quite different forms. Goux's poststructuralist reading of the parallels between linguistic and financial abstraction associates the ending of the gold standard with deferment and loss, whereas Michaels's emphasis on the materiality of aesthetic abstraction privileges a text that doesn't seek mimetic representation. For Goux, the loss of gold is on a continuum with a loss of symbolic authority and the real (a line amplified in the postmodernism of both Fredric Jameson and David Harvey), whereas for Michaels the goldbug aesthetic is a materialist one that brings us closer to the possibility of a meaning that can occur without reference.[19]

Modernism's concern with different forms of money was as political as it was theoretical or aesthetic. The radical instabilities in the major world currencies that took place in the 1920s and 1930s, the experience of depression and hyperinflation, resulted in sustained experimentations with alternatives to sovereign currencies and the gold standard upon which they often relied. C. H. Douglas's work on social credit was particularly influential, and Alec Marsh has explored the ways in which Ezra Pound and William Carlos Williams responded to his work, placing them, respectively, in the longer historical lineages suggested by the divergence between Thomas Jefferson's emphasis on hard money and Alexander Hamilton's acceptance of soft.[20] Douglas was certainly not alone in seeking alternatives to a gold-based currency in these decades. Fredrick Soddy, Howard Scott, Arthur Kitson, and A. R. Orage all experimented with alternative economic systems and their thinking about using credit, energy and fossil fuels, technology, and a minimum social wage seem prescient and even progressive – even as the antisemitism that often accompanied their attacks on the financial elite certainly does not. These experimentations with alternative forms of currency were often as imaginary and rhetorical as they were political. The currencies of science fiction discussed in Chapter 14 can be traced through modernist writing and are apparent in the energy-currencies suggested in H. G. Wells's *The Shape of Things to Come* (1933), the transmutations of electric beings in Mina Loy's *Insel* (published posthumously in 1991), and the *Amazing Stories* of the Gernsback pulps that Mark Morrison adroitly links to modernism's lingering fascination with the possibilities of alchemy.[21]

Exchange and Gender in the Work of Modernist Women Writers

These three broad approaches to economics – an engagement with the literary marketplace, with emerging strains of economic and

countereconomic thought, and with alternatives to the money form itself –
were frequently interwoven through the lives and works of many modernists. This was especially pronounced for the woman modernist writer who
often occupied a deeply ambivalent status, at once the subject and object
of modernism's real and symbolic economies. This awareness shaped how
women modernists represented and understood the connections between
cultural, biological, and financial reproduction in the most compelling and
far-reaching ways.

The positioning of woman as a currency is deeply embedded in money's
rhetorical languages. A Marxist tradition that placed money's debasement
of the social on a continuum with prostitution's debasement of the
intimate – an androcentric conflation that relied on the assumed infirmity
and exchangeability of women, which Marx took from Shakespeare – was
to be elaborated in the writing of figures such as Walter Benjamin, Charles
Baudelaire, and Georg Simmel.[22] For many modernists, as Janet McCabe,
among others, has suggested, the prostitute's "flagrant disregard for natural
procreation and love of artifice" rendered the feminine body "desirous only
as a petrified one. Sexual pleasure and sexuality – to be sold and consumed
without love – are reduced to a morbid exhibitionism" and the exchange of
money in prostitution was given a "dialectical function," buying pleasure
but expressing shame.[23] Yet the centrality of the exchange of women is not
confined to the money economy but is similarly privileged in the traditions
assumed to counter it. Mauss's *The Gift* begins by noting that "everything – food, women, children, property, talismans, land, labor services,
priestly functions, and ranks – is there for passing on, and for balancing
accounts" and this was only reinforced in the later work of Claude Lévi-
Strauss, whose analysis was so important in establishing Mauss's work as
an economic system.[24]

For women writers, often entirely dependent on patrons, family,
friends, and lovers, assumptions of their exchangeability were often painfully and literally rendered. The covert language of prostitution pulses
through the writing of Jean Rhys, Katherine Mansfield, and Zora Neale
Hurston, for example, and is often associated less with the theoretical
debasement of capitalist abstractions than with the complexities of surviving in an economy in which every transaction is shaped by race, class, and
gender. These writers were profoundly vulnerable, occupying economically, socially, and racially marginal positions, and the biographies and
extensive correspondence of each provide detailed accounts of the ways in
which their very ability to write and publish depended on the sometimes
cruel, and often capricious, succor of others.[25] Jean Rhys, most

memorably, asks the reader to enter into the logic of this intimate abjec-
tion when Sasha, the protagonist in *Good Morning, Midnight* (1939),
associates the feminization of the consumer economy with her own
degradation. Sasha proclaims her need for "money, for the night" only to
make clear that the money binds, rather than frees, her from status as both
consumer and consumed: "money, for the night. Money for my hair,
money for my teeth, money for shoes that won't deform my feet (it's not
so easy now to walk around in cheap shoes with very high heels), money
for good clothes, money, money. The night is coming."[26]

   Mansfield deploys the figure of the prostitute as she both traces and
disturbs the sexual and racial hierarchies that belied the fantasy of a
liberated cosmopolitan avant-garde that she, a New Zealander travelling
in England and France in the 1910s, desperately sought and by which she
was continually frustrated. These feelings of bathos are often captured in
Mansfield's recurring stories of travel. The most pointed of these difficulties frequently involve handling money – knowing when to pay, when not
to pay, how much to pay, and what money to pay with. These transactions
are given one of their most complex forms in her 1918 short story "Je Ne
Parle Pas Francais," in which Mansfield replaces the vulnerable young
woman through whom much of her fiction is focalized with the liminal
figure of Raoul Duquette – white but with "olive" skin, male but "plump
like a girl."[27] Duquette is a *flâneur* who stands above a decadent cosmopolitanism. He describes himself as a "Customs official" who judges those
who come before him by asking, "Have you anything to declare? Any
wines, spirits, cigars, perfumes, silks?" For him, the "moment of hesitation
as to whether I am going to be fooled just before I chalk that squiggle, and
then the other moment of hesitation just after, as to whether I have been,
are perhaps the two most thrilling instants in life."[28] Duquette's undoing
in the narrative is his identification with Mouse, the woman who can speak
no French (the "je ne parle pas francais" of the story's title belongs to her)
and is callously abandoned in Paris by her lover. In retelling her story,
Duquette reveals the single memory he has of his own childhood, of an
"African laundress" who "took me into a little outhouse . . . caught me up
in her arms and began kissing me. Ah, those kisses!"[29] He recounts that he
was given a "little round fried cake covered with sugar" in recompense and
although both the act and the payment are "prettily" rendered they
represent the loss of innocence from which he is constituted: "from that
very first afternoon my childhood was 'kissed away.' I became very languid,
very caressing, and greedy beyond measure."[30] The story allows him to
explain that he, like the silenced and abandoned Mouse, has suffered a ruin

that sets him adrift without family or connections in Paris and that, even now, if he ever finds himself "in need of right-down cash – well, there's always an African laundress and an outhouse, and I am very frank and *bon enfant* about plenty of sugar on the little fried cake afterwards."[31] The ending of the story, however, completes the reversal of the narrative signaled by the "hyper-disruptive" presence of the African laundress[32] as Duquette is revealed to be the procurer rather than the procured, and his sympathetic identification with Mouse is belied by his admission of his exploitation of her vulnerability: when the "piano starts playing a 'mouse' tune'" his reverie of reconciliation is interrupted by "some dirty old gallant" to whom he can promise that he has "the little girl for you, *mon vieux*. So little ... so tiny."[33] Duquette's avaricious pleasure in Mouse's physical vulnerability allows Mansfield to reveal the privilege that his identification with Mouse disavows, a privilege that short-circuits the apparent endless fungibility of exchange.

That the rendering of the female body as a type of currency should be coded by race as well as class was especially true in the early twentieth-century United States, where the battles over the money form, especially the distinction between gold and credit, had long taken an explicitly racial form.[34] The narrative of different kinds of value is played out very differently in Zora Neale Hurston's short story "The Gilded Six-Bits" (1933). Hurston was an anthropologist and collector of folk tales who was associated with the Harlem Renaissance in the 1920s, and experienced a particularly ignominious fate in its aftermath. She was only brought back to literary history by the work of feminist critics, including Alice Walker, in the 1970s. In "The Gilded Six-Bits," Hurston describes the corruption of the relationship between a young and happy couple, Joe Banks and Missie May, at the hands of Otis Slemmons, a newcomer who disrupts their community with the false promise of gold. Missie and Joe are both fascinated by Slemmons's ostentatious displays of wealth, his "five-dollar gold piece for a stick pin" and "ten-dollar gold piece on his watch chain" and claims that "women give it all to'im."[35] When Joe returns home from work unexpectedly early one evening, yearning "painfully for Missie" – "[c]reation obsessed him ... They ought to be making feet for little shoes" – he finds Slemmons in his stead.[36] Slemmons escapes Joe's fury, leaving his gold dollar behind, and its presence becomes an inadvertent taunt to the couple. When they eventually sleep together again Joe leaves the coin under Missie's pillow, and her hope that they have been reunited is dashed when she realizes that he, as Slemmons before him, has rendered her a prostitute. The couple's estrangement is only resolved when Joe decides to help the now pregnant Missie with her domestic tasks, just as they realize that Slemmons's gold was merely gild and they had both been duped. The story was published in the same year as President Roosevelt ended the gold standard in the United States, in order to finance the New Deal, and has been read by critics such as Michael Tratner through the libidinous terms of a liberalized credit economy. Other critics, such as Hildegard Hoeller, have suggested that the story accords with the dominant financial codes of the time: silver is linked to "a playful, working class, gift-giving community and gold money to the deceptively seductive lures of the city and its corporate structure."[37] Yet the celebration of the birth of the son at the end of the story, without the resolution of the question of his paternity that hangs over the entire structure, also suggests Hurston's quiet rejection of the racial and gendered lines, the insistence on purity, upon which the story otherwise relies.

Women modernist writers, such as Edith Wharton and Virginia Woolf, who were often writing from less vulnerable class positions, were able to explore the possibilities of *refusing* to accede to this logic of exchange and presented protagonists who seek to subvert their status as a currency and manifestos that exhort currency to be invented anew. Lily Bart's apparent ability to resist being spent in Edith Wharton's *The House of Mirth* (1905), for example, renders her a tragically compelling heroine. Bart demonstrates a pyrrhic resistance to realizing her own value in the loveless but lucrative marriage market of the upper middle classes because of her love for the principled, but unpropertied, Lawrence Selden. The novel, as Wai-Chee Dimock has argued, lays bare the economics of the social and reveals that "the power of money lies not so much in its pristine form as in its claim as a model, in its ability to define other things in its own image. The fluidity of currencies in *The House of Mirth*, the apparently endless business possibilities, attests to the reduction of human experiences to abstract equivalents for exchange."[38] Yet Lily's refusal of this economy, her withdrawal from exchange, is presented as far from radical when it functions to preserve the racial purity of New York's established upper middle class just as it is threatened with dilution by the "new" – a barely veiled code for Jewish – money. As Jennie Kassanoff has argued, there is more at stake than simply the pleasure of the male observers in the precision Wharton assigns to Lily's "art of blushing at the right time." For Kassanoff, such skills speak to Lily's embodiment of the "paradigm of apotheosis, sacrifice, and extinction. Wharton captures and immobilizes her at the moment of racial perfection, a fate preferable, she implies, to a slow demise in New York's competitive wilderness."[39]

The possibility for withdrawing from exchange entirely, for spending the gendered coin differently, finds probably its most famous realization in Virginia Woolf's *Three Guineas* (1938). This is one of Woolf's most clearly political works and offers a detailed and explicitly gendered critique of the patriotic imperialism of interwar Britain. The essay uses coins to code both the rejection of hegemonic middle class masculine imperialism and the proposal of a feminized alternative. The eponymous guinea was no longer actually a currency by the time Woolf was writing. It had been replaced by the pound over a century earlier and by the late 1930s was a symbol of class privilege: land, horses, and art were priced in guineas while tradespeople and servants were paid in pounds. Woolf contrasts this anachronistic shibboleth of inherited privilege against the shiny transformational "sixpence" that she associates with the 1919 Sex Disqualification Removal Act: "[I]n every purse there was, or might be, one bright new sixpence in whose light every thought, every sight, every action looked different."[40] For Woolf, the sixpence is a "sacred coin" for the "educated man's daughter" and is represented in an explicitly feminized way: "[T]he moon even, scarred as it is in fact with forgotten craters, seemed to her to be a white sixpence, a chaste sixpence, an altar upon which she vowed never to side with the servile, the signers-on."[41] The coin is thus a symbol of a new kind of feminist life, in which "the money element has been removed" from private and intimate interactions. The woman who is able to earn, rather than be given, her money "no longer" has to "use her charm to procure money from her father or brother. Since it is beyond the power of her family to punish her financially, she can express her own opinions."[42]

Woolf's sixpence is reclaimed in order to resist the state capitalism that it also represents. When Woolf rhetorically asks how women can use the sixpence, "this new weapon . . . to prevent war" she differentiates between it and the guinea on more than monetary value: "[I]f our point of view is the same as yours then we must add our sixpence to your guinea: follow your methods and repeat your words. But, whether fortunately or unfortunately, that is not true."[43] In this instance, then, the refusal to spend is associated with a more radical possibility for the economy:

> It falls to us now to go on thinking: how are we to spend that sixpence? Think we must. Let us think in offices; in omnibuses; while we are standing in the crowd watching Coronations and Lord Mayor's Shows; let us think as we pass the Cenotaph; and in Whitehall; in the gallery of the House of Commons; in the Law Courts; let us think at baptisms and marriages and funerals. Let us never cease from thinking – what is this "civilization" in which we find ourselves? What are these ceremonies and why should we take part in them?[44]

We might usefully read the unspent sixpence as a currency for Woolf's "Outsiders' Society," part of what Rebecca Walkowitz has termed modernism's "critical cosmopolitanism" that aims to unearth new imaginative possibilities by revealing the "customs and conventions, social and psychological, that control what can be seen and what can be said."[45]

Yet not all of Woolf's coins went unspent. Scholars have also made evident the ways in which her view of money was shaped through the self-consciously gendered and politicized practices of consumption. As Jessica Berman has made clear, this support of consumerism was deeply bound up with Woolf's gendered support of internationalism. Berman demonstrates that the Woolfs diverged from the Fabian, trade union, and cooperative movements because these movements failed to disassociate themselves from the masculine and imperialist nationalism rejected in *Three Guineas*. In their place, Berman suggests, Woolf supported the more contingent yet radical politics of the Women's Cooperative Guild, which effaced the divisions between nations, classes, and even public and private. Berman traces a line from Woolf's identification with the WCG's symbolic "Woman with the Market Basket" to the "possibility of community not only without charismatic leaders but also without any structure like that of state, nation, or party" offered by *The Waves* (1931).[46]

Literary modernism, then, was steeped in the economic debates of the opening decades of the century: writers were concerned not only about their own, often vexed, economic status, but also with responding to the economic upheavals that surrounded them as the meanings of value, credit, exchange, consumerism, and currency were being actively contested and rewritten. The engagement of the modernist woman writer with these debates was often a deeply troubled one. Such writing reveals that both the symbolic and literal languages of exchange were consistently and persistently gendered, riven with assumptions about biological and social as well as financial reproduction, which these writers were never able entirely to escape.

Notes

1 On the "great divide," see Andreas Huyssen, *After the Great Divide: Modernism, Mass Culture, Postmodernism* (Bloomington: Indiana University Press, 1986).

2 Lawrence Rainey, *Institutions of Modernism: Literary Elites and Public Culture* (New Haven, CT: Yale University Press, 1998), 144. See also John Guillory, *Cultural Capital: The Problem of Literary Canon Formation* (Chicago: University of Chicago Press, 1993).

3 Joyce Wexler, "Who Paid for Modernism?" *The Sewanee Review* 94.3 (1986), 440–449; 443. See also Aaron Jaffe, "Publication, Patronage, Censorship: Literary Production and the Fortunes of Modernist Value," in *The Oxford Handbook of Modernisms*, edited by Peter Brooker, Andrzej Gąsiorek, Deborah Longworth, and Andrew Thacker (Oxford: Oxford University Press, 2010), 315–334; Paul Delany, *Literature, Money, and the Market: From Trollope to Amis* (New York: Palgrave Macmillan, 2002).

4 Bonnie Kime Scott, *The Gender of Modernism: A Critical Anthology* (Bloomington: Indiana University Press, 1990).

5 Nathan Huggins, *Harlem Renaissance* (New York: Oxford University Press, 1971); Ralph D. Story, "Patronage and the Harlem Renaissance: You Get What You Pay For," *CLA Journal* 32.3 (1989), 284–295.

6 Piero V. Mini, *Keynes, Bloomsbury, and* The General Theory (London: MacMillan, 1991), 110.

7 Jennifer Wicke, "Mrs. Dalloway Goes to Market: Woolf, Keynes, and Modern Markets," *Novel: A Forum on Fiction* 28.1 (1994), 5–24; 14, 21.

8 Bill Maurer, "Redecorating the International Economy: Keynes, Grant, and the Queering of Bretton Woods," in *Queer Globalizations: Citizenship and the Aftermath of Colonialism*, edited by Arnaldo Cruz-Malave and Martin F. Manalanasan (New York: New York University Press, 2002), 111.

9 Patrick Brantlinger, *Fictions of State: Culture and Credit in Britain, 1694–1994* (Ithaca, NY: Cornell University Press, 1996), 3; Jed Esty, "National Objects: Keynesian Economics and Modernist Culture in England," *Modernism/Modernity* 7.1 (2000), 1–24; 9.

10 Michael Tratner, *Deficits and Desires: Economics and Sexuality in Twentieth-Century Literature* (Stanford: Stanford University Press, 2001); Alissa G. Karl, *Modernism and the Marketplace: Literary Culture and Consumer Capitalism in Rhys, Woolf, Stein, and Nella Larsen* (New York: Routledge, 2009), 14.

11 Matt Seybold, "Astride the Dark Horse: T. S. Eliot and the Lloyds Bank Intelligence Department," *T. S. Eliot Studies Annual* 1 (2017), 131–156; 137.

12 Rebecca Colesworthy, *Returning the Gift: Modernism and the Thought of Exchange* (Oxford: Oxford University Press, 2018).

13 See Jeanne Scheper, "The New Negro *Flâneuse* in Nella Larsen's *Quicksand*," *African American Review* 42.3–4 (2008), 679–695.

14 Rebecca Walkowitz, *Cosmopolitan Style: Modernism Beyond the Nation* (New York: Columbia University Press, 2007).

15 Jean-Michel Besnier and Amy Reid, "Georges Bataille in the 1930s: A Politics of the Impossible," *Yale French Studies* 78 (1990), 169–180.

16 Georges Bataille, *The Accursed Share, Vol. 1: An Essay on General Economy* (1949; London: Zone Books, 1991), 13.

17 See Hugh Rockoff, "The 'Wizard of Oz' as a Monetary Allegory," *Journal of Political Economy* 98.4 (1990), 739–760.

18 See Martha Woodmansee and Mark Osteen, eds., *The New Economic Criticism: Studies at the Intersection of Literature and Economics* (London: Routledge, 1999).

19 Jean-Joseph Goux, *The Coiners of Language*, translated by Jennifer Curtiss
    Gage (1984; Norman: University of Oklahoma Press, 1994); Walter Benn
    Michaels, *The Gold Standard and the Logic of Naturalism: American Literature
    at the Turn of the Century* (Berkeley: University of California Press, 1987).

20 Alec Marsh, *Money and Modernity: Pound, Williams, and the Spirit of Jefferson*
    (Tuscaloosa: University of Alabama Press, 1998)

21 Mark Morrison, *Modern Alchemy: Occultism and the Emergence of Atomic
    Theory* (Oxford: Oxford University Press, 2007).

22 See Nicky Marsh, "Reproduction," in *The Routledge Companion to Literature
    and Economics*, edited by Matt Seybold and Michelle Chihara (New York:
    Routledge, 2018), 315–323.

23 Janet McCabe, "Textual Debaucheries and the *Flâneur*: Prostitution as
    Paradoxical Discourse in Walter Benjamin's *The Arcades Project*," *New
    Formations* 54 (2004), 154–168; 160.

24 Marcel Mauss, *The Gift: The Form and Reason for Exchange in Archaic Societies*,
    translated by W. D. Halls (1925; New York: W. W. Norton, 2000), 18.

25 See Claire Tomalin, *Katherine Mansfield: A Secret Life* (London: Penguin,
    1998); Lilian Pizzichini, *The Blue Hour: A Portrait of Jean Rhys* (London:
    Bloomsbury, 2014); Carla Kaplan, *Zora Neale Hurston: A Life in Letters* (New
    York: Knopf Doubleday, 2004).

26 Jean Rhys, *Good Morning, Midnight* (1939; New York: W. W. Norton, 1986), 144.
    See Cynthia Port, "'Money, for the night is coming': Jean Rhys and Gendered
    Economies of Ageing," *Women: A Cultural Review* 12.2 (2001), 204–217.

27 Katherine Mansfield, *The Collected Stories* (London: Penguin, 2001), 68.

28 Ibid., 44.

29 Ibid., 82, 79–80.

30 Ibid., 80.

31 Ibid., 82

32 Elleke Boehmer, "Mansfield as Colonialist Modernist: Difference Within," in
    Celebrating Katherine Mansfield: A Centenary Volume of Essays, edited by Gerri
    Kimber and Janet Wilson (London: Palgrave, 2011), 57–71; 68. See also
    Pamela Dunbar, *Radical Mansfield: Double Discourse in Katherine Mansfield's
    Short Stories* (London: Palgrave, 1997).

33 Mansfield, *Collected Stories*, 91.

34 See Michael O'Malley, *Face Value: The Entwined Histories of Money and Race
    in America* (Chicago: University of Chicago Press, 2012); Michael Germana,
    Standards of Value: Money, Race, and Literature in America (Iowa: University
    of Iowa Press, 2009).

35 Zora Neale Hurston, "The Gilded Six-Bits," in *The Norton Anthology of
    African American Literature*, edited by Henry Louis Gates, Jr. and Nellie
    Y. McKay (New York: W. W. Norton, 1997), 1011–1019; 1014.

36 Ibid., 1015.

37 Hildegard Hoeller, "Racial Currency: Zora Neale Hurston's 'The Gilded Six-
    Bits' and the Gold-Standard Debate," *American Literature* 77.4 (2005),
    761–785; 762–763.

38 Wai-Chee Dimock, "Debasing Exchange: Edith Wharton's *The House of Mirth*," *PMLA* 100.5 (1985), 783–792; 784.
39 Jennie A. Kassanoff, "Extinction, Taxidermy, Tableaux Vivants: Staging Race and Class in *The House of Mirth*," *PMLA* 115.1 (2000), 60–74; 70.
40 Virginia Woolf, *Three Guineas* (1938; London: Houghton Mifflin, 2006), 16.
41 Ibid., 16.
42 Ibid., 17.
43 Ibid.
44 Ibid., 62–63.
45 Rebecca Walkowitz, *Cosmopolitan Style: Modernism Beyond the Nation* (New York: Columbia University Press, 2006), 99.
46 Jessica Berman, "Modernist Fiction," in *Cosmopolitanism and the Politics of Community* (Cambridge: Cambridge University Press, 2001), 148.

CHAPTER 6

Economic Logics and Postmodern Forms

Laura Finch

More than any other critic, Fredric Jameson has been responsible for theorizing postmodernism as the cultural correlate to the economic period of late capitalism. Focusing on the United States, Jameson dates the start of the economic shift into late capitalism from the 1950s onwards, with the emergence of a postmodern mindset in the cultural upheavals of the following decade. For Jameson, late capitalism's constitutive features include the dominance of multinational corporations, the international division of labor, new technologies and automation, the outsourcing of production to the Global South, and gentrification.[1] It also includes financialization, which will become increasingly central to Jameson's later work on postmodernism such that by his 1997 essay "Culture and Finance Capital," he argues that "what is called postmodernity articulates the symptomatology of yet another stage of abstraction ... finance capitalism."[2] Accompanying these economic shifts is the new cultural dominant, post-modernism, whose features include a new "flatness or depthlessness,"[3] the fragmentation of subjectivity and waning of affect, a weakening of histo-ricity and its replacement by nostalgia, the eclipse of parody by pastiche, and the end of the subject's ability to understand their place in relation to the vastness of global finance capital, which Jameson terms a failure of "cognitive mapping."[4]

Another constitutive feature of Jameson's postmodernism is that "the prodigious new expansion of multinational capital ends up penetrating and colonizing those very precapitalist enclaves (Nature and the Unconscious) which offered extraterritorial and Archimedean footholds for critical effec-tivity."[5] It is, therefore, a particularly suffocating stage of capitalism where "even overtly political interventions ... are all somehow secretly disarmed and reabsorbed."[6] Despite this suffocating hegemony, the language of colonizing and territorializing may give us a sense that if there are possi-bilities of exception, they are spatial. In his essay "Third-World Literature in the Era of Multinational Capitalism" (1986), Jameson suggests that the

Global South offers the missing Archimedean point from which to better theorize late capitalism. This essay has been critiqued by many, in particular Aijaz Ahmad, who in "Jameson's Rhetoric of Otherness and the 'National Allegory'" (1987) argues against the universalism and essentialism of Jameson's idea of both "First World" and "Third World," writing "there is no such thing as a 'Third World Literature' which can be constructed as an internally coherent object of theoretical knowledge."[7]

While Jameson has been critiqued for his instrumentalizing of the Global South to provide a contrast to Western postmodernity, this chapter will focus on a similar critical aporia in his assessment of the hegemonic postmodernity within the United States. Given the extremity of the wealth inequity and the sharp segregation of over- and underdeveloped spaces within the United States (an unevenness that falls out along class lines but also along other lines, including race and ethnicity), the theory of postmodernity as a universal condition of contemporary life in the USA is at odds with the vastly different lived relations to capital in that country. When confronted with the idea of racial capitalism, work on postmodernism in the USA has often fallen into what Madhu Dubey calls "the romance of the residual," which "beguiles so much postmodern thinking about race."[8] That is, rather than an expansion, or to follow Frantz Fanon's language, a "stretching" of the idea of postmodernism to include the intersections of race and class, postmodernism is located as a white experience, while "African Americans are fetishized as the guarantors of everything that is felt to be at risk in the postmodern era – bodily presence, palpable reality, political intentionality."[9]

This chapter opens by considering how white American postmodernism has positioned Blackness within the United States, and how Black authors have reckoned with this "Third Worlding," where Blackness, as bell hooks writes, is "associated solely with concrete gut level experience conceived either as opposing or having no connection to abstract thinking and the production of critical theory."[10] I then turn to Jameson's theory of postmodernism, in particular his use of ethnicized city space as an outside other to the slick surfaces of white postmodern architecture. Reading a key scene from Bret Easton Ellis's *American Psycho* (1991) as an example of a canonical instance of white postmodernism, the chapter then turns to a more extended reading of Toni Cade Bambara's *Those Bones Are Not My Child* (1999), set in the financially booming city of Atlanta, Georgia, over the three-year period of 1979–1981 when at least thirty Black children went missing or were found murdered in the city.[11] Reading these two novels together reveals that as Blackness is central to the economic form of late capitalism, so too is it central to the theorization of postmodernism, and there is no way of understanding economic logics and postmodern forms in the United States without reckoning with Blackness and anti-Blackness.

Black Postmodernisms

The following claim from Toni Morrison should give us pause when considering the argument that all of Western society moved into the postmodern period at the same time: "Black women had to deal with 'postmodern' problems in the nineteenth century and earlier. These things had to be addressed by black people a long time ago."[12] Given the long experience of dislocation and ontological fracturing that African Americans have experienced in the United States during and in the wake of slavery, Madhu Dubey argues that "we would expect African-American literature to form a vital resource for debates about postmodernism"; however, "it is conspicuously missing."[13] Instead, African American culture becomes a useful limit point or outside for postmodernism, such that Blackness becomes the bearer of an authenticity that is being lost in white culture. While white cis-male authors are free to inhabit the realm of postmodern nonreferentiality, literature by nonwhite authors is forced into what Theodore Martin calls the "ethnographic reporting of direct experience," a "pseudosociological imperative that literature reflect its author's 'own experience.'"[14] This historic expectation that literature by minority writers must use the tools of realism to display social truths is one that was felt by Toni Cade Bambara, who was at times worried that postmodernism took her away from an ability to talk to some of the Black audience she was trying to reach:

> I am not as linguistically nimble as I used to be when interviewing various sectors/strata of the community, for I've just blown a gabfest on identity, belonging, and integration at the dentist's through an inability to bridge the gap between the receptionist, a working-class sister from the projects, who came of age in the sixties and speaks in nation-time argot, and the new dental assistant, a more privileged sister currently taking a break from Bryn Mawr, who speaks the lingo of postmodern theory.[15]

Black theorists and writers have pushed back on the exile of Black thought and experience from white postmodernism in a variety of ways. One way is to disrupt its periodization, by insisting – with Morrison – that Black people have experienced postmodernism centuries before it was identified by Anglo-European theorists in the 1960s. In *The Black Atlantic* (1993), Paul Gilroy addresses Anglo-American and European postmodernism, writing that "much of the supposed novelty of the postmodern evaporates when it is viewed in the unforgiving historical light of the brutal encounters between Europeans and those they conquered, slaughtered, and enslaved."[16] Black peoples, but also other nonwhite populations and Indigenous peoples, are not a primitive holdout against the creep of postmodernism, but rather were dealing with, living, and theorizing postmodern ideas well before white Western culture.

Another critique of white postmodernism comes from the standpoint of ethics and politics. While Patricia Hill Collins points to the usefulness of postmodernism, she also warns that it "rejects ethical positions that emerge from absolutes such as faith. It also eschews social policy recommendations ... [Therefore,] postmodernism undercuts selected dimensions of African-American women's political activism."[17] Bambara, who used a variety of postmodern formal techniques in her fiction, was also aware of the ambivalent necessity of a distinctly nonpostmodern appreciation of empirical data and facts: "[A]s a mother, teacher, writer, community worker, neighbor, I am concerned about accurate information, verifiable facts, sound analyses, responsible research, principled study, and people's assessment of the meaning of their lives."[18] Bambara's commitment to history and ethics within the Black postmodern experience, and especially the Black experience within the increasingly financialized spaces of urban capitalism, offers a powerful counter-argument to the deracinated urban experiences defined by white postmodernism.

Cognitive Mapping and Financial Space

The rest of this chapter will focus on the racialized experience of urban downtown centers in the 1980s as depicted in two postmodern novels of finance. I choose this specific lens through which to think about economic logics and postmodern forms as Jameson uses the architecture of downtown Los Angeles, specifically the Bonaventura Hotel, as his primary example of postmodernism, arguing that architecture is "of all the arts that closest constitutively to the economic, with which ... it has a virtually unmediated relationship."[19] It is also a useful point of comparison for the novels, as *American Psycho* – a canonical instance of postmodern fiction – and *Those Bones Are Not My Child* – a book that has a definitively postmodern form and yet is not always thought of as such[20] – are both invested in depicting the effect of global circuits of capital on the shape of downtown New York and Atlanta respectively.

Jameson's turn to architecture as a key example of postmodernism also leads to the spatial conclusion to his essay, which is his theory of cognitive mapping:

> So I come finally to my principal point … [Postmodernism] has finally succeeded in transcending the capacities of the individual human body to locate itself, to organize its immediate surroundings perceptually, and cognitively to map its position in a mappable external world … [It] is the incapacity of our minds, at least at present, to map the great global multinational and decentered communicational network in which we find ourselves caught as individual subjects.[21]

Jameson reads the disorienting spaces of the Bonaventura Hotel as an example of a universalized inability to theorize the lived experience of global capital. However, within his description, the universal application of the postmodern experience is undermined, as race and ethnicity are simultaneously evoked and erased in order to demonstrate the novelty of the hotel.

Jameson builds a novelistic description of experiencing a postmodern built environment, leading the reader through the streets with his prose:

> mounting what used to be Raymond Chandler's Beacon Hill from the great Chicano markets on Broadway and 4th St. in downtown Los Angeles, suddenly [one] confronts the great free-standing wall of the Crocker Bank Center (Skidmore, Owings, and Merrill) – a surface which seems to be unsupported by any volume.[22]

For Jameson, the presence of the market abutting the bank provides a visual example of time passing, where the ethnically marked place of trade contrasts neatly with the postmodern blankness of the bank. As José Eduardo Limón notes, "in the great Chicano market is to be found depth as well as other counter values to the defining attributes of Jameson's postmodernism."[23]

However, Jameson's argument for postmodernism is that it signals the end of a resistance from within the Global North – he locates the possibility of resistance only in the Global South. If nonwhite populations within the USA are implicated and integrated into the seamless web of late capitalism, are at the center not the periphery, then they do not fit into Jameson's schema except as anachronistic examples. In this sense they take on a comparable role to a romanticized idea of Indigeneity in the USA, out-of-time reminders of a more "authentic" and material existence before the latest stage of capitalism. As Limón's work shows, however, "although 'below,' [the market] is, nonetheless, in the same political semiotic universe as Andy Warhol paintings and the Bonaventura Hotel."[24]

Just as Limón points to the racialized outside of smooth postmodern space, Mike Davis's work also offers a similar critique of Jameson's description of the Bonaventura, arguing it is a building whose purpose is to create a "systematic segregation from the great Hispanic-Asian city outside."[25] To Jameson's account of the architecture of downtown LA, Davis adds it was the perceived threat to whiteness of the urban uprisings of the 1960s that motivated the "cordoning off [of] the downtown financial districts, and other zones of high property values, from inner-city residential neighborhoods."[26] Davis stresses not just the segregating effect of postmodern architecture, but also the "decisive role of urban counterinsurgency in defining the essential terms of the contemporary built environment."[27] Thus, while Jameson points to city space as the archetypal location of postmodern forms, his work fails to register both the ongoing presence of the racialized "outside" of this smooth postmodern space, and also the perceived threat to whiteness of racialized and ethnicized violence that was constitutive of this kind of postmodern architecture and urban design in the first place.

Ellis's *American Psycho* can be read as a fictionalized playing out of the contradictions and aporias surrounding race and ethnicity in Jameson's theory of postmodernism. In its usual critical reception, it is read as a novel about the effects of postmodern culture on Patrick Bateman, a white man working on Wall Street whose sense of abstraction, fragmentation, and unreality is raised to such heights that he turns to serial murder in a desperate attempt to recapture an embodied experience. However, a closer attention to the scenes where the serial killer/financier protagonist Bateman is most unable to map his experiences onto the city around him reveals that it is not the Bonaventura-like spaces of the Central Business District that lead to his disorientation, but rather the experience of moving through a city that has been violently splintered by racialized urban segregation in service to the creation of a pristinely white financial district.

By the mid-1970s, New York had transformed into the archetype of a financialized landscape, becoming the laboratory for testing out the limits of financialization. Throughout the twentieth century, corporate interests had been reshaping lower Manhattan from a mixed-use industrial port area to the rebranded "Central Business District" (CBD) through an aggressive use of zoning regulations.[28] The financial crisis of New York in the

1973–1975 recession led to a seizing of the city's finances that David Harvey has termed "a coup by the financial institutions against the democratically elected government of New York."[29]

Bateman exists in a world of Bonaventuras. However, he does not experience disorientation when he is with his colleagues or acquaintances – all white and extremely wealthy – in the endless round of bars, restaurants, nightclubs, and Wall Street offices he frequents. Rather, the failure to locate himself in space occurs only when Bateman interacts with nonwhite, working-class characters. While the novel is insistent on the concrete naming of locations throughout (there are 139 specific addresses and/or places named in the book), the ability to map the social deserts Bateman when he is forced out of his entirely white social circle. To give just one brief example, we see Bateman visiting a dry cleaners he has chosen specifically for its distance from Wall Street, as he is taking in items stained by the blood of his most recent murder victim, "located twenty blocks up from my apartment on the West Side, almost by Columbia, and since I've never actually been there before the distance shocks me."[30] The cleaner, whom Bateman identifies as Chinese, is unable to get the bloodstains out of the sheets, leading him to spit a tirade of racist insults at her until, "jolted by the sound of a real voice, I turn around and it's someone I recognize from my building."[31] In a city so devastatingly divided by finance capital, Bateman cannot map the collision of a wealthy white woman from his building with a working class nonwhite woman. The collapse of the "real voice" of his neighbor with the dry cleaner – so alien that she is no longer even real to him – leads Bateman to lose all geographic bearings:

> shaken, I walk away, hailing a taxi, and heading toward Hubert's in it I hallucinate the buildings into mountains, into volcanoes, the streets become jungles, the sky freezes into a backdrop, and before stepping out of the cab I have to cross my eyes in order to clear my vision. Lunch at Hubert's becomes a permanent hallucination in which I find myself dreaming while still awake.[32]

What this disorientation indexes is the fact that, as Madhu Dubey writes, while "the rhetoric of growth (focused on downtown areas) and the rhetoric of crisis (focused on the 'underclass') seem to run along separate and parallel tracks,"[33] the city that they cocreate is in fact a dialectical whole. The separation of downtown and "underclass" in the urban discourse of the 1970s and '80s "disabl[ed] the recognition of how redevelopment policies themselves have contributed to urban immiseration."[34] It is the failure to recognize this that is registered throughout Ellis's novel, as Bateman can only map the tiny arena of upperclass locations in which he exists. Ellis's novel shows that the failure of cognitive mapping is not a universalized experience of urban space in the post-1970s United States, but is in fact a function of antagonisms across race and class.

Cognitive Remapping

I turn now to Toni Cade Bambara as an author who proposes a postmodern form centered on and in Blackness that can more fully reckon with the centrality of racial capitalism to the deracinated vision of "late capitalism." Reading Bambara's *Those Bones Are Not My Child* as a novel of postmodernism and finance challenges taxonomies of postmodernism that can obscure how finance capital is experienced differently depending on class, race, and gender. Bambara's writing moves seamlessly between her own personal experiences of living in Atlanta during the missing and murdered children crisis, the experiences of her female protagonist Zala (Marzala) and Zala's husband Spence (Nathaniel), as their son Sonny (Sundiata) goes missing, and the response of the community at large to these events. Instead of placing these local experiences as a nonfinancialized counterpoint to theorizations of the circuits of global finance capital that were being routed through Atlanta in the 1970s and '80s, Bambara shows how the creation of Atlanta as a global hub was built through the segregation of the population of the metropolitan Atlanta area, and the disinvestment and demolishment of historically Black neighborhoods. Further, by taking the ethical risk of bringing together a narrative about the murder of real children with a critique of finance capital, Bambara's work draws attention to the inadequacies of theorizing capital without theorizing the complexity of its lived experience, while also demanding that the reader witness the terribly violent costs of this failure to understand the connections between the financialized city spaces of postmodernity and Black death. While Atlanta was busy fashioning itself into a post-racial paradise – "The City Too Busy to Hate," as it became known in the 1960s – and the keystone of the New South, which by the 1970s "was claiming half the annual foreign industrial investment expended in the United States,"[35] Bambara's novel demands that the racial capitalism of the United States be reckoned with in its newly financialized iteration; or, as one character succinctly puts it, not New South, but "Noose South, father, Noose South."[36]

The embodied nature of the increasingly financialized economy runs through the whole novel. Bambara's protagonist too embodies finance.

Near the start of the book, when Zala's oldest son Sonny has already gone missing but Zala has a moment of hope for his return, "she felt lighter somehow. The knot toward the top of her spine – just under the one clenched for the overdue rent – loosened."[37] Here, the extraction of profit through the exploitation of housing lives in Zala, adjacent to the worry over her missing child. While this is an embodiment of finance capital every bit as much as Bateman's knife-wielding financier, it is not typically read as a postmodern experience because Black women exploited by the debt relation of rent in a city of increasingly unaffordable housing are not included in white Euro-American theorizations of postmodernity.

While Ellis's novel plays out the violent disorientation of whiteness newly subjected to the economic pressures of a contracting American Empire, Bambara's novel diagnoses this link between finance capital and anti-Blackness, but also offers resources for resistance. In particular, the novel focuses on the experience and knowledge of space as a tool for finding the murderer(s) and for understanding and therefore arming oneself against the rule of finance capital. Bambara's novel shows again and again the ability of a multiplicity of different characters to engage in the mapping of global capital, as well as the theorizations of the real-life group Committee to Stop Children's Murders, organized by the mothers of the missing children, who "charged that the authorities were dragging their feet because of race; because of class; because the city, the country's third-busiest convention center, was trying to protect its image and was trying to mask a crisis that might threaten Atlanta's convention trade dollars."[38] Here, finance is added as a term that is as socially distorting as race and class. In metonymically naming the city itself as "the country's third-busiest convention center," Bambara succinctly nails one of the main problems of Atlanta's urban planning in the previous twenty years, where Black neighborhoods were cordoned off from downtown by new highways that connected the white suburbs to the emerging complex of skyscrapers and convention centers downtown.[39] It is this, not the glassy fronts of skyscrapers, that causes cognitive failure; the only moment of spatial hallucination comparable to Patrick Bateman's is when Zala and Spence think about their missing son: "a tape, a ruler, a yardstick, whatever they chose would be off too. Inches, feet, yards foreshortened. The conventional laws of perspective shot. Their son at the vanishing point."[40]

In response to the impossibility of comprehending a city that, despite being labelled the "Black Mecca of the South" by *Ebony* magazine in 1971, was also a place that willfully ignored the deaths of so many Black children, Zala sets about remapping the city.[41] Bambara's prose is multiclaused and accretive as she describes Zala moving through space. While the prose of Ellis's *American Psycho* is also famously one of lists and details, an effect that is typically described as creating a form of postmodern repetition that relies on surface and simulacra, the piling up of details in Bambara serves other ends:

> Zala had always prided herself on her knowledge of the city; its back roads, parks, and campuses; its architecture and monuments ... the voting districts that kept shifting their lines since the day Primus King cast the first Black ballot down in Columbus, Georgia. Her first training had come from her dad ... Atlanta, the real one, was documented in the sketchbooks, the scrapbooks, the photo albums, the deeds, family Bibles, in the memories and mouths of the elders ... Later, they'd sit outside the house, their mouths stuffed with candy, while he guided her hand drawing maps of the terrain and she dutifully recited, prying her jaws apart with her sticky fingers, the history learned on that day's trip.[42]

The density of the layers of historical period invoked here, the variety of modes of alternate memory, and the sweet sensory recall Zala has of these lessons, refutes postmodernism's thesis that true historical consciousness has waned into mere pastiche. Instead, Zala's "submerged geographies," as Jodi Melamed argues, "direct the reader to look at Atlanta's contemporary racial geography as no fait accompli but a terrain of struggle."[43]

While Zala is deeply cathected to this moment of intergenerational mapping, this map is not a stationary one. Building on her childhood knowledge of the city, Zala is hard at work on mapping the effect of finance capital on the city:

> Now, leaning hard across the steering wheel on the lookout for blinking detour signs, she realized that the downtown area she'd mastered at five, then remastered at ten ... was a confusion of sawhorse barriers, open ditches, plank sidewalks, and sandy pathways for yellow Caterpillars carrying boulders in their maws. She ... ducked instinctively when a line slung across the narrow street slackened and a clamshell bucket dropped a dollop of cement on her roof. She peered past the windshield lest she miss the new entry onto 75/85 north.[44]

The "leaning hard" and the intuitive recoil from the attack of the cement are redolent of Sara Ahmed's idea of a "sweaty concept," which is one that "might come out of a bodily experience that is trying"[45] and is Zala's response to a cityscape whose rate of change has accelerated over her lifetime. Within this dense paragraph, we are given the city of the '50s, the reshaping of downtown in the '60s, and the pace of change in the 1980s of Zala's present, where the landscape is literally being rebuilt before her eyes. Bambara's use of personification for the machinery nods to the structural analysis of this roadwork as part of the global change orchestrated at the behest of global capital, rather than focusing on the workers in the machines or even local political interests.

Bambara's novel makes clear that the true postmodern reshaping of urban space is not the glittering high rises, but the destruction of traditionally Black neighborhoods. While Atlanta also received its share of Bonaventuras – in fact, the architect of that hotel, John Portman, also designed the Peachtree Center in Atlanta – for Zala, the division of the city along lines of race and class is more informative than reading the CBD: "It was an impressive skyline, Zala supposed – the glass towers, the skyscraper hotels, the banks, the revolving club lounges on the top floors of buildings ... Too literal, she decided – too literal a statement about its intention to be a major city."[46] Not worth the novel's penetrating analysis, the true work of financial city-shaping takes place at eye-level, not in the glassy enclaves of the CBD.

While Zala's remapping may be at ground level, it is as international as the finance capital of the downtown skyscrapers. The novel makes frequent allusion to the breadth and depth of Black diasporic imaginations: "Tell me we aren't a cosmopolitan people ... Tell me we aren't one big family with kinfolks scattered all over the world. Mississippi. Grenada. Alabama. Soweto. Brooklyn."[47] The revolutionary international imaginaries that *Those Bones* considers are breathtaking in their scope and too numerous to outline here, spanning anti-Imperial protests across the Global South and their twinned protests in the United States, the exploitation of working class Black and Latino populations to fight in Vietnam, the national and international effects of the war on drugs, the link between the sterilization of women in Puerto Rico, of Native Americans, and of African Americans, the parallels between white supremacists in South Africa and in the USA, and the parallels between neoliberal urban planning in the USA and in Brazil.

Zala exhibits impatience at the media who refuse to cover the mass murder of Black children as they deem it too local. Speaking to a journalist, Zala is told:

> "What can I tell you? Blacks just aren't news anymore, Mrs. Spencer ... The problem is – and I don't mean to sound insensitive to your situation – but the Atlanta story lacks scope" ...
> "Please! There's terrorism right here in Atlanta. Atlanta, I'm talking about, the 'New International City.'"[48]

Zala's invocation of Atlanta's international status when it comes to capital (a status reinforced by its choice as host of the 1996 Olympics), but not when children are murdered, is testament to her claim that "convention dollars speak so much louder than an invisible community silenced by their very wealth of pigment and their very lack of dollars."[49] By linking race and capitalism in this way, Zala is also arguing that the creation of Atlanta as a global international hub is directly linked to the serial murders of Black children, and the serial and unconscionable failure of the local police and FBI to investigate these crimes. It is not just that Black deaths occur and the need to keep Atlanta's image as international financial center means they must be hushed up; it is that the hypertrophic investment in the CBD in order to "protec[t] lawyers, bankers, consultants, and regional executives from the intrusion of low-income neighborhoods"[50] and the concurrent segregation and deinvestment of nonwhite spaces is the kind of urban planning that leads to Black deaths – here, by a serial killer or killers, but more widely through other modes of premature death, exacerbated by ghettoizing Black life into defunded portions of the city.[51]

As well as showing that Black urban space is as much postmodern space as the skyscrapers of downtown, Bambara's novel also offers the possibility for resistant forms of mapping. Even amid the horror of the death of Black children, the novel shows that Black space is not just violence and underinvestment, tied only to the glittering global postmodern city by being its inverse. After Sonny has returned, traumatized but alive, his parents devote energy to trying to find out where he has been held captive for the months he was missing. In an unlikely twist, they manage to get hold of a videodisc from a government source, a real piece of technology made by MIT in the 1970s that "can store as many as 54,000 stills . . . any visual can be segued to allow the viewer to reconceptualize or recontextualize a particular site, detail, or relationship"[52] – in short, an early version of Google Street View. This is an appropriation of a technology of the state, in particular of surveillance, a mode of technology deployed disproportionately against people of color, and in particular African Americans.[53] With the unexpected turn to a technology that is far from obviously utopian, Bambara's novel shows that the disruptive technologies of postmodernism can help solve the case of the missing and murdered children: "With the aid of a videodisc, an entire city could be learned . . . [even] the killer's route."[54] This is in opposition to the official Task Force investigating the killings, who showed a "stubborn resistance to acknowledge the links a map made obvious."[55] Bambara uses the postmodern forms of repetition and listing, and the postmodern technology of remapping space, but repurposes them. Importantly, as Carole Anne Taylor has argued, "however easily the term 'postmodern' might suggest [*Those Bones's*] polyvalent, trans-generic qualities, the work ultimately appropriates them"[56] and puts them to emancipatory ends.

Remapping Black spaces is to insist not only on their link to the postmodern financial spaces of Central Business Districts, but also the necessity of these Black spaces to finance capital. Capital needs to label some sites as "nonpostmodern" to allow for the "spatial fix" of expansion and investment. In the present day, this looks like "capital disinvestment, white flight, gentrification, urban renewal, incarceration, and policing," all of which "demonstrate the reliance of capital on [the] notion of empty, lifeless, Blackened spaces."[57] While finance capital writes off Black spaces as "empty, lifeless," to the extent that even the death of Black children means nothing, Bambara claims postmodern spaces as sites of Black revolutionary internationalisms, mutual aid and empowerment, techno-logical mastery, and given the return of Sonny – hope. And this is in part because, unlike Jameson's postmodern actors, "caught as individual subjects ... [in the] great global multinational and decentered communi-cational network,"[58] Bambara's characters do not confront this global network as individual subjects, but as a community with shared resources.[59] If, for Jameson, "the political form of postmodernism, if there ever is any, will have as its vocation the invention and projection of a global cognitive mapping, on a social as well as a spatial scale,"[60] then Bambara's novel is surely it.

Notes

1 Fredric Jameson, *Postmodernism, or, The Cultural Logic of Late Capitalism* (1991; London: Verso, 2019), xix.
2 Fredric Jameson, "Culture and Finance Capital," *Critical Inquiry* 24.1 (1997), 246–265; 252.
3 Jameson, *Postmodernism*, 60.
4 Ibid., 64–65.
5 Ibid., 87.
6 Ibid.
7 Aijaz Ahmad, "Jameson's Rhetoric of Otherness and the 'National Allegory,'" in *In Theory: Classes, Nations, Literatures* (London: Verso, 1992), 95–112; 96–97.
8 Madhu Dubey, *Signs and Cities: Black Literary Postmodernism* (Chicago: University of Chicago Press, 2014), 8.

9 Frantz Fanon, *The Wretched of the Earth* (1961; New York: Grove Weidenfeld, 1991), 5.

10 bell hooks, "Postmodern Blackness," in *Yearning: Race, Gender, and Cultural Politics* (New York: Routledge, 2015), 23–32; 23.

11 While Wayne Williams was only charged with two murders, and both victims were adults, the case was closed with his conviction. The official Task Force list recognized only twenty-eight murders; however, lists kept by the Atlanta community ran much higher, including some deaths after Williams's incarceration.

12 Toni Morrison, "Living Memory: A Meeting with Toni Morrison," in Paul Gilroy, *Small Acts: Thoughts on the Politics of Black Cultures* (London: Serpent's Tail, 1993), 175–182; 178.

13 Dubey, *Signs and Cities*, 2.

14 Theodore Martin, "Crime Fiction and Black Criminality," *American Literary History* 30.4 (2018), 703–729; 716, 723.

15 Toni Cade Bambara, "Deep Sight and Rescue Missions," in *Deep Sightings and Rescue Missions*, edited by Toni Morrison (New York: Random House, 2008), 146–178; 147.

16 Paul Gilroy, *The Black Atlantic: Modernity and Double Consciousness* (1993; London: Verso, 2007), 42.

17 Patricia Hill Collins, *Fighting Words: Black Women and the Search for Justice* (Minneapolis: University of Minnesota Press, 1998), 125.

18 Toni Cade Bambara, "What It Is I Think I'm Doing Anyhow," in *The Writer on Her Work*, edited by Janet Sternburg (New York: W. W. Norton, 1980), 153–168; 155.

19 Jameson, *Postmodernism*, 56–57.

20 For an exception, see Martyn Bone's excellent essay "Capitalist Abstraction and the Body Politics of Place in Toni Cade Bambara's *Those Bones Are Not My Child*," *Journal of American Studies* 37.2 (2003), 229–246.

21 Jameson, *Postmodernism*, 83–84.

22 Ibid., 62.

23 José Eduardo Limón, *Dancing with the Devil: Society and Cultural Poetics in Mexican-American South Texas* (Madison: University of Wisconsin Press, 1994), 107–108.

24 Ibid., 111.

25 Mike Davis, "Urban Renaissance and the Spirit of Postmodernism," *New Left Review* 151.1 (1985), 106–113; 112.

26 Ibid., 111.

27 Ibid.

28 Proxies were used, such as the Regional Plan Association, founded in 1922 by Morgan bankers, Rockefeller Foundation directors, and real estate developers, and the Downtown Lower Manhattan Association created by David Rockefeller in 1958. For more on this, see Laura Finch and Jessica Hurley, "From the Bomb to the Crash: Geographies of Disaster in the American Century," https://fromthebombtothecrash.squarespace.com/.

29 David Harvey, *The Limits to Capital* (Chicago: University of Chicago Press, 1982), 397. See also Christina B. Hanhardt, *Safe Space: Gay Neighborhood History and the Politics of Violence* (Durham, NC: Duke University Press, 2013) and Neil Smith, *The New Urban Frontier: Gentrification and the Revanchist City* (London: Routledge, 1996).

30 Bret Easton Ellis, *American Psycho: A Novel* (New York: Vintage, 1991), 81.

31 Ibid., 84.

32 Ibid., 86.

33 Dubey, *Signs and Cities*, 64.

34 Ibid.

35 James C. Cobb, *Selling the South: The Southern Crusade for Industrial Development, 1936–90* (Chicago: University of Illinois Press, 1993), 188.

36 Toni Cade Bambara, *Those Bones Are Not My Child* (1999; New York: Knopf Doubleday, 2009), 173.

37 Ibid., 53.

38 Ibid., 16.

39 For this history, see Ronald H. Bayor, *Race and the Shaping of Twentieth-Century Atlanta* (Chapel Hill: University of North Carolina Press, 2000); Larry Keating, *Atlanta: Race, Class, and Urban Expansion* (Philadelphia: Temple University Press, 2010); Kevin Michael Kruse, *White Flight: Atlanta and the Making of Modern Conservatism* (Princeton, NJ: Princeton University Press, 2007); and Charles Rutheiser, *Imagineering Atlanta: The Politics of Place in the City of Dreams* (London: Verso, 1996).

40 Bambara, *Those Bones*, 122.

41 Thanks to Jessica Hurley for her generous comments on this piece, and in particular for her suggestion that Bambara is engaged not in a mapping, but in a remapping.

42 Bambara, *Those Bones*, 83–84.

43 Jodi Melamed, *Represent and Destroy: Rationalizing Violence in the New Racial Capitalism* (Minneapolis: University of Minnesota Press, 2011), 128.

44 Bambara, *Those Bones*, 85

45 Sara Ahmed, *Living a Feminist Life* (Durham, NC: Duke University Press, 2017), 13.

46 Bambara, *Those Bones*, 82.

47 Ibid., 170

48 Ibid., 273–274.

49 Ibid., 152.

50 Carl Abbott, *The New Urban America: Growth and Politics in Sunbelt Cities* (Chapel Hill: University of North Carolina Press, 1983), 143.

51 Bambara is not alone in this analysis – see also James Baldwin's *The Evidence of Things Not Seen* (New York: Holt, Rinehart, and Winston, 1985).

52 Bambara, *Those Bones*, 643.

53 See Simone Browne, *Dark Matters: On the Surveillance of Blackness* (Durham, NC: Duke University Press, 2015).

54 Bambara, *Those Bones*, 644.

55 Ibid., 416.
56 Carole Anne Taylor, "Postmodern Disconnection and the Archive of Bones: Toni Cade Bambara's Last Work," *Novel: A Forum on Fiction* 35.2–3 (2002), 258–280; 259.
57 Adam Bledsoe and Willie Jamaal Wright, "The Anti-Blackness of Global Capital," *Environment and Planning D: Society and Space* 37.1 (2019), 8–26; 13.
58 Jameson, *Postmodernism*, 83–84.
59 The book is deeply communal and social, both within its pages and in its publication history; Toni Morrison edited the unfinished manuscript after Bambara's death in 1995.
60 Jameson, *Postmodernism*, 92.

CHAPTER 7

Writing Postcolonial Capitalism

Cheryl Narumi Naruse

Postcolonial capitalism names a form of capitalism that is practiced, rationalized, and imagined with respect to a historical and geopolitical consciousness of colonial subordination. Whether ideologically articulated by individuals or operating at the scale of state discourse, the historical consciousness of colonialism that undergirds postcolonial capitalism frames capitalism as a politicized response to the injustices of colonialism and racial capitalism, even as it reproduces and sustains the very systems that facilitated their spread.[1] The "post" in postcolonial here – a prefix that has been rightly questioned by postcolonial and Indigenous scholars for the implication that colonialism is over – marks the formal shift in political power that accompanied decolonization and the rise of independent states.[2] But such a historical shift does not suggest the irrelevance of what came before. Rather, the "post" recognizes that with statehood comes a new configuration of power and thus new questions of accountability as empire takes on an informal role. As an analytical framework, postcolonial capitalism asks how postcolonial subjectivities, contexts, and ideologies produce capitalism and how histories of colonialism are actively, deliberately, strategically instrumentalized. As historical developments show, postcolonial capitalism hardly looks to overturn the imperial legacies of racial capitalism – it instead accepts the terms of capitalism's uneven structure and works within it. Addressing the role of the postcolonial – whether referring to a subject, a history, a geopolitical position, an academic field, or a body of theory – in perpetuating capitalism is to find appropriate objects of capitalist analysis and critique. How does postcoloniality sanction the global coproduction of capitalism?

Although there are a number of critical works that take up the *theme* of postcolonial capitalism, the term itself has had surprisingly limited use. While its coinage cannot be easily pinned down to an origin – after all, adjectival usage of "postcolonial" is a commonplace descriptor – postcolonial capitalism's most thorough engagement comes from economist Kalyan Sanyal, who studies the particularities of capitalist formations in postcolonial India. Drawing on Robert Brenner, Sanyal writes: "[T]he story of capitalist transformation must begin by recognizing that the superstructure" – that is, the cultures, behaviors, ideologies, and institutions that sustain capitalism – "has an important role to play."[3] Because of their ability to represent discourse, layers of history, and narrative logics, literary engagements with postcolonial capitalism provide the objects of study to investigate the workings of the superstructure that Sanyal highlights. Besides offering insights into the ideologies and cultures of postcolonial capitalism, "the category of literature, like that of the postcolonial," as my coauthors and I have previously observed, "has underwritten diverse and powerful modalities of anticapitalist critique, even as it has helped normalize the systematic use of raw materials from particularized locales toward the production of aesthetic goods."[4] Literatures of postcolonial capitalism are thus not united in function and for our analytical purposes can serve a dual purpose: as the stuff of superstructure and as a mode of critique.

Critiques of postcolonial capitalism unpack the complexity of political agency in a world laden with determinative structural forces and histories of oppression. Within postcolonial studies – and indeed cognate literary fields such as ethnic American literature where histories of oppression and difference are also fundamental concerns – comprehending forms of political resistance is key for deconstructing perceptions of power as totalizing, which is itself a discursive technique of oppression. In this way, "agency" – as Tina Chen notes – is often "leveraged by marginalized and disavowed subjects to establish positions that subsequently enable the articulation of rights and resistance to oppression."[5] But a critical emphasis on agency that operates in service of "major narratives around resistance and romanticized notions of liberal free speech," as Hentyle Yapp puts it, potentially obscures the ways in which postcoloniality as a historical, material, and cultural condition might function as its own force of power.[6] Certainly, traumatic histories of racial capitalism have dispossessed and "pauperized" what we now know as the postcolonial world, as Couze Venn writes.[7] But as illustrated by, say, the economic differentiation within the postcolonial world, such histories can take unexpected turns and can produce an ideological range within the scope of "resistance."

Even while critiques of postcolonial capitalism call attention to the ways that agential resistance to colonialism does not always result in resistance to capitalism, they keep the question of agency in critical view in order to overturn Eurocentric or elitist forms of knowledge. Critical approaches to postcolonial capitalism build on methodological insights from subaltern studies: scholars like historian Ranajit Guha argue that histories from "the people" reveal a politics and power dynamic not apparent in dominant narratives of history.[8] The former colonies take on a similar structural position to Guha's reference to "the people" insofar as they have been subject to the material and psychic violence of racial capitalism as enabled by colonialism.

As a critical paradigm, postcolonial capitalism resists installing Europe as the active center from which capitalism emanates and the nonwest as a compliant, passive site.[9] Sandro Mezzadra argues that postcolonial capitalism enables the recognition of "diverse scales, places, and histories" of labor in a global context.[10] The diversity of labor challenges cohesive, universalizing theories of abstract or free labor – the basis of many Marxian conceptions of capitalism. In Sanyal's work, the heterogeneous character of capitalism is key for arresting simplified accounts of capitalism's hegemony that undergird the assumptions of developmental economics. For Sanyal, comprehending postcolonial capitalism means thinking through the "complex hegemony" of postcolonial capitalism, or the ways in which "tradition and modernity, capital and pre-capital, converge, coalesce, and constitute each other."[11] Such complexity, he argues, "militates against a mechanical view of class struggle."[12] Whether as what Aihwa Ong might describe as "an analytical angle that allows us to examine the shifting lines of [capitalist] mutation" or as a naming of a particular historical development, postcolonial capitalism – by reframing the so-called periphery as an active, distinctive site of capitalism – problematizes normative approaches to capitalism.[13]

While postcolonial methodologies that underscore the agential subject and the multiplicity of historical developments have been useful for overturning normative, Eurocentric approaches in other fields, postcolonial capitalist agency is not the kind of agency that the field of postcolonial studies itself tends to place much emphasis upon. Though postcolonial capitalism might share with subaltern accounts of history a general "notion of resistance to elite domination," as Guha writes, it does not lead to a radical politics since the autonomy it promises appears only to further entrench colonial ideologies.[14] Just as Sanyal and Mezzadra look to the historical development of postcolonial capitalism as evidence against universalist accounts of capitalism that generate formulaic understandings of its dynamics, within the scope of postcolonial studies, postcolonial capitalism warns against the "mechanical view" that Sanyal describes, but in this instance, of political resistance. In other words, postcolonial capitalism is a reminder not to overvalorize marginalized or subaltern subjects for their political resistance. Examining the ways in which postcoloniality functions as a capitalist force pushes at postcolonialism's discursive limits by exposing the ideological heterogeneity of what "postcolonial" might describe. The concept also ensures that postcolonial theory's anticolonial intellectual roots do not produce the effect of overlooking or disavowing the ways that postcoloniality works in service of capitalism. That so many postcolonial sites once considered part of the economic margins are now central to the operations of global capitalism – Brazil, India, Kenya, Korea, Singapore, South Africa – suggests a broader pattern that postcolonialists are well-equipped to investigate.

The Postcolonial Entrepreneur, the Anticolonial Logics of Commodifying Difference, and Postcolonial Capitalism in the Marketplace

In the context of the "marketplace," the site of commodity exchange, postcolonial capitalism renders postcoloniality as a marker of historical and thus cultural difference, an essentialized condition that is leveraged for financial, social, or cultural capital and navigates the racial dynamics of colonial consumption. Although the term is not directly used, this manifestation of postcolonial capitalism has been best theorized through Graham Huggan's notion of the "postcolonial exotic."[15] In the 1990s, postcolonial critics called attention to the emergence of postcoloniality as academic capital, particularly as it was figured through the diasporic intellectual working in the United States. As Huggan puts it, these critiques draw attention "to the commodifying processes by which generalized cultural differences are manufactured, disseminated, and consumed," and the "literatures/cultures of the 'non-Western' world" turned "into saleable exotic objects."[16] Huggan's notion of the postcolonial exotic illustrates how postcoloniality can be instrumentalized, wielded, and leveraged. What Huggan and other thinkers like Sarah Brouillette, Arif Dirlik, Stuart Hall, Timothy Brennan, and Rey Chow recognize is the agency of, in this case, subjects who use postcoloniality in order to gain financial or social advantage. Similar concepts appear in allied fields, such as Asian Americanist Yến Lê Espiritu's notion of the panethnic entrepreneur.

A key figure of this particular articulation of postcolonial capitalism is the entrepreneur, a person who operates their own business. Although the entrepreneur in the twenty-first century is typically thought of as a figurehead for corporations, I use the entrepreneur here to name the celebrated heroes of capitalism that are regarded as creative individuals who achieve financial success amid difficult market conditions, regardless of their historical context. If already the entrepreneur is seen as navigating the precarious circumstances of capitalism, the postcolonial entrepreneur faces even greater uncertainty, given the structural disadvantages accorded by the histories of racial capitalism. In this way, the successful postcolonial entrepreneur is celebrated not only for their business acumen: capital gain is read as a symbol for their ability to successfully navigate systematized, historical limitations. Such figures are especially prevalent in recent post-colonial texts: the Guide from Cathy Park Hong's *Dance Dance Revolution* (2006), Balram of Aravind Adiga's *The White Tiger* (2008), Phoebe from Tash Aw's *Five Star Billionaire* (2013), Chiah Deng of Hwee Hwee Tan's *Mammon Inc.* (2001), Rajkumar of Amitav Ghosh's *The Glass Palace* (2000), the unnamed protagonist of Mohsin Hamid's *How to Get Filthy Rich in Rising Asia* (2013), and Vimbai of Tendai Huchu's *The Hairdresser of Harare* (2010), to name a few. Moments of a postcolonial entrepreneurial spirit are also evident in works, both fictional and critical, now considered classic. Consider, for example, the market scene in which Tambuzai of Tsitsi Dangarembga's *Nervous Conditions* (1988) sells mealies in order to pay for her school tuition or Epeli Hauʻofa's reference to his Tongan friend in "Our Sea of Islands" (1994), an enterprising, resourceful man described as having "never heard of dependency."[17] I turn here to Derek Walcott's *Omeros* (1990) and Chimamanda Ngozi Adichie's *Americanah* (2014), two texts that explore themes of postcolonial entrepreneurship, though not explicitly using such terms.

In Walcott's epic poem *Omeros*, readers are introduced to Helen – a woman characterized as having a "tongue too tart for a waitress to take orders" – amid her frustration with the sexual harassment she faces from her tourist customers.[18] Tired of subjecting herself to her customers' whims, Helen instead decides to set up her own business: "She braided the tourists' flaxen hair with bright beads / cane-row style, then would sit apart from the vendors."[19] The early part of *Omeros* depicts Helen as a controversial, sexualized, and highly desired character, but what is also notable about this mini narrative arc is how Walcott conveys the complexities of postcolonial agency under (global) capitalism. Insofar as Helen moves from a position where she is managed to one where she holds more control over her circumstances, readers are to understand Helen's trajectory as improved, or at least as one that allows her to maintain some element of autonomy and thus dignity. That Helen's empowerment is built on a hair braiding business is also symbolically significant. Such a business typifies how racial difference is commodified for tourist consumption, and Walcott subtly ironizes the profitability of, in this instance, mimicry of the postcolonial subject by the colonial-tourist, racially marked as white by the text through their "flaxen hair." As the very description of the "cane-row" style braids reminds readers, the braids are not simply a symbol of difference, they are a symbol of colonial history – in this case, the history of enslaved labor for sugar plantations in the Caribbean. Helen's business savviness, in this instance, is based on her understanding of how colonial desire operates.

Certainly, for the ways that tourism commodifies difference for pleasure and consumption, the St. Lucian context in *Omeros* provides an apt and convenient stage to explore the workings of postcolonial capitalism. The touristic framework can be expanded to discuss the writing career of Walcott, as Sarah Brouillette has in her discussion of postcolonial writers and the global literary market.[20] Walcott's literary works, which grapple with the complex legacies of colonial enslavement, have been celebrated for their original and empowering depictions of Caribbean life. Yet, as a critical approach to postcolonial capitalism might ask: what new forms of power and oppression accompany, in this case, the (warranted) celebration of Walcott's work? When considering this question, Walcott cannot be read separately from his sexual harassment scandals while at Oxford and Harvard – scandals arguably facilitated by the institutional prestige accorded to Walcott's work. The postcolonial character of Walcott's work – in terms of the historical period and of its imperial critique – is at political odds with and obscures (if not excuses) his misogyny. Although a critical reading of postcolonial capitalism might begin with a reading of capitalist agency, it also always seeks its limits – in this instance, the limits of Helen's entrepreneurial efforts and the limits of Walcott's ability to represent a woman as a character with depth.

In contrast to Helen in terms of her classed position, another more contemporary literary example that depicts the ambivalence of instrumentalizing postcoloniality as an entrepreneur in the globalized anglophone literary market is Ifemelu of Adichie's *Americanah*. Readers first encounter Ifemelu at the height of her career in a time of life transition: she is at Princeton with a prestigious writing fellowship and has just closed her well-read blog, *Raceteenth or Various Observations About American Blacks (Those Formerly Known as Negroes) by a Non-American Black*, and is about to move back to Lagos, Nigeria. Throughout the novel, readers are given Ifemelu's backstory of her childhood in Nigeria, which in turn provides the context for her status as a "non-American black," the postcolonial ethos and thus perspective that is the basis of her successful blog. As Ifemelu explains to her boyfriend Blaine, an African American professor at Yale: "It's different for me and I think it's because I'm from the Third World ... To be a child of the Third World is to be aware of the many different constituencies you have and how honesty and truth must always depend on context."[21] The use of "Third World," which Blaine dismisses as a lazy usage, is ambiguous insofar as it might refer to Nigeria's economic status as an underdeveloped nation or refer to the solidarity movement among non-aligned nations.[22] In either possibility, Ifemelu's use of "Third World" calls attention to her consciousness of colonial and postcolonial history, a consciousness she embraces for the way it decenters US hegemony and that she leverages into a commodifiable form. The hegemony of American thinking, as portrayed through Blaine's scorn for Ifemelu's explanation, resonates in tone with the universalist accounts of capitalism that Sanyal seeks to undo. *Americanah* problematizes the rise in power which accompanies Ifemelu's successful commodification of postcolonial difference by calling attention to the class divide between her and other African immigrants in the USA and by highlighting the ways that Ifemelu's postcolonial subjectivity sanctions her sometimes dismissive takes on antiblackness in the USA.

Furthermore, Ifemelu as postcolonial entrepreneur operates as a reflection of the conditions through which former colonies become visible to imperial colonizers as cultural capital. Ifemelu's sense of triumph over her successful blog is undercut by the career opportunities that her blog creates.[23] At invited talks, she finds herself working in the service of diversity initiatives at schools and corporations and simply repeating "what they wanted to hear, none of which she would ever write on her blog."[24] Though *Americanah* clearly problematizes how institutionalized diversity creates a marketplace that tokenizes racial difference, the text also shows how Ifemelu does not – and perhaps cannot – overturn the very structures she critiques.

Notably, both Helen and Ifemelu's successful trajectories are also marked with a sense of loss. After she performs her hair-braiding, Helen "then would sit apart from the vendors." The reader is not privy to Helen's thoughts and whether the cause of her separation is self-imposed or the result of unspoken hostilities, but the text indicates that the social alienation Helen faces is an outcome related to her business. Ifemelu experiences a similar sense of loss after a scathing critique of her blog – and thus of her – from her boyfriend's sister: "She's writing from the outside,"

Shan declares, "She doesn't really feel all the stuff she's writing about . . . If she were African American, she'd just be labeled angry and shunned."[25] As Ifemelu contends with the idea that her outsider status is both the source of the insights that she is able to commodify *and* the basis of her perceived inauthentic politics, she is left feeling "an embittered knot, like bereavement, in her chest."[26] Both Helen's alienation and Ifemelu's grief call attention to the social sacrifice demanded by postcolonial capitalism as a historical phenomenon. As a critical framework, postcolonial capitalism helps us to understand that whatever empowerment might accompany the successful commodification of postcolonial difference is destabilized by the loss of community, solidarity, and social relations. Even when economic differentiation works in favor of the postcolonial subject, it is a deeply ambivalent outcome.

Postcolonial Capitalism as Political Rationality

Despite their opposing political positions, in subaltern forms of capitalism and contemporary state discourse postcolonial capitalism appears as a rationality, justifying capitalist formations by cultivating the idea that financial wealth is some kind of restorative justice. Within postcolonial studies there has been increasing critical attention to "Dalit capitalism." Akshya Saxena explains how Dalit capitalism is about "the transformation of a low-caste life, marked by humiliation and poverty, into a life rich with purchasing power."[27] Indeed, capitalist accumulation as a mode of challenging histories of oppressive power is evident in a number of kindred formations such as "Indigenous capitalisms," described by anthropologist Alexis Celeste Bunten as "a distinct strategy employed by Indigenous communities to take part in national and international level political economies while negotiating and asserting self-determination";[28] "neotribal capitalism," theorized by Elizabeth Rata as historically rooted in the history of Māori land dispossession;[29] and "Black capitalism," explained by Black Panther Party cofounder Huey P. Newton as "Black control of another one of the institutions in the community."[30] Taken together, these subaltern forms of capitalism underscore a desire for respect and articulate capitalist ideologies through liberatory rhetoric. In doing so, they create the view that the problems of capitalism might be resolved by new figures of power. But as postcolonial histories have taught us, formal decolonization did not produce decoloniality.

Similar logics appear in postcolonial state rhetoric. During the 2019 Amazon rainforest fires, for example, Brazilian president Jair

Bolsonaro rejected the G7's offer of aid, as led by French President Emmanuel Macron, to fight the fires. Emphasizing Brazil's sovereignty, Bolsonaro accused Macron of a "colonialist mentality."[31] The strategy of positioning the Brazilian nation-state as subaltern was clearly a ruse for Bolsonaro to maintain the extractive, industrial practices – and profitability – of deforestation. In contrast is the earnest political rhetoric from the Bandung Conference of 1955. Many speeches throughout the meeting of heads of state of the newly decolonized, sovereign nations called for economic cooperation across Asia and Africa. "[W]hat we certainly can do is co-operate closely amongst ourselves in the economic field ... to devise ways and means to increase inter-regional trade, and gradually stay independent in the economic sense," Ali Sastroamidjojo, then Prime Minister of Indonesia, declared.[32] As Samir Amin writes: "The Bandung era, with the triumph of the ideology of development, was based on a range of seeming truths, specific to each region of the world but all deeply rooted in prevailing beliefs: Keynesianism; the myth of catching up through third world interdependence."[33] In other words, the anticolonial desire for liberation and autonomy, as embodied by developmentalism, further entrenched and obscured capitalist logics (even while they were more socialist in orientation).

As Rajkumar of Amitav Ghosh's *The Glass Palace* illustrates, the triumphs of subaltern capitalism both rationalize and problematically obscure the violences of capitalism. A historical, multigenerational, transnational novel centered on Burma (though spanning British India and Malaya), *The Glass Palace* explores the complex power dynamics of British imperialism, beginning with the British invasion of Burma in 1885 and extending to contemporary Myanmar under military rule. A key protagonist of the novel is Rajkumar, whom readers follow from his beginnings as an orphaned child seeking work in Burma and as he eventually commands a commercial business in the teak industry. Rajkumar's story – and indeed the novel as a whole – provides a different gloss on understandings of postcoloniality by calling to the historical antecedents of the subaltern capitalism of the twenty-first century, in this instance as it is rooted in an economy based on extractive capitalism and colonial governance.

In order to create a steep narrative arc in which capitalist success is made all the more dramatic, the novel begins with Rajkumar as an orphaned boy in the unfamiliar land of Burma – a character, in other words, devoid of social advantage. Readers are later made to understand that Rajkumar is from a low caste, which not only makes the accomplishment of his teak business remarkable, but the fact of his financial assistance to Bengalis in

Rangoon even more surprising. As a letter from one of his beneficiaries reveals: "At home in India a man like Rajkumar-babu would stand little chance of gaining acceptance in the society of people like ourselves."[34] In contrast to Helen and Ifemelu, who experience social rejection as a result of their entrepreneurial endeavors, Rajkumar keeps his alienated sociopolitical status in tension with the social expectations that accompany his improved class status. At a dinner among colonial dignitaries, "Rajkumar glanced impatiently at the knives and forks that surrounded his plate. Then, as though in exasperation at the profusion of cutlery, he held up his right hand and snapped his fingers. Even before he had completed the gesture U Ba Kyaw had appeared at his side, to hand him the appropriate utensil. This took no more than an instant, but everyone in the room took startled notice."[35] In this curious moment, Rajkumar at once performs the historical effects of his low-caste – he does not know the proper decorum for European meals – and asserts his newly accrued class power by calling on his servant. In this way, Rajkumar transforms his caste status into a colonial critique by refusing to enter fully into the expectations of class behavior. Rather than performing an assimilative respectability politics, Rajkumar instead emphasizes his awkward fit in the elite class of which he is now a part. In doing so, Rajkumar reveals the rationality of postcolonial capitalism. Rajkumar's marginalized sociopolitical status at once sanctions his power – as the underdog with whom readers and other characters sympathize – and further maintains his image as exceptional. Rajkumar's exceptionality, however, proves the rule of caste rather than critiquing or challenging it.

Through the depiction of boat journeys across the Bay of Bengal, *The Glass Palace* calls attention to the ways in which the exceptionality of subaltern capitalism obscures the consequences of new oppressions created by this emergent form of power and problematically absolves the subaltern capitalist of political accountability. When Rajkumar asks Saya John for a loan to finance his business, Rajkumar returns to India to find the indentured servants – Indian coolies – for his labor needs. The passage across the Bay is harrowing. Ghosh provides a graphic description of the ship's hold as "covered with vomit and urine ... [that] welled back and forth with the rolling of the ship" – conditions so wretched that many attempt suicide.[36] Readers know that Rajkumar's childhood experience of the Bay was also traumatic because his mother died by his side during his crossing. Such a shared history of trauma or even nominally shared social position does not result in Rajkumar's sympathies for his newly accrued coolies, however. The narrative instead tracks the choices Rajkumar makes in order eventually to accumulate the savings he needs to buy a timber-yard. In doing so, the novel illustrates how the narrative's centering of Rajkumar's ascendency – and the readerly affective attachment to him – obfuscates his exploitative role. This point is at first made indirectly through the rather brief (though vivid) depiction of how coolies are inhumanely treated. It is only later through a conflict with another character, Uma, that the novel calls more direct attention to Rajkumar's exploitative actions: "You – an animal, with your greed, your determination to take whatever you can – at whatever cost. Do you think nobody knows about the things you've done to people in your power – to women and children who couldn't defend themselves? You're no better than a slaver and rapist, Rajkumar."[37] *The Glass Palace* emphasizes that accountability must accompany any assertion of agency, especially as agential expressions that resist oppressive structures of power may act as justifications and motivations for postcolonial capitalism.

Postcolonial Capitalism, Solidarity Movements, and New Configurations of Power

As the political rhetoric from the meeting of Asian and African heads of state at the 1955 Bandung Conference illustrated, postcolonial capitalism can be the basis of a political solidarity movement that emphasizes a history of shared colonial oppression. In more recent developments, postcolonial capitalism has emerged as a quasi-solidarity movement in the form of economic blocs and free trade agreements – in other words, postcolonial solidarity has been transformed into a neoliberalized alignment. The leaders of the BRICS nations (Brazil, Russia, India, China, and South Africa), for example, "persist in presenting their group . . . in the warm and fuzzy framework of benevolent South-South cooperation, an essential counterweight to the 'old' West and a better partner for the poor masses of the developing world."[38] Such state-serving use of anticolonial rhetoric has been widely critiqued, however. In 2018, the "Break the BRICS" coalition groups in South Africa organized a march as a way of protesting what they described as "the capitalist nature of the BRICS states, their anti-working class behaviour, and their environmentally destructive policies."[39] Through such protests, we observe how postcoloniality is itself a site of competing power claims, one mired in the dynamics of neoliberalized, global capitalism.

Aravind Adiga uses the protagonist Balram's narrative address to the Chinese Premier in *The White Tiger* as a way of portraying postcolonial capitalism as the basis of understanding and cooperation between post-colonial states, calling attention to its new configuration of power and the ways in which western power is displaced. In this way, *The White Tiger* aligns with a number of postcolonial texts that explore the waning appeal and colonial reach of the Euro-American west through return narratives as seen in *Americanah*, Tash Aw's *Five Star Billionaire*, Sefi Atta's *A Bit of Difference* (2012), and Kevin Kwan's *Crazy Rich Asians* trilogy (2013, 2015, 2017). Such texts do not imagine displacement as some sort of postcolonial revenge, but as a decentering of the west by reforming the periphery as the metropole. The novel opens with Wen Jiabao's visit to Bangalore – Balram's city of residence – and his desire to "meet some Indian entrepreneurs and hear the story of their success from their own lips."[40] The Chinese Premier's visit thus becomes the occasion for Balram to tell his story of how he became an entrepreneur despite his low-caste beginnings. Balram's tone is (over)familiar with the narratee in its emphasis on their shared marginalized historical status caused by western imperialism, though also deferent when acknowledging that China has never been colonized.[41] While the novel's epistolary form performs a kind of intimacy, it also calls attention to how that intimacy is mediated through the Anglophone: "I read about your history in a book, *Exciting Tales of the Exotic East*, that I found on the pavement."[42] The novel seems humorously to problematize the orientalist production of knowledge about China, but also dismisses it. The received knowledge does not come from a powerful colonial institution like a school, but is a discarded object, accidentally found, and no longer quite holding command over the colonized subject.

The symbolism of *Exciting Tales of the Exotic East* speaks to the shifting power dynamics that accompany postcolonial capitalism: with the emergence of postcolonial economic blocs also comes the issue of how global (economic) orders are reconfigured by the emergence of post-colonial power. With his own entrepreneurial success and China's development as evidence, Balram declares the twenty-first century as the century "of the *yellow* and the *brown* man."[43] An interesting element of Balram's reference to the Asian Century, as it is comprised of "New India" and "Rising China," is his racial reference as opposed to a national one. The emphasis on race rather than nation could simply be read as part of Balram's grandiose speech; it also draws on colonial terms of racial categorization from the eighteenth century. In this way, Balram draws from a historical consciousness of colonial marginalization even as he is confident in the emergent power of postcolonial capitalism. Though Balram's discourse retains the legacies of imperialism, western power and knowledge systems – while still at play – are positioned as *a* power rather than *the* power in the context of the Asian Century.

Balram's former status as a servant is a social and historical reminder of the caste system; it further serves as a reminder of the increased, exploited migrant and domestic labor upholding postcolonial and global capitalism. As illustrated by the proliferation of postcolonial literatures on forms of servitude, the materialization of postcolonial capitalist power is not simply about the displacement of western power, but also the production of new oppressions. Looking at what he describes as "Philippine reproductive fiction," for example, Alden Sajor Marte-Wood argues that the ways in which authors like Mia Alvar, Jose Dalisay, Sophia G. Romero, Marivi Soliven, and Catherine Torres narrate stories about Overseas Filipino Workers (OFW) track "the subtle ways nationalist fantasies of reconciliation have become increasingly untenable in the era of global capital's turn toward flexible accumulation."[44] Ragini Tharoor Srinivasan's examination of call center literature by authors such as Chetan Bhagat and Bharti Mukherjee similarly considers how new subjectivities of postcolonial capitalism augment understandings of national literatures, finding surprising continuities between the call center agent and Indian expatriate writers.[45]

Both Marte-Wood's and Srinivasan's works draw out the importance of postcolonial capitalism as a periodizing concept, one that allows for the thinking of earlier histories of developmentalism together with the contemporary moment of neoliberalism. Such ideologies are typically associated with the modernizing push for socioeconomic development through industrial, manufacturing economies on the one hand and then with market deregulation and a push towards privatization on the other. Developmentalism and neoliberalism are often depicted as historically distinct as, for example, David Harvey's portrayal of neoliberalism illustrates when he writes of 1978–1979 as a watershed historical moment that would "remake the world around us in a totally different image."[46] The postcolonial era instead brings these two historical periods together while also keeping the history of colonialism in critical view.

Philippine reproductive literature and Indian call center literature describe the Anglophone formations of migrant worker literature. In postcolonial sites such as Singapore and Taiwan, nations highly dependent on migrant domestic labor and construction work, writing competitions generate migrant worker literature that does not typically reach western audiences. Occasionally, as was the case with Saud Alsanousi's *The Bamboo Stalk* (2012), a novel originally written in Arabic, migrant worker literature enters the Anglophone literary market through translation. The full body of migrant worker literature, however, is quite limited in terms of its translation and circulation. As postcolonial capitalism generates further gradations of power differentials, comparative literary approaches will provide a fuller scope for comprehending postcolonial capitalism. Migrant worker literature, particularly that written by workers foreign to the postcolonial site, will be important for further rethinking categories of national literature and for helping us track the moments in which postcolonial capitalism takes on colonizing impulses.

Notes

1 Gargi Bhattacharyya explains that racial capitalism "is a way of understanding the role of racism in enabling key moments of capitalist development – it is not a way of understanding capitalism as a racist conspiracy or racism as a capitalist conspiracy" (*Rethinking Racial Capitalism: Questions of Reproduction and Survival* [London: Rowman and Littlefield, 2018], ix).

2 See, for example, Alice Te Punga Somerville, "OMG Settler Colonial Studies: Response to Lorenzo Veracini: 'Is Settler Colonial Studies Even Useful?'" *Postcolonial Studies* 24.2 (2021), 278–282; or the preface to Ann Laura Stoler, *Duress: Imperial Durabilities in Our Times* (Durham, NC: Duke University Press, 2016), ix–x.

3 Kalyan Sanyal, *Rethinking Capitalist Development: Primitive Accumulation, Governmentality, and Post-Colonial Capitalism* (London: Routledge, 2013), 2.

4 Cheryl Narumi Naruse, Sunny Xiang, and Shashi Thandra, "Literature and Postcolonial Capitalism," *ARIEL: A Review of International English Literature* 49.4 (2018), 1–21; 2.

5 Tina Chen, "Agency/Asiancy" in *The Routledge Companion to Asian American and Pacific Islander Literature*, edited by Rachel Lee (London: Routledge, 2014), 56–67; 60.

6 Hentyle Yapp, *Minor China: Method, Materialisms, and the Aesthetic* (Durham, NC: Duke University Press, 2021), 2.

7 Couze Venn, *After Capital* (London: Sage, 2018), 67.

8 Ranajit Guha, "On Some Aspects of the Historiography of Colonial India," in *Postcolonialisms: An Anthology of Cultural Theory and Criticism*, edited by Gaurav Desai and Supriya Nair (New Brunswick: Rutgers University Press, 2005), 403–410; 405.

9 Vivek Chibber would describe this as the "Conventional Story" and critiques the Subaltern Studies use of it as a strawman argument. See *Postcolonial Theory and the Specter of Capital* (London: Verso, 2013).

10 Sandro Mezzadra, "How Many Histories of Labour? Toward a Theory of Postcolonial Capitalism," *Postcolonial Studies* 14.2 (2011), 151–170; 166.

11 Sanyal, *Rethinking Capitalist Development*, 92.

12 Ibid., 25.

13 Aihwa Ong, *Neoliberalism as Exception: Mutations in Citizenship and Sovereignty* (Durham, NC: Duke University Press, 2006), 12.
14 Guha, "On Some Aspects," 406.
15 Graham Huggan, *The Postcolonial Exotic: Marketing the Margins* (London: Routledge, 2001).
16 Ibid., 10.
17 Epeli Hau'ofa, "Our Sea of Islands," *The Contemporary Pacific* 6.1 (1994), 147–161; 160.
18 Derek Walcott, *Omeros* (1990; New York: Farrar, Straus, & Giroux, 1992), 36.
19 Ibid.
20 See Sarah Brouillette, *Postcolonial Writers in the Global Literary Marketplace* (London: Palgrave Macmillan, 2007), 1–12.
21 Chimamanda Ngozi Adichie, *Americanah* (New York: Anchor, 2014), 396.
22 Ibid.
23 Ibid., 375.
24 Ibid., 378.
25 Ibid., 418.
26 Ibid.
27 Akshya Saxena, "Purchasing Power, Stolen Power, and the Limits of Capitalist Form: Dalit Capitalists and the Caste Question in the Indian English Novel," *ARIEL: A Review of International English Literature* 52.1 (2021), 61–90; 79.
28 Alexis Celeste Bunten, "A Call for Attention to Indigenous Capitalisms," *New Proposals: Journal of Marxism and Interdisciplinary Inquiry* 5.1 (2011), 60–71; 61.
29 Elizabeth Rata, "The Theory of Neotribal Capitalism," *Review* 22.3 (1999), 231–288; 234.
30 Huey P. Newton, "Black Capitalism Re-Analyzed: June 5, 1971," in *The Huey P. Newton Reader*, edited by David Hilliard and Donald Weise (New York: Seven Stories Press, 2002), 227–233; 229.
31 See Chloe Taylor, "Brazil's Bolsonaro Accuses French President of 'Colonialist Mindset' After Calls for Action on Amazon Fires," *CNBC*, August 23, 2019, www.cnbc.com/2019/08/23/brazils-bolsonaro-hits-back-at-frances-macron-over-amazon-fires.html.
32 *Asia-Africa Speaks from Bandung* (Jakarta: Ministry of Foreign Affairs, 1955), 37.
33 Samir Amin, *Theory is History* (New York: Springer, 2014), 63.
34 Amitav Ghosh, *The Glass Palace* (New York: Random House, 2000), 116.
35 Ibid., 123.
36 Ibid., 109.
37 Ibid., 214.
38 Pascal Fletcher, "BRICS Chafe Under Charge of 'New Imperialists' in Africa," *Reuters*, March 26, 2013, www.reuters.com/article/uk-brics-africa-idUKBRE92P0GF20130326.
39 "Homepage," *BRICS from Below*, www.bricsfrombelow.org/.
40 Aravind Adiga, *The White Tiger* (New York: Free Press, 2008), 2.

41 Ibid., 3.

42 Ibid.

43 Ibid., 4, emphases in original.

44 Alden Sajor Marte-Wood, "Philippine Reproductive Fiction and Crises of Social Reproduction," *Post45* 1 (2019), https://post45.org/2019/01/philippine-reproductive-fiction-and-crises-of-social-reproduction/.

45 See Ragini Tharoor Srinivasan, "Call Center Agents and Expatriate Writers: Twin Subjects of New Indian Capital," *ARIEL: A Review of International English Literature* 49.4 (2018), 77–107.

46 David Harvey, *A Brief History of Neoliberalism* (Oxford: Oxford University Press, 2007), 1.

PART II

Contemporary Critical Perspectives

CHAPTER 8

The Economy of Race

Michael Germana

Value and race have always been constitutive fictions – social constructions that do not exist outside the legal, political, and cultural frameworks through which they are reiterated or the social transactions through which they are validated. Both are reduplicated through feedback loops that are at once discursive and material: economic instruments and racial signifiers have currency insofar as the social contracts that maintain them are operational, and, conversely, these contracts are operational inasmuch as their realization guarantees exchangeability. Complicating things further is that value and race are also *mutually* constitutive, each social contract partially underwriting the other, the feedback loops locked in a feedback loop. Lindon Barrett examines this isomorphic relationship in his book *Blackness and Value* (1999) when he argues that whiteness is fundamentally expropriative, acquiring value through a parasitic relationship to blackness. The asymmetric demarcation of racial boundaries, in turn, is economically generative within the system Cedric Robinson identifies as racial capitalism – a system predated by and predicated upon racial taxonomies and their reevaluation. This dialectic is succinctly summarized by Barrett when he writes, "the valuelessness of African Americans is always proclaimed *unreasonably* in the *name* of value," and "Value ... remembers itself by dismembering the Other."[1] Authors of literary fiction have long revealed the economy of race (as a signifying system) and the economics of race (as a lived reality of relationships to power) to be inextricably intertwined (and unreasonably unreasonable). But literary critics have only recently begun to explore the isomorphism between race and value outside of a Marxist purview. This chapter charts the emergence and development of post-Marxist economic literary criticism in general and its bearing on the study of race since the 1980s – a history that, like the economic history it parallels, neatly bifurcates at the point of the 2008 economic collapse.

The economic turn in literary and cultural studies coincides with two interdependent upheavals that, taken together, have radically reshaped capitalist societies since the late 1970s: neoliberalism and postmodernism. Neoliberalism, writes David Harvey, is "a theory of political economic practices that proposes that human well-being can best be advanced by liberating individual entrepreneurial freedoms and skills within an institutional framework characterized by strong private property rights, free markets, and free trade" – a theory that was put to the test in China, Britain, and the United States as Deng Xiaoping, Margaret Thatcher, and Ronald Reagan rose to power in the years 1978–1980.[2] In practice, the consolidation of neoliberalism was characterized by and enacted through a broad shifting of burdens onto individuals that had formerly been distributed across collectives and supported after the World War II via state interventions into market processes including but not limited to the setting of wage standards and the establishment of welfare systems.[3] This shifting assumed many forms, including the abandonment of social democratic policies, the deregulation of industry and concomitant privatization of public enterprise, the introduction and maintenance of austerity measures to ensure precarity, and, according to Harvey, the restoration of class power to economic elites through the acceleration of capital accumulation. This acceleration and the concentration of wealth it enabled was accomplished in no small part through the increasing abstraction of economic instruments that disintermediated the commodity form and allowed investors to make money directly from money on a scale Karl Marx could never have anticipated.[4] The ensuing centralization of financialized capitalism came with increased risk, and this risk, as Annie McClanahan observes, was disproportionately transferred "to the most vulnerable economic subjects."[5]

As neoliberalism was "bring[ing] all human action into the domain of the market" and simultaneously dematerializing that market via financialization, late capitalism was assuming a complementary cultural logic in the form of postmodernism, which raised the de-realization of the world – what Jean Baudrillard calls the "liquidation of all referentials" and "their resurrection in the system of signs" – to an aesthetic.[6] Critical theory, in turn, responded to financialization and its abstractions – the derealization of the postindustrial economy – by shifting away from a Marxian critique that relied upon "the suturing of value to production" and toward a post-Marxist analysis of the autonomy of representation in a new marketplace that, like mass cultural forms themselves, was increasingly characterized by simulacra and simulation.[7] Late capitalism and postmodernism, in other words, were both exemplified by and emphatically committed to the contractual and contingent nature of value, be it economic or epistemic, and literary theory did its part to make the tilt toward a postindustrial economy and the emergence of post-realist cultural forms appear to be two sides of the same coin. This helps explain, among other things, literary theory's growing skepticism toward realism as a relevant genre for expressing the contingencies of either a nascent cultural turn or a new financial world whose relationship to the tangible world of goods and commodities was fraught at best.

Coemerging with and bridging the gap between these two "turns" was a corresponding engagement with economic theories in literary and cultural studies that originated in the early 1980s – one that explicitly challenged hitherto prevailing Marxist interpretive paradigms while conforming to the methodologies of poststructuralism. Applying the latter's anti-foundationalist assumptions to economic discourse, these scholars treated economics not as an instrumental science but as another sign system of differential relations – an operational simulation. Moreover, they observed how economic symbolization was not only reflected in but also inextricable from every other signifying system. Or, as Jean-Joseph Goux notes in *Symbolic Economies* (1990), "the monetary metaphor that haunts discussions of language – not in accidental poetic incursions but quite coherently, in the site of substitutions – seems to betray an awareness, as yet veiled and embryonic, of the correspondence between the mode of economic exchange and the mode of signifying exchange."[8] This suggestion – that economic and linguistic sign systems aren't just analogous but homologous – is reflected in the pioneering work of Deirdre McCloskey and Kurt Heinzelman, who used the *words* of economists to critique the *worlds* of economists. In her book *The Rhetoric of Economics* (1985), McCloskey collapses the disciplinary boundaries between rhetoric and economics to suggest that economists aren't the "hard" scientists they appear to be, but are instead rhetoricians deploying the *signs* of scientific observation in ways that facilitate the reiteration of economic systems. Recognizing that genres of economic writing, like their literary counterparts, are less windows onto the world than frameworks through which the world is read, interpreted, and transformed, McCloskey declares economics to be "a collection of literary forms, not a science."[9] And if, as McCloskey asserts, economics is fundamentally literary, then Heinzelman shows that the converse is also true: the imaginary, of which literature is an integral part, is shaped by and reflective of something he calls "our economic consciousness," which "is so integral to our ordinary thought process that we constantly think *with* economic terms when we wish to think *about* noneconomic matters which affect moral and aesthetic values."[10]

Marc Shell historicizes the emergence of this phenomenon in his book *Money, Language, and Thought* (1982), arguing that language and thought are bound by, as well as expressions of, the economic systems from which they spring. As economic models came and went, argues Shell, so too did the logic of literary representation change.[11] This line of inquiry would be extended, in subsequent years, to studies of literary genre and form, and it became an enduring feature of what Mark Osteen and Martha Woodmansee dubbed "the New Economic Criticism" (hereafter NEC), a mode of inquiry "predicated on the existence and disclosure of parallels and analogies between linguistic and economic systems."[12] While NEC was not a homogeneous movement, its practitioners were, on the whole, indebted to critical theory's skepticism of Marxist and neo-Marxist approaches to literature. And as the texts glossed above indicate, these scholars often adopted poststructuralism's insistence upon the inseparability of textual meaning from systems of power-knowledge and applied it to texts that historically predated the cultural turn, sometimes by centuries.

NEC wasn't the only genre of economic criticism to emerge during the period, however. Another, which originated within the adjacent fields of Black studies and sociology, provided an *effective* bookend to NEC's *affective* treatment of economics. Whereas NEC's adherents explored the homologous relationship between economics and literature, scholars in these disciplines interrogated the complex relationship between economics and race. The core text around which this body of criticism grew is Cedric Robinson's *Black Marxism: The Making of the Black Radical Tradition* (1983), in which Robinson articulates the theory of racial capitalism – a system in which value extraction is dependent upon and integral to taxonomies of racial difference. Robinson's argument, in a nutshell, is that "racial order," as he calls it, didn't develop as a form of capitalist exploitation but was instead an integral part of European civilization out of which capitalism developed. Capitalism, he argues, is inseparable from and reliant upon racist ideas and practices – a fact that histories and theories of historical materialism mystify in order to preserve the illusions of superiority upon which racist mythologies – and, by extension, the relations of capitalism – continue to depend. "As part of the inventory of Western civilization," writes Robinson, racism

> would reverberate within and without, transferring its toll from the past to the present. In contradistinction to Marx's and Engels' expectations that bourgeois society would rationalize social relations and demystify social consciousness, the obverse occurred. The development, organization, and expansion of capitalist society pursued essentially racial directions, so too

did social ideology. As a material force, then, it could be expected that racialism would inevitably permeate the social structures emergent from capitalism.[13]

In sum, "capitalism was less a catastrophic revolution (negation) of feudalist social orders than the extension of these social relations into the larger tapestry of the modern world's political and economic relations."[14] Succinctly paraphrased by Jodi Melamed, "capitalism ... was always-already racial capitalism."[15]

While Robinson illustrates how the frameworks through which the body is read transform physical differences into racial signifiers of differing value in the service of slavery, colonialism, and other forms of economic exploitation, scholars like Stefano Harney and Fred Moten detail how, under racial capitalism, blackness becomes a debt that is accrued (or rather imposed) through the (re)production of whiteness. "Whiteness," they write, "is nothing but a relationship ... to blackness in its relationship to capital" – a relationship that conforms to and thereby validates the terms of the racial contract through which white supremacy is maintained.[16] Like Lindon Barrett, Harney and Moten document how value, both symbolic and material, is stolen from Black people, and accrues to the beneficiaries of racial capitalism (i.e., white people). White people, in turn, become the bearers of unearned credit, which is whiteness itself. Adding insult to injury, those in debt are offered credit – both cultural and financial – by those to whom it has unjustly accrued. Socioculturally speaking, non-white people in general and Black people in particular are invited to "earn" back the value that was stolen from them in the first place through "accrediting" institutions (e.g., university) whose norms were organized around whiteness. At the same time, the indebted become the targets of predatory lending practices, reluctant participants in alternative financing schemes, and bearers of the risk that accompanied debt securitization, which accelerated the concentration of wealth into the hands of white economic elites.

These two threads would eventually converge when scholars began exploring race, value, and literature as homologous systems standing in interaction. These scholars asked: if the economy reiterates itself through economic writing, which consists of literary forms, and the real is refracted through literature, which relies upon economic forms to make sense, then how does literature intervene in and/or intersect with racial capitalism? More to the point, how does literature engage the language and logic of economic instruments and policies in ways that denaturalize the processes integral to racial formation, the economic foundation of racial capitalism? What if economics is an engine of white supremacy, not only because of the way economic policies promote the maintenance of asymmetric power relations (e.g., neoliberalism's restoration of class power to predominantly white economic elites), but also because the ongoing interaction between economic and racial discourses reiterates and naturalizes the subject positions of white and nonwhite persons as the subjects and objects of market forces, respectively? What if economics is both *effective* (as racist policy) and *affective* (as part and parcel of what Heinzelman called the economic imagination), and the terms of the racial contract were negotiated – and renegotiable – within the latter?

What follows is a brief history of those economic literary critics who, since the mid-1990s, have used these new and emerging methodologies to describe and explain how literary texts engage and/or intersect with racial capitalism. Like the authors they study, these scholars are less concerned with documenting the material consequences of racism, which have their own economic weight, than they are with interrogating the systemic logic of the sociocultural frameworks through which race is reiterated and racist policy is rationalized. Specifically, they illustrate how literary authors explicitly engage the language and logic of economic theory and/or policy in an attempt to destabilize racism's ideological underpinnings, which are often invisible to racial capitalism's beneficiaries. This is not to suggest that these scholars downplay the brutal forces of racial capitalism or the violence with which its terms were reinforced or renewed. Rather, they seek to show how these forces are not just reflected in but also rehearsed and even enacted through symbolic economies.

This line of inquiry was inaugurated by Michael O'Malley in his 1994 essay, "Specie and Species: Race and the Money Question in Nineteenth-Century America." In this essay, O'Malley illustrates how a ubiquitous analogy whereby the money of the nation was likened to the blood of the body, when paired with hegemonic hard money rhetoric (i.e., the idea that only precious metals like gold and silver constitute "good" money), was used to prop up essentialist definitions of race and thereby support discriminatory social and political policies that relied upon race as a stable system of classification. Of particular interest to O'Malley is the homologous relationship between Reconstruction-era monetary policies and post-Civil War racial politics. While O'Malley's essay is written by an historian for historians, it nevertheless demonstrates how novels like Mark Twain and Charles Dudley Warner's *The Gilded Age: A Tale of Today* (1873) and Charles Chesnutt's *The Marrow of Tradition* (1901) are informed by the homological relationship O'Malley interrogates between anti-inflationary monetary politics and essentialist racial politics. The former, writes O'Malley, "connected the enterprise of racial and gender equality to inflated value," while the latter rehearses white Americans' anxieties over "the possibility of the market remaking the meaning of racial difference" at a time when Black Americans sought to renegotiate their identities in a rapidly diversifying labor market.[17]

John Ernest identified another example of the crosstalk between race, economics, and literature the following year when he illustrated how Frances E. W. Harper's novel *Iola Leroy* (1894) applies Gresham's Law, the economic theory that "bad" money tends to drive "good" money out of circulation, to Harper's exploration of race in America. Ernest, who in an earlier essay noted that *Iola Leroy* "is primarily a study of discursive systems, one that recognizes the ability of one discursive system to inscribe its impression on another," illustrates how the name of the eponymous protagonist's white suitor, Dr. Gresham, alludes to the common practice, under the bimetallic and later gold standards, of hoarding money whose value as bullion exceeds its face value.[18] Dr. Gresham, writes Ernest, "begins by finding it inconceivable to kiss an African American and ends by wanting to marry Iola," essentially "asking her to pass for white" so that he can take her out of circulation and hoard her for himself.[19] Simultaneously identifying the anti-Black sentiment of this request (her perceived value depends upon her proximity to whiteness) and extending the monetary analogy, Iola resists Dr. Gresham by resisting identification with white people who use their "position to 'minister to a selfish greed of gold and a love of domination.'"[20] Iola, together with many of the novel's characters, chooses "to circulate among those with whom they have been cast, and not with those among whom they could pass," refusing to serve as "shadow" currency in support of a racial gold standard (i.e., whiteness).[21] "In effect," concludes Ernest, "they resist Dr. Gresham's temptation and thus Gresham's law."[22]

Hildegard Hoeller takes a similar approach in her reading of Zora Neale Hurston's short story "The Gilded Six-Bits" (1933) as an extended allegory for the suspension of the domestic gold standard in America – a standard whose deflationary principles were hostile to the working classes in general and to Black laborers in particular. "Hurston's story," she writes, "racializes the debate about the color (and substance) of legal currency as it tracks the destructive repercussions of the gold standard's arrival in an African American community."[23] Hoeller specifically identifies the domestic gold standard, which was revoked the same year Hurston's story was published, as "represent[ing] a universal white supremacy" because each ascribes intrinsic value to arbitrary signifiers (gold and whiteness) while making them "guarantor[s] of *all* value."[24] The story's climax and dénouement revolve around the elimination of this standard and the white cultural norms to which it is sutured throughout the story – the "racial currency" to which the essay's title alludes.

Whereas Ernest and Hoeller take synchronic approaches to the race/value homology, I take a diachronic approach in *Standards of Value: Money, Race, and Literature in America* (2009) to show how economic and racial discourses coevolved over the course of a century, with popular cultural inflections of the "money question" framing the discussion about racial difference in American fiction from the 1850s to the 1950s. In it I contend that American authors incorporated "the language, logic, and imagery of U.S. monetary policy reforms as they were popularly understood (or misunderstood) into their texts" in an ongoing attempt to renegotiate the value of racial difference in America, and that by doing so these authors produced racial counter-projects that were necessary but insufficient to bring about systemic social change.[25] Harriet Beecher Stowe's *Uncle Tom's Cabin* (1851–1852) , for example, revolves around a monetary metaphor born of the coinage act of 1834, which initiated a slippage between the bullion value and nominal value (the "body" and the "face") of silver dollars – a slippage whose racial implications were rehearsed on the minstrel stage and later brought into the novel's symbolic economy to redirect minstrelsy's class-inflected critiques of "wage slavery" to abolitionist ends. George Washington Cable's *The Grandissimes* (1880), by extension, is an extended allegory for the coinage act of 1873, popularly known among monetary populists as "The Crime of 73." Through this allegory, Cable's novel brings the utilitarian rhetoric of Reconstruction-era political economy to bear on an examination of the rights of the formerly enslaved and their descendants in the New South. *Standards of Value* also shows how, from 1900 to 1933, the "passing" novel, as a genre, conforms to the logic of the gold standard in ways that extend Hoeller's argument outlined above. The book concludes by showing how Ralph Ellison's *Invisible Man* (1952) is structured by an extended allusion to L. Frank Baum's *The Wonderful Wizard of Oz* (1900), whereby Ellison draws an analogy between the end of the gold standard and the dismantling of racial essentialism to show how each retains a spectral presence much like the fiat money satirized in Baum's original text. In so doing, I argue, Ellison anticipates postmodernism's insistence upon authenticity's relocation in performance to show that such insistence can, when misapplied, help mask rather than ameliorate racist practices.

Jeffory A. Clymer brings US legal history into the mix in his essay "Family Money: Race and Economic Rights in Antebellum US Law and Fiction" (2009), which would become a core part of his book *Family Money: Property, Race, and Literature in the Nineteenth Century* (2012). As its name suggests, "Family Money" documents the attempts some white enslavers made to pass their inheritances down to their enslaved or formerly enslaved offspring – attempts that were litigated in court cases throughout the antebellum years. Clymer explores the "tropic interaction" between law and literature to examine the legal formalization of white ethno-nationalist ideologies in America, on the one hand, and their destabilization in American fiction, on the other. Teasing out the homology between legal opinions and literary expression, Clymer writes, "reading judges' legal opinions alongside fiction brings into view and context the symbolic and metaphoric aspects of their language. Just as reading fiction through the lens of legal history illuminates fiction's economic framework, bringing literature to bear on the law exposes the enabling tropes and techniques of representation that judges mobilize to create and justify a particular social order."[26] After quoting Rosemary Coombe's assertion that "law generates the signs and symbols – the signifying forms – with which difference is constituted and given meaning," Clymer asserts that "law, like literature, exists within rather than outside or above culture more generally, and produces and describes some forms of subjectivity while declining or failing to produce others."[27] Accordingly, he argues that two antebellum novels, Frank Webb's *The Garies and Their Friends* (1857) and Harriet Beecher Stowe's *Dred: A Tale of the Great Dismal Swamp* (1856), "negotiated the incompatibility between economic rights and interracial emotional bonds in the southern family, and both track the psychological warping that black and white characters experience under slave law's economic regime, a crucial feature of slavery that critics have generally neglected."[28] Methodologically, Clymer uses court cases like *Hinds v. Brazealle* (1838), *Vance v. Crawford* (1848), and *Mitchell v. Wells* (1859) to contextualize Webb's and Stowe's novels while also showing how the latter problematize the former. Specifically, Clymer shows how the judges in these cases "argued that the family itself was gravely threatened and defended it by making family, whiteness, and Americanness both synonymous and exclusionary."[29] Webb's and Stowe's novels, in turn, "represent nothing less than an ultimately flawed, if utopic, effort to

imagine a redistribution of American wealth from white families to formerly enslaved persons."[30]

As Clymer's essay and *Standards of Value* were working their way
through the publication pipeline, the credit crisis that climaxed in the
2008 financial collapse was already underway – a collapse that, as Annie
McClanahan shows in her book *Dead Pledges: Debt, Crisis, and Twenty-
First-Century Culture* (2017), was tied to the coemergent processes of
deindustrialization and debt securitization. By the end of the twentieth
century, she writes, "the development of debt securitization (which
allowed debt to function as a tradable financial instrument) meant that
consumer credit was no longer simply an aid to consumption but an
industry in itself."[31] And when the bottom fell out in 2008, "the resulting
crisis revealed the earlier, more intractable problem that capital had temporarily deferred: the absence of any real productive opportunities in the
wake of deindustrialization."[32] In the wake of this crisis, scholars like Arjun
Appadurai have shifted their attention to the financial instruments that
helped bring the system to its breaking point. In the process, however, the
role of racial symbolization in the reiteration of racist social systems fell by
the wayside. Appadurai, for example, focuses primarily on the derivatives
market and instruments like credit default swaps, which, given their
contractual nature, are accessible to linguistic and cultural analysis.
Indeed, the primary claim of Appadurai's book *Banking on Words: The
Failure of Language in the Age of Derivative Finance* (2016) is that "the
failure of the financial system in 2007–8 in the United States was primarily
a failure of language."[33] And, just as the risks inherent in the system had
been shifted onto those most vulnerable, so too did Black and Brown
families bear the brunt of the collapse as they became, in Lindon's Barrett's
turn of phrase, Others dismembered in the name of value.[34]

The shift in economic criticism toward the language and logic of
derivative finance has its congruent turn in literary studies toward what
Alison Shonkwiler calls "the financial imaginary" with its "circulations
between economic and cultural forms" and its formalization in what
Mark Fisher calls "capitalist realism."[35] (Read: The object of analysis
remains what Shell called "tropic interaction," only now the tropes are
financial rather than monetary.)[36] Capitalist realism, as Shonkwiler and
Leigh Claire La Berge illustrate in their collection *Reading Capitalist
Realism* (2014), is both an "ideological formation in which capitalism is
the most real of our horizons, the market-dominant present that forms the
limits of our imaginaries" and a mode of realism, and they ask "whether
our current forms of representation are equipped to comprehend and

historicize" late capitalism in general and neoliberalism in particular.[37] "As an ideological formation," they argue, "it describes the pervasive logic of capitalism in the present. As a mode, however, it potentially conjoins both conservative and critical impulses – on the one hand retaining the conservatism of representational realism in its commitment, as Jameson puts it, to the status quo, while on the other hand modeling the very transformative capitalist processes of commodification and financialization that it records."[38] Capitalist realism, in other words, reflexively announces its own complicity in extending – and thereby naturalizing – the logic of capitalism. "Ultimately," they write, "capitalist realism might describe . . . how realism undergoes the precise processes of capture and subsumption into the circuits of capital that it claims to represent."[39] Capitalist realism also rehearses its own complicity in *racial* capitalism, as La Berge's own reading of Tom Wolfe's *The Bonfire of the Vanities* (1987) illustrates. In particular, La Berge uses Wolfe's novel to show that the financial imaginary is forged in anti-blackness, with blackness figured as the antithesis – and undoing – of white financial subjectivity.[40]

Demonstrated in La Berge's reading of Wolfe's novel but generally underexamined in economic criticism is the centering of whiteness within the financial imaginary – an imaginary coterminous with capitalist consciousness – the primary effect of which is the invisibility of racial capitalism to its primary beneficiaries. Capitalist realism may make this centering apparent, but it doesn't remedy the processes by which it is contractually obligated and perpetually renewed. And, given whiteness's parasitic relationship to blackness, capitalist realism is also complicit in the anti-blackness of the financial imaginary – an anti-blackness that is most glaring in genres like financial fiction (or fi-fi) whose authors are almost exclusively white, or in the gross underrepresentation of Black economists in higher ed economics departments, even at historically Black colleges and universities.[41] But even when it's not as readily apparent or compartmentalized within a genre or mode, anti-blackness remains ubiquitous in economic writing, both imaginative and instrumental, with the abstractions of finance providing cover for the violence of racial capitalism.

The exacerbation of racial capitalism's deleterious effects (and affects) in the wake of the 2008 collapse necessitates new approaches for authors as well as scholars who examine the intersection of economics, race, and literature. Of particular importance is the need to hone a more critical approach to capitalist realism – one that foregrounds its role in validating the racial contract. In his exploration of capitalist realism, Fisher laments the operational inevitability and inescapability of capitalism – its status in the contemporary imagination as a system without alternatives – by noting that "it is easier to imagine the end of the world than it is to imagine the end of capitalism."[42] I would extend this formula by suggesting that the intractability of capitalist realism as both an ideological formation and a mode, combined with a financial imaginary that recenters whiteness and naturalizes racial capitalism, means that it is also easier to imagine the end of the world than it is to imagine the end of racism. Just as imposed neoliberal austerity measures and our perpetual participation in capitalism have been elevated (or reduced) to brute realities whose alternatives are always-already foreclosed, so too does racism appear to have outlived the possibility of its eradication. Like capitalism to which it is inextricably bound (hence racial capitalism), "it is now impossible even to *imagine* a coherent alternative to it," at least not through the capitalist realist mode.[43]

Aimee Bahng cuts clean through this Gordian knot in her book *Migrant Futures: Decolonizing Speculation in Financial Times* (2018) by examining minoritarian authors who move toward speculative futures as a way to circumvent the conventions (and conventional wisdom) of capitalist realism. While illustrating how contemporary authors slip the yoke of capitalist realism's limitations, Bahng treats their texts as overt attempts to decolonize the (financial) imagination and explicitly addresses the need to locate and interrogate race within a financial-temporal context. Speculative finance and speculative fiction, she argues, rely on homologous forms of "extrapolative figuration" as they participate in "the cultural production of futurity."[44] Because imagined futures rely on present collective social understandings and their materialization, notes Bahng, narrative speculation can often assume a neo-colonial guise (or function). Marginalized and/or racialized subject positions that exist in the present, for instance, can be extrapolated into the future, rationalizing otherwise chaotic, contingent, and iterative phenomena. By treating "works of speculative fiction by people of color not as antidotes in and of themselves to racialized global capitalism but as affecting experiments that, in the process of imagining another way of being in time, point to the limitations of the new world order's ongoing drive toward modes of privatization and securitization," Bahng treats her objects of analysis as integral to the decolonization of the imagination.[45] In the process, Bahng transforms "the minoritarian sector" of the genre of speculative fiction into an affective racial and financial counterproject, one that offers "a counterpoint to other forms of speculation – specifically, a financial speculation assumptive of a naturalized empiricism and universal financial subject, which may pretend not to care about race but that nonetheless traffics across histories of racialized capitalism."[46] The goal, in many ways, is to liberate the future from the "certainties" of a present always-already shaped by colonialism, racism, and other forms of oppression. This, she asserts, is part and parcel of the radical work of the global undercommons.

As NEC gradually gives way, in the aftermath of the financial collapse, to what Paul Crosthwaite, Peter Knight, and Nicky Marsh have recently coined "the Economic Humanities," it becomes clear that while many things have changed between the two paradigms, some things remain the same.[47] In some ways, scholarship in the Economic Humanities extends the work done by NEC scholars on race in literature. However, the differences are significant: in addition to demonstrating greater expertise in and facility with the discourses of business and finance, the newer scholarship tends to focus on contemporary authors, is unconstrained by NEC's New Historicist bent, assumes a more global approach, and broadens the scope of its treatment of race outside of a Black/white racial calculus. This being said, there remains a distinct need for critics to expand the scope of Black authors' engagement with and interrogation of the commerce between racial and economic discourses, especially in a contemporary context (even Bahng's book examines only one Black author: Nalo Hopkinson). How, I ask, might we more fully address what Fred Moten calls "the historical reality of commodities who spoke" in the context of the financial turn and in a world that has outlived postmodernism's purchase?[48] Moten asserts that Black performances inhere in "a revaluation or reconstruction of value, one disruptive of the oppositions of speech and writing, and spirit and matter."[49] Through and/or within these performances, "apparent nonvalue functions as a creator of value."[50] Moten's observations point toward the need to specifically address Black authors' performative indictments of the anti-blackness that structures the financial imaginary and, by extension, the genres of (racial) capitalist realism.

Notes

1 Lindon Barrett, *Blackness and Value: Seeing Double* (Cambridge: Cambridge University Press, 1999), 93, 128; emphases in original.
2 David Harvey, *A Brief History of Neoliberalism* (2005; Oxford: Oxford University Press, 2011), 2.
3 Ibid., 10–11.
4 See Arjun Appadurai, *Banking on Words: The Failure of Language in the Age of Derivative Finance* (Chicago: University of Chicago Press, 2016), 5.

5 Annie McClanahan, *Dead Pledges: Debt, Crisis, and Twenty-First-Century Culture* (Stanford, CA: Stanford University Press, 2017), 10.

6 Harvey, *Brief History*, 3; Jean Baudrillard, *Simulacra and Simulation*, translated by Sheila Faria Glaser (1981; Ann Arbor: University of Michigan Press, 1994), 2.

7 Leigh Claire La Berge, *Scandals and Abstraction: Financial Fiction of the Long 1980s* (Oxford: Oxford University Press, 2015), 17.

8 Jean-Joseph Goux, *Symbolic Economies: After Marx and Freud*, translated by Jennifer Curtiss Gage (Ithaca, NY: Cornell University Press, 1990), 96.

9 Deirdre N. McCloskey, *The Rhetoric of Economics* (Madison: University of Wisconsin Press, 1985), 55.

10 Kurt Heinzelman, *The Economics of the Imagination* (Amherst: University of Massachusetts Press, 1980), 73; emphases in original.

11 Marc Shell, *Money, Language, and Thought: Literary and Philosophic Economies from the Medieval to the Modern Era* (Baltimore: Johns Hopkins University Press, 1993), 4.

12 Martha Woodmansee and Mark Osteen, "Taking Account of the New Economic Criticism: An Historical Introduction," in *The New Economic Criticism: Studies at the Intersection of Literature and Economics* (London: Routledge, 1999), 3–50; 14.

13 Cedric J. Robinson, *Black Marxism: The Making of the Black Radical Tradition* (London: Zed, 1983), 2–3.

14 Ibid., 10.

15 Jodi Melamed, "Racial Capitalism," *Critical Ethnic Studies* 1.1 (2015), 76–85.

16 Stefano Harney and Fred Moten, *The Undercommons: Fugitive Planning and Black Study* (Wivenhoe: Minor Compositions, 2013), 55–56.

17 Michael O'Malley, "Specie and Species: Race and the Money Question in Nineteenth-Century America," *American Historical Review* 99.2 (1994), 369–395; 369.

18 John Ernest, "From Mysteries to Histories: Cultural Pedagogy in Frances E. W. Harper's *Iola Leroy*," *American Literature* 64.3 (1992), 497–518; 500; John Ernest, *Resistance and Reformation in Nineteenth-Century African-American Literature: Brown, Wilson, Jacobs, Delany, Douglass, and Harper* (Jackson: University Press of Mississippi, 1995), 202.

19 Ernest, *Resistance and Reformation*, 202.

20 Ibid.

21 Ibid., 202–203.

22 Ibid., 203.

23 Hildegard Hoeller, "Racial Currency: Zora Neale Hurston's 'The Gilded Six-Bits' and the Gold-Standard Debate," *American Literature* 77.4 (2005), 761–785; 762.

24 Ibid., 763; emphasis in original.

25 Michael Germana, *Standards of Value: Money, Race, and Literature in America* (Iowa City: University of Iowa Press, 2009), 3.

26 Jeffory A. Clymer, "Family Money: Race and Economic Rights in Antebellum US Law and Fiction," *American Literary History* 21.2 (2009), 211–238; 213.

27 Ibid., 231.

28 Ibid., 214.

29 Ibid., 215.

30 Ibid., 214.

31 McClanahan, *Dead Pledges*, 5.

32 Ibid., 13.

33 Appadurai, *Banking on Words*, 1.

34 See McClanahan, *Dead Pledges*, 5; Paula Chakravartty and Denise Ferreira da Silva, "Accumulation, Dispossession, and Debt: The Racial Logic of Global Capitalism – An Introduction," *American Quarterly* 64.3 (2012), 361–385; 364.

35 Alison Shonkwiler, *The Financial Imaginary: Economic Mystification and the Limits of Realist Fiction* (Minneapolis: University of Minnesota Press, 2017), xi.

36 Shell, *Money, Language, and Thought*, 11.

37 Alison Shonkwiler and Leigh Claire La Berge, "Introduction: A Theory of Capitalist Realism," *Reading Capitalist Realism* (Iowa City: University of Iowa Press, 2014), 1–25; 2, 3.

38 Ibid., 15.

39 Ibid., 10.

40 La Berge, *Scandals and Abstraction*, 95.

41 See "Almost No Black Economists at the Nation's Highest-Ranked Universities," *Journal of Blacks in Higher Education* 50 (2005), 18–20; "The American Economic Association: Where Racial Diversity Takes a Back Seat," *Journal of Blacks in Higher Education* 54 (2006), 42–43.

42 Mark Fisher, *Capitalist Realism: Is There No Alternative?* (Winchester: Zero Books, 2009), 2.

43 Ibid., emphasis in original.

44 Aimee Bahng, *Migrant Futures: Decolonizing Speculation in Financial Times* (Durham, NC: Duke University Press, 2018), 2.

45 Ibid., 7.

46 Ibid., 10.

47 Paul Crosthwaite, Peter Knight, and Nicky Marsh, "The Economic Humanities and the History of Financial Advice," *American Literary History* 31.4 (2019), 661–686.

48 Fred Moten, *In the Break: The Aesthetics of the Black Radical Tradition* (Minneapolis: University of Minnesota Press, 2003), 6.

49 Ibid., 14.

50 Ibid., 18.

CHAPTER 9

American Literature and the Fiction of Corporate Personhood

Peter Knight

In the eyes of the law, corporations count as people. This means that collective organizations (including both for-profit and nonprofit) have some of the same rights – but also in theory some of same responsibilities – as individuals. There has been a struggle over the last two centuries to define what is termed the legal fiction (i.e., convention) of corporate personhood, which has focused public attention on the similarities and differences between corporations and natural people. The legal debates have revolved around questions of identity, responsibility, intentionality, and agency. Is a corporation (and its legal rights) merely an extension of the individuals that own it, or does it have an existence in its own right? Is a corporation immortal, since its existence continues after the death of its founders? To what degree is a corporation responsible for negligence or the criminal acts of its agents? These kinds of issue have been thrashed out in a raft of legal cases and legislative acts over the last two centuries.[1]

But what does the legal fiction of corporate personhood have to do with literary fiction? In terms of straightforward content, literature has been strangely reluctant to engage with the corporate world. There are few major novels about business corporations. (This chapter focuses on American literature, but the same is true of British literature, for example.) This is not surprising, as the novel has tended to concentrate on the moral dilemmas and social entanglements of individuals, rather than the more impersonal realm of economic activity. As Brook Thomas notes, "focusing on the social interaction of individualized characters, the novel has to stretch to its generic limits to represent the dynamics of collective forms of organization."[2] Yet the changing legal nature and increasing importance of corporations has forced some writers to reimagine what it means to be human, creatively rethinking the relationship between individual and collective agency. This chapter considers three phases in the literary representation of corporations: as monster, as system, and as story.

The Corporation as Monster

Until the 1840s, corporations were primarily organized for public good rather than private profit. They were usually created by special acts of state legislatures to engage in large-scale civic or charitable projects, such as building a canal or establishing a college. Unlike partnerships, corporations could continue beyond the lifetime of the original founders, becoming in a sense immortal. The notion of the corporation as solely a creature of the state began to change with the 1819 Supreme Court case of *Dartmouth College* v. *Woodward*. It revolved around the question of whether the New Hampshire legislature could overturn the college's original charter in its plan to convert Dartmouth College from a seminary into a secular, public university. The court decision recognized that a corporation indeed owed its existence to state decree: it was "an artificial being, invisible, intangible, and existing only in contemplation of law."[3] But the Supreme Court broke with legal tradition by insisting that corporations should have some of the same legal protections as individuals – in this case, the argument was that the college's original charter was in fact a contract entered into by its trustees as a group of individuals, and therefore should not be interfered with by the state.

The landmark Dartmouth College case also gave impetus to revisions in how corporations could be formed, with states increasingly allowing them to be set up by simple application rather than special legislative act. As corporations grew larger and more numerous, their ownership (through tradable shares) became more diffuse and anonymous, increasingly far removed from a tight-knit group of the original founders. For much of the nineteenth century, however, lawyers in fact resisted claiming that corporations were legal persons. Instead, they insisted that the legal rights that corporations enjoyed were derived solely from the rights of the individual owners of the firm. Corporations, on this line of thinking, were merely aggregates of individuals, rather than a special kind of metaphysical being whose identity was independent of its owners. But the introduction of limited liability (the idea that a company's owners were only liable for its debts to the tune of what they invested individually) made it less plausible for lawyers to claim that a corporation was merely an aggregation of individuals. Rather, they began to argue that corporations were special kinds of beings with rights of their own.

Although few works of antebellum American literature in the nineteenth century directly represented these new kinds of organization, many writers did engage indirectly with the wider questions about the nature of collective agency and unfair privileges that corporate legal decisions raised. The setting for James Fenimore Cooper's novel *The Bravo* (1831), for example, is not the emerging realm of American industry, but political intrigue in Venice. But by focusing on the Venetian city state as an incorporated body, the novel provides an extended reflection on the problems that the growth of business corporations posed to the fledgling American republic when Cooper was writing. Should the future of the United States be shaped by the Jeffersonian faith in an agrarian republic of civic-minded equals, or by the Hamiltonian vision of a liberal state that encouraged private business interests to flourish? On the one hand, corporations came under suspicion because they smacked of undemocratic privilege, with corporate charters a modern form of feudal largesse that could easily foster corruption. On this line of thought, business corporations were antithetical to the ideals of a republic, because they appealed to private greed rather than public-minded virtue, especially if they were merely aggregations of individual shareholders. On the other hand, the collective organization of the "body corporate" resembled the "body politic" of a republic, with both creating a whole that was more than the sum of its parts. As Stefanie Mueller argues, the real protagonist of Cooper's novel is not the titular "bravo" (the secret agent) who carries out the wishes of the state, but the Venetian city corporation itself, as an impersonal, disembodied collective agent (in contrast to the personal embodiment of power in a monarchy). Cooper, Mueller explains, "set out to narrativize the corporation and to show his readers how a collective entity acts in the world: to make corporate agency visible and readable."[4]

In the nineteenth century the genre of the Gothic allowed writers to explore the confusing legal and metaphysical status of corporations, especially as they began to grow to enormous size and wield an outsized influence on the economic life of the nation. Corporations might hold some of the same legal rights and duties as individuals, but they were also completely unlike actual people in that they could in theory endure forever (although, in reality, many businesses failed). Recalling the central dilemma at the heart of *Frankenstein* (published the year before), the *Dartmouth* v. *Woodward* case in effect decreed that corporations could not be killed off by the state that had created them. These artificial beings were invisible and intangible (in the words of the *Dartmouth* decision), and thus seemed to possess a life and even a mind of their own. Gothic tropes of ghostliness, haunting, and the uncanny powers of supernatural creatures thus provided a way of thinking about the status of corporation. The work of Edgar Allan Poe, for instance, can be read as investigating the uncanny doubleness of corporate immortality and immateriality. Poe's "Silence. A Sonnet" (1839–1840) provides a meditation on the question of personhood and the immortality of the soul in the era of the corporation. Poe's sonnet ostensibly considers the mysterious "double life" of having a body and being a soul. Silence is described as "two-fold," because it involves the silence of both the material, dead body in the grave, and the more troubling possibility of eternal silence for a person's soul.[5] That second silence is personified as a creature (an "elf") come back to life, "Who haunteth the dim regions where hath trod / No foot of man." Written in the aftermath of the devastating financial panic of 1837 that saw many banks and other business fail, Poe's language draws attention to these parallel meanings. One of the "incorporate things / That have a double life" is the "corporate Silence" of graveside mourning. As Peter Jaros notes, "the corporate form, in Poe's hands, has become a tool for exploring, even undermining, the subjectivity of natural persons, a new way to complicate human identity on the pattern of the corporation's ghostly legal paradoxes of mortality and immortality, singularity and plurality."[6] In short, the legal fiction of corporate personality forced writers to contemplate how a corporation could resemble a person – and vice versa.

Although in the nineteenth century American literature tended to engage with the questions raised by corporate capitalism only obliquely, in the twentieth century more writers took the corporation as their primary focus. Published in 1901 but providing a reworking of historical events that took place in the 1880s, Frank Norris's *The Octopus* was the first part of a projected trilogy on the production, financing, and consumption of wheat as a commodity. The novel tells the story of a land dispute in California that leads to a violent confrontation between wheat farmers and the Pacific and Southwest Railroad (a thinly veiled version of the Southern Pacific Railroad).[7] The novel is in part a populist attack on the railroad corporation as an impersonal and implacable enemy that destroys the livelihood – and even the lives – of the naïve farmers. One of the P. & S. W. locomotives roaring across the farmers' land is described as "the galloping monster, the terror of steel and steam, with its single eye, cyclopean, red, shooting from horizon to horizon." But the narrator realizes that the engine is merely "the symbol of a vast power, huge, terrible . . . leaving blood and destruction in its path." The railroad trust is not merely a locomotive, but "the leviathan, with tentacles of steel clutching into the soil, the soulless Force, the iron-hearted Power, the monster, the Colossus, the Octopus."[8] The concluding term of this passage is in keeping with the many satirical cartoons from the period that depicted the rapidly emerging corporate giants as malevolent octopuses. The corporation is figured as both an anthropomorphized monster, and an impersonal abstraction that seemingly has a will of its own: "the Trust was silent, its ways inscrutable . . . It worked on in the dark, calm, disciplined, irresistible" (1: 60).

Norris's novel is mainly told from the point of view of Presley, a poet who is trying to write an epic about the West. He comes to realize that the real story is the struggle between the farmers and the railroad, but his difficulty as a writer is in representing the corporate enemy. The local representative of the P. & S. W. is S. Behrman, a corpulent embodiment of the corporation's greed. Like a corporation, Behrman's all too human flesh is seemingly immortal, impossible to kill off, despite two attempts to kill him. Seemingly unmoved by one of the assassination attempts, Behrman comments "Well, that don't show no common sense.... . What could you have gained by killing me?" (2: 335). He is seen by the farmers as the source of their woes (the plot revolves around the P. & S. W.'s plan to gain monopoly control of both railroad traffic and farm produce by raising its freight rates in order to drive the farmers to ruin, and then selling off the lands to its own dummy buyers). "There was no denying the fact," the narrator comments, "that for [the farmers], S. Behrman was the railroad" (1: 64). But Behrman deflects their complaints by insisting he has no power to alter the decision. He is merely the railroad's agent, "placid, unperturbed, unassailable" (1: 172). The real power lies higher up the chain of command in the person of Shelgrim, who is "a giant figure in the end-of-the-century finance, a product of circumstance, an inevitable result of conditions, characteristic, typical, symbolic of ungovernable forces" (1: 99–100). Shelgrim is both a physical being (he is described as an octopus, with a giant head and arms like tentacles) and an abstract symbol. After the deadly encounter between the farmers and the railroad that sees five of his friends killed, Presley finds himself one day passing the unassuming headquarters of the P. & S. W. in San Francisco. On the spur of the moment, he decides to go in and confront Shelgrim: "Why not see, face to face, the man whose power was so vast, whose will was so resistless, whose potency for evil so limitless, the man who for so long and so hopelessly they had all been fighting" (2: 279). But the meeting does not turn out as he had expected. Presley "had been prepared to come upon an ogre, a brute, a terrible man of blood and iron, and instead had discovered a sentimentalist and an art critic" (2: 284).

Shelgrim insists that even he is not in control of the railroad trust, because it obeys only the impersonal economic laws of supply and demand:

> "Believe this, young man," exclaimed Shelgrim, laying a thick powerful forefinger on the table to emphasize his words, "try to believe this – to begin with – THAT RAILROADS BUILD THEMSELVES. Where there is a demand sooner or later there will be a supply ... Do I build the Railroad? You are dealing with forces, young man, when you speak of Wheat and the Railroads, not with men. There is the Wheat, the supply. It must be carried to feed the People. There is the demand. The Wheat is one force, the Railroad, another, and there is the law that governs them – supply and demand. Men have only little to do in the whole business. Complications may arise, conditions that bear hard on the individual – crush him maybe – BUT THE WHEAT WILL BE CARRIED TO FEED THE PEOPLE as inevitably as it will grow. If you want to fasten the blame of the affair at Los Muertos on any one person, you will make a mistake. Blame conditions, not men."
>
> "But – but," faltered Presley, "you are the head, you control the road."
>
> "You are a very young man. Control the road! Can I stop it? I can go into bankruptcy if you like. But otherwise if I run my road, as a business proposition, I can do nothing. I can *not* control it. It is a force born out of certain conditions, and I – no man – can stop it or control it." (2: 285–286; emphasis in original)

The vision of power that Shelgrim evokes is one in which human actors are mere conduits for the sublime, impersonal, and natural forces that flow through them. Other than the personified abstractions of the wheat and the railroad themselves, there is no individual at the top of the chain of command. The legal fiction of corporate personality was a way of ascribing agency to complex collective institutions, but in Shelgrim's vision neither the railroad chief nor the corporation itself are in control of their own actions. Looked at one way, *The Octopus* is a rabble-rousing attack on the corporation as an iron-hearted monster whose legal ruses allow it to escape blame for murder: "Was no one, then, to blame for the horror at the irrigating ditch. Forces, conditions, laws of supply and demand – were these then the enemies, after all?" (2: 286). But the novel also ends up naturalizing corporate capitalism as if it is an irrepressible biological force, rather than a hotly contested political and economic arrangement. The final conclusion that the novel reaches is that individual agency is insignificant in the face of the cosmic forces of nature and corporate capitalism.

The Corporation as System

The first decades of the twentieth century saw efforts – only partially successful – to restrict the monopoly power of the vast corporate trusts. State regulation of the market became a more pressing concern after the Wall Street Crash of 1929. At the same time, corporations themselves turned to public relations to try to convince politicians and the public of their friendly, public-spirited nature, partly in order to ward off government interference.[9] The period after World War II was the golden era of corporate welfare capitalism, that uneasy bargain between labor and capital that brought consumerist affluence to the masses, albeit limited primarily to white Americans. No longer an evil octopus, the postindustrial corporation positioned itself as a benevolent employer and paternalist supporter of the community.

However, the nature of white collar work in the ever-expanding realm of corporate bureaucracy gave many sociologists and writers cause for concern. In *The Lonely Crowd* (1950), for example, David Riesman warned that Americans were in danger of losing their moral compass, as they lost a rugged sense of self-reliance and instead became merely "other-directed."[10] In a similar vein, William Whyte in *The Organization Man* (1956) claimed that corporate culture had diminished individuals' sense of self, as their desires came to be conditioned by corporate advertising and public relations. The fear was that American men had supposedly been turned soft by their smothering mothers, the emasculating influence of living in the suburbs, and the loss of rugged individualism as a result of working for a vast corporation. Employing military metaphors, Whyte insisted that men "must fight The Organization" because "the peace of mind offered by organization remains a surrender."[11]

Postwar novelists also repeatedly gave voice to these concerns. Sloan Wilson's *The Man in the Gray Flannel Suit* (1955), for example, tells the story of Tom and Betsy Rath, a young couple living in a commuting town outside New York. Each feels a vague but oppressive sense of dissatisfaction with their suburban lives. Having never really adjusted to the dullness of civilian life after the excitement and trauma of the war, Tom gives up his job working for a nonprofit and goes to work for the United Broadcasting Corporation, in the vague hope that making more money in the corporate world will improve his life through the comforts of affluence. In his new job Tom becomes a PR ghostwriter for his boss, the corporation's president. He spends much of the novel endlessly redrafting a speech for the CEO, a meaningless act of corporate ventriloquism whose aim is merely to whitewash the company's reputation. As part of his job application for UBC he is asked to complete an "autobiography" beginning "[f]rom the point of view of the United Broadcasting Corporation, the most significant fact about me is ..." At first, he feels he has to double-guess what the corporation wants him to say. But, in the spirit of remaining true to yourself that is the novel's central theme, he ends up insisting that he will only take the job on his own terms: "I will be glad to answer any questions which seem relevant, but after considerable thought, I have decided that I do not wish to attempt an autobiography as part of an application for a job."[12] The irony, however, is that Tom's rebellious refusal to fully become a corporate man is actually valued as refreshing honesty by his boss. By the end of the novel, he has had a number of promotions – even though he ultimately rejects the offer of further advancement, as he does not want to sell his soul to the company.

Novels such as *The Man in the Gray Flannel Suit* and Richard Yates's *Revolutionary Road* (1961) tell the story of men who feel their individuality and masculinity diminished by working for a faceless corporation that no longer values the independent spirit of a Rockefeller or Ford. As Riesman puts it, "If a man founded a firm, this was his lengthened shadow. Today the man is the shadow of the firm."[13] These novels are written in the mode of realism, striving to maintain an elegance of style that sets itself up in opposition to the disingenuous PR-speak of the organization. In contrast, writers such as William S. Burroughs, Joseph Heller, Ken Kesey, Thomas Pynchon, Philip K. Dick, and Don DeLillo have tended to adopt non-realist modes of writing in their tales of individuals as the victims of vast but often vague conspiracies that control their lives, their bodies, and even their desires.[14] Where Wilson's and Yates's protagonists nurture the hope of artistic independence outside the constraints of the corporation, the anti-heroes of these paranoid postmodernists find themselves inhabiting worlds in which the bureaucratic logic of the corporation has entirely taken over society.

Catch-22 (1961), for example, is set in a US Army bombing squadron in World War II, but, unlike *The Man in the Gray Flannel Suit*, the wartime experience is not framed as more "real" in contrast to the dull uniformity of civilian life. Instead, the military is presented as a synecdoche for the penetration of corporate bureaucracy into all aspects of national life in the 1960s. As Heller explained, "*Catch-22* is about the contemporary, regimented business society depicted against the backdrop of universal sorrow and inevitable death that is the lot of all of us."[15] The novel's protagonist, the bombardier Capt. Yossarian, is told that he can only be relieved of further near-suicidal bombing missions if he is medically certified as insane; the catch, however, is that to seek to avoid flying is itself a sign of sanity and reason to continue flying. The novel's absurdist mode highlights how irrationality is internalized as normality in a bureaucracy.

Where Whyte urges his readers to think of corporate business like "combat" and to "fight" the organization in order to regain a sense of masculine agency, Heller suggests that the war – and the military-industrial complex more generally – is itself part of a larger corporate form of organization. Part of the novel deals with the activities of Lieutenant Milo Minderbinder, a lowly mess hall officer who is running a vast, multinational supply cartel called M&M Enterprises. This shadowy organization is the model of the postindustrial business corporation, which profits less from actual industrial production than from financial sleight-of-hand, as it operates a complex web of interconnected trades and shadow companies. Minderbinder has no national loyalty, and war becomes merely another business opportunity. At one point, he does a deal with the American army to bomb a bridge in Italy, while also agreeing a contract with the Germans to defend the same bridge. He also conducts a bombing raid on his own squadron. At first, his superior officers condemn the attack, but when they discover how profitable it was, they turn a blind eye.

At the end of *Catch-22*, Yossarian is offered the choice of a dishonorable discharge (if he gives up his campaign to reduce the number of bombing missions) or a promotion and a hero's welcome back home (if he accepts their irrational logic). Instead, he opts to escape the entire national-military-corporate system by fleeing to Sweden. This fantasy of escape from control and emasculating domesticity (a repeated trope of American literature) also occurs in Kesey's *One Flew Over the Cuckoo's Nest* (1962). Where *Catch-22* imagined capitalist society as the military, Kesey's novel is set in a state psychiatric hospital. The novel's protagonist, Randle McMurphy, tries to lead his fellow patients into rebelling against Nurse Ratched, who controls her ward through rewards and shame, rather than physical punishment. The novel is narrated by Chief Bromden, a patient of Native American and white ancestry whom everyone believes to be deaf and mute. He calls the hospital regime "the Combine," and it is a figuration of American society at large as an evil, corporate bureaucracy presenting itself as benevolent. Although at the end of the novel McMurphy is forcefully lobotomized and loses his sense of individuality, Chief Bromden regains his sense of self and prodigious masculine strength, breaking his way out of the facility to freedom. The story suggests, however, that some of the inmates have become institutionalized, having voluntarily internalized the Combine's desires as their own.

The penetration of corporate power into the life of the individual is taken to an extreme in Pynchon's *Gravity's Rainbow* (1973). Like *Catch-22*, it is set in World War II, but is also an allegory for contemporary multinational capitalism. The protagonist of this dazzling and bewildering novel is Tyrone Slothrop, an American army officer whose nightly sexual conquests in London mysteriously anticipate the exact location of V-2 rocket bomb attacks. It turns out that as a child Slothrop was the unwitting participant in a series of perverse medical experiments that tried to apply Pavlovian conditioning to sexual stimuli derived from mass media imagery. The experiments were in fact conducted by multinational corporations working loosely with the German state and their US affiliates, suggesting not only that Slothrop's innermost desires have been entirely constructed by corporate consumerism, but that the war itself is merely a superficial distraction that masks the underlying system of global capitalism. Where fictional heroes like Yossarian and McMurphy try to preserve their residual individuality by fashioning an escape, in *Gravity's Rainbow* the problem is that there is no untainted self to which Slothrop can cling. There is nowhere that is outside the vast reach of the corporation. Instead, in the second half of the novel, his character slowly disperses as a single, identifiable being, meaning that "they" can no longer conspire against him, because "he" is no longer there. In place of the fiction that a corporation is like a person, in *Gravity's Rainbow* a person becomes like a corporation.

The Corporation as Story

In the 2010s, two controversial Supreme Court cases further extended the constitutional rights of corporations. In the *Citizens United* case of 2010, for example, the Supreme Court ruled that corporations, including political campaign finance organizations like the conservative group Citizens United, are protected by the First Amendment defense of free speech for individuals. The ruling overturned an existing law that had restricted business corporations and labor unions from contributing to political campaigns close to an election. In a similar fashion, the *Burwell* v. *Hobby Lobby* case of 2014 revolved around the question of whether Hobby Lobby, a family-run chain of craft stores, could opt out on religious grounds from including contraception in health insurance plans for female employees. The ruling agreed that closely held corporations were entitled to similar protections of religious expression as individuals. The *Citizens United* and *Hobby Lobby* cases thus extended the legal fiction of corporate personhood to include political and religious beliefs.[16]

But if a corporation is in the eyes of the law a person, what kind of personality does it have? This is the question asked, for example, by Joel Bakan in his documentary *The Corporation* (2003).[17] Bakan's answer is that if a corporation is a person, then it is a psychopath, untroubled by conscience, morality, honesty, or memory. Although in the era of corporate welfare capitalism large companies at times assumed a sense of reciprocal loyalty to stakeholders including employees and local communities, since the 1970s the prevailing understanding of the ultimate purpose of a publicly held corporation is to maximize return on investment to its shareholders, and little else matters.[18] However, theorists of business organization have also begun to explore the role of storytelling in creating a sense of corporate purpose and brand identity.[19]

Two of the most interesting recent literary texts to engage creatively with the idea of the corporation as story are Richard Powers's *Gain* (1998) and Joshua Ferris's *Then We Came to the End* (2007). *Gain* weaves together three narrative strands. The first tells the story of the Clare Corporation (and American capitalism more generally), from Clare's origins in the nineteenth century as a soap manufacturer, to a vast multinational conglomerate in the present. At first the biography of the company is identical with that of its founding partners, the three sons of Jephthah Clare, called Samuel, Resolve, and Benjamin, each with different talents and personalities. This part of the story is written in a mock-heroic style, matching the old-world characters of the three brothers, and befitting the preferred mode of the authorized "corporate biography" as a tale of struggle and near inevitable triumph. But as the family-owned business expands it is incorporated, first as "S, R, & B Clare," and then as the publicly owned "Clare, Incorporated," becoming a "legally created person."[20] The eldest brother, Samuel, agrees to give up personal control of the company because incorporation will allow it to "live forever," in keeping with his strong sense of religious and familial duty: "It carried on beyond the span of any owner's life ... That vision of continuance clinched Samuel's choice" (177). The firm's identity – and the narrative style – then diverges from closely following the thoughts and actions of the founding brothers, as Clare begins to develop an identity and a purpose of its own. "The law now declared," the narrator explains, "the Clare Soap and Chemical Company one composite body: a single, whole, and statutorily enabled person" (170). In the narrative Clare becomes the grammatical subject, as if a heroic person in its own right: "Clare took up its corporate destiny" (179), and "Clare, lathered but unbowed, proudly refused that sore temptation" (208). Although the Clare brothers become the initial office holders in the new corporation, the company is no longer identical to their individual will, as it takes on a collective agency of its own: "Composite bodies might still need a titular head. Yet from Samuel's vantage, a corporation president had precious little to say about the firm's development" (206). Instead of the company being an expression of its founders' personalities, now its officer holders can merely hope to internalize its desires and intentions as their own. The divergence continues in the twentieth century, with a future boss of Clare (no longer one of the family dynasty) finding it amusing, "drawing the salary he does, how little say a CEO has about anything." He is merely the "corporation's point man, the passive agent of a collective bidding" (349). Once Clare is no longer the heroic story of its founding brothers, it becomes an "amorphous jelly-fish of fifty thousand people" (296), virtually unknowable and unrepresentable. Like Presley in *The Octopus*, a disgruntled local resident contemplates bombing the corporation. But the problem is that Clare is both everywhere in general and nowhere in particular, making it impossible to target: "Then the imaginary dust settles, and it dawns on him. The board? The board's not even close to ground zero. Nor is the CEO's office, or the CFO's, or the majority stockholder's, or any other target that [he] will ever be allowed to walk past" (256).

The corporation's name – Clare – sounds homely and familiar, yet the second narrative thread makes clear to the reader it is anything but. It focuses on Laura Bodey, a forty-something woman dying of ovarian cancer who is convinced that her illness is caused either by carcinogenic chemicals in her household cleaning products made by Clare, or by environmental pollution from living in Lacewood, a midwestern town dominated by Clare factories. Lacewood is a one-company town, its fate symbiotically conjoined with that of Clare Soap and Chemical: "The company cuts every other check, writes the headlines, sings the school fight song. It plays the organ at every wedding and packs rice that rains down on the departing honeymooners" (6). Laura's corporeal existence has become fatally entangled with the incorporated body of Clare, which makes both the chemicals that have poisoned her, and the chemotherapy medicines that are being used (in vain) to cure her. The malignant cancer taking over Laura's body matches the way that Clare has metastasized in Lacewood, such that removing the parasitic company would kill its host town. Laura in effect is a victim of what economists call externalities: those costs (such as pollution) that result from a company's activities, but that are not charged to it. In contrast, *Gain* suggests that it is impossible to understand the corporation without documenting its interconnectedness with the lives of the people it affects. The story of the collective agency that is Clare therefore needs to be larger than a simple corporate biography, or a singular drama of the human-scale effects of its actions. Ultimately, as Lisa Siraganian argues, in *Gain* neither Laura nor the Clare brothers are the narrative subjects. Rather, the novel attempts to tell the nonhuman story of the insatiable drive for uncontrolled growth of cancer and the corporation-as-cancer.[21]

The third narrative strand of *Gain* comprises interspersed fragments from an imagined corporate archive including publicity brochures, advertising materials, and an authorized corporate biography. As Richard Hardack notes, corporations constitute a dispersed network (a "nexus of contracts," according to one influential line of legal thought), but advertising makes them appear as a coherent individual, speaking in its own voice.[22] Although these snippets do not add anything of significance to the plot, they do provide an important additional dimension. The uneasy combination of the three story elements undermines any pretension to narrative omniscience, or a totalizing perspective on contemporary capitalism. Instead, the tension between the different narratives demonstrates how the cause-and-effect model of realism has come unstuck in the age of large-scale, interconnected systems that are too complex to represent or control.

A corporation speaking in its own voice creates an uncanny effect. Ferris's *Then We Came to the End* focuses on this uncanniness through a simple yet disarming narrative device. The novel features a group of insecure millennials working for a Chicago advertising agency. Its tale of aimless dissatisfaction among precarious cubicle-dwellers is in itself not that remarkable, but what makes the novel stand out is its assignment of the first person plural to the narrator. It remains unclear who exactly constitutes this "we," which is alternately omniscient and limited, sometimes making authoritative pronouncements but at others merely recirculating rumor. On the one hand, it might simply be the central cluster of characters whose identities have merged into a hazy collective. Often the "we" is a collection of disgruntled individuals who feel alienated from their employer: "We were fractious and over-paid. Our mornings lacked promise."[23] Yet as more workers get laid off, it becomes unclear who actually remains to form this communal voice. On the other hand, the "we" might be the collective identity of the corporation itself, whose voice the workers have internalized, in odd phrasings such as, "Ordinarily jobs came in and we completed them in a timely and professional manner. Sometimes fuckups did occur" (3). The affectless narrative is at times the corporation speaking. As Ferris explained, "Companies tend to refer to themselves in the first-person plural in annual reports, corporate brochures, within meetings and internal memos, and, in particular, in advertising. What used to be the 'royal we' might be thought of as the 'corporate we.'" But, Ferris continues, the novel shows that this "we" is "a collection of messy human beings – stripped of their glossy finish and eternal corporate optimism."[24] The corporation is thus no longer simply the "shadow of a man," or a monstrous octopus, or even a self-regulating yet strangely sinister cybernetic system. Whatever else a corporation is, it is a story.

Notes

1 For a summary of the legal history, see Adam Winkler, *We the Corporations: How American Businesses Won Their Civil Rights* (New York: Liveright, 2018).

2 Brook Thomas, *American Literary Realism and the Failed Promise of Contract* (Berkeley: University of California Press, 1997), 239.

3 *Trustees of Dartmouth College v. Woodward*, 17 US 518 (1819).

4 Stefanie Mueller, "The Silence of the Soulless Corporation: Corporate Agency in James Fenimore Cooper's *The Bravo*," *Law & Literature* (2020), doi: 10.1080/1535685X.2020.1754022.

5 Edgar Allan Poe, "Silence. A Sonnet," *Burton's Gentleman's Magazine* 6 (1840), 166.

6 Peter Jaros, "A Double Life: Personifying the Corporation from *Dartmouth College* to Poe," *Poe Studies* 47.1 (2014), 4–35; 26.

7 It is therefore significant that in the case of *Santa Clara County v. Southern Pacific Railroad*, 118 US 394 (1886), the Supreme Court ruled that corporations have the same rights as natural persons in regard to the Fourteenth Amendment, which had granted legal protections to recently freed slaves after the Civil War.

8 Frank Norris, *The Octopus: A Story of California*, 2 vols. (Garden City, NY: Doubleday, 1901), vol. 1, 48; references hereafter noted parenthetically.

9 See Roland Marchand, *Creating the Corporate Soul: The Rise of Public Relations and Corporate Imagery in American Big Business* (Berkeley: University of California Press, 1998).

10 David Riesman, *The Lonely Crowd: A Study of the Changing American Character* (New Haven, CT: Yale University Press, 1950).

11 William H. Whyte, *The Organization Man* (1956; Harmondsworth: Penguin, 1960), 372.

12 Sloan Wilson, *The Man in the Gray Flannel Suit* (Cambridge, MA: Da Capo, 1955), 14.

13 Riesman, *Lonely Crowd*, 146.
14 The best introduction to this strand of American writing is Timothy Melley, *Empire of Conspiracy: The Culture of Paranoia in Postwar America* (Ithaca, NY: Cornell University Press, 2000). Although some women writers (e.g. Joan Didion and Diane Johnson) and some African American writers (e.g. Ralph Ellison and Ishmael Reed) have explored similar themes, what Melley terms "agency panic" is rooted in a paranoid fear of a loss of masculine sovereignty and white privilege.
15 Quoted in Thomas Blues, "The Moral Structure of *Catch-22*," *Studies in the Novel* 31.1 (1971), 64–79; 64.
16 In both cases, however, the justices returned to older arguments that these protections resulted from the rights of the corporate owners as individuals.
17 Joel Bakan, *The Corporation*, directed by Mark Achbar and Jennifer Abbott (2003).
18 The article that started the so-called shareholder revolution is Milton Friedman, "The Social Responsibility of Business Is to Increase Its Profits," *New York Times Magazine*, September 13, 1970, 32–33, 122–124.
19 For an overview of this area of research, see Birgitte Norlyk, "Corporate Storytelling," in *The Living Handbook of Narratology*, edited by Peter Hühn et al., www.lhn.uni-hamburg.de/article/corporate-storytelling.
20 Richard Powers, *Gain* (New York: Picador, 1998), 45; references hereafter noted parenthetically.
21 Lisa Siraganian, "Theorizing Corporate Intentionality in Contemporary American Fiction," *Law & Literature* 27.1 (2015), 1–25; see also Ralph Clare, *Fictions Inc.: The Corporation in Postmodern Fiction, Film, and Popular Culture* (New Brunswick, NJ: Rutgers University Press, 2014).
22 Richard Hardack, "New and Improved: The Zero-Sum Game of Corporate Personhood," *Biography* 37.1 (2014), 36–68.
23 Joshua Ferris, *Then We Came to the End* (New York: Little, Brown, 2007), 3.
24 Joshua Ferris, "Reading Group Guide," *Then We Came to the End* (New York: Back Bay Books, 2008), 4.

CHAPTER 10

Political Economy, the Family, and Sexuality

David Alderson

In his *Treatise on the Family* (1981; enlarged 1991), Gary Becker offers an account of that institution's dynamics based on the rational choice theory that fundamentally informs neoclassical economics: the assumption that individuals behave in ways that maximize utility, or benefits to themselves. However, his avowedly scientific – indeed, algebraic – descriptions of family dynamics also amount to a defense of the family against the economic and ideological pressures that challenged its integrity during the 1960s, primarily through the extension of state welfare, but also in the form of feminist and countercultural critique. If neoliberals such as Becker have mostly claimed to be advocates of freedom, they have none-theless tended to converge with neoconservatives in respect of the family: as Melinda Cooper has argued in detail, while the latter see a primarily moral value in family life beyond any market function it might serve, the former "wish to re-establish the private family as the primary source of economic security and a comprehensive alternative to the welfare state."[1]

However, Becker also offers a more traditional apologia for the family: effectively, that it humanizes us and, by extension, our societies. He argues that even a selfish person will tend to realize that the advantages sought from the family are best achieved through altruism. Whereas selfishness is efficient in the marketplace, then, altruism is efficient in the family, which functions as a kind of firm in which all (supposedly) pull together for the benefit of the whole. Moreover, since the family plays a substantial role in economic activity, "altruism is much more important in economic life than is commonly understood."[2]

Becker's claim is vulnerable on various counts. First of all, behavior designed ultimately to get what one wants is not usually regarded as altruistic; it sounds more like cynicism. Perhaps we learn this from the family. Second, we might easily draw a different conclusion from the analogy Becker advances between the family and the firm: that it is not only, or even principally, individuals who compete in capitalist societies, but also families. Indeed, one of the defenses of inheritance is that the desire to provide for one's own is a spur to competitive, entrepreneurial activity, and therefore admirable in terms of both the motive and the resulting wealth creation. This logic is strangely pervasive: even in Alan Hollinghurst's novel *The Line of Beauty* (2004), in which the power dynamics and hypocrisies of the central family, the Feddens, are laid bare, there is a suggestion that the decision of the arch-Thatcherite, Barry Groom, to disinherit his children on principled grounds is of a piece with his general bigotry.[3]

Groom is representative of those wealthy types who believe their children should become independent by making their own fortunes, but this comes at the expense of continuity. It is this latter principle that has been upheld by other economists as the great advantage of family inheritance, with which I am substantially concerned here: they offer a different account of the family's humanistic potential that is linked to the category of culture, and therefore literature. In *The Constitution of Liberty* (1960), Friedrich Hayek argues against those for whom inheritance represents an obstacle to greater meritocratic equality. The family is "desirable as an instrument for the transmission of morals, tastes, and knowledge," he asserts, and "this will be achieved only if it is possible to transmit not only immaterial but also material advantages."[4] The implicit corollary of this must surely be that families who have little, if anything, to pass on must also be deficient in "morals, tastes, and knowledge": culture *belongs* to traditional elites. The argument reflects the explicit influence of Edmund Burke on Hayek, a surprising one, perhaps, in a figure who rejects the label "conservative" in the same work.[5] However, as we have already begun to see, attitudes toward the family have a tendency to confound the usual political-economic distinctions. The socialists Mary McIntosh and Michèle Barrett have polemicized against "the anti-social family" as an institution that both privatizes relations of reciprocity and solidarity at the expense of noninstrumental bonds beyond it and also functions to reproduce inequality.[6] They are not necessarily representative, though: Cooper identifies a tradition among some on the left who critique neoliberalism for its corrosive effects on the family.[7]

The arguments of McIntosh and Barrett, as well as Cooper, are anticapitalist, but they are also influenced by feminism and the sexual liberation movements. I write from a similar perspective, and this chapter focuses on the persistence and evolution of Burkean ideas specifically in literary and other discourses over the course of the nineteenth and twentieth centuries in response to major political-economic transformations.

I emphasize that, while Burke defended elite familial traditions and relations as the defining features of a supposedly humane social order, his simultaneous commitment to free-market principles in opposition to any paternalist sense of responsibility for the poor contributed to an increasing nineteenth-century preoccupation with the need for the procreative sexuality of the working class to be regulated, initially in ways especially influenced by Thomas Malthus, and subsequently the discourse of eugenics. Burkean thought continued to inform a disdain for popular sexuality – whether familial or extra-familial – in the "mass society" of the twentieth century, but it also determined a hostility toward the "liberated" sexuality of women and queers, and a defense, by contrast, of privacy and tact. I discuss literary texts that draw on and contribute powerfully to such traditionalism, as well as various kinds of utopian writing that advocate erotic liberty, but finally go on to show that the commodification of sexual freedoms has led to new forms of socio-cultural conflict at the heart of our contemporary politics.

Class, Inheritance, and Disciplinary Independence

It is important to remember that, in his *Reflections on the French Revolution* (1790), Burke idealized specific kinds of family on the grounds that they were not merely dominant within, but constitutive of, the British socio-political order:

> In this choice of inheritance we have given to our frame of polity the image of a relation in blood; binding up the constitution of our country with our dearest domestic ties; adopting our fundamental laws into the bosom of our family affections; keeping inseparable, and cherishing with the warmth of all their combined and mutually reflected charities, our state, our hearths, our sepulchres, and our altars.[8]

The French alternative represented a state both alienated from family morals and affections, and simultaneously wicked, because its promise of liberty could only result in the overthrow of an essentially chivalric, gentlemanly order whose manners held an ultimately evil human nature in check. The march of thousands of Parisian citizens on the royal palace at Versailles in October 1789, and – at least in Burke's account – the sexualized violation of Marie Antoinette's dignity in which it culminated, was the inevitable result of all that. Reviewing the conduct of the Revolution in 1796, Burke claimed that its legislators "think everything unworthy of the name of publick virtue, unless it indicates violence on the private."[9]

Burke's sense that an organic principle connected the generations made little sense in relation to the lives of the poor: "When, in countries that are called civilized, we see age going to the workhouse and youth to the gallows, something must be wrong in the system of government," wrote Tom Paine in scathing response.[10] The poor, who had little to bequeath, were subject to a secular, punitive discipline. However, according to the emerging political-economic discourse of the time, their lives were not untouched by providence. In expressing his opposition to the proposed extension of the Speenhamland System, which made poor relief more generous, in *Thoughts and Details on Scarcity* (1795), Burke argued that the interests of workers lay with the profit-seeking endeavors of their employers, since

> It is ... the first and fundamental interest of the labourer, that the farmer should have a full incoming profit on the conduct of his labour. The proposition is self-evident, and nothing but the malignity, perverseness, and ill-governed passions of mankind, and particularly the envy they bear to each other's prosperity, could prevent their seeing and acknowledging it, with thankfulness to the benign and wise disposer of all things, who obliges men, whether they will it or not, in pursuing their own selfish interests, to connect the general good with their own individual success.[11]

If, for Burke, providence determines things as they are – whether the political government of the gentry and aristocracy, or the agricultural market in labor and goods – discontent with them must suggest a more generally disordered condition. Sexual passion is implicitly a component of that, and it is one that, soon after these words were written, became the focus of an explicit, and influential, argument in political economy.

In *Against the Market* (1993), David McNally argues that in the social order that was emerging in the late eighteenth century, it was increasingly asserted that workers needed to be both disciplined *and* independent in a socially specific sense. McNally demonstrates that the autonomy that was once associated with possession of a modest landholding and access to the commons came to be stigmatized as tending to encourage laziness and dissolute habits, just as the long process of enclosure that resulted in the consolidation of larger farms, the eradication of the commons, and the consequent displacement of poorer landholders was reaching its full extent. A labor market, by contrast, would produce greater discipline in workers by forcing them to rely on their own efforts. Thomas Malthus was a key figure in the transformation of attitudes in this respect by encouraging a hostility toward poor relief that survived the repudiation of his alarmism about population growth.[12] For followers of Malthus, it became imperative that the poor should be independent in order to take full responsibility for their dependents by limiting their number. The principle remains active: in 2017, the Conservative British government introduced a cap of two on the number of children per family who might qualify for state benefits.

Few political economists more zealously promoted Malthusian ideas in the nineteenth century than John Stuart Mill, who, as Gregory Claeys has demonstrated, also regarded the family, not the individual, as the basic unit of society: it must be the object of responsibility, and should therefore define the limits to personal liberty, whose extent must consequently be variable according to wealth.[13] Mill's Malthusian anxieties made him an enthusiastic advocate of contraception: at the age of seventeen, he was prosecuted for obscenity for promoting it in a working-class area of London.[14] This particular paternalistic gesture anticipated the activities of a later political movement similarly committed to the improvement, not merely of the individual, but also the race, through management of the family. Francis Galton, in *Hereditary Genius* (1869), objected strongly to the general Malthusian principle that marriage should be delayed until middle age on the grounds that, if it were to apply to all classes, its failure to discriminate between the congenitally prudent and imprudent would lead to the latter dominating the former. "It may seem monstrous that the weak should be crowded out by the strong," he wrote, "but it is still more monstrous that the races best fitted to play their part on the stage of life, should be crowded out by the incompetent, the ailing, and the desponding."[15] The state's preoccupation with the family must focus not merely on reproduction in a quantitative, but, even more urgently, a qualitative, sense.

One passage in Galton's influential work suggests that one of the major influences on his thinking was a literary one that is rich in significance for my purposes here: Alfred Tennyson's *In Memoriam* (1850). First, Galton:

> We are exceedingly ignorant of the reasons why we exist, confident only that individual life is a portion of some vaster system that struggles arduously onwards towards the ends that are dimly seen or wholly unknown to us, by means of the various affinities – the sentiments, the tastes, the appetites – of innumerable personalities who ceaselessly succeed one another on the stage of existence.
>
> There is nothing that appears to assign a more exceptional or sacred character to a race than to the families or individuals that compose it. We know how careless Nature is of the lives of individuals; we have seen

how careless she is of eminent families – how they are built up, flourish and decay: just the same may be said of races, and of the world itself; also, by analogy, of other scenes of existence than this particular planet of one of innumerable suns. Our world appears hitherto to have developed itself, mainly under the influence of unreasoning influences; but, of late, Man, slowly growing to be intelligent, human, and capable, has appeared on the vast scene of life and profoundly modified its conditions ... He has introduced a vast deal of civilization and hygiene which influence, in an immense degree, his own well-being and that of his children; it remains for him to bring other policies into action, that shall tell on the natural gifts of his race.[16]

This alludes to, but appears to revise, Tennyson's view of Nature as "So careful of the type she seems, / So careless of the single life."[17] Actually, Galton suggests, she is more generally indifferent, but this trait has been corrected by the emergence of purposeful, rational Man in a way that endows him with a powerful responsibility to the future. This sentiment is not really out of keeping with Tennyson's larger argument, however, which Galton ventriloquizes so faithfully here that it is no surprise that the particular reference occurs to him. In *In Memoriam*, the poet overcomes his grief and loss of faith through the conviction that his friend Arthur Hallam's earthly existence not only testified to the existence of an evolutionary principle, but so embodied the highest form of racial development as to be prefigurative of a yet higher, wholly spiritual condition that could only be realized through his death. Tennyson is clear that the race he has in mind is specifically Anglo-Saxon, not Celtic. The evolutionary principle informing his thinking is therefore clearly less scientific than Burkean: Section CIX of the poem defends a gradualist English freedom against the "The blind hysterics of the Celt," and Section CXXVII disdainfully alludes to the violence of the third French Revolution of 1848.

Galton's point about Man's ignorance of the reasons for his existence, yet confidence that there must be a purpose to it, also seems to me indebted both conceptually and linguistically to Tennyson:

> Let knowledge grow from more to more,
> But more of reverence in us dwell;
> That mind and soul, according well,
> May make one music as before,
>
> But vaster.

This well-known passage from the Prelude is echoed in Galton's sense of the individual as "a portion of some *vaster* system" (the emphasis I have

added here echoes Tennyson's through his placement of that word both at
the end of a sentence and opening of a new stanza). Both writers suggest
that a developing genius helps us to grasp this larger entity. Moreover, the
evidence for Tennyson's poem as proto-eugenicist is reinforced by another
work that similarly sought to synthesize science, art, religion, and politics
in ways that would reinforce the family: the ardent promoter of contraception to the poor Marie Stopes used the first two lines of these stanzas as
the epigraph to the conclusion of her pioneeringly explicit guidance to
couples, *Married Love* (1918).[18]

Indeed, the exalted, Tennysonian language of Galton and Stopes is a
feature of eugenicist discourse more generally, and is allied to a veneration
for the individual who will emerge from a sexuality that is managed and
directed in the right way. The political-economic implications of this view
are evident in William and Catherine Whetham's *The Family and the
Nation* (1909), one of the most widely referenced instances of the time.
They argue at one stage that, even if the state at some point in the future
might wholly control capital,

> health, character, and ability are assets which cannot be divorced from the
> individual. They must yield an annual return of interest on which he and
> his family may flourish and multiply. Such qualities are an inherent
> possession of the individual. They are his to use and to hand on as he will,
> for the advantage of the nation. No collectivist state can deprive him of
> their possession, and any environment which makes him disinclined to use
> or to transmit this innate capital is an irremediable misfortune to the
> community. The inborn qualities of mankind, whether good or bad, may
> be established, maintained, and extended in a family by, and only by,
> appropriate marriages. In past ages long and honourable lines of descent
> were based jointly on ability and inherited wealth. If, at some future time,
> the latter condition be set aside, the former can yet remain; and we may
> look with confidence to the continuance in high position, from generation
> to generation, of those families whose members choose their mates for all
> good qualities of mind and body.[19]

Here, the economically productive individual, the family he sires, and the
nation that is the expression of a racial spirit are aligned against a potentially debilitating, secular, and artificial state, a mode of collectivity that
drags the individual down. If the landed elite specifically may be a thing of
the past, an irrepressible racial elite will nonetheless prosper. The assumption here is not that financial inheritance inhibits independence, as Mill
strikingly argued in supporting the taxation of it,[20] but rather that it is the
mark of individual superiority. These kinds of ideas were so influential

they had to be addressed by early proponents of state welfare: Arthur Pigou, in *The Economics of Welfare* (1920), devoted a chapter to refuting the idea that his proposals would lead to a progressive deterioration in "the quality of the people."[21]

Manliness, Queerness, and Utopia

Perhaps it was Tennyson's decision to end his poem with a celebration of marriage that especially commended his work to proponents of eugenics: it is through this institution that the reproduction of noble types such as Hallam will occur. This is a specific expression of what I have elsewhere called heterosacramentality: the redemption of which sexuality is in need is supplied by its procreative, "spiritual" function.[22] The poem's glorification of this principle is evident not merely in its outward depiction of this ritual, but also the subjective development of the poet himself: in ultimately appreciating the full significance of Hallam, and no longer grieving abjectly over his corporeal absence, the poet achieves a manhood that disavows the gender confusion and hints of same-sex intimacy that mark the earlier sections of the poem in ways that have been discussed by Alan Sinfield. Instead, feelings are moderated, and proximity is now wholly spiritualized; the poet recovers his self-possession. As Sinfield also shows, these earlier sections subsequently made Tennyson feel the need to disavow any hint of sexual passion for Hallam in the context of political alarm over socialist agitation, imperial anxieties over the fall of Khartoum and the threat of Irish Home Rule, and the 1885 Criminal Law Amendment Act, which made sexual acts between men specifically illegal: in all of these, the ideal of manliness was at stake.[23] *In Memoriam* establishes in a particular way a more generally held view – asserted, for instance, in the conservative development of psychoanalysis – that forms of queerness represent modes of immaturity that threaten not only morality, but also the sacrosanct principle of progress. The arguments of queer theorist Lee Edelman are of interest in this regard: he has polemically attacked a discourse of "reproductive futurism" that symbolically invests the sentimentalized figure of the child with hope in ways that serve to regulate sexuality.[24]

Edelman's argument, however, is a highly abstract one; no wonder it counsels the abandonment of optimism. In response to it, others have reaffirmed utopian possibilities more in keeping with the politics I ultimately wish to assert here.[25] I want therefore to turn to a novel that attempts something of this sort in relation to the historical conjuncture of which Tennyson made such powerful ideological sense: Sylvia Townsend

Warner's historical novel, *Summer Will Show* (1936). Written after Warner had joined the Communist Party, it focuses on protagonist Sophia Willoughby, who travels from her English estate, Blandamer, to revolutionary Paris in 1848. Having travelled there in order to try to persuade her estranged husband Frederick to help her conceive a child and heir after the deaths of their other children, she instead becomes sexually involved with his former lover, the Jewish actor and revolutionary, Minna Lemuel, and politically active in the revolutionary circles in which Minna mixes. Orphaned in a Lithuanian antisemitic pogrom, Minna is a Romantic figure, defiant of social norms and conventions, regardless even of her own well-being. Sophia discovers in their relationship the antithesis to her former existence governed by the Burkean principles of conjoined familial and social duty – "a world policed by oughts," as she remembers it. That is not to say, however, that her English life was merely cold or unfeeling; rather, "Behind every love or respect stood a monitorial reason, and one's emotions were the expression of a bargaining between demand and supply, a sort of political economy."[26]

Sophia's thought here is exceptionally complex and worth pausing over. It suggests that the supposedly private affective self is rather subject to a kind of internalized surveillance (monitorialism) governed by those norms that determine social approval and permissible intimacy. This subjectification is not necessarily stable, however, as emotional needs encounter the problem of scarcity (non-, partial, or conditional reciprocity), and may therefore go more or less unsatisfied; the equilibrium of "love" appears unlikely. This is because the marketplace of emotional life is hardly genuinely free, but rather exists within a determinate social structure that empowers some while disempowering others, as Sophia's motives for travelling to Paris in the first place perfectly exemplify. Her obligations, however, are dissolved by Frederick's confiscation of her property – his right as her husband – in response to the dubious relations she has cultivated. Propertyless, her interests come to be aligned with (other) proletarians.

Minna, by contrast, offers Sophia an erotic liberty from the values imposed by social regulation, because both she and it are scandalous: Sophia had earlier imagined her as "half actress, half strumpet; a Jewess; a nonsensical creature bedizened with airs of prophecy" (29). Their relationship is therefore wholly gratuitous, and Minna herself resembles the ideal, unaccountable artwork, since "her artfulness was for art's sake ... Calculating with unscrupled cunning on the effect she might have [on others], her calculations stopped short there, she was unconcerned as to whether the effect of the effect would advantage her or no" (238). Minna's social and artistic performances – the two are barely distinguishable – are focused on the moment itself, not on any benefit that might subsequently accrue to her from it. There is therefore a transcendent quality to their relationship that Warner nonetheless insists is socially determined. In its specifically erotic dimension, it consists in what Herbert Marcuse once described as the reification of the body – pleasure taken in it for its own sake, the "ill-reputed privilege of whores, degenerates, and perverts."[27] As Warner, too, consistently emphasizes, then, a certain freedom could be experienced through marginalization from that "world policed by oughts."

Shame, the Family, and the Commodity

In history as it has unfolded, however, sexual freedom has not taken the forms hoped for it by either Warner or Marcuse, even if heteronormative restrictions no longer carry anything like the force they once did, but that is because such freedom has been substantially commodified.

For Aldous Huxley, in *Brave New World* (1932), this fact is integral to his dystopian vision of a Fordist society based on conveyor-belt production and mass consumption. Crucially, families have been eradicated from the wholly paternalistic World State, and culture, as represented by Shakespeare especially, has been suppressed. This is no coincidence: John the Savage acquires his dissident sense of morality directly from the plays. The full force of his misogynistic judgmentalism is directed at those women, Linda and Lenina, who deny him the proper intimacies of maternal affection and monogamous devotion that his masculine dignity demands: in being shameless, they shame him. John, then, is no Caliban; indeed, he aspires to be a Ferdinand. However, his commitment to the principle of love also renders him the novel's naïve figure, and consequently its Miranda: he is the one who speaks the words of hers from *The Tempest* that give the novel its title. Lenina would not fit the bill, as she is neither chaste nor capable of the true poetry by and through which the World State is ironically judged; inheriting nothing from the past, she is consubstantial with the consumerist doggerel she speaks.

The family has to be eradicated from the World State because it is the source of the kind of subjectively disruptive emotional intensities with which Shakespeare's plays deal. Moreover, the family would also promote powerful, *private* attachments disruptive of the public good. This privacy, however – precisely because it is counterposed with the state and informs the formal reflection of art – is associated, not with narcissistic individual*ism*, but with a specifically cultivated and humanistic independence through the capacity for detachment and (self-)reflection. It is this that establishes the Burkean emphasis of the novel, which resonates, of course, with other cultured protests of the time at the emergence of a "mass society." The literary critic, F. R. Leavis, for instance, argued that good culture was threatened by the relentless spread of the standardization evident in popular forms.[28]

The odd thing about Huxley's novel is that its logic runs counter to Henry Ford's own belief in the value of the family as a means of ensuring precisely the kind of subjective stability that assisted in establishing work discipline: it was the pursuit of fun through dissolute behaviour, by contrast, that rendered people unpredictable and therefore unproductive.[29] However, under Fordism – the regime of accumulation that dominated western societies after World War II – the specific form the family took was disdained by some. Indeed, it was the economic role the popular family played that sponsored a kind of elitist disparagement of it. In *Notes towards the Definition of Culture* (1948), T. S. Eliot observed that "by far the most important channel of transmission of culture remains the family," but went on to qualify this claim, since

> this is a term that may vary in extension. In the present age it means little more than the living members. Even of living members, it is a rare exception when an advertisement depicts a large family or three generations: the usual family on the hoardings consists of two parents and one or two young children. What is held up for admiration is not devotion to a family, but personal affection between the members of it: and the smaller the family, the more easily can this personal affection be sentimentalized.[30]

The nuclear family is here identified with its mode of representation, which is oddly both historical, in the sense of being of a particular time, yet simultaneously unhistorical, in the sense that it is fixed in that moment, outwith temporal continuity. It therefore embodies only the cheapest emotions, by contrast with the spirituality (the "devotion") that dignifies those with a pedigree.

Both Eliot and Huxley were, in their own ways, right, however: on the one hand, the family has been sold to us as an ideal through the family cars, family properties, and family sizes in everything that will satisfy our demand; and yet, because it is obviously not in the interests of capital that we should be satisfied, the ideal self-sufficiency of family life is simultaneously undercut. Moreover, the stimulation of dissatisfaction is not merely achieved through the advertising on the hoardings that Eliot disparages, but also through the spatial deprivatization of that sanctified familial space, the home, by the proliferation of specific kinds of technology that claim our intimacy: radio, television, computers, smart phones (there is a telling trajectory here). The contemporary potential for such deprivatization is perhaps best exemplified by the predominantly gay male "chemsex" parties that have recently become the focus of moral panic. The term no doubt serves to reify a range of practices and experiences, but such drug-fueled events typically entail opening up the home to a sexualized public through invitations issued through phone apps; self-possession gives way to heady abandonment.[31] If this represents a freedom from what Freud called the reality principle, it is frequently held to account in the end: former addicts speak of ruined careers and relationships.

At an earlier stage in the development of the kind of technology I am speaking of here, Herbert Marcuse noted it as a crucial component of the emergence of "one-dimensional man" – a society in which oppositional forces had been substantially assimilated – and Marcuse's arguments have been developed in Fredric Jameson's account of a postmodern world governed by commodity logic, not least through the prodigious expansion of a popular culture.[32] The principal critique of this condition in Martin Amis's novel, *Money: A Suicide Note* (1984), however, as with Huxley's satire on Fordism, is that it is shameless. In this novel, though, disinhibition is not cultivated as a mode of regulation, but is rather the product of a society that appears out of control. Families barely figure at all in the novel, though that is not because they are a matter of unconcern: John Self's sense of his origins is mistaken, insofar as he believes Barry to be his father, and clouded in mystery in relation to his mother, a spectral figure in his memory whose absence, we infer, deprives him both of love and of a female relation whom he might actually have respected, because sexually off-limits. The implication is that his spectacularly desublimated relations with women result as much from this as from his addiction to pornography.

Self, though, is a child of the sixties, he tells us.[33] This is important: it suggests that the eighties are the apotheosis of trends evident in postwar Fordism, rather than an abrupt, neoliberal departure from them, and the continuities in this respect become apparent in a number of ways. Here, for instance, is Self in the "porn emporium" he occasionally visits in London:

> Down here, you get all sorts. Odds and sods and no longer any shame, no shame. Everyone is determined to be what they are: it's the coming thing. Women want out from under us men. Faggots and diesels won't be humped by the hets. Blacks have had it with all this white power. Street criminals prefer to go about their business without being vexed by the *police*, who keep trying to *arrest* them and put them in *jail*. Now even the

paedophile – the type of human being so keen on violation that only children will do – dares show his shadowed face: he wants a little respect around here. Turn up the lights: nothing matters.[34]

The reactionary suggestion in this passage is that Black and countercultural expressions of pride have culminated in the effrontery of the criminal and depraved. Some critics nonetheless discern a subversive potential in the novel at odds with this message. Emma Parker, for instance, suggests that *Money* offers a critique of John Self's masculinity, and that it also represents gender as fluid in ways that conjure up queer possibilities.[35] This is undoubtedly true, but such fluidity is part of the world Amis satirizes. The novel may best be regarded as a dramatic monologue in prose, and Self's persona as a mask for the indirect articulation of authorial sentiments; indeed, Amis's metafictional techniques encourage us to see things this way. The Amis-Self relation is apparent in this passage in the inconsistency of the awareness that "nothing matters" with Self's usually *un*selfconscious embodiment of that same principle. The pathos evoked by the figure of the pedophile's child victim is hardly an approving vindication of antinormativity; it is rather the ultimate indictment of the collapse of the inhibitions the family instils, especially through the culture it passes on (among some).

As I began by noting through the work of Melinda Cooper, the corrosive potential of commodification in relation to the family has been widely noted by different political traditions. Likewise, it is not only conservatives such as Amis who have highlighted the importance of the market in determining the emergence of countercultural forces. In *Insult and the Making of the Gay Self* (2004), for instance, Didier Eribon celebrates the subcultures that have emerged for the most part in cities and have exerted such a powerful attraction on those fleeing provincial condemnation.[36] He draws on the work of John d'Emilio, who argued that capitalism made such lesbian and gay communities possible.[37]

However, in *Returning to Reims* (2013), Eribon subsequently went on to reflect on the inverse process that attended his own flight to the city and the cosmopolitan life he enjoyed there: the shame he felt for his working-class family origins, about which he felt compelled to maintain silence.[38] In the same book, he also charts his father's political transition from Communist voter to National Front supporter, substantially in response to neoliberalization and the attendant political neglect of class by both parties and intellectuals. It is a narrative whose allegorical power in relation to much of the world has surely only intensified over time, given the success globally of various reactionary populisms through their attacks on "liberal elites" and frequent claims to be upholding family values.

Ironically, though, those same populists are in most cases truly elite beneficiaries of one major vector of the dramatically expanding inequality that has characterized neoliberalism's hegemony: the accumulation of wealth through familial inheritance that has been highlighted by Thomas Piketty, among others.[39] These recent developments and dynamics further highlight one of the principal conclusions I wish to draw from the history I have been tracing here: to speak of "the family" may be defensible at one level of abstraction, but it also represents a failure to acknowledge the complex and diverse roles played by that institution in societies that are variously fragmented, unequal, and unjust. Certainly, Becker's view that it promotes altruism looks extraordinarily naïve on the basis of the history recounted here.

With all of this in mind, I shall conclude briefly – and, given the prevailing conditions, somewhat gesturally – by returning to debates that have significantly determined the discussion I have given here: those relating to revolutionary France and the purposes of queer dissidence. As part of his critique of reproductive futurism, Lee Edelman notes that the central figure of Eugène Delacroix's famous painting, *Liberty Guiding the People* (1830), bares her breasts as a symbol of her nurturing potential.[40] Several decades before Edelman, however, Marcuse noted the dialectical properties of her gendered symbolism. She is also carrying a gun; hence, "the end of violence is still to be fought for."[41]

Notes

1 Melinda Cooper, *Family Values: Between Neoliberalism and the New Social Conservatism* (New York: Zone Books, 2017), 9.
2 Gary S. Becker, *A Treatise on the Family*, enlarged ed. (Cambridge, MA: Harvard University Press, 1991), 303.
3 See Alan Hollinghurst, *The Line of Beauty* (London: Picador, 2004), 476–477.
4 F. A. Hayek, *The Constitution of Liberty* (London: Routledge & Kegan Paul, 1960), 90.
5 See F. A. Hayek, "Why I Am Not a Conservative," in *Constitution of Liberty*, 397–411.
6 Mary McIntosh and Michèle Barrett, *The Anti-Social Family*, 2nd ed. (London: Verso, 1991).
7 Cooper, *Family Values*, 9–16.
8 Edmund Burke, *Reflections on the Revolution in France*, edited by L. G. Mitchell (1790; Oxford: Oxford University Press, 2009), 34.
9 Edmund Burke, *Letters on a Regicide Peace* (1795–1796; Indianapolis, IN: Liberty Fund, 1999), 127.

10 Thomas Paine, *Rights of Man*, in *Rights of Man, Common Sense, and Other Political Writings*, edited by Mark Philp (Oxford: Oxford University Press, 1998), 271.

11 Edmund Burke, *Thoughts and Details on Scarcity* (1795; London: F. and C. Rivington, 1800), 11.

12 David McNally, *Against the Market: Political Economy, Market Socialism, and the Marxist Critique* (London: Verso, 1993), 19–24.

13 Gregory Claeys, *Mill and Paternalism* (Cambridge: Cambridge University Press, 2013), 178–180.

14 Richard Reeves opens his biography with this striking incident: *John Stuart Mill: Victorian Firebrand* (London: Atlantic Books, 2007), 1–2.

15 Francis Galton, *Hereditary Genius: An Inquiry Into its Laws and Consequences* (London: Macmillan, 1869), 357.

16 Ibid., 351–352.

17 Alfred Tennyson, *In Memoriam*, in *Tennyson: A Selected Edition*, edited by Christopher Ricks (Harlow: Longman, 1989), section LV, 357.

18 Marie Stopes, *Married Love*, edited by Ross McKibbin (1918; Oxford: Oxford University Press, 2008), 102.

19 William and Catherine Whetham, *The Family and the Nation: A Study in Natural Inheritance and Social Responsibility* (London: Longmans, Green, and Co., 1909), 86.

20 For a summary of his views in this respect, see Claeys, *Mill and Paternalism*, 70–76.

21 Arthur Pigou, *The Economics of Welfare* (1920; London: Macmillan, 1952), 106–122.

22 David Alderson, *Sex, Needs, and Queer Culture: From Liberation to the Postgay* (London: Zed Books, 2016), 71–72.

23 Alan Sinfield, *Alfred Tennyson*, (Oxford: Blackwell, 1986), 143–153.

24 Lee Edelman, *No Future: Queer Theory and the Death Drive* (Durham, NC: Duke University Press, 2004), especially 1–33.

25 See, for instance, José Esteban Muñoz, *Cruising Utopia: The Then and There of Queer Futurity* (New York: New York University Press, 2009).

26 Sylvia Townsend Warner, *Summer Will Show* (1936; New York: New York Review Books, 2009), 237–238; references hereafter noted parenthetically.

27 Herbert Marcuse, *Eros and Civilization: A Philosophical Inquiry into Freud* (1955; Abingdon: Routledge, 1987), 201.

28 F. R. Leavis, "Mass Civilization and Minority Culture," in *The Penguin Book of Twentieth-Century Essays*, edited by Ian Hamilton (London: Penguin, 1999), 169–191.

29 Antonio Gramsci highlights this point: see "Americanism and Fordism," *Selections from the Prison Notebooks*, edited and translated by Quintin Hoare and Geoffrey Nowell Smith (London: Lawrence and Wishart, 1971), 304–305.

30 T. S. Eliot, *Notes towards the Definition of Culture*, 2nd ed. (London: Faber and Faber, 1962), 31.

31 The panic was given a significant boost by the production of the film, *Chemsex* (Vice Media, 2015).

32 Herbert Marcuse, *One-Dimensional Man: Studies in the Ideology of Advanced Industrial Society* (1964; London: Routledge, 2002), especially 59–86; Fredric Jameson, *Postmodernism, or The Cultural Logic of Late Capitalism* (London: Verso, 1991), 1–54.

33 Martin Amis, *Money: A Suicide Note* (1984; London: Picador, 2005), 153.

34 Ibid., 323–324; emphases in original.

35 Emma Parker, "Money Makes the Man: Gender and Sexuality in Martin Amis's *Money*," in *Martin Amis: Postmodernism and Beyond*, edited by Gavin Keulks (Harmondsworth: Palgrave Macmillan, 2006), 55–70.

36 Didier Eribon, *Insult and the Making of the Gay Self*, translated by Michael Lucey (1999; Durham, NC: Duke University Press, 2004), 18–23.

37 John d'Emilio, "Capitalism and the Making of Gay Identity," in *Making Trouble: Essays on Gay History, Politics, and the University* (New York: Routledge, 1992), 3–16.

38 Didier Eribon, *Returning to Reims*, translated by Michael Lucey (2009; Los Angeles: Semiotext(e), 2013).

39 Thomas Piketty, *Capital in the Twenty-First Century*, translated by Arthur Goldhammer (Cambridge, MA: Belknap Press of Harvard University Press, 2014); Cooper suggests that family wealth has accumulated through the appreciation of assets consequent on the anti-inflationary emphases of neo-liberalism, as well as its attacks on welfare (*Family Values*, 119–166).

40 Edelman, *No Future*, 11.

41 Herbert Marcuse, *Counter-Revolution and Revolt* (Boston: Beacon Press, 1972), 78.

CHAPTER 11

The Literary Marketplace and the Rise of Neoliberalism

Paul Crosthwaite

Perhaps the greatest overlaps between literary and economic domains lie in the commodity status of literature itself. For centuries, the very institution of literature has been constituted – both conceptually and materially – by the existence of a literary marketplace, even (or especially) where attempts have been made to position the production and circulation of literature in opposition to market logics. Since the 1960s, structural shifts in the publishing industry and the wider economy – commonly denoted by the term "neoliberal" – have expanded and intensified the commercial pressures on the literary field.[1] This chapter examines how the ratcheting up of these pressures has affected that historically most commercial of literary forms – prose fiction. It argues that a mounting demand to satisfy perceived market preferences has not only influenced how authors go about their writing, but has also become the core subject matter of many of the most significant works of contemporary fiction. This tendency is especially marked among writers in the United States and (to a slightly lesser extent) the United Kingdom, with their particular proximity and sensitivity to the bastions of global publishing power, centered on New York and London. Analyzing exemplary texts by four high-profile American authors (Kate Zambreno, Eugene Lim, Jordy Rosenberg, and Helen DeWitt) and one major British novelist (Rachel Cusk), this chapter further argues that while ambitious contemporary writers necessarily stand at odds to the "neoliberalization" of the literary field, they nevertheless recognize the equal necessity of devising means to navigate and negotiate this shifting landscape. In contrast to influential critical accounts that have identified the decisive assertion of autonomy as the only politically meaningful authorial gesture vis-à-vis the market,[2] my reading shows how market logics may, in certain circumstances, be conducive to – or strategically harnessed in the service of – authors' aesthetically and politically radical or subversive objectives, even as such authors also highlight the market's more general tendency to foster orthodoxy and conservatism.

In the chapter's first section, I identify the specific forms that the political and economic phenomenon known as neoliberalism has taken in the world of publishing and bookselling. I then examine how recent novels by Zambreno, Lim, and Rosenberg self-consciously negotiate the publishing industry's simultaneous yet conflicting demands for novelty and familiarity, especially as they relate to expectations surrounding representations of femininity, race, ethnicity, and trans identity. In the concluding section, I read recent fiction by DeWitt and Cusk as meditations on how – rather than simply decrying, or capitulating to – the growing power of literary marketing and promotion, the "serious" contemporary writer might – at least in principle – utilize that power precisely in order to stimulate consumer appetite for seriousness as a desirable literary quality.

Selling Stories: How Publishing Became Neoliberal

"Neoliberalism" is a crucial concept in contemporary critical thought, but one that is too often invoked casually and indiscriminately. As Simon Springer, Kean Birch, and Julie MacLeavy observe, while "most scholars tend to agree that neoliberalism is broadly defined as the extension of competitive markets into all areas of life," the concept "is in need of unpacking."[3] The most crucial distinction to be drawn is between theory and practice, or between neoliberal doctrine and what has been called "actually existing neoliberalism."[4] As a theoretical movement (or "thought collective"),[5] neoliberalism is the product of elite intellectual and academic institutions, including the Mont Pelerin Society, the American Enterprise Institute, and the Economics Department and Business School at the University of Chicago. While neoliberal theory is itself complex and diverse, its adherents share a basic belief in the superiority of market structures relative to other systems of economic organization, and an insistence that the evaluation of "all institutions and spheres of conduct" should be subject "to a single economic concept of value."[6] If much of the world we inhabit today conforms to this neoliberal vision, this is only partly because of the influence of neoliberal thought on policymakers, business leaders, and other elite actors, however. It is equally the consequence of an accumulation of piecemeal reforms undertaken in pragmatic efforts to find workable solutions to specific, contingent challenges.

The neoliberal restructuring of the global publishing industry is a case in point. In the 1980s, as neoliberal ideas increasingly entered mainstream discourse, some commentators did make the case that, as a matter of principle, market success represented the only meaningful measure against which a work of literature could be judged.[7] Yet insofar as the dominance of this mode of evaluation is now something close to a reality, it has less to do with ideological polemics than with publishing houses' attempts to resolve internal succession crises or "intractable . . . financial problems" by agreeing to sell or merge their businesses, and with acquiring corporations' strategic efforts to achieve "synergies" between books and other media, boost growth, or expand into new territories.[8] It is this process of consolidation that has given rise to a situation in which a "neoliberal" market model of evaluation is internalized in day-to-day professional practice at every level of mainstream publishing, even as it sits uneasily both with the industry's preferred mode of self-presentation, and with many of its workers' personal sympathies and inclinations.

The "conglomerate era," as Dan N. Sinykin has called it, began in earnest in the 1960s with the leading American electronics and communications corporation RCA's acquisition of one of the most distinguished New York publishers, Random House.[9] Since then, successive waves of conglomeration have seen dozens of once-independent presses absorbed into a contracting group of multinational companies, where they persist in the form of imprints – residual markers of legacy and distinction within increasingly homogeneous corporate structures. At the time of writing, Penguin Random House is in the process of acquiring Simon & Schuster, which will reduce the "Big Five" global publishers to a "Big Four," each sitting within an even larger parent corporation: Penguin Random House is owned by Bertelsmann, Hachette Livre by the Lagardère Group, HarperCollins by News Corp, and Macmillan by Holtzbrinck Publishing (Simon & Schuster was put up for auction in 2020 by ViacomCBS).

As Sinykin observes, the crucial outcome of this process is that "conglomerate publishers have increasingly committed themselves to profitability in submission to shareholder value."[10] Thus, to a much greater extent than when publishers' lists primarily "reflect[ed] the idiosyncratic tastes and styles of their owners and editors," authors are today "confronted with the demand that their work be sellable. Literary fiction is no different than other texts in this regard."[11] Timothy Aubry notes that as literary culture has become increasingly shaped by "a market-orientated submission and editorial process designed to maximize profitability," publishers' "ability to gamble on experimental, idiosyncratic, or innovative fiction" has contracted.[12]

Importantly, while the "conglomerate era" has seen the consolidation of many formerly independent publishers, some legacy houses have retained their independence, while the falling costs of entry to the industry have allowed numerous small-scale indies to begin business. The "independent" segment of the industry ranges from small nonprofits (such as the Minneapolis-based Graywolf Press and Coffee House Press) to vanguard startups (like Brooklyn's Melville House) to storied names founded in the heyday of European and American modernism (most notably Faber & Faber in London and New Directions in New York) to large multinational companies whose structures in many ways resemble those of the conglomerates (including Bloomsbury Publishing, which has been listed on the London Stock Exchange since 1994). While the independents' varying organizational arrangements and revenue models permit greater or lesser degrees of latitude in editorial decision-making, all are to some extent subject, as John B. Thompson suggests, to a "logic of the field" dictated by the conglomerates' norms and priorities.[13] The dominance of the field by the brand-name authors and tried-and-tested genres favored by the conglomerates was exacerbated in the 1990s and 2000s, first by the growth of the "big box" book retail chains (with their own tendency to prioritize name recognition and market-proven modes), and later by the rise of Amazon (whose recommendation functions similarly tend to reinforce the industry's longstanding preference for familiar-with-a-twist offerings).[14]

These, then, are the main routes via which the publishing industry and book retail business have participated in a wider neoliberal shift toward market logics and narrowly economic models of value. While these industry transformations have been extensively charted by cultural sociologists and book and publishing historians, literary scholars have only recently begun to pay significant attention to the effects of these shifts on the forms and contents of works of literature themselves.[15] In a previous contribution to this emerging field of critical inquiry, I argued that one of the major consequences of the intensification of market pressures on writers of fiction is the emergence of a mode I term "market metafiction."[16] Texts in this vein, I argue, meditate self-reflexively on their own appeals or resistances to market approval precisely in the process of performing them. Elements of this style are evident in works of innovative or experimental fiction spanning the "conglomerate era," including novels by B. S. Johnson, Gilbert Sorrentino, Kathy Acker, Martin Amis, Iain Sinclair, Bret Easton Ellis, David Foster Wallace, Dave Eggers, Chris Kraus, and Percival Everett. It has emerged as perhaps the defining mode of "advanced" fiction over the past decade, especially in the United States: in addition to the texts by Zambreno, Lim, Rosenberg, DeWitt, and Cusk considered below, it is exemplified by the work of leading contemporary authors including Teju Cole, Ben Lerner, Sheila Heti, Nell Zink, Joshua Cohen, and Barbara Browning. In the following sections, I explore how this form of self-consciousness about a text's market positioning functions in a series of key recent examples. Alongside an acute awareness of the dominance of the literary field by market logics, these texts, I argue, demonstrate a grasp of those logics' complexity and multivalence: how they may afford openings for experimentation and subversion, even as they foreclose the possibility of pure or uncompromised autonomy or resistance.

Sell Yourself: Identity and the Market in Contemporary Fiction

Kate Zambreno's 2020 novel *Drifts* is characteristic of what I call "market metafiction" in the way in which it meditates on the commercial and economic pressures that inform its own composition. Like Zambreno herself, the text's unnamed narrator occupies "the precarious life of a writer":[17] the income from her own writing and from a string of adjunct teaching positions in and around New York City is never sufficient for economic security, especially when – in the book's latter part – she finds herself unexpectedly pregnant. In attempting to produce work that will elicit sufficient enthusiasm in the publishing world for her to sustain herself and her family, the narrator confronts a double bind that Zambreno has described: the common demand from publishers that new titles should be at once like and unlike other popular works.

The expectation of conformity is manifest in the publishing industry's strategy of evaluating books in terms of comparisons or "comps." In Zambreno's words, "to get published by a larger press" (*Drifts* itself was eventually picked up by Riverhead Books, an imprint of the world's largest publisher, Penguin Random House), "you must present your work in direct comparison with a work that's been commercially and critically successful, preferably a bestseller." Voicing a widespread concern about the ubiquity of this practice, Zambreno observes that "it waters down work to have it compared" in this way, "especially the onus on it selling well."[18] In *Drifts*, Zambreno's narrator is especially conscious of the extent to which expectations of her work are defined by the category of "woman writer." She writes to a female friend (also a writer) of her "irritation" at "appearing only on ... lists of women writers" and of "being referenced only in the context of other women writers" (38). She thus "dread[s] the comparisons" (38) that will be imposed on her current project. As if in confirmation of how far the commercial imperatives of the "comp" have been internalized in the writing profession (especially as they are defined in reductively gendered terms), a student, who "wants to make money writing," asks the narrator, "Didn't you write, like, one of those 'girl' novels" (127) – presumably referencing Zambreno's own *Green Girl* (2011), whose resemblance to bestselling thrillers such as Gillian Flynn's *Gone Girl* (2012) and Paula Hawkins' *The Girl on the Train* (2015) is both superficial and coincidental, but might look to the uninformed eye like a deliberate comping strategy.[19] A male acquaintance's success in publishing a novel written "from the point of view of a young woman" with a "prestigious experimental press" (53) points to a double standard in the gendering of contemporary fiction, as do the reviews that compare the author to a litany of male giants – "Beckett, Calvino, Cortázar" (53) – who occupy a position of "universality" in literary history rarely afforded to women.

If *Drifts* reflects Zambreno's awareness of demands to conform to publishing industry norms, then it also registers the pressures imposed by the industry's simultaneous thirst for novelty. In this latter regard, *Drifts'* conspicuously autobiographical qualities presented an obstacle for at least one editor, who "rejected the book by telling my agent he was bored with autofiction," as Zambreno recalls.[20] In the novel, the narrator expresses her frustration that she and the "women and non-binary writers"[21] with whom she corresponds are assumed simply to be tilling an autofictional furrow ploughed by a more celebrated male author: "a prominent writer of so-called autofiction, with a half-million dollar advance on his last book, wins the so-called genius grant ... The writer's name had become synonymous for the type of first-person narrative we also wrote, and yet no one found our struggles worthy of reward" (75). (The author in question is transparently Ben Lerner, though the phrase "our struggles" gestures toward the other contemporary writer most closely associated with autofiction, Karl Ove Knausgård, author of the six-volume *Min kamp* or *My Struggle* series, whom the narrator resents being "supposed to read" [217]). The narrator wants her own work-in-progress, which she calls *Drifts*, and which has presumably resulted in the text we are now reading, "to be completely new, as if from a completely different writer" (38).

Drifts, then, foregrounds the competing and often confounding commercial imperatives shaping the production of contemporary fiction. Yet in drafting the novel Zambreno also evidently succeeded in reconciling these demands sufficiently to secure the backing of one of the industry leader's most prominent imprints. The published text emphatically demonstrates that there is nothing inherently "narrow" or "limiting" about the kinds of concerns most frequently associated with writing by women. Zambreno filters such concerns (sex, beauty, embodiment, motherhood, female friendship) through an oblique, elliptical narrative style that comes close to realizing the narrator's desire to produce, not so much the "novel" with "characters" and things "happen[ing]" that the "publishing people" (5, 15) expect, as "a small book of wanderings, animals. A paper-thin object, a ghost. Filled with an incandescence toward the possibility of a book, as well as a paralysis" (5). *Drifts* demonstrates the potential for an author able to negotiate the industry's simultaneous demands for adherence to and departure from convention to produce compelling syntheses of established and innovative forms.

A similar interplay between pressure toward and resistance to literary convention arises in relation to questions of racial and ethnic identity. In recent decades, African American authors such as Percival Everett, Paul Beatty, Zinzi Clemmons, and Brandon Taylor have gained prominence with novels that, with greater or lesser degrees of explicitness, critique and subvert heavily commodified stereotypes of Black life.[22] Significant contemporary Asian American novelists have likewise sought alternatives to overfamiliar cultural narratives. For authors such as the Korean Americans Eugene Lim, Yongsoo Park, and R. O. Kwon; Chinese Americans Tan Lin, Ling Ma, and Alexandra Chang; or Vietnamese American Ocean Vuong, the long-prevailing expectation that Asian American writing should "be *generic*, its worth measured by how capably the writer executes the essential elements of the expected immigrant narrative" is to be challenged.[23]

Eugene Lim (born to South Korean immigrants to the United States in 1974) has remarked that "for a long stretch of my life, alternatives or subversions of a necessary but increasingly familiar Asian American assimilation tale were very hard to find."[24] His own *Dear Cyborgs* (2017) is an important contribution to such reimagining. The novel's opening pages ostensibly suggest a conventional story of the immigrant child's search for identity, introducing the Korean American narrator and his friend Vu, the son of Vietnamese refugees, as they negotiate the challenges of being virtually the only "Asian kids" in their patch of rural Ohio in the 1980s.[25] The narrative abruptly scrambles its generic codes, however, in moving to an alternate present-day New York City, where a band of off-duty superheroes meets to exchange downbeat monologues on art, capitalism, protest, and their mundane day jobs. In the novel's closing section, it transpires that these characters – the inhabitants of the *Team Chaos* universe – are the creations of Vu and the narrator, lifetime devotees of "Nerddom" (10) who are reunited by chance as adults at an East Village comic book store and set about writing and illustrating their own series. The frame narrative involving Vu and the unnamed protagonist is itself ambiguously framed by the appearance, in the final pages, of a mysterious book entitled *Dear Cyborgs*. If it is presumably not quite the novel we have been reading (it is presented as the "fictionalized" autobiography of Vu's estranged father [154]), this volume nonetheless bears a striking resemblance to it in its complexly ramifying form: "An odd story, it was composed of many shorter, similar stories. It was a confessional novel it [*sic*] was also a puzzle with a fractal structure, and it mutated and yet duplicated its shape by my changing focus and perspective on it" (155).

Lim embeds within this nested arrangement of stories a satirical response to the "confessional novel" of identity-formation that Asian American writers have long been expected to produce, and which *Dear Cyborgs* initially appears to be. One member of Team Chaos, who goes by the alias Frank Exit, is a writer by day – or at least tries to be. He describes how, following a collection of stories that was "a minor hit" with "decent sales," he was contracted to write a novel whose "assignment," though never expressly articulated, "was clear as day":

> What was expected was a slightly modified coming-of-age novel that traded on my Korean-American identity. Something not too obviously an assimilation tale – and above all clever – yet also something not too much a deviation from that sellable idea, so that the marketplace of culture could easily absorb my story without being too discomfited. (40)

Unable to muster the requisite combination of earnestness and irony, Frank remains blocked until, "hurting for money" (40), he accepts a commission to ghostwrite a Chinese American politician's autobiography (the two put together simply because "we were both Asian American" [41]). Suggesting how an effect of ethnic "authenticity" may in fact rely on contrived techniques or methods of "strategically fictionaliz[ing] ... identity" (42), Frank now finds himself able to "use all of the underhanded emotionally manipulative tricks I couldn't have borne to see enter the world under my own name," and efficiently performs his contribution to "this glossy and heavily marketed product" (42). Lim's novel, then, satirizes – and aims to redress – the exclusions and misrepresentations perpetuated by the "marketplace of culture."

Similar resistance to the commercial imposition of one-dimensional codes of representation on complex identities is also increasingly evident in writing by queer, trans, nonbinary, and other gender nonconforming or sexually dissident authors. Since its fully recognizable emergence in the latter decades of the twentieth century, trans literature has been especially subject to channeling by the publishing industry into a specific genre: the memoir. As Juliet Jacques notes, "trans memoir, thanks to the workings of the market and the prejudices of editors and publishers, remains far more prominent than fiction."²⁶ Over the past decade, however, authors such as Jordy Rosenberg, Andrea Lawlor, Akwaeke Emezi, McKenzie Wark, Juliana Huxtable, Torrey Peters, Paul B. Preciado, Shola von Reinhold, and Jacques herself, have sought to displace the expectations of confession and self-exposure inherent to the memoir form by drawing not only on fictional strategies, but also on theory and other modes of cultural, social, and economic analysis in their accounts of trans lives. While acknowledging the value of memoir as a means of giving voice and visibility to trans experience, Jordy Rosenberg, author of the 2018 novel *Confessions of the Fox*, has expressed his unease at publishers' "huge thirst around transgender memoir" and editors' recurrent message that "if this person would just write a memoir, that's what we want."²⁷

Like other authors discussed in this chapter, Rosenberg makes his novel's deliberate swerving of publishing industry expectations an overt feature of the narrative itself. *Confessions of the Fox* centers on the discovery of a mysterious manuscript by a literature professor "at the flagship campus of a demoralized and floundering public institution" (Rosenberg himself teaches literature at University of Massachusetts, Amherst).²⁸ The document purports to be the autobiography of Jack Sheppard, and suggests that the notorious thief and jailbreaker, whose audacious escapes from Newgate made him a folk hero of eighteenth-century England, was a trans man. Rosenberg's scholar-protagonist, Dr. Voth, is pressured into editing the manuscript for publication by the *"North-Northeast Senior Marketing Director of P-Quad Publishers and Pharmaceuticals."* Noting that the company is a "subsidiary," the director quips, *"You know how it is with neoliberalism these days ... everything's a subsidiary of everything!"*, marking him as one of Voth's least favored "types," the "corporate meta-neoliberal comedian" (119–120; italics in original). The publisher intends to market the volume as *"the earliest authentic confessional transgender memoirs known to history"* (121; italics in original), and the novel suggests how such insistence on transparency and truth-telling may be continuous with what the trans theorist Talia Mae Bettcher calls "reality enforcement," the "common-sense folk view about sex" whereby genitalia are understood to "play the role of 'concealed truth' about a person's sex."²⁹ Accordingly, the marketing director insists that "READERS NEED TO BE ABLE TO VISUALIZE" the specific meaning of the "proto-sexological" term "Sexual Chimera" (132; caps in original) and demands that Voth provide the "voyeuristic depiction of Jack's genitalia" (109) that the manuscript does not in fact contain. Taking a leaf (almost literally) out of Lawrence Sterne's *Tristram Shandy* (1759–1767), the novel features a marbled page where a graphic illustration of this kind might be expected to appear, and Voth eventually satisfies the director's prurience by passing off a photoshopped image of a dead slug as the "very explicit description of genitalia" that he demands (272, 251).

Like *Dear Cyborgs*, however, *Confessions of the Fox* is a refutation of mainstream publishing norms – and of the wider structures of financial and corporate capitalism – that was released under the aegis of one of the world's largest media conglomerates (Lim's novel was published by Farrar, Straus, and Giroux, part of Macmillan, the key constituent of the Stuttgart-based Holtzbrinck Publishing Group; Rosenberg's appeared with the One World imprint, which sits within the Random House division of the biggest publisher of all, Penguin Random House, itself a subsidiary of another German multinational, Bertelsmann). In these cases, publishers' desires for novelty evidently overrode their equally internalized inclinations towards conventionality (it's no coincidence that One World and the FSG Originals imprint under which *Dear Cyborgs* appeared are conspicuously branded as the "edgier," risk-taking faces of their parent companies). One could thus easily see confirmation here of the claim voiced in Lim's novel that, "in our current marketplace," a distinctive, "identifiable" artistic innovation is liable "to be richly compensated and then quickly desaturated by co-optation" (29) or that "the omnipotent digestive juices of the market's gut – it eats it all!" (75). Rosenberg's reflections on his experiences with One World are instructive in this regard, however. He describes how – contrary to prevailing industry pressures for trans writers to confine themselves to memoir – the imprint's publisher and editor-in-chief Chris Jackson and editor Victory Matsui (to whom Rosenberg dedicated the novel) "really wanted to support a transgender author writing fiction." While an element of strategic calculation – of seeking to capitalize on the growing cultural visibility of trans issues via a logical expansion into fiction – can hardly be discounted here, Jackson and Matsui's eschewal of the customary "demand for disclosure" – "They never once asked, 'Which parts of this are true and which are not?'" Rosenberg recalls – lends credence to One World's avowed ambition of providing "a home for writers . . . unconstrained by genre . . . who seek to challenge the status quo [and] subvert dominant narratives."[30] Similarly, a novel like *Dear Cyborgs* suggests that there is some substance to FSG Originals' stated mission to be "driven by voices . . . who are compelled to show us something new [and] defy categorization and expectation."[31] These cases might be considered illustrative instances of a situation in which market signals and unorthodox authorial intentions are unusually well aligned. They would suggest, then, that there are scenarios in which the very shaping of the contemporary literary field by market logics may be conducive – rather than solely obstructive – to both political and aesthetic nonconformity.

The Hard Sell: A Market for Difficulty?

The idea that texts liable to present challenging or defamiliarizing reading experiences may not be inherently or necessarily incompatible with a market-dominated literary field is central to recent fictional works by Helen DeWitt and Rachel Cusk. DeWitt's 2018 short story collection *Some Trick* contains oblique meditations on her own career, which at least to some extent illustrates the potential for corporate publishers and other major institutions of the conglomerate era to place works of innovative or experimental writing in the hands of a large readership. Having been rejected by a succession of editors as "too dense, too difficult," as DeWitt recalls,[32] her debut novel *The Last Samurai* was eventually published in 2000 by Talk Miramax, the publishing wing of Talk Media, a key plank of Bob and Harvey Weinstein's Miramax empire in the late 1990s and early 2000s. As well as prize nominations and enthusiastic reviews, the novel garnered English-language sales of over 100,000 copies and numerous foreign rights acquisitions (having succeeded in generating the requisite level of industry "buzz" at the 1999 Frankfurt Book Fair).[33] Demonstrating the extent to which contemporary writers are at the mercy of media transnationals' high-level restructurings, however, DeWitt's opus fell out of print after the Miramax imprint was absorbed by Disney's Hyperion Books in 2005 as part of the Weinsteins' withdrawal from their relationship with the Walt Disney Company, which had acquired Miramax twelve years earlier.

It would be around a decade – more than enough time for it to accumulate the status of a lost classic – before *The Last Samurai* was reissued, initially by New Directions in 2016. In the Afterword to the 2018 Vintage reissue, DeWitt pointed to the potential for mainstream publishing's promotional mechanisms to be used to generate a new large-scale market for her novel, and other works like it: "It's not hard to imagine a world where the effect of the book on what has been a coterie of readers is multiplied to the point where general assumptions about what is possible are changed. We have only to imagine a world in which Oprah Winfrey picks up *The Last Samurai*."[34] Since the launch of Oprah's Book Club in 1996, Winfrey has played a key role in shaping Americans' reading habits via a range of media outlets. DeWitt suggests that, if the most widely influential literary tastemakers promoted more (ostensibly) "challenging" or "difficult" fare than is their wont, then the very market dynamics that have tended to marginalize such writing might work to grant it a new centrality. Echoing an idea crucial to the novel itself – that "no one is put off by difficulty only by boredom and if something is interesting no one will care how hard it is" – DeWitt argues that mainstream literary culture has failed to attend to and cultivate "the unknown capabilities of the reader."[35]

DeWitt's collection *Some Trick*, published by New Directions in 2018, repeatedly depicts scenarios in which artistic and intellectual principles fall almost magically into line with market conditions. In one story, a team of Sundance-garlanded NYU film students, who are reluctant to make the "guaranteed bankable and commercial" feature their producers demand, consent to undertake "the one commercial project they [can] even *contemplate*" – an adaptation of a beloved series of children's books – and achieve "succe[ss] beyond [their] wildest dreams," "such that they can select their own projects."[36] Another piece, "My Heart Belongs to Bertie," concerns a math professor who has had an unexpected hit with another children's book, a collection of "robot tales" (27) explaining elementary mathematical concepts. The "leverage" (41) over his corporate publisher that comes from sales of half a million copies (31) allows the author to insist on retaining the complex technical elements that he sees as essential to the integrity of his followup. DeWitt's story itself contains an array of mathematical formulae, specialized vocabulary, statistical visualizations, and programming code – features of the kind that, in her own experience over the past two decades (as she describes in a 2018 essay), publishers have been almost uniformly unwilling to countenance.[37] New Directions' preservation of its original avant-garde spirit (it was founded in 1936 by the steel fortune heir James Laughlin at the instigation of Ezra Pound) makes it virtually the only New York house of significant stature receptive to DeWitt's brand of literary experiment and risk-taking.

New Directions – which has published DeWitt since 2011's *Lightning Rods* – plays a key role in *Some Trick*'s centerpiece story, "Climbers." The narrative focuses on a group of New Yorkers working in and around the publishing industry, who alight upon a reclusive Dutch writer living in Vienna named Peter Dijkstra, and set about transforming him into the next global literary celebrity. Their models are W. G. Sebald and Roberto Bolaño, both of whose ascents to international stardom (posthumously in Bolaño's case) were launched by New Directions' publication of English translations of their works (81, 84, 89–90, 92). Almost overnight, a bidding war for the obscure Dijkstra's writing is incited amid projections of "the next *2666*" (89, 92), a reference to Bolaño's opus, which appeared in English to huge acclaim in 2008, becoming a bestseller in the United States. The story is at once a satire – of book world "hustling" (84); of American monolingualism; and of the enduring appeal of melancholic, oracular foreigners for a particular type of New York literary hipster – and an exercise in authorial wish fulfillment, in which "genius" (90) (a word applied so often to DeWitt's work that commenting upon its ubiquity has itself become a journalistic cliché) finally receives its just financial rewards.

That it is at least conceivable that the publishing industry would throw its full weight behind an uncompromisingly serious or challenging body of writing is also a key implication of Rachel Cusk's 2018 novel *Kudos*, the concluding volume of her *Outline* trilogy. In one of several discussions of the condition of literary culture in the novel, the showily cynical German publisher of Faye, the narrator, tells her that he sees little point in defending "great writers" – such as Dante, Robert Musil, and T. S. Eliot – from know-nothing derision.[38] Faye's response is one of the few moments across the trilogy in which we hear her own opinion, rather than neutral reports of others' views, reflections, or confessions. She counters the publisher's attitude of wry resignation by arguing that he in fact has a responsibility to honor "justice ... for its own sake" and to defend Dante and his ilk "at every opportunity" (42).

This unexpectedly solemn response to the teasing and worldly remarks of Faye's companion is echoed in a literary world encounter later in the novel. Faye is meeting another publisher, Paola, who complains that, "like the Siberian tiger," book world people "are always being threatened with extinction, as though novels likewise had once been fierce and [are] now fragile and defenceless" (176). Paola suggests, however, that it is not so much the tyranny of the market that has brought about the near-extinction of serious literature as the failure of writers and publishers to market their wares aggressively enough:

> Somewhere along the line ... we have failed to promote our product, perhaps because the people who work in the literary world are those who secretly believe their interest in literature is a weakness, a kind of debility. ... We publishers ... proceed on the assumption that no one cares about books, whereas the makers of cornflakes convince everyone that the world needs cornflakes like it needs the sun to rise in the morning. (176)

While it is risky to take anything that a character in the trilogy (perhaps even Faye herself) says as enjoying full narratorial or authorial endorsement, the convergence of Paola's reflections here with Faye's ardent reaction to her publisher earlier in the novel suggests that the position they jointly articulate has some measure of privileged status. What their remarks suggest is that, if the thoroughgoing marketization and commodification of literature is an accomplished fact, then those who sell books must respond in kind. Other literary world professionals whom Faye meets take the view that it is futile to promote "great" or "landmark" (105) works of literature in the face of public indifference or hostility. Yet as Faye and Paola both imply, while markets impose limitations on producers, they may also be created, shaped, and expanded: it is the duty of writers and publishers like themselves, the novel suggests, to ensure that books of serious literary merit and significance are consumed and read as widely as possible, and thus they must use their platforms to make the maximally compelling case for such books' value and necessity in people's lives.

While entertaining such honorable aspirations, however, both Cusk's novel and DeWitt's short story collection acknowledge that, in actuality, publishers' tendency to adopt a reactive stance in relation to the marketplace inevitably generates pressure on authors to make concessions to perceived consumer demands for familiarity, transparency, and immediate accessibility. For the German publisher in *Kudos*, for example, "the holy grail ... of the modern literary scene" is a "cultural product" that, while it displays some superficial "connection to the values of literature," requires no "hard work" and makes "no demands" on its readers (37, 40, 39). Similarly, DeWitt describes attempts by the would-be publisher in "My Heart Belongs to Bertie" to "dilute" (31) the mathematician-author's vision for his book. And even the literary "genius" at the center of DeWitt's "Climbers" has come to the conclusion that the "cult classic" status he has earned from the English translation of "two novellas and some stories" won't keep "his credit cards afloat," and that he must adapt his writing practice to appeal to "the big boys" – the leading corporate publishing houses – "who wouldn't touch a novella with a bargepole" (85).

As DeWitt and Cusk suggest, the fact remains that – both in its perpetually changeable weather and in its underlying climate of conservatism – the market, and the publishing industry that seeks to forecast its conditions, cannot provide an environment that fosters ambitious literary expression with any degree of consistency. Perhaps some future experiment in mass writers' subsidies – or indeed the establishment of a form of universally guaranteed economic security along the lines of a Universal Basic Income – would be capable of instituting the material underpinnings that a genuinely diverse literary culture requires. For the time being, we might at least hold open the possibility – as the narrator of Zambreno's *Drifts* does – of "some utopian and impossible arrangement I can't imagine," in which the demands to meet the costs of such necessities as "paternity leave … the hospital bill, the midwives, [and] childcare" – in short, "to pay for everything" – are alleviated, and it is possible simply to "think and write and make things" (315, 294).

Notes

1 On the notion of the literary field, see Pierre Bourdieu, *The Rules of Art: Genesis and Structure of the Literary Field*, translated by Susan Emanuel (1992; Cambridge: Polity, 1996).

2 See Nicholas Brown, *Autonomy: The Social Ontology of Art under Capitalism* (Durham, NC: Duke University Press, 2019); Walter Benn Michaels, *The Beauty of a Social Problem: Photography, Autonomy, Economy* (Chicago: University of Chicago Press, 2015).

3 Kean Birch, Julie MacLeavy, and Simon Springer, "An Introduction to Neoliberalism," in *The Handbook of Neoliberalism* (Abingdon: Routledge, 2016), 1–14; 2.

4 See Neil Brenner, Jamie Peck, and Nik Theodore, "Actually Existing Neoliberalism," in *The Sage Handbook of Neoliberalism*, edited by Damien Cahill, Melinda Cooper, Martijn Konings, and David Primrose (London: Sage, 2018), 3–15.

5 See Philip Mirowski, *Never Let a Serious Crisis Go to Waste: How Neoliberalism Survived the Financial Meltdown* (London: Verso, 2013), especially ch. 2.

6 William Davies, *The Limits of Neoliberalism: Authority, Sovereignty, and the Logic of Competition* (London: Sage, 2014), 21.

7 See Margaret Doherty, "State-Funded Fiction: Minimalism, National Memory, and the Return to Realism in the Post-Postmodern Age," *American Literary History* 27.1 (2014), 79–101; 86.

8 John B. Thompson, *Merchants of Culture: The Publishing Business in the Twenty-First Century*, 2nd ed. (Cambridge: Polity, 2012), 104.

9 Dan N. Sinykin, "The Conglomerate Era: Publishing, Authorship, and Literary Form, 1965–2007," *Contemporary Literature* 58.4 (2017), 462–491; 470.

10 Ibid., 470.

11 Thompson, *Merchants*, 103; Sinykin, "Conglomerate Era," 472.

12 Timothy Aubry, *Reading as Therapy: What Contemporary Fiction Does for Middle-Class Americans* (Iowa City: University of Iowa Press, 2011), 9–10.

13 Thompson, *Merchants*, 11–12.

14 See Laura Miller, *Reluctant Capitalists: Bookselling and the Culture of Consumption* (Chicago: University of Chicago Press, 2007); John B. Thompson, *Book Wars: The Digital Revolution in Publishing* (Cambridge: Polity, 2021), ch. 6.

15 In addition to scholarship cited elsewhere in this chapter, important studies in this emerging field of literary studies include Sarah Brouillette, *Literature and the Creative Economy* (Stanford, CA: Stanford University Press, 2014); Amy Hungerford, *Making Literature Now* (Stanford, CA: Stanford University Press, 2016); and Jeremy Rosen, *Minor Characters Have Their Day: Genre and the Contemporary Literary Marketplace* (New York: Columbia University Press, 2016).

16 Paul Crosthwaite, *The Market Logics of Contemporary Fiction* (Cambridge: Cambridge University Press, 2019).

17 Kate Zambreno, *Drifts* (New York: Riverhead, 2020), 25; references hereafter noted parenthetically.

18 "Ten Questions for Kate Zambreno," *Poets & Writers*, May 19, 2020, www .pw.org/content/ten_questions_for_kate_zambreno. On the ways in which "comps perpetuate the status quo" (especially in racial terms), see Laura B. McGrath, "Comping White," *Los Angeles Review of Books*, January 21, 2019, https://lareviewofbooks.org/article/comping-white/.

19 Lee Konstantinou and Dan Sinykin remark that "the presence of a girl in the title can serve as a kind of marketing gimmick ... For a moment, neoliberal publishing's top profit-guaranteeing gimmick was simply *a girl*" ("Literature and Publishing, 1945–2020," *American Literary History* 33.2 [2021], 225–243; 233; italics in original).

20 "Ten Questions."

21 Sara Black McCulloch, "In the Margins: A Conversation with Kate Zambreno," *Los Angeles Review of Books*, September 13, 2019, https:// lareviewofbooks.org/article/in-the-margins-a-conversation-with-kate-zam breno/.

22 On the often narrow and reductive industry expectations imposed on African American writers, see John K. Young, *Black Writers, White Publishers: Marketplace Politics in Twentieth-Century African American Literature* (Jackson: University Press of Mississippi, 2006). On the stark and ongoing racial inequalities in American publishing, see Richard Jean So, *Redlining Culture: A Data History of Racial Inequality and Postwar Fiction* (New York: Columbia University Press, 2020).

23 Betsy Huang, *Contesting Genres in Contemporary Asian American Literature* (New York: Palgrave Macmillan, 2010), 12; emphasis in original.

24 Eugene Lim, "American Classics that Influenced *Dear Cyborgs*, Mostly in Pairs," Library of America website, June 6, 2017, https://loa.org/news-and-views/1287-eugene-lim-american-classics-that-influenced-_dear-cyborgs_-mostly-in-pairs.

25 Eugene Lim, *Dear Cyborgs* (New York: Farrar, Straus, and Giroux, 2017), 9; references hereafter noted parenthetically.

26 Juliet Jacques, "Forms of Resistance: Uses of Memoir, Theory, and Fiction in Trans Life Writing," *Life Writing* 14.3 (2017), 357–370; 369.

27 Megan Labrise, "Jordy Rosenberg," *Kirkus*, July 2, 2018, www.kirkusreviews .com/news-and-features/articles/jordy-rosenberg/.

28 Jordy Rosenberg, *Confessions of the Fox* (London: Atlantic, 2018), 168; references hereafter noted parenthetically.

29 Talia Mae Bettcher, "Trapped in the Wrong Theory: Rethinking Trans Oppression and Resistance," *Signs* 39.2 (2014), 383–406; 392; "Evil Deceivers and Make-Believers: On Transphobic Violence and the Politics of Illusion," *Hypatia* 22.3 (2007), 43–65; 48.

30 Labrise, "Jordy Rosenberg"; One World website, www.oneworldlit.com/about-ow.

31 FSG Originals website, www.fsgoriginals.com/about.

32 Morten Høi Jensen, "*Bookforum* Talks to Helen DeWitt," *Bookforum*, 22 Sept. 2011, www.bookforum.com/interviews/bookforum-talks-to-helen-dewitt-8389.

33 See Christian Lorentzen, "Publishing *Can* Break Your Heart," *New York*, July 11, 2016, www.vulture.com/2016/07/helen-dewitt-last-samurai-new-edition.html.

34 Helen DeWitt, *The Last Samurai* (2000; London: Vintage, 2018), 485.

35 Ibid., 399, 484.

36 Helen DeWitt, *Some Trick: Thirteen Stories* (New York: New Directions, 2018), 63, 64; emphasis in original; references hereafter noted parenthetically.

37 See Helen DeWitt, "The Wrong Stuff," *Los Angeles Review of Books*, May 29, 2018, https://lareviewofbooks.org/article/the-wrong-stuff/.

38 Rachel Cusk, *Kudos* (London: Faber & Faber, 2018), 41; references hereafter noted parenthetically.

CHAPTER 12

World-Systems and Literary Studies

Stephen Shapiro

World-systems analyses emerged in the 1970s as attempts to fuse a Marxist-informed critique of developmental economics with historical sociology. They are most well-known through the writings of Immanuel Wallerstein (1930–2019) who produced a multi-volume (and incomplete) series about the history of the capitalist world-system from the sixteenth century, wrote dozens of essays, led a research center at SUNY, Binghamton, and edited two successive journals, *Review* (1976–2015) and *Journal for World-Systems Research* (1995–present).[1] The focus on Wallerstein, however, creates two challenges. First, while Wallerstein was active in crafting world-systems, he insisted initially that it was not a *theory*, but a *perspective*, a guiding outlook on ways of handling complex historical and social materials. Even as world-systems *did* rest on a set of basic premises, Wallerstein eventually argued that it was better seen as a collective *knowledge-movement*, "a reorientation of the ways we organize our understanding of the world. In the case of world-systems analysis, it is based on a rejection of social science categories inherited from the nineteenth century. It proposes to replace these categories with a new historical social science."[2] In this movement toward a new way of thinking, the citation of Wallerstein is at once necessary, but also antithetical to the spirit of the project. Additionally, because Wallerstein intentionally insisted on a constant repetition of his claims and chosen terms, the host of scholars working in conjunction with Wallerstein or inspired by his work, many lesser known, often give more concise summaries as well as generate the most useful extensions, revisions, and implementations of world-systems approaches. Readers are encouraged to consider writings by such associates as Wilma A. Dunaway, Walter L. Goldfrank, Terence K. Hopkins, Christopher Chase-Dunn, and Thomas R. Shannon.[3]

A second problem emerges for literary and cultural studies. World-systems perspectives insist on the need to overcome the separation of inquiry from the disciplinary categories created by Western universities throughout the nineteenth century (economics in one faculty, literature in another). Wallerstein rarely considered the arts and humanities, and his discussion of culture seems deeply rooted in a social scientist's assumptions. For instance, when he begins his discussion of ideology as a medium for managing "a deep and possibly unbridgeable gap of conflicting interests," he claims that ideologies are "more than prejudices and presuppositions"; they "are political metastrategies."[4] Most cultural studies scholars would consider this definition as far too limited and homogenizing, especially with regards to the very intersectionality of lived experience that world-systems approaches otherwise enable. In this way, the burden has been on humanities scholars to first educate themselves on world-systems approaches, and then draw out their uses for literary studies. Below I will outline some of the more important presuppositions and then indicate their implications for existing scholarship and future directions.

Premises of World-Systems Perspectives

World-systems analyses began as alternatives to forms of developmental and stage theories. Initially a specialist in decolonizing Southern Africa, Wallerstein found that dominant theories of development held that non-Western nations should follow the historical stages of progression enacted by the so-called industrialized (usually Western) nation-states. While these claims predate World War II, developmental economics, political science, and sociology came to dominate government policy and academic approaches during the ensuing phase of American power, especially through the Cold War years of (military) Keynesianism. If these claims were usually found within "the West," there were likewise mechanistic assumptions within the Soviet Union that there was a conveyor belt of revolutionary steps on the way to socialism. To escape both these rigidities, Wallerstein drew on different intellectual traditions to come up with a better way of understanding the binds that African postcolonial states faced. Because Wallerstein felt that a deep understanding of capitalism's logistics and recurring features was necessary in order to provide a context for the new African states, he was led to investigate a longer history of capitalism, going back to its sixteenth-century roots. If world-systems' initial motivation was to better understand the power relations between the "North" and the "South," Wallerstein realized it would be necessary to discover how the "North" became capitalist in the first place.

He began this project just as some South American writers, like Raúl Prebisch and Andre Gunder Frank, were also challenging the notion of equal opportunities among nations to pursue development. Prebisch argued against Ricardo's notion of comparative advantage among international trading partners to claim that capitalism structurally created inequality in ways that produced, as Frank would famously put it, the development of underdevelopment, a system of creating the subordination of the world's nations to the United States and Europe.[5] These ideas gave rise to notions of a set of "core" trading nation-states and a larger one of the "periphery."

To the assumption that nations were structurally made unequal with one another within capitalism, Wallerstein brought together other intellectual resources, namely German and central European historical sociology, French historiography, and Marxism.[6] The work of Weber, Polanyi, and Schumpeter helped world-systems move away from nation-centric approaches, categorize variations of market activity (reciprocity, redistribution, and the price-setting market), and discover the existence of a crisis-driven business cycle. From the historiography of Fernand Braudel and the *Annaliste* historians came the retreat from "event" history, often one of great men and dates, to look at longer spans of time and the rhythms of change that superseded the individual. Marxism's discussion of "social conflict among materially based human groups" and capitalism's basic drive for endless accumulation, especially with the seizure by capitalism in so-called primitive accumulation "through the expansion of Europe (colonies, precious metals, slave trade) and the reorganization of agricultural production (enclosure, capitalist ground rent)," provided an explanation for historical transformation.[7]

The legacy of and commitment to an open Marxism became more explicit in Wallerstein's later writing.[8] Unlike many of his contemporaries, Wallerstein did not become entangled with many of the more abstruse Marxist economic debates, such as the so-called transformation problem about the relationship of price to value. Indeed, Wallerstein, and world-systems analysts, take the published volumes of *Capital* as essentially correct and without needing major revision, even if Marx's understanding of capitalism was circumscribed by the conditions historically possible for him to consider in the mid-nineteenth century. Rather than seek alterations to *Capital*, the world-systems knowledge movement can be taken as an effort to complete it. Marx's initial outline for *Capital* was to include volumes on the state, foreign trade, and world markets.[9] While Volume I was published, and revised by Marx through the course of multiple editions and translations, the second and third volumes were put together after Marx's death by Engels. The remaining volumes were unwritten, and one way to consider Wallerstein's body of work is as an attempt to fill out descriptively and suggestively what may have been included in these volumes. This goal has led Wallerstein to consider capitalism in a less Eurocentric fashion, by taking in a wider horizon of labor divisions than Marx's preliminary discussions in *Capital* volume I.

In this sense, world-systems perspectives believe in the historical existence of three social totalities (and the possibility of a fourth) based on each one's dominant modes of production and division of labor. These named totalities are minisytems, world-empires, and a capitalist world-economy. The fourth is a vision of a socialist world, one not yet seen, since the prior and existing "communist" nation-states are not considered as having broken free from the magnetic force of the capitalist world-system.

A minisystem is a small, self-contained group that has an internal division of labor (often by gender or age), but a homogeneous culture, faith, or customary belief system. Minisystems are often the topic of the academic discipline of anthropology, and world-systems writers tend to believe these groupings exist more in the imagination of Western observers than in actual historical reality. The presence of this idyllic grouping is like many economists' fantasy of a world that reciprocally exchanged goods before the use of money as a medium of equivalence. Minisystems have received little attention within world-systems, despite some archaeological studies that use a world-systems approach.[10] Consequently, there has been little consideration of how a world-empire form emerges. Hence, the minisystem to world-empire transition operates something in the same way as assumed tales of primordial human declension, as with the tale of Eden's paradise lost or Rousseau's mourning of human existence untarnished by social relations. If there is a literary form inherent to minisystems, it belongs to archaic myths.

Considering the difference between world-empires and a capitalist world-system, world-systems approaches tend to reinforce a great divide between the so-called pre-modern and modern societies. The world-empire form tends to be viewed as a historical precedent that, while having historical variations and regional differences, is the social form that is enacted, more or less, by all human societies until the emergence and expansion of capitalism. While the imperial form has sometimes been sought after the rise of capitalism (for example, by Napoleon or Hitler), these attempts are believed to be doomed to fail after the short-term.

A world-empire contains multiple cultures within it, but is controlled by a single political entity. The empire allows its sub-regions to continue to have their own society, religious faith, and system of local elites, so long as the political authority of the center is not challenged, and the processes of an upwards redistributive economy is unthreatened. The basic economic-social function of a world-empire is the form of accumulation through taxes or agricultural surpluses handed over to the center's authorities, or their emissaries, in return for protection against invasion and starvation. They tend to gain surplus from land-based, rather than labor-based sources.

The logistic of the world-empire involves knowability. The subordinates' redistribution to the center occurs within the bounds of convention. The center can hoard wealth, but so long as this acquisition is within the boundaries of familiarity it is felt to be part of the "natural" order of hierarchy. The crisis that world-empires often face is this loss of predictability in what is considered personal relations of domination and servitude. The ruled know whom they pay, and, in turn, they know who bears responsibility for their survival. The opening scene of *Oedipus Rex* stages this scenario. The plague in Athens has caused hunger, and the city's inhabitants come directly to Oedipus the king to demand that he resolve the crisis, as is the responsibility of the imperial ruler.

The center's acquisition does enable the existence of a small strand of artisans, merchants, administrators, and the military, but the latter two exist to maintain order and protection, while the former two provide a limited amount of luxury goods (from long-distance trade) and ornamental status markers to elites. New technologies that might disturb the balance are also suppressed, except in times of dire emergency. The risk that world-empires must guard against is if redistributed wealth gets diverted by local warlords so that it cannot be recirculated by the center, or the cost of protection goes beyond expected outlays, as is often the case when an empire faces military invasion or a catastrophe in the form of an ecological or disease emergency. The crisis of one suzerain falling is usually resolved by their replacement with another one. This substitution may involve the rise of foreign invaders or the rise of newly-empowered minor elites, but in any case the structure of the world-empire remains fundamentally the same, even if its specific actors change.

One European variation of the world-empire form appears with the rise of feudalism. Feudalism, however, differs from other world-empires in its narrowing of scale as rule becomes a matter of smaller regional units, due to Europeans' inability to oversee larger tracts of land as a result of not being able to find new sources of slave labor and an arable geography that could enable larger-scale farming. With smaller and fewer resources than prior world-empires, the European feudal order fell into a century-long crisis as a result of the Black Death.[11] The loss of many peasants due to disease gave a tactical advantage to the surviving lower classes who demanded better conditions of servitude. With too few laboring plebeians that could create wealth, the various lords began to fight each other for control in long struggles (the Fronde, the War of the Roses, etc.) in ways that often left all the antagonists impoverished. A crisis of seigniors and the State was then joined by a challenge to the authority of the Roman Catholic Church, now felt to have become too entangled within and supportive of aristocratic rule. For Wallerstein, the *coup de grâce* was the collapse of the Mongol Empire due to the Black Death. As the Mongol empire collapsed, Europe became cut off from the Silk Road and other links to China. Without these corridors, a weakened Europe had no avenue for a replacement empire to come to the rescue. Consequently, a spectrum of minor nobility and aspirational merchants began to develop a new system, one without historical precedent: a capitalist world-system.

The global definition of and distinction between world-empires and the capitalist world-system roughly from the sixteenth century has two initial implications for literary studies. The comparative outlook suggests that all writing anywhere in the globe similarly addresses the same social conditions of world-empires. If the epic is a form that consecrates a new imperial order, then Virgil's or Homer's are not civilizationally different from or superior to those in contemporaneous China or Africa. Second, the break after feudalism consequently rejects the idea of a (national) unique literary tradition, especially if it rests on philological particularities. The study of the Gawain poet's supposed linguistic inferiority to Chaucer has interest as a means of gauging the relative cultural responses to the feudal order's disassembly, but from a world-systems perspective, they both belong to a different object of knowledge than writing produced after the onset of the capitalist world-system. In this way, there is little need to believe in the "development" of English literature from proclaimed roots in Middle (or Old) English or for students to be taught these writings as chronologically necessary for acquisition of the subject. Because the language differences relate to the break from a globe of world-empires to a capitalist world-system, the study of Old and Middle English has little direct influence on the cultural formations of a post-world-empire world.

The modern world-system (modern in the sense of existing from the sixteenth century) emerged with the following defining features:

> a single axial division of labor existed within its boundaries, with a polar-ization between core-like and peripheral economic activities; the principal political structures, the states, were linked together within, and constrained by, an interstate system whose boundaries matched those of the axial

division of labor; those who pursued the ceaseless accumulation of capital prevailed in the middle run over those who did not.[12]

Unlike the world-empire's combination of multiple cultures within a single political order, a capitalist world-system combines multiple cultures within a multiple inter-state system of sovereign rulers. The dream of resurrecting a lost empire is replaced by a system that internalizes conflict in order to extend its exploitation of laborers. This inter-state system replaces the imperial center with a core, which is not to be understand as a single *center*, but as a group of states that compete against one another for advantage, while collaborating with one another in the sense of granting recognition of rival states' right to police their borders and subjects (both citizens and denizens), and control commodity exchange through internal taxes and external tariffs.

A world-system's peripheries' populations are more numerous than those of the core, and their trade is highly directed to what is often their former colonial ruler. Another distinction between the two rests in the nature of their long-distance commodity trade. World-empires tend to use long-distance trade for rare or luxury goods (preciosities) for the spectacular and sumptuary consumption by elites. The capitalist world-system tends increasingly to commodify everything within a price-setting marketplace and vastly increases the scale, mass, and speed of international trade, but these are usually for mass-market food staples and other primary (unfinished) secondary goods. In this way, the unequal exchange between the core and the peripheries involves a geographical division between regions of "highly capitalized, higher-wage, higher-profit activities" in the core and "less capitalized, lower-wage, lower profit activities" in the periphery.[13]

In addition to the core and the periphery, world-systems thought has added the category of the semiperiphery. Semiperipheries have been considered nation-states that combine core-like and periphery-like production processes, but do not have their own unique kind of production processes. Often described as intermediary nodes in the circulation of goods across long-distance trade, the semiperipheries' main function, for Wallerstein, is to act as a political buffer zone. Rather than the core nations directly controlling the peripheries, they, in essence, subcontract the policing of the peripheries to the semiperipheries. Additionally, in times of profitability crisis, core nations often relocate previously higher-waged industries to the lower-waged ones in the semiperiphery. Some semiperipheries can use these industries to later gain entry into the core. For instance, the

People's Republic of China, as the receptacle for the production of high-tech goods for Western consumers made out of raw materials from the periphery, is an example of a rising semiperiphery.

As places that calibrate the tensions of the world-system, the semiperipheries are recognized as the regions that are often most likely to have new political and cultural formations in response to historical transformations. The structural addition of the semiperiphery is not simply a new element, but it exemplifies how world-systems approaches make the traditional binary oppositions of Marxist political economy into one that is more varied. The classical Marxist claim that capitalist activity tends to massifying and binarizing opposition is balanced against the presence of a more multifactorial system.

A similar allowance for multiplicity comes as Wallerstein defines capitalism as the search for endless accumulation, rather than the onset of waged labor. Here world-systems introduces the concept of the semiproletarian household, often found in larger numbers in the semiperipheries. Capitalism seeks always to lower wage costs for making a commodity, and for this reason it seeks to pay laborers as little as possible for their life maintenance. In this sense, a highly proletarianized working force is not the most desired situation because this requires more wages to be paid. Instead, capitalism seeks to employ workers within semiproletarianized households, where some members' work is unwaged, but, nonetheless, helps ensure the waged worker's survival. If a household's members' unwaged work goes to meet the survival needs of a laborer, a capitalist can then pay laborers less money than they would otherwise need. Since the provision of household support (sometimes called social reproduction, as it involves domestic maintenance, food preparation, and child rearing) is usually highly gendered (and racialized), Wilma A. Dunaway describes this phenomenon as the pairing of proletarianization and "housewifization."[14] Here world-systems link the capitalist world-system's macro-economic cartography to micro-economic patterns of socialization and identity formation.

One way the geography of these linkages can be traced is by following the trajectory of specific commodity chains, where a commodity can be seen as "the outcome of a long series of production processes" that are "typically geographically extensive and contain many kinds of production units within their multiple modes of remunerating labor."[15] While Korzeniewicz, Gereffi, and Korzeniewicz consider a commodity chain as "competition embedded in time and space," it can also be better considered as *exploitation and seizure* embedded in time and space.[16]

World-Systems for Literary Studies

The notion of a capitalist world-system of inequality created by the search for endless accumulation that can be traced through the transit of a commodity that contains within it varieties of waged and unwaged labor, proletarianized and housewifized production, presents some initial opportunities for literary studies. Given that the dominant features of literary transmission in the modern period exist through the separation of the authorial producer from an unknown consumer, wherein a price-setting marketplace mediates the links between them, a world-systems commodity chain analysis can register the role and fate of narrative forms and contents as they move through the interchanges between the core, semiperipheries, and peripheries.

Such a move was first begun in literary studies by Susan Willis's 1979 discussion of economic dependency in William Faulkner's short fiction.[17] In 1992, Fredric Jameson then invoked the perspective as a way to consider cinema in *The Geopolitical Aesthetic: Cinema and Space in the World System.*[18] But the first persistent use was by Franco Moretti, who began incorporating world-systems frameworks into his discussion of literary markets, cultural geographies, consumer cycles, and literary forms. Indeed, one chapter of his *Atlas of the European Novel, 1800–1900* (1997) first appeared in Wallerstein's *Review.*[19] The reliance on world-systems became explicit in Moretti's "Conjectures on World Literature" (originally published in 2000), where he proposed an "initial hypothesis from the world-systems school of economic history, for which international capitalism is a system that is simultaneously *one*, and *unequal*; with a core, and a periphery (and a semi-periphery) that are bound together in a relationship of growing inequality."[20] Moretti's notion that literary consecration and popularity could be indexed by the shape of the capitalist world-system confronted ideas that literature should be considered solely within insulated nationalist containers. Pascale Casanova took the concept of competition within cores and peripheries as a way to understand literary canonization in the 1999 study (translated 2004) *The World Republic of Letters.*[21] Both Moretti and Casanova challenge the notion that aesthetic value can be determined transcendentally or that texts become "world literature" through the act of translation alone.

Yet neither Moretti nor Casanova takes up seriously the world-systems knowledge movement's focus on labor conditions and modes of production. In this light, the most dedicated use and exploration of world-systems for literary and cultural studies has been with the "Warwick School," a loosely-affiliated group of scholars within the UK's Four Nations and the Republic of Ireland, many of whom have had some institutional connection to the University of Warwick. The "Warwick School" uses revisions of classical Marxism within a world-systems outlook in order to supersede the division between Eurocentric and "postcolonial" criticism.

One formation of these scholars, publishing as the Warwick Research Collective (WReC), implemented Trotsky's arguments about the role of combined and uneven development to argue that "world literature" is "the *literature of the world-system* – of the modern capitalist world-system."[22] By invoking Jameson's argument that there are not alternative modernities, but one, WReC sees the experience of capitalism's changes in the world-system as being registered by and through particular narrative forms. Similarly, this school has used world-systems to consider the rise of popular religion, gothic and weird fiction, and the relations of the literary within neoliberalism.[23]

An additional focus of figures within the Warwick School, has been on energy resource commodity chains and their role in writing. Drawing on the world-systems ecohistory of Jason W. Moore, studies that have used world-systems to produce work within the environmental humanities include work by figures such as Sharae Deckard, Michael Niblett, Kerstin Oloff, Treasa de Loughry, Graeme Macdonald, and Sorcha Gunne. Matthew Eatough has reviewed some of these initial approaches for literary studies.[24] Andrew Milner also used world-systems geographies as a means to understand science fiction's alternative lifeworlds, and Ruth Jennison has done likewise for modern American poetry.[25]

Beyond world-systems' conception of space, its discussion of time also presents a new approach to literary studies. World-systems' rejection of developmentalism has also led it to downplay a linear history that uses a sequential periodization of ensuing phases leading towards the present. World-systems looks instead to different kinds of periodic recurrences within capitalism, such as the cyclical rhythms of 40–60 years (often called Kondratieff waves) and secular trends of about 150–200 years. The cyclical rhythm involves a sinusoidal, equally expanding and contracting, economic phase that results in "regular slow-moving but significant geographical shifts in the loci of accumulation and power, without however changing the fundamental relations of inequality within the system."[26]

These rhythms are a result of the contradictions created within capitalism by its drive for accumulation. The cycles are named after Soviet economist Nikolai Kondratieff (1892–1938). Kondratieff asked the question, why had capitalism been able to survive past what had been thought of as its terminal crises? After all, Marx predicted that the economic crash of the 1870s was the starting bell of capitalism's end. And yet, as Lenin, Luxemburg, and Hobson noted, capitalism managed to avoid that demise through the rise of imperialism and new financial mechanisms. Kondratieff, writing in the 1920s, also became interested in how capitalism had been able to contain the spread of Bolshevik revolutions and continue forwards. His explanation that capitalism lived on the systolic-diastolic of rhythms of profitability that used crisis to thrive was not one that would be tolerable to Stalin's endorsement of the inevitability of global communist revolution. Whatever the factors that create a K-wave (military expenditures, epidemics, ecological catastrophes, or crises of profitability), world-systems approaches returned to Kondratieff's work as a basic feature of understanding capitalist-created time patterns.

The meaning of these spirals of time for literary studies is that the rise and fall of cultural productions at one moment in a K-wave or secular trend can be compared against an analogous point of another. This study of comparative periodicity, rather than lateral periodization, not only counters the study of literature as formed by a sequential tradition (or "anxiety of influence") or linear development, but it also counters the notion of translation as existing only as result of a core nation's power. For instance, when Gramsci wondered why the Italian working class in the twentieth century preferred to read novelists of nineteenth-century France rather than contemporary Italian fiction or poetry, he invoked a claim of periodicity. He felt that the Italian working class was experiencing the social conditions that French writers had addressed earlier, while contemporary Italian writing was preoccupied by avant-garde concerns that were dictated by internationalist modernisms. The Italian working class was not backward in the sense of being anti-modern, but it sought expressions that spoke to its feelings and experiences.

Beyond the constellation shifts of a cyclical rhythm, there are longer secular trends. These trends are the result of successive K-waves, where every effort to go beyond a contractive period creates a workable compromise. But at a certain point these compromises add up to become so unworkable that a larger reorganization must occur. Wallerstein argues that there have been two complete secular trends within capitalism, one ranging from the sixteenth century until the French Revolution, and another lasting until "1968," the years of social discontent. Now, we are either in the first moments of another secular trend, or, perhaps as Wallerstein suggested, the actual end of the capitalist world-system entirely.

The study of secular trends has an even more fundamental challenge to literary studies. As Wallerstein argues, the French Revolution had two main long-lasting effects in the new second secular trend of the capitalist world-system. First, it made the notion of change normal. Transformation was no longer an aberration or something to be avoided. The world-empire form depended on the promise of permanence in structure, even if certain players rose and fell. Capitalism's first secular trend tried still to hold onto these ideals even while developing a system based on capitalist transformation. Well into the eighteenth century, economic thinkers insisted on the possibility of systemic equilibrium and a harmonic whole. From the Physiocrats, who still looked backwards to land-based systems, to Adam Smith, with his theory of mutually-satisfying exchange, the proposition remained that while corrupting influences might derange economic trade, these degenerating aspects could be identified and removed to allow the marketplace to function "naturally" in an amicable fashion. Thomas Malthus's significance for economic history is not simply for the argument about what is known as "Malthusian pressures," the tendency for a rising population to exceed the food and other resources that it needs to survive. Regardless of the truth of that claim, Malthus stands as the first post-Enlightenment era writer to argue that crisis is not an accident, but an intrinsic part of the modern economic system's process.

The second aspect of the French Revolution was the recognition of the inescapability of popular sovereignty – the shift from lineage societies to ones of democratic rule. From these elements of change and popular rule came the strategic responses in the forms of three ideologies: conservatism, radicalism, and centrist liberalism. The conservatives wanted to limit popular transformations as much as possible and sought to highlight preexisting institutions, such as the aristocracy, religion, or the family, as the repositories of reactionary values. Radicalism, especially after the 1840s springtime of revolutions, sought to accelerate demotic change and smash the institutions that the conservatives highlighted. Centrist liberalism sought to moderate and guide change by foregrounding individuals of talent or merit who were to manage or administer society, often having been trained in institutions of higher education. For Wallerstein, bourgeois centrist liberalism became so dominant throughout the nineteenth century that it forced even conservatives and radicals to adapt to and often covertly adopt centrist liberal perspectives. The second secular trend is this age of centrist liberalism.

In order for nations to be managed well, centrist liberalism proposed the idea that the university should be a research institution beyond merely functioning as a site of undergraduate quasi-aristocratic "finishing," as a cultivation of behavior. A feature of the liberal university was that knowledge was divided and given to specialist disciplines as their field of expertise. So for instance, economics was granted rights over the market, political science, the State, and so on. Similarly, literary studies was divided into ostensibly self-enclosed national literatures, as in the department of *English* or *German* or *American* literature. The legacy of these distinctions forms, after all, this collection's titled project, which is to bring together what liberal centrists forms of knowledge had rent asunder, separating commentary on the economic from the cultural.

A final feature of liberalism was its production of a series of other civil society divisions, such as the separation of public from private spheres. The division on which world-systems focuses is the rise of universalism and racism/sexism. On the one hand, liberalism's response to popular transformation was the idea of universalism, the equality of representation initially enacted through the expansion of suffrage, the right to vote. Yet these claims of equality would clash with a capitalist economics that depends on and cannot exist without the production of inequality as the primary means of creating surplus-value. In this sense universalism was only allowed in capitalism as the liberal nation-state created status (or identity) distinctions that established forms of social death or limits to waged proletarian existence. The chief forms of exclusion were racism and sexism (although other divisions might include homophobia, disability, and criminality).

For literary studies, several implications follow from these premises. First, the second secular trend gave rise to cultural objects and communications that helped constitute and are indicative of liberalism. For example, the "novel" was one out of many existing forms of long-form fiction, but it came to overly dominate others as it housed and epitomized liberal assumptions. Yet if it functioned as a commodity chained to the deployment of racism and sexism, like all liberal-era commodities, then every literary study needs to acknowledge its texts (and training in techniques of reading) as structurally shaped by anti-popular forms of exploitation and prejudice. Today, we hear calls to decolonize the curriculum, and world-systems critiques belong to this trend.

Second, if the category of "literature" and the academic discipline of literary studies were products of the liberal-era secular trend, then neither functions adequately in a post-liberal one. Although Wallerstein rarely used the term, another way of describing this post-'68 phase is *neoliberalism*, given his belief that the prior one was dominated by centrist liberalism. The world-systems knowledge movement understands that the loss of liberal culture is not an unfortunate matter of social network incivility, but a foreseeable effect of the end of a secular trend. Similarly, the university and its divisions of knowledge into separate disciplines are also breaking down because the university, too, as we know it is a product of a now near-finished secular trend.

Today, the literary and cultural configurations of this new third secular trend are far from clear, but, in any case, the world-systems knowledge movement provides useful tools for thinking about its possibility. Yet even if literary and cultural studies informed by the world-systems knowledge movement is in its first steps, current transformations in the capitalist world-system suggests that its most promising work is still to come.

Notes

1 This discussion of Wallerstein draws on *The Modern World-System I: Capitalist Agriculture and the Origins of the European World-Economy in the Sixteenth Century* (New York: Academic Press, 1974); *The Modern World-System II: Mercantilism and the Consolidation of the European World-Economy, 1600–1750* (New York: Academic Press, 1980); *The Modern World-System III: The Second Era of Great Expansion of the Capitalist World-Economy, 1730s–1840s* (New York: Academic Press, 1989); *The Modern World-System IV: Centrist Liberalism Triumphant, 1789–1914* (Berkeley: University of California Press, 2011); *The Capitalist World-Economy* (Cambridge: Cambridge University Press, 1979); *Historical Capitalism* (London: Verso, 1983); *The Politics of the World-Economy: The States, the Movements, and the Civilizations* (Cambridge: Cambridge University Press, 1984); *Geopolitics and Geoculture: Essays on the Changing World-System* (Cambridge: Cambridge University Press, 1991); *After Liberalism* (New York: The New Press, 1995); and Immanuel Wallerstein and Terence K. Hopkins, *World-Systems Analysis: Theory and Methodology* (Beverly Hills: Sage, 1982).
2 Immanuel Wallerstein, "World-Systems Analysis as a Knowledge Movement," in *The Routledge Handbook of World-Systems Analysis*, edited by Christopher Chase-Dunn and Salvatore Babones (London: Routledge, 2012), 515–521; 515.
3 Wilma A. Dunaway, "The Double Register of History: Situating the Forgotten Woman and Her Household in Capitalist Commodity Chains," *Journal of World-Systems Research* 7 (2001), 2–29; Walter L. Goldfrank, "Paradigm Regained? The Rules of Wallerstein's World-System Method," *Journal of World-Systems Research*, 6 (2000), 150–195; Wallerstein and Hopkins, *World-Systems Analysis*; Christopher Chase-Dunn, *Global Formation: Structures of the World-Economy* (London: Basil Blackwell, 1989);

and Thomas R. Shannon, *An Introduction to the World-System Perspective* (Boulder, CO: Westview Press, 1992).

4 Wallerstein, *Modern World-System IV*, 1.

5 Raûl Prebisch, *The Economic Development of Latin America and Its Principal Problems* (New York: United Nations, 1950); Andre Gunder Frank, *Capitalism and Underdevelopment in Latin America: Historical Studies of Chile and Brazil* (New York: Monthly Review Press, 1969).

6 Walter L. Goldfrank, "The Long Road," *Social Problems* 28 (1981), 513–514.

7 Goldfrank, "Paradigm Regained," 163.

8 Luca Meldolesi, Nicolette Stame, and Immanuel Wallerstein, "Immanuel Wallerstein's Thousand Marxisms," *Jacobin*, September 11, 2019, www .jacobinmag.com/2019/09/immanuel-wallerstein-marxism-world-systems-theory-capitalism; Marcello Musto and Immanuel Wallerstein, "Read Karl Marx! A Conversation with Immanuel Wallerstein," *Marx 200*, April 10, 2018, https://marx200.org/en/blog/read-karl-marx-conversation-immanuel-wallerstein.

9 Ernest Mandel, "Introduction," in Karl Marx, *Capital: A Critique of Political Economy* (1867; New York: Vintage, 1977), 11–86.

10 Thomas D. Hall and Christopher Chase-Dunn, "The World-Systems Perspective and Archaeology: Forward into the Past," *Journal of Archaeological Research* 1.2 (1993), 121–143.

11 Immanuel Wallerstein, "The West, Capitalism, and the Modern World-System," in *China and Historical Capitalism: Genealogies of Sinological Knowledge*, edited by Timothy Brook and Gregory Blue (Cambridge: Cambridge University Press, 1999), 10–56.

12 Wallerstein, *After Liberalism*, 128.

13 Immanuel Wallerstein, *Labor in the World Social Structure* (Beverley Hills: Sage, 1983), 17.

14 Wilma A. Dunaway, "The Semiproletarian Household over the *Long Dureé* of the Modern World-System," in *The Longue Durée of the Modern World-System*, edited by Richard Lee (Albany, NY: State University of New York Press, 2012), 97–136.

15 Immanuel Wallerstein and Terence K. Hopkins, "Commodity Chains in the World-Economy Prior to 1800," *Review* 10 (1986), 157–170.

16 Miguel Korzeniewicz, Gary Gereffi, and Roberto P. Korzeniewicz, "Introduction: Global Commodity Chains," in *Commodity Chains and Global Capitalism*, edited by Miguel Korzeniewicz and Gary Gereffi (Westport, CT: Greenwood Press, 1994), 4.

17 Susan Willis, "Aesthetics of the Rural Slum: Contradictions and Dependency in 'The Bear,'" *Social Text* 2 (1979), 82–103.

18 Fredric Jameson, *The Geopolitical Aesthetic: Cinema and Space in the World System* (London: John Wiley & Son, 1992).

19 Franco Moretti, *Atlas of the European Novel, 1800–1900* (1997; London: Verso, 1998).

20 Franco Moretti, "Conjectures on World Literature," *Distant Reading* (London: Verso, 2013), 43–62; 46; emphases in original. See also Franco

Moretti, *Graphs, Maps, Trees: Abstract Models for Literary History* (London: Verso, 2005).

21 Pascale Casanova, *The World Republic of Letters*, translated by M. B. DeBevoise (Cambridge, MA: Harvard University Press, 2004).

22 WReC (Warwick Research Collective), *Combined and Uneven Development: Towards a New Theory of World-Literature* (Liverpool: Liverpool University Press, 2015), 8.

23 Stephen Shapiro and Philip Barnard, *Pentecostal Modernism: Lovecraft, Los Angeles, and World-Systems Culture* (London: Bloomsbury, 2017); Stephen Shapiro, "The Cultural Fix: Capital, Genre, and the Times of American Studies," in *The Fictions of American Capitalism: Working Fictions and the Economic Novel*, edited by Vincent Dussol and Jacques-Henri Coste (London: Palgrave, 2020), 89–108; Sharae Deckard and Stephen Shapiro, "World-Culture and the Neoliberal World-System: An Introduction," in *World Literature, Neoliberalism, and the Culture of Discontent*, edited by Sharae Deckard and Stephen Shapiro (London: Palgrave Macmillan, 2019), 1–48.

24 Jason W. Moore, *Capitalism in the Web of Life: Ecology and the Accumulation of Capital* (London: Verso, 2015); Matthew Eatough, "The Literary History of World-Systems, I: Marxist Lineages," *Literature Compass* 12.11 (2015), 591–602; Matthew Eatough, "The Literary History of World-Systems, II: World Literature and Deep Time," *Literature Compass* 12.11 (2015), 603–614.

25 Andrew Milner, *Again, Dangerous Visions: Essays in Cultural Materialism* (Leiden: Brill, 2018); Ruth Jennison, *The Zukofsky Era: Modernity, Margins, and the American Avant-Garde* (Baltimore: Johns Hopkins University Press, 2012).

26 Immanuel Wallerstein, "The Rise of East Asia, or the World-System in the Twenty-First Century," in *The End of the World as We Know It: Social Science for the Twenty-First Century*, edited by Immanuel Wallerstein (Minneapolis: University of Minnesota Press, 1999), 34–48; 35.

CHAPTER 13

Crisis, Labor, and the Contemporary

Liam Connell

When the narrator of Alice Furse's novel, *Everybody Knows This is Nowhere* (2014), discovers that her coworker, "Young Nathan," is "working on a novel" about "working in an office," she presses him on the plot. "I'm trying to decide between two options," he explains, "either there'll be an apocalypse . . . Or nothing at all."[1] Nathan's humorous dilemma is useful for thinking about the difficulties of representing the idea of work in fiction and about the approaches that contemporary novels have adopted in trying to address them. To a degree, this is a problem solely of literary representation; work is often repetitive and boring and, as David Foster Wallace demonstrated in *The Pale King* (2011), the accurate depiction of workaday activities requires lengthy passages of undifferentiated prose.[2] Consequently, novelists trying to write about the workplace are likely pushed to the excessive (an apocalypse) or to the minimalist (utilizing slight plot lines lacking incident). Furse's own novel tends towards the latter. Although it divides evenly between depictions of work and home, the plot-incidents largely concern home life rather than the narrator's office work. The main arc of the plot is a domestic story about the narrator's relationship with her live-in boyfriend set against the largely undifferentiated pattern of office life. Coworkers come and go, but this has little impact on the nature of her work, which remains mostly unaltered.

Furse is not the only novelist whose depictions of work tend toward the mundane. In Halle Butler's *The New Me* (2019) and Heike Geissler's *Seasonal Associate* (2014), nothing much happens at all. In *The New Me*, Millie works as a receptionist at a design firm, hoping to convert a temporary contract into the permanent position that her employment agency has promised her. However, the senior receptionist finds something "a little off-putting about" Millie and engineers to terminate her contract. Although her dismissal appears to trigger a bout of depression, the potential for crisis is unfulfilled and the novel concludes with an oddly discordant epilogue in which Millie is now a long-term employee, "a cautionary thing, a reminder" to a new generation of temps "not to stay in the same job for too long."[3] *Seasonal Associate* follows broadly the same narrative arc, describing a freelance writer whose precarious finances require her to take a temporary Christmas job at an Amazon processing center. The prospect of permanent work runs through Geissler's novel but, in this case, it appears as a threat rather than a lure and one that eventually becomes unbearable, prompting the narrator to decide, "it's enough," and to leave her job two weeks before her contract expires.[4]

By contrast, other novels about work veer toward the spectacular. Ling Ma's *Severance* (2018) is set during a global pandemic and deploys the zombie-contagion genre to recount the story of Candace, who works to keep an office running while her colleagues succumb to a deadly disease. The victims of Sheng fever lose the capacity for high-level thought but appear able to continue "mimicking old routines and gestures" that are locked into their "lizard brain": the fevered can "operate the mouse of a dead PC," but cannot talk or interact with others.[5] The novel includes several instances where fevered victims carry on working despite this lack of cognition. In a prominent example, Candace discovers that Juicy Couture's flagship store in New York appears unaffected by the decay that has blighted the mostly-abandoned city. A zombie shopworker is still inside and maintains this illusion by "folding and refolding pastel polo shirts ... clearly good at her job, even in her fevered condition."[6] Ma's presentation of the zombie at work utilizes a common metaphor for contemporary labor.[7] However, her novel stands out partly because it combines both a literal and a metaphoric use of the zombie figure. *Severance* extends a series of comparisons between the zombie and the uninfected through a presentation of repetition. Among the parallels with the fevered are Candace's dementing mother, shoppers that buy the uniform products of consumer capitalism, and the everyday tasks of work. When, for instance, a colleague of Candace's becomes fevered, he is found "sequestered in his office ... sitting at his computer" having spent the weekend sending out emails to suppliers in Hong Kong.[8] Significantly, the description of his fevered working differs little from the descriptions of Candace's occupation elsewhere in the novel.

Hilary Leichter's *Temporary* (2020) deploys magical-realist techniques to tell the story of a serial temp whose CV includes spells as a ghost, pirate, barnacle, and witch's assistant. The use of these fantastical placements does not detract from a portrayal of the mundanity of the contracts. Her work as a ghost involves a strict schedule of door opening, which she must complete "every forty minutes, every day, all day long." The regime of work imprints itself onto her whole being so that she learns to complete every task in forty minutes, stretching out shorter tasks "for the sake of clarity and precision." When she makes friends with the temporary ghost of the neighboring house, the need to keep dashing back inside to complete her routine offsets the pleasure of friendship.[9] Sitting alongside the narrator's story is a mythical fable of "the first temp," employed by the gods to carry out work that they have tired of doing. This story emerges gradually across the novel, punctuating the main narrative as a kind of explanatory key that makes sense of the narrator's condition of perpetual temporariness. Superficially, Leichter's novel represents temporary work as cover for permanent workers who are temporarily on leave. Framed this way, the novel becomes a quest narrative in pursuit of "the permanence" or "steadiness." Each placement earns the narrator progress toward this goal. However, the mythical story of the first temp suggests that the condition of temporariness is an enduring one. Describing how the first temp gives birth to a species of temporaries in response to the deficiencies of a universe built around "a fallacy of permanence," Leichter suggests that the temps evolve to fill the gaps in the world of work. This fable functions as a kind of allegory for the nature of contemporary work. It stands simultaneously as a fanciful picture of Darwinian evolution and as a metaphor for the worker's need to develop new skills to adapt to frequently changing employment. "In this way," she suggests, "the temporaries had a sort of elastic permanence of their own."[10]

If Nathan's dilemma highlights a problem of literary representation this is, unsurprisingly, reflected by a relatively sparse field of critical studies on literature and work. In the last decade, several books on literary economics have afforded attention to the subject of work. In *Literature and the Creative Economy* (2014), Sarah Brouillette explores the entangling of creative work with neoliberal notions of the cultural worker as a model of flexible self-management. Brouillette offers insightful analysis of the writer as a form of creative worker, whose labor produces marketable products, but also a class-positionality that purports to place the author outside the normal patterns of labor and capital. In her readings of novels, Brouillette focuses on how characters' labor mirrors that of writers. For instance, reading Ian McEwan's *Saturday* (2005), she sees the protagonist as a figure of entitled elitism and interprets the culminating act of surgical compassion toward the antagonist, Baxter, as a display of "professional competence," allowing Henry Perowne to inhabit "the moment of his labor [and] transcend the local and the particular" with all of its attendant anxieties.[11] Although Brouillette offers some persuasive fictional readings, her focus is more often on authors as exemplars of the creative worker, and on the literary market as a space where these ideas about creative work get played out. My own book, *Precarious Labour and the Contemporary Novel* (2017), places more focus on literary depictions of labor and suggests that the fictional representation of office work crystallizes social anxieties about the declining link between work and security. For instance, looking at Jenny Turner's *The Brainstorm* (2007), I reflect how the novel narrates the production of competitive work economies through its use of setting and plot. The novel's depiction of a contemporary geography of capital, actualized in the building of new office blocks and in the worker's daily commute, allows it to demonstrate how the organization of work contributes to the stratification of different kinds of workers.[12]

Other recent studies have tended to approach the topic of work more indirectly, often taking other economic categories as their primary focus. Ralph Clare's *Fictions Inc.* (2014), for instance, proposes a twentieth-century struggle between capital and organized labor to frame an analysis of fictional US Corporations. Clare combines an armory of Marxist terminology, such as alienation or free labor, with an historicist approach that reads fiction against concurrent changes to the labor market. For instance, he reads Thomas Pynchon's fiction against the mid-century growth of white-collar employment and reads Joshua Ferris's *Then We Came to the End* (2007) and Ed Park's *Personal Days* (2008) as illustrations of a twenty-first-century cooption of workers into the corporate identity.[13] Similarly, in *The Microeconomic Mode* (2018), Jane Elliott treats the topic of labor obliquely; Elliot argues that the modelling of choice within recent fiction sheds light on the nature of contemporary work but rarely focuses on fiction that depicts labor itself. For instance, she reads Gillian Flynn's *Gone Girl* (2012) as a narrative about the "transition from industrial to immaterial labor" but does this by focusing on the novel's narrative of gamification – whereby the character's life and death decisions take on the form of a competitive puzzle that needs to be won or lost.[14] The novel's depiction of redundancy and career-transition is a minor element used only to establish the narrative.

It is not only literary studies that have struggled with the representation of work as an object of analysis. As Kathi Weeks notes, political theory has been relatively silent on the question of work in comparison with the attention it affords to the "meaningfulness of commodities."[15] In Weeks's view, this analytic preference plays out Karl Marx's account of commodity fetishism, in which the processes of exchange obscure the labor required to produce commodities. For Marx, labor is only visible as the values of commodities, which are in reality "the material expressions of the human labor spent in their production." Although, for Marx, work is everything, "we are not aware of this"; in his account, labor appears as *nothing* because it is only visible in the form of the commodity.[16] Marx's emphasis on the calculable product of labor echoes the preoccupation with value in classical economics, which led to a narrow definition of work. One of Adam Smith's starting propositions, for instance, was that we could measure the wealth of the nation as the proportion of people employed in useful labor. Similarly, throughout *The Wealth of Nations* (1776), Smith frames labor as a commodity, as something with calculable value that people can purchase.[17] Contemporary economists tend to share this narrow definition of work, often treating labor only as a "factor of production" or as "work time and work effort that people devote to producing goods and services."[18] Even the branch of labor economics tends to study the supply and distribution of productive labor rather than interrogate the meanings of work as a category.[19]

Defining work only through its relation to a productive economy presents a problem for representation. As sociologists and political theorists have pointed out, there are numerous examples where changes to the labor market transform voluntary or social activities into forms of paid work.[20] These shifting boundaries create persistent problems for economics because the same work activity can be both an economic activity and noneconomic domestic work.[21] One of the challenges novelists face when trying to depict work is that they need to represent the social relations that define work as labor just as much as the tasks of work undertaken. Furse hints at this problem when Nathan claims to be "working on a novel" and "working in an office." These two occupations might closely resemble one another as tasks: Nathan likely writes his novel on a computer in much the same way that he enters data at the office. However, economically these two occupations are quite different. Nathan's office job is waged-labor where he makes commodities that profit his employer. When writing, he is unpaid and, though his unfinished novel may represent a future commodity, writing would not meet a narrow economic definition of work that depends upon the production of calculable value. From the opposite direction, the narrator recalls her time working for McDonald's when, during slack periods, workers were made to keep busy carrying out unnecessary tasks. She comments that she was initially "irked" at being unable to "tell the difference between a real and an imaginary task" but soon "stopped caring" because she "liked feeling useful."[22] Economically, the real and the imaginary task are identical because they involve the exact same employer-employee relation: the tasks are work because the worker's time is directed and remunerated. In her desire to appear "useful," Furse's narrator accepts that her employer's control over her actions is paramount and subscribes to a narrow economic definition of work that depends upon her productive utility.

The question of what constitutes work has also been central to feminist economics, which has highlighted the forms of domestic work that take place without pay. The tendency to overlook this kind of work is apparent in both classical and Marxist economics. For instance, Smith appears to regard the question of social reproduction as chiefly a question of pricing and assumes that a gendered division of labor will bear upon such calculations. In his discussion of wages, he considers the cost of bringing up a family as an additional factor in the "sufficient" wage but draws a clear distinction between the wage for men and the wage for "the wife" who, "because of her necessary attendance on the children," will only "provide for herself."[23] In this formulation, the work of caring removes women from the realm of economic calculation and becomes invisible as a form of labor.[24] Although Marx was well aware that the social reproduction of the working class was a crucial economic factor in capitalism, his writing suggests that the organization of this work was left to workers to resolve rather than being a key element in the systematic organization of capitalist economics.[25]

According to Weeks, feminist economics developed two approaches to address the tendency to assign this unpaid work to women. First, feminists conceded the devaluing of unpaid work and tried to improve women's access to paid employment: second, feminists tried "to revalue unwaged forms of household-based labor ... making this socially necessary labor visible, valued, and equitably distributed."[26] As Weeks notes, both approaches run the risk of reencoding the conventional equivalence of work with productive value. Nevertheless, varieties of feminist economics that grew out of the Italian Operaist movement were able to grasp this problem by combining the call for domestic wages with the refusal of work as a strategy for moving beyond work as the organizing principle of capitalist economies. Silvia Federici, writing in the mid-1970s, argued that the purpose of the wage is to hide "all the unpaid work that goes into profit."[27] Consequently, "the demand for a wage makes our [unpaid] work visible, which is the most indispensable condition to begin to struggle against it."[28] It is useful to note Federici's emphasis on making work visible as work, especially for thinking about the novel. The fictional depiction of domestic work as a kind of labor may contribute to Federici's strategy toward the refusal of work. To that end, it is significant that novels by women often grapple with how to represent domestic work and, as more women have entered the workplace, this fiction has often depicted the continuing difficulty that women face in juggling paid and unpaid labor.

Contemporary novels about work frequently depict women taking on the tasks of cleaning and caring alongside their paid employment. Again, Furse's novel illustrates this tendency when the domestic story that makes up the main narrative arc troubles an easy distinction between the domestic and the work life. The narrator is constantly irritated by the work she is required to do to maintain the home – from putting away shopping and cooking, to cleaning away condensation on the widows or mold off the walls – while her boyfriend reads magazines or plays video games. This inequality fuels their arguments that culminate in their breakup, but it is also entangled with the narrator's experience of and feelings about her paid work. Her complaints about her boyfriend's indolence are also complaints about his contentment with their present situation, set against her own sense of being trapped in a job she hates. These feelings are partly captured by the way the novel narrates her work life, which places a strong emphasis on the undifferentiated character of her routines. Like other novelists, Furse's description of the working day pays considerable attention to the journey to and from the office. This is also a notable feature of *Severance*, where the narrator demonstrates the disconnect between work and her emotional life with the repeated incantation, "I got up. I went to work in the morning."[29] Furse's novel differs from this in the quantity of description that it gives of different aspects of the commute, supplying repetitive details about the regular passengers on each train journey, about where the narrator stands on the platform, and daily weather reports. Similarly, there is a conspicuous use of the word "usual," which the narrator frequently applies to the performance of her work duties, and to social aspects of the working day such as where she chooses to take her lunchbreak. Unlike in *Severance*, where Candace uses the mundane routine of work to inoculate herself from her grief over her parents' deaths, an unplanned pregnancy, or the sudden breakup with her boyfriend, Furse's narrator blurs her personal and her work life by borrowing the language of the office to describe the intimate conflicts with her boyfriend. For instance, in the midst of a familiar argument about the bathroom, she describes the exchange as "a recycled conversation. A photocopy of a photocopy," suggesting that office and home life are alike, comprising acts of routine duplication.[30]

The similarity of home and office life are further emphasized by the gendered character of work in the office. Her employer has different expectations of male and female workers: female staff share the work of answering the phone, and the narrator's boss expects women to carry out "trivial tasks" in his stead. Office conversations between female colleagues, which frequently center on the domestic, show that these gender divisions carry through to the domestic sphere. For instance, Mary (the office manager) advises the narrator to keep hold of her boyfriend, as he compares favorably with her own sons who still live at home and demand that she cook separate menus for them at every meal. Such examples draw together the story about domestic life with the story of office life. As twin spheres of work, they are fundamentally inseparable, even sharing a vocabulary to express the narrator's dissatisfaction with both. Unpaid work becomes visible when it is the explicit focus of the novel but also when it takes on the character of work by borrowing the lexical and structural vocabulary of paid employment.

In many respects, *Everyone Knows* resembles second-wave women's fiction that depicted women trapped in unsatisfying marriages who sought fulfillment through access to the labor market. While the narrator already works, the novel ends with her planning a move to London in the hope that changing her home and job will alleviate the stultification of her clerical work and suburban life. In this respect, the text is relatively conservative and appears to maintain a belief in the liberating potential of work. This is matched, aesthetically, by the broadly realist form of the text. As readers, we live in the world of the protagonist and can imagine her as an autonomous subject alive in the world. The novel presents her with problems, some work-related, but offers her the possibility of individual solutions that stem from her agency as a subject. Indeed, in keeping with a tradition of second-wave feminist writing, the plot requires her to call upon this agency – to make the decision to change – in order to achieve narrative resolution. For many critics, realism is an important genre for making legible historical forces that might otherwise evade comprehension and has been particularly significant in the twenty-first century for narrating the 2007–2008 financial crisis and its aftermath. Katy Shaw, for instance, claims that the success of the realist novel during the nineteenth century was due to its capacity to foreground "the horror of a financial crash." According to Shaw, the novel was uniquely equipped to represent financial crises through its capacity to tell "the life stories of individuals and communities" in the tides of economic fluctuations. When discussing contemporary fiction, Shaw conflates literature with realism and, consequently, opts for "crunch lit" novels, such as Sebastian Faulks' *A Week in September* (2009) or John Lanchester's *Capital* (2012), that echo

Victorian novelists such as Dickens or Trollope.[31] More subtly, Annie McClanahan points to critical work that connects the emergence of the novel to the development of credit economies, to explain the prevalence of what she calls "the credit-crisis realist novel."[32] McClanahan is critical of the idea that these novels humanize complex financial systems, but argues that their desire to situate the individual historically within the present crisis allows them to represent "kinds of social totality" that "could function both individually and collectively."[33]

In their different ways, Shaw and McClanahan echo Georg Lukács who defended realism's attempt to "represent reality as it truly is." For Lukács, moments of crisis revealed the totality of capitalism, by making "manifest the unity of processes" that otherwise appear "individually independent."[34] Following from Marx, Lukács's sense of crisis is the general crisis of over accumulation. Nevertheless, it does seem useful for thinking about the fiction that immediately followed the 2007–2008 financial crash. However, when considering the contemporary work economy it may be necessary to think of a slightly different notion of crisis. Certainly, one immediate indicator of the late 2000s recession was rising unemployment, especially in Southern European nations, which were fiscally constrained by the price of the Euro. However, since the crisis, unemployment has fallen to comparatively low rates.[35] Although the threat of unemployment remains significant, a more diffuse sense of crisis arises from the changing character of the labor market. Whereas in the immediate postwar period work was commonly associated with security, the shift toward a financia- lized economy from the mid-1970s led to increasingly casualized (flexible) and precarious patterns of labor.[36] This altered the contract between employer and employee, decreasing the benefits of employment and passing economic risk from employer to employee. Recent legal disputes over the employment status of workers in the "gig economy" clearly exemplify this pattern. These cases asked whether workers for companies such as Uber and Deliveroo were employees or self-employed and, there- fore, whether they were entitled to statutory employment rights.[37] Such disputes illustrate a wider trend in which the notion of a firm's obligation to its workers has cumulatively narrowed. For instance, the growth of so- called zero-hours contracts intensified the commoditization of work, reframing workers as contractors who supply hours of work on-demand and employers as customers who buy labor only when they need it. Under these conditions, the value of worker's labor declines and a significant crisis of contemporary work has been a crisis of remuneration in which the rewards of work cannot meet the growing cost of living. Perhaps the most emblematic illustration of this crisis has been persistently buoyant housing markets, where the costs of renting and home-ownership have risen disproportionately in relation to wages.[38]

When trying to capture this different sense of crisis, it is not clear that realism is the most effective means, and various nonrealist strategies in recent fiction seem better placed to depict a crisis of work. For instance, like Furse's *Everyone Knows*, Leichter's *Temporary* employs a single unnamed narrator who narrates her story in the first person. However, the fantasy elements of Leichter's novel seem better able to connect this individual story to the structural unevenness of the employment contract. *Temporary's* episodic structure, for instance, propels the narrator from one appointment to another but also reveals that this serial employment cannot provide the narrative of progress that Furse's conclusion imagines. Moreover, the central conceit of the temporary as a replacement links the experience of different individual workers who are effectively inter-changeable. By presenting different workers as modular counterparts, Leichter undermines the equivalence of the worker with work as a com-modity. What is more, the narrator rarely meets the permanent workers whom she notionally replaces. Instead, the novel is populated by an army of temporaries each moving from contract to contract. Indeed, even some of her employers, such as the hitman Carl, take "temporary jobs when work gets slow."[39] This device also allows Leichter to engage the debate surrounding domestic work when, in the section "Home Work," a young boy employs the narrator to work as his mother since his "real mother" has disappeared. In a superbly effective critique of the relegation of emotional labor, the boy pays the narrator to cook, clean, read bedtime stories, and discipline him, but chastises her when she spends her wages on medicine or presents because she has overstepped her duties and is not paid to care.[40]

Geissler's *Seasonal Associate* provides further evidence of the successful nonrealist narration of contemporary work. Instead of the fantastical ele-ments of *Temporary* or *Severance*, it utilizes metafictional strategies of narrative self-consciousness to mount an explicit critique of work as a form of social relations that limits the potential for aesthetic appreciation, care, or solidarity. Most prominently, the narrative voice switches between narrat-ing the events of the novel in the first and second person. Although the narrator is an "I" who appears to have already experienced the episodes described, she narrates these events as happening to "you," a proximate version of her own personae, in the present. Geissler's "I" and "you" are not identical, although "I" appears to know everything that "you" is experienc-ing, "having thought your thoughts before you."[41] This structural prolepsis, and the narrative focalization, allows "I" to meditate upon "your" experience of work and, extrapolating from there, on the nature of paid work as an economic relation. A key element of this meditation is the question of the worker's agency, the limits of which animate the narrative throughout. The narrator frequently reflects on whether she is in control of the choices she makes, and this leads her to demand that "you" prove her subjectivity through some gesture of rebellion that will demonstrate "to your employer that you're alive." Finally, she insists, "we're not leaving this book until you've taken action."[42] This insistence resembles Hannah Arendt's writing on the distinction between labor and work, in which she posits action as the entry into politics.[43] Action for Geissler also appears to be the opposite of work, although the question at the end of the novel is whether walking away from her job constitutes "action or not."[44]

The gap between the two pronouns also illustrates differing attitudes toward permanence. This is neatly captured in an episode where "you" becomes infatuated with a forklift driver at work. Describing "you's" flustered reaction to her coworker's presence, the narrator diagnoses her problem as a kind of false consciousness born of cultural standards that are external to the worker herself:

> I know you, and I know where your feelings come from: you've just watched too much TV. You'd never admit it but you think of this simple solution: You enter the forklift driver's heart, whereupon the forklift driver skilfully manoeuvres you into a permanent contract. He carries you over the actual threshold of the company. From there on in, you have a life that can be narrated in easily understandable phrases.[45]

By linking a permanent contract to the romance narrative, Geissler implies that the security of work is a kind of fantasy, and suggests that neither romance nor paid work are in the woman's interest. Geissler is clearly not advocating a retreat to unpaid work here, and her imagery, which transforms the female worker into inventory (maneuvered by the forklift driver) and then into a bride (carried across a threshold), highlights the negative force of the fantasy. The claim that permanency and marriage will render the worker's life through a simplified narrative demonstrates that both are reductive. This claim also sustains one of the novels repeated images by presenting work as a kind of performance. The narrator sees workplace transactions as theatrical but also complains that these stage plays lack quality because they are "simply ripped off from reality."[46] Notably, this speaks to the idea of agency. If work is a play, then the worker cannot be an agent because she only delivers scripted lines. To become an agent, "you" must leave work.

Geissler's suggestion that agency and work are incompatible appears to constitute something like the autonomist idea of the refusal of work. The narrative form is crucial to expressing this idea in the novel, in particular the use of pronouns. This is best illustrated by the use of the first person plural to demand action from her character. Significantly, this repeats the use of "we" when the narrator considers a form of collective action that involves an imagined act of a mass absenteeism. When contemplating this possibility, the narration unites the different pronouns in a single body of commuting workers: "I think of solidarity . . . You think: We can stop the traffic if we step onto the street."[47] It is possible to think of this vision of solidarity, like the concluding renunciation of her contract, as a validation of the refusal of work. Certainly, the strategy of the refusal of work included the kind of spontaneous disruptions that the narrator contemplates.[48] This reading is made more compelling by the fact that the novel's critique of work is couched within a wider critique of capitalism that centers upon the worker's compliance with her employer. The narrator is well aware that compliance stems from a double structure: the economic structure of the wage, which compels the worker to work in the absence of other means of support, and the intellectual dominance of work, which is the only idea "suitable for daily life." In the face of this necessity, the narrator tries to imagine the "potential" of a collective refusal, speculating that, "perhaps nothing can be made out of this crowd of people, nothing at all."[49] The idea of nothing here seems especially powerful given the inability of economics to imagine work as practice, and the word seems to be doing a number of things in Geissler's text. On the surface, the narrator seems only to bemoan the lack of solidarity and action as politics. The possibilities she imagines cannot materialize in the context of a capitalist economy that places waged labor at its center. However, it is possible to glimpse another meaning and to suggest that within this economy, waged labor is nothing. It is not simply that capitalism makes refusal impossible – its incapacity to define work renders the worker "nothing at all."

Notes

1 Alice Furse, *Everybody Knows This Is Nowhere*, Kobo ed. (Portishead: Burning Eye, 2014), "Clive."
2 David Foster Wallace, *The Pale King: An Unfinished Novel* (2011; London: Penguin, 2012). The frequently discussed §25 depicts a group of tax collectors working in silent communion by repeatedly stating that a character "turns a page."

3 Halle Butler, *The New Me* (London: Weidenfeld & Nicholson, 2019), 2–3, 15, 189.

4 Heike Geissler, *Seasonal Associate*, translated by Katy Derbyshire (2014; South Pasadena, CA: Semiotext(e), 2018), 199–203.

5 Ling Ma, *Severance*, Kobo ed. (Melbourne: Text Publishing, 2018), ch. 2.

6 Ibid., ch. 22.

7 The internet comedy *The Working Dead* (2014) depicts workers as zombies, who carry out tasks without conscious agency, www.theworkingdead.tv/ watch. The film *Dead Man Working* (2012), directed by L. E. Salas, imagines zombie workers coming back to resume their former jobs. In business literature on worker engagement, the zombie metaphor describes employees who produce no discernible value for their employer: Anna Bruce-Lockhart, "Is Your Colleague a Zombie Worker?" World Economic Forum (2017), www .weforum.org/agenda/2017/10/is-your-colleague-a-zombie-worker/; James O'Brien, "The Working Dead: How to De-Zombify Your Business," American Express OpenForum (2014), www.americanexpress.com/us/small-business/openforum/articles/the-working-dead-how-to-de-zombify-your-busi ness/.

8 Ma, *Severance*, ch. 18.

9 Hilary Leichter, *Temporary: A Novel* (Minneapolis, MN and Brooklyn, NY: Coffee House Press, 2020), 58–61.

10 Ibid., 164–166.

11 Sarah Brouillette, *Literature and the Creative Economy* (Stanford, CA: Stanford University Press, 2014).

12 Liam Connell, *Precarious Labour and the Contemporary Novel* (London: Palgrave Macmillan, 2017).

13 Ralph Clare, *Fictions Inc.: The Corporation in Postmodern Fiction, Film, and Popular Culture* (New Brunswick, NJ: Rutgers University Press, 2014).

14 Jane Elliott, *The Microeconomic Mode: Political Subjectivity in Contemporary Popular Aesthetics* (New York: Columbia University Press, 2018), 91.

15 Kathi Weeks, *The Problem with Work: Feminism, Marxism, Antiwork Politics, and Postwork Imaginaries* (Durham, NC: Duke University Press, 2011), 2.

16 Karl Marx, *Capital: A Critique of Political Economy* (1867; London: Lawrence & Wishart, 1970), 72–74.

17 Adam Smith, *The Wealth of Nations* (1776; New York: Modern Library, 2000).

18 John Sloman, Jon Guest, and Dean Garratt, *Economics* (Harlow: Pearson Education, 2017), 7; Michael Parkin, *Economics, Global Edition* (Harlow: Pearson Education, 2018), 39.

19 Pierre Cahuc and André Zylberberg, *Labor Economics* (Cambridge: Massachusetts Institute of Technology Press, 2004).

20 Andrew Abbott, "Sociology of Work and Occupations," in *The Handbook of Economic Sociology*, edited by Neil J. Smelser and Richard Swedberg (Princeton, NJ: Princeton University Press, 2005), 307–330; 308.

21 Diane Coyle cites the familiar anecdote of the widower who reduces GDP when he marries his maid: see *GDP: A Brief but Affectionate History*, revised edition (Princeton, NJ: Princeton University Press, 2014), 108.

22 Furse, *Everybody Knows*, "RTW."

23 Smith, *Wealth of Nations*, 77.

24 Smith generally treats care for children as a transactional consideration, looking at birth rates, infant mortality, and family size as a metric only of wages.

25 David Harvey, *A Companion to Marx's* Capital (London: Verso, 2010), 252.

26 Weeks, *Problem with Work*, 12–13.

27 Silvia Federici, *Revolution at Point Zero: Housework, Reproduction, and Feminist Struggle* (Oakland, CA: PM Press, 2012), 16.

28 Ibid., 19.

29 Ma, *Severance*, ch. 14 (four times), 17, 18 (twice), 22 (twice).

30 Furse, *Everybody Knows*, "Mark."

31 Katy Shaw, *Crunch Lit* (London: Bloomsbury, 2015), 5–7.

32 Annie McClanahan, *Dead Pledges: Debt, Crisis, and Twenty-First-Century Culture* (Stanford, CA: Stanford University Press, 2017), 3–4, 22–25.

33 Ibid., 30–32.

34 Georg Lukács, "Realism in the Balance," in *Aesthetics and Politics*, edited by Ronald Taylor (1977; London: Verso, 1980), 28–59; 32–33.

35 In the UK, unemployment peaked in October 2011 at 8.5 percent before dropping to an average of 4 percent prior to the COVID-19 lockdown: Office for National Statistics, "Unemployment Rate (Aged 16 and Over, Seasonally Adjusted)" (2020), www.ons.gov.uk/employmentandlabourmarket/peopleno tinwork/unemployment/timeseries/mgsx/lms. Unemployment in the worst affected European nations (Portugal, Italy, Greece, and Spain – referred to derogatively by some commentators as the "PIGS") remains stubbornly high, but across the EU unemployment rates are, at the time of writing, between 6 percent and 7 percent, having fallen from a high of 12.1 percent in 2013: Eurostat, "European Commission\Eurostat\Employment and Unemployment (LFS)\Data\Database" (2020), https://ec.europa.eu/eurostat/web/lfs/data/ database.

36 Brett Neilson and Ned Rossiter argue that this "Keynesian" conception of work was a brief and geographically-limited break from the norm: see "Precarity as a Political Concept, or, Fordism as Exception," *Theory, Culture, and Society* 25.7–8 (2008), 51–72.

37 The UK High Court ruled that Deliveroo riders were self-employed in December 2018. In the same month, the Court of Appeal ruled that Uber drivers were employees. In the United States, drivers are classed as contractors but a 2019 law in the state of California reclassified them as employees.

38 Indexed to 2015, the cost of housing has risen in every EU country with the exception of Italy. By comparison, average wages have fallen in every European OECD country with the exception of Spain. Across the EU, the median

increase in house prices between 2015 and 2019 was 24.7 percent while the median fall in wages was 5.5 percent: Eurostat, "European Commission \Eurostat\Housing Price Statistics\Data\Database" (2020); OECD, "Annual Average Wages" (2020), https://ec.europa.eu/eurostat/web/housing-price-sta tistics/data/database.

39 Leichter, *Temporary*, 72.
40 Ibid., 151–163.
41 Geissler, *Seasonal Associate*, 139.
42 Ibid., 169–170.
43 Hannah Arendt, *The Human Condition*, 2nd ed. (Chicago: University of Chicago Press, 1998).
44 Geissler, *Seasonal Associate*, 211.
45 Ibid., 151.
46 Ibid., 33, 42, 186–188.
47 Ibid., 138.
48 See Steve Wright, *Storming Heaven: Class Composition and Struggle in Italian Autonomist Marxism* (London: Pluto Press, 2002).
49 Geissler, *Seasonal Associate*, 139–140.

CHAPTER 14

Speculative Fiction and Post-Capitalist Speculative Economies: Blueprints and Critiques

Jo Lindsay Walton

Mark Fisher describes "capitalist realism" as "the widespread sense that not only is capitalism the only viable political and economic system, but also that it is now impossible even to *imagine* a coherent alternative to it."[1] Yet sometimes, quite straightforwardly, speculative fiction does seem to imagine coherent alternatives. Deep economic transformations may be driven, for example, by climate change, by AI and other automation, or by changes to the nature of family and kinship. In consequence, speculative fiction sometimes depicts forms of work, distribution, production, exchange, ownership, consumption, finance, planning, evaluation, bookkeeping, decision-making, and so on, that differ from what really occurs in any capitalist economy – or even any economic system that has ever existed.

Such thought experiments thrive in utopian and dystopian fiction, often framed as provisional proposals or cautionary tales. These arrangements may be fictional, but they also proclaim (or whisper): this is how things really could be. In Edward Bellamy's utopia *Looking Backward: 2000–1887* (1888), a time traveler visits a future United States where all forms of production and distribution are governed as one big commons. This post-capitalist economy has dismantled all its market systems, and done away with money, as well as most or maybe all trade. Its democratic processes appear principally designed against risks of economic exploitation, rather than of political oppression. Bellamy offers plenty of justifications, elaborations, exceptions, and qualifications, and it's easy to get lost in the detailed worldbuilding. But its heart is a democratically-governed commons where every stakeholder contributes equally and enjoys equal benefits.

Ursula K. Le Guin's *The Dispossessed* (1974) depicts Anarres, a post-revolutionary society with no private property, police or prisons, or government or law.[2] One big difference from Bellamy's utopia is that work is voluntary. It's also decoupled from consumption: everyone scoops up whatever they need from communal depositories. Anarres is rich with voluntary associations, involving both communities of interest and communities of place. The closest thing they have to a government is Production and Distribution Coordination (PDC), staffed by sortition (that is, a kind of lottery), and observing strict four-year term limits. It's up to the PDC to coordinate aggregate supply and demand: to act as a "clearing house" for the demand and supply priorities of myriad syndicates, community groups, and individuals across society. Exactly *how* close PDC strays to acting like a government is one of the novel's key themes.

If Bellamy sets out a state-socialist vision, then Le Guin sets out an anarchist-syndicalist one. Of course, it's best to use such labels lightly. Speculative fiction deserves leeway to provide visions of society that don't fit neatly into political theory's pigeonholes. Besides, the novels don't just depict different economic arrangements – they depict them in very different ways. We might say that Bellamy's USA belongs to a tradition of "blueprint" utopia, and Le Guin's Anarres to that of "critical" utopia. Take the representation of labor. A key puzzle for Bellamy's utopians is how they know they really *are* all contributing roughly their fair share to the commons. They are keenly aware that different jobs *feel* very different, and present different risks: it wasn't long ago that "the most perilous, severe, and repulsive labor was done by the worst paid classes."[3] The best solution they can think of is to continually calibrate the balance of work and leisure within each occupation, to make all occupations equally attractive, despite their many qualitative differences. The underlying hunch is that if your job is less pleasant than most people's, well, at least you get to knock off work earlier. Rather optimistically, they also seem to believe that this same balancing practice can match the work put into an occupation with the demand for its goods and services.

What argues for *Looking Backward* as a "blueprint" utopia is that Bellamy mostly just *asserts* that labor is organized in just this way. He is interested in incentive design but lacks Le Guin's perpetual preoccupation with how designs don't always function as intended, and her insights into how participants in institutions become partisan observers and unreliable narrators of those institutions. By contrast, Le Guin evokes a culture where labor is entirely voluntary in *theory* . . . but really, everyone experiences a deep unshakeable compulsion to work, and many Anarresti toil in personally unfulfilling ways. True, no one works unless they want to, but do they all *want* to want to? More generally, her novel exposes deeply discomfiting processes of mutual socialization that underpin Anarres's economy. In this sense, it is a "critical" utopia, dwelling intently on the flaws, fragilities, and hypocrisies of the very arrangements it advocates.

Within speculative fiction studies, blueprint utopias have often been seen as the compulsive worldbuilding of schemers and crackpot tinkerers, and critical utopias as potentially politically illuminating and useful.[4] All the same, we should probably take this distinction with a pinch of salt. For example, set beside Joanna Russ's closely contemporary *The Female Man* (1975), even *The Dispossessed* begins to look rigid and programmatic. Russ's feminist utopia of Whileaway is proffered in fragments, inviting readers to reassemble them in many possible patterns. In particular, as Heather J. Hicks puts it, "where work is concerned Whileaway is a riddle."[5] Whileaway's emissary Janet complains ferociously about over-work. Young adults bear an especially hard burden, relentlessly rotated through assignments so that by twenty-two, "the typical Whileawayan girl is able to do any job on the planet, except for specialties and extremely dangerous work."[6] Janet herself has previously worked as a "Safety and Peace" officer, whose duties include hunting down those "run mad and unable to bear the tediousness of [their] work," apparently so that they can duel to the death.[7] Yet an equally insouciant fragment reveals that "the Whileawayan work-week is sixteen hours."[8] How do we reconcile these facts? Probably the Whileawayans regard any mandated work, even a mere sixteen hours a week, as insultingly tedious – and occasionally worth fleeing to the ends of the earth and battling assassins to avoid. But it's also likely that, when the Whileawayans talk about their relentless work, they're including socially reproductive labor: work such as housework, childcare, and *ad hoc* socialization, teaching, and therapy. The full scope of Whileawayan work and its relationship to those sixteen hours are features left to the imagination.

Despite their differences, all three narratives are "permeated with the social material of the present," as much tools for thinking critically about the present as they are proposals about the future.[9] Neither Bellamy, Le Guin, nor Russ really offers a rigid and detailed set of model policies. Rather, all mobilize utopianism to provoke, to suggest, to anticipate objections, and to recruit readers into collaborative practices of world-building. Bellamy's early audience certainly didn't treat his utopia as a take-it-or-leave-it *fait accompli:* it inspired countless rejoinders, variations, and unofficial sequels.[10] As Ruth Levitas points out, *too* much zeal for openness may make utopia "a vehicle only of critique rather than of transformation."[11] Celebrating a text's reflexivity can even subtly castigate it for having utopian pretensions in the first place: "well done, good utopian text, you know your dreams are flawed!" As Samuel R. Delany puts it, "one cannot *revise* an image until one *has* an image to revise."[12] And when a story stages its own skeptical responses to its most radical ideas, this may prompt readers into active and critical revisions – but it also risks predetermining the scope and emphases of their response.

Post-Capitalisms Old and New

Pretending that a text was written yesterday can help awaken its contemporary relevance. Speculative fiction invites something similar – the pretense that it was written tomorrow. Yet the post-capitalist systems depicted by speculative fiction are not only suspended "above" history: they are also products *of* history, marked by the respective moments when they were imagined. Capitalism itself changes: although post-capitalist stories are in dialogue, they are not merely different angles on the same set of problems. The post-capitalisms they depict are not all "post" the same thing. Likewise, the concepts available to theorize capitalism and its alternatives have changed. "Value" and "price" make a good illustration.

In Bellamy's *Looking Backward*, there is common ownership of all goods and services, and each utopian chooses their own mixture from the commons. But what is worth a lot, and what a little? Without markets to propose values, how can you be sure you've enjoyed your fair share and no more? Their answer is to fix the value of each good or service as an estimate of the difficulty involved in supplying it, emphasizing the amount of work woven into it. They also allow leeway to adjust values to avert a glut or a shortage, whenever levels of demand wander unexpectedly. Suspending for a moment how workable this idea is, how *radical* is it? Judged from the perspective of the mainstream western economics of most of the twentieth century, it would feel like a completely wild idea, implicated in dozens of unanswered and possibly unanswerable questions.

But it would seem wild not because it was an unprecedented concept, but because it was a concept that had recently fallen out of fashion. The subjective theory of value, emerging in the late nineteenth century, more or less abandoned the idea that things have any inherent social values. Léon Walras, William Stanley Jevons, and Carl Menger shifted attention to how crowds of potential users might interact to produce the movements of prices, always assuming that every individual's acts of valuation arise from highly subjective inner processes intractable to economic analysis. On these foundations, later economists built vigorous defenses of the private ownership of means of production (land, machinery and tools, and so on). Economists like Ludwig von Mises and Friedrich Hayek hoped to show

how Soviet experiments with nonmarket valuations, at first based on material balances planning, and later on research into mathematical optimization, were doomed from the start. But in the later part of the twentieth century, with the end of the Cold War, and the growing influence of fields like market design and computational economics, the pendulum perhaps began to swing back again. Bellamy's assumption, that to value a disparate set of things we need a "recipe" rooted in some mixture of moral reasoning and instrumental pragmatism – that we need, in other words, an algorithm – might today not be dismissed quite so quickly by mainstream economists.

Russ and Le Guin likewise speak from a very particular moment in economic history. Russ's interests in automation and cybernetics were informed both by second-wave feminist critiques of labor in the private sphere and by the post-work strand of New Left thinking. The participatory-democratic localism of Le Guin's Anarres belonged, in Fredric Jameson's words, to an "agenda of decentralization" that was deradicalized in the shift from Fordism to Post-Fordism, in part because "flexible capitalism can arrogate the virtues of multiplicity and difference to itself, in the way in which computerization enables niche production and the systematic variation of products."[13] Put another way, *The Dispossessed* comes a little too early in the development of financial capitalism and in the integration of ICT into the world economy to really appreciate the distinctive neoliberal mode of decentralized governmentality as it later unfolded. In the world of *The Dispossessed*, curtailments of freedom arise primarily from social and cultural collectivism or from economic centralization, and are most visible as a homogeneity of manners, morality, and mores. That makes it a far from ideal space in which to understand the key neoliberal dynamic of *decentralized* economic oppression operating across socially and culturally *atomized* populations – while also cultivating and celebrating any diversity compatible with neoliberalism's basic premises.

It's trickier to historicize very recent fiction, but it's worth trying. Cory Doctorow's *Walkaway* (2017) – its working title was *Utopia* – explores online models of collaboration, especially the tools that coordinate and inform crowdsourced labor, and enable projects like Wikipedia. *Walkaway* asks how we might elaborate and generalize such tools across all aspects of economic life, even, for example construction work. At the same time, *Walkaway* mounts a polemic on a particular class of such collaboration tools, those that organize economic activity as a gamified meritocracy.[14] In this sense, *Walkaway* can be read as Doctorow's reckoning with his own earlier *Down and Out in the Magic Kingdom* (2003), written just before the appearance of platforms such as Uber, Airbnb, and Deliveroo. Unlike *Walkaway*, *Down and Out* offered a guardedly optimistic account of capitalism getting replaced by gamified social relationships, reliant on ubiquitous data collection and peer-to-peer reputation metrics.[15]

But in the interval between the two books, much has been revealed about what economic activity on such a pattern may look like in practice. *Walkaway* is underpinned by a rejection of platform capitalism's rhetoric of "sharing"; by a recognition that it is difficult and probably undesirable for any large group to govern its activity through aggregated peer-to-peer reputational rating; by a familiarity with these platforms' characteristic forms of surveillance, disciplinarity, precarity, and exploitation; and to some extent, by a recognition of their permeability to older forms of financial capital. In this sense, *Walkaway* also participates in a wave of critiques of data-intensive capitalism appearing in the late 2010s: Will Davies's *The Happiness Industry* (2015) and Nick Srnicek's *Platform Capitalism* (2016), for example, appeared just before *Walkaway*, and Shoshana Zuboff's *The Age of Surveillance Capitalism* (2018) just afterward.

Nevertheless, the novel technically remains a techno-utopia, nurturing the hope that digital networks can take over from capital to coordinate collective decision-making. In this sense, *Walkaway* is also part of a lively resurgence of post-scarcity politics, including Srnicek and Williams's *Inventing the Future* (2015), Paul Mason's *PostCapitalism* (2015), and anything to do with Fully Automated Luxury (Space and/or Gay) Communism.[16] Post-scarcity, too, is of course a historically-contextual concept, and abundance in *Walkaway* is nothing like the medieval plenty of the Land of Cockayne, where honey-roast doves flap to your lips at the first pang of hunger.[17] Rather, what abundance means in *Walkaway* is informed by recent and potential socio-technological changes to the nature of productive capital, and to the nature of wants and needs. In *Walkaway*, labor is changing, as the open source ethos supplants the work ethic, and a plethora of tools become available to mediate between "skilled" tasks and the "unskilled" workers who want to tackle them. Doctorow's account of a building site, for example, explores the awkward interface between open collaboration and quality control, sketching an automated quality assurance regime that's as much about what is *not* scrutinized as about what *is*. Equipment is also changing, as 3D-printing grows more accessible, and it becomes possible to 3D-print 3D-printers. Raw materials are changing, with hints of a much more circular economy, and obsolescent and unwanted things practically floating up to 3D-printer input funnels like those delicious undead pigeons of Cockayne. On the flip side, *Walkaway* is interested in how quantifiable demand relates to happiness and/or to the good life more broadly. Scenes fill up with long, unhurried conversations, sex, communal onsen bathing, and the cooking and sharing of food, and the novel contrives atmospheres suggestive of voluntary simplicity, degrowth, post-growth, and growth-agnostic thinking. The influence of Thomas Piketty's *Capital in the Twenty-First Century* (2014) is apparent in its critique of meritocracy, and its understanding of poverty and hardship as questions of distribution rather than scarcity. The influence of Rebecca Solnit's *A Paradise Built in Hell* (2009) and David Graeber's *Debt: The First 5,000 Years* (2011) is apparent in its treatment of mutual aid and reciprocity.

Speculative Fiction as Capitalist Ideology

Speculative fiction may challenge conventions about what should or shouldn't belong to economic analysis in the first place, and about what concepts and theories we should use to construe something in economic terms. If the main theme of economics is the alternative uses to which scarce resources are put, that raises the issue of what determines which bits of reality are treated as "resources" in the first place, how they are made "scarce," and which "alternative uses" are considered rational to explore. Speculative fiction has often joined disciplines at the edges of mainstream economics – such as critical management studies, political theory, economic anthropology and sociology, and so-called heterodox economics – in reinscribing the ethical, ecological, and socio-cultural dimensions that mainstream economics sought to reject in the early twentieth century, much to its detriment. Correspondingly, speculative fiction has also anticipated the tentative turn toward pluralism that parts of the economics profession has seen over the past several years.

Has mainstream economics, for all its love of mathematical models, been slow to integrate the significance of informatics and cryptography? A reader of Doctorow's *Walkaway* or Neal Stephenson's "The Great Simoleon Caper" (1995) – notable for its pairing of e-currency and cryptography, anticipating certain aspects of Bitcoin – may well think so. Has mainstream economics paid insufficient attention to the production, manipulation, transformation, and legitimation of desire? The directly inspectable and editable selves of *Walkaway* as well as, for instance, Greg Egan's "Reasons to be Cheerful" (1997), Ted Chiang's *Exhalation* (2008),

Makena Onjerika's "Disassembly" (2020), and numerous works featuring robotic or posthuman characters, may make the case that it has. And does the mainstream "production of goods and services" paradigm tend to suppress affective and biopolitical agencies, including socially reproductive labor and socially transformative labor? Le Guin's *The Dispossessed*, Russ's *The Female Man*, and, to pick just a few more, Charlotte Perkins Gilman's *Herland* (1915), Pamela Zoline's "The Heat Death of the Universe" (1967), and Starhawk's *Fifth Sacred Thing* (1993), have such labor at their hearts. The economics of reproductive labor in a more literal sense is thematized in works like Margaret Atwood's *The Handmaid's Tale* (1985), Octavia Butler's "Bloodchild" (1984), and Jeanette Winterston's *Frankissstein* (2019). The overlapping subgenres of post-apocalyptic fiction, speculative ecofiction, climate fiction, and solarpunk argue for the centrality of ecology to economics, in works such as Frank Herbert's *Dune* (1965), Le Guin's *The Word for World is Forest* (1972), Ernest Callenbach's *Ecotopia* (1975), Karen Tei Yamashita's *Through the Arc of the Rainforest* (1990), and Kim Stanley Robinson's *The Ministry for the Future* (2020).

Even so, the post-capitalist societies of Bellamy et al. constitute a tiny sliver of the futures typically imagined by speculative fiction. Pick a future at random from a shelf, and you're more likely to read that capitalism has spread among the stars, or that its decline has made way for neofeudalism or for Hobbes's *bellum omnium contra omnes*. For example, there is a rich seam of right-libertarianism running through modern and contemporary speculative fiction, and perhaps particularly US science fiction. This includes outright polemics, such as Ayn Rand's *Atlas Shrugged* (1957), Robert Heinlein's *The Moon is a Harsh Mistress* (1966), and Lionel Shriver's *The Mandibles: A Family, 2029–2047* (2016), but it is often subtler. An easy fit exists between right-libertarianism and "Golden Age" science fiction: when these heroes are trapped in impossible situations, they prefer to triumph through reason, resilience, and self-reliance, rather than to whinge. "Hard" science fiction has never been very satisfactorily defined, but we might say that some science fiction "acts hard" when it attempts to expand the ambit of real-world technoscience to new subject matter, potentially fantastical ones. Such work risks endorsing the pretensions of some parts of economics to function as a natural science. And in military science fiction, the Bugs of Robert A. Heinlein's *Starship Troopers* (1959) and "Buggers" of Orson Scott Card's *Ender's Game* (1985) exemplify a fondness for monstrous hyper-collectivist societies as villains.[18]

Speculative fiction that uncritically celebrates capitalism, or roots its criticism in a fantasy of "unfettered" capitalism functioning "as it should," can nevertheless be a source of useful post-capitalist thinking. For instance, it can let us scrutinize the legitimations offered for capitalist institutions from unusual angles and in strange lights. Shriver's *The Mandibles* tacitly responds to the eurozone sovereign debt crises from 2009 onward, and the implementation of austerity measures in many parts of the world. Although the novel essentially defends such government policies, it also thinks through some alternatives in ways that fiscally hawkish political rhetoric often doesn't. It at least attempts to imagine concretely what the US government defaulting on its national debt might actually look like in practice. It provokes us to ask not only, "How credible is it that the debt will get 'too big'?" but also, "Under what circumstances would this be more or less credible? What else would need to be possible, for this to be possible?"

Yet the converse also holds: speculative fiction critical of capitalism – and keen to explore its alternatives – may unwittingly elaborate the assumptions of capitalist economics across time and space. For example, some post-apocalyptic fiction purports to show where capitalism unchecked may lead us, while also giving us tantalizing glimpses of a post-money future. Scarce resources are circulated through barter, mutual aid, theft, tribute, largesse, or self-provisioning such as scavenging. Where there is a kind of money, it is often a commodity whose use value takes precedence over its representative value, such as water in the desert world of *Mad Max* (1979), or dirt in the water world of *Waterworld* (1995). But money, on close inspection, proves a curiously tenacious presence. When characters use metaphors involving money, are these mere innocuous figures of speech? Or are their minds really still shaped by the use of money? As for barter, a tense standoff between two armed parties on an irradiated wasteland may make sense within the logic of the world, but it scarcely reflects the historical realities of barter. What it reflects are the sensibilities of a certain kind of market society, whereby economic coop-eration is only tenable if interlocking sets of individual self-interest are written up as contracts and enforced by cops. In other words, such post-apocalyptic narratives don't show us a post-money society. They show us an assemblage of people and things that fails to become a society precisely because of the money-shaped hole at its heart. Paradoxically, it may often be the speculative fiction that seeks to re-imagine money, such as Karen Lord's *Galaxy Game* (2014) or Adam Roberts's *By the Pricking of Her*

Thumb (2018), rather than abolish it outright, that most successfully articulates a post-money futurity.

The purported anti-capitalism of cyberpunk is another interestingly complex case. Extravagant new forms of corporate villainy, or the commodification of new areas of life, may carry an air of dystopian satire, but at the same time tacitly indict democratic governance for failing to protect us. Cyberpunk has a tendency to fetishize entrepreneurial loner mavericks, and to disparage or satirize corporate power only to the extent that it resembles state power. Fresh, intelligent cyberpunk works like Lauren Beukes's *Moxyland* (2008), Malka Older's *Infomocracy* (2016), and Tim Maughan's *Infinite Detail* (2019) may dodge such clichés, but must still navigate the tension between critiquing capitalism by extrapolating its future forms, and normalizing the inevitability of these developments.

Estranging Economics

An alternative term for "speculative fiction" is "non-realist fiction": but then again, for many of its theorists, the power and appeal of speculative fiction is precisely that it contains *more* reality than other kinds of literature. Ordinary literature merely shows us things that really do happen. Speculative fiction, on the other hand, shows us things that really *could* happen, and perhaps even things that really *will* happen. Yet it doesn't do so principally through being a source of design proposals or futures scenarios. For one thing, when we interpret with reductive literalism, we risk missing all the literary and aesthetic qualities that distinguish a work as speculative fiction in the first place. As Fredric Jameson suggests, "SF seems particularly well-suited – or should I say vulnerable? – to paraphrase."[19] That said, let's not exaggerate this vulnerability. The more "applied" aspects of speculative fiction – its models, hypotheses, theories, designs, and so on – cannot somehow be separated from its status as culture. Rather, speculative fiction's very instrumentality is fundamental to how it operates *as* culture. On the flip side, the myriad speculative practices of activists, designers, futurists, policymakers, military and business strategists, and so on also possess their own rich aesthetic qualities. In that sense, these practices constitute a kind of speculative fiction.

Nonetheless, speculative fiction often generates knowledge or exercises agency in much more intricate and indirect ways as well, operating through satire, allegory, metaphor, and estrangement. Octavia Butler's duology consisting of *The Parable of the Sower* (1993) and *The Parable of the Talents* (1998) makes an excellent case study. Butler's narrative opens in California in 2024, in the midst of interconnected ecological and economic crises. Despite their relative affluence, Lauren Oya Olamina's family live precarious and hardscrabble lives in a gated community. Lauren knows the slow and unevenly distributed apocalypse will find her eventually, and when it does, she is as prepared as she can reasonably be. In the context of loss and trauma, Lauren sets out on a perilous journey and lifelong project of world-making, intent on founding a kind of secular religion, Earthseed, that is more rational and robust than the political and economic systems whose disintegration she is enduring. God, according to Earthseed, is Change: indifferent to you, but potentially something you can shape. In such a context, Butler's representation of cash may feel rather curious. Yes, there are hints in *Parable of the Sower* of hyperinflation. But for the most part, cash is sought after with a special fervor. This reliability of money in this free-for-all world of cannibals and pyromaniac drug addicts could be interpreted as just another small but significant failure of the science-fictional imagination: another example of money's curious tenacity through the downfall of capitalism and beyond.[20]

Then again, Butler's representation of money is inseparable from her exploration of slavery. For Butler, the cycle of acquiring and using money *may* imply autonomy, but she is crystal clear that it does not *always* imply this.[21] The company town is a repeated motif: "[Emery Mora] had been a debt slave ... The debts were accumulated because she worked for an agribusiness corporation that underpaid its workers in company scrip instead of money, then overcharged them for food and shelter, so that they could stay in ever-increasing debt."[22] With this in mind, perhaps the duology does not "transcendentalize" money as an unchanging and compulsory feature of any possible future economy. Nor does it advocate for any particular future form or forms for money. Rather, it articulates a sense of money's immanence in history as a particular distribution of tools and traps.

For Lauren, any given bundle of cash is just another locus of "Change," one with its own distinct features, and one that is often versatile, unpredictable, and – on the long time-scale on which Lauren thinks – ephemeral. When Lauren hides and then retrieves caches of money, her acts suggest Matthew 25:14–30, "The Parable of the Talents," about a rich man and the stewards of his estate. In this parable, two stewards please their master by trading actively and growing his wealth, while the third angers him by merely burying and then retrieving the money. The lessons of doing what you can with what you are given, and of thinking long-term – the Kingdom of Heaven may take a while! – are clearly relevant.

But Butler complicates and even resists such lessons. Significantly, debt slavery was a pervasive condition in the Ancient Near East, and the word often translated as "servants" in "The Parable of the Talents" is probably better translated as "slaves." Butler pairs the figure of God as one who "reaps where he has not sown" with the figure in Matthew 13:1–23, "The Parable of the Sower," who sows (at least *some* seeds) where he cannot reap. So should this composite Sower be understood in a broadly anti-theodicean manner, as a representation of the unfathomable nature of God's goodness? Possibly, although Butler tends to deploy religious discourse in service of a more secular idea of justice. Both Lauren and the disfavored slave confront God as something entirely without mercy. Whereas the two slaves who have traded actively are rewarded by being "set over" a large part of his estate, the slave who perhaps quite reasonably refuses to risk increasing his debt to such a master is rebuked and "cast into the outer darkness" – an image that takes on a more ambiguous resonance in a narrative that is, ultimately, about yearning to travel to space.

Bringing finance into dialogue with theology, Butler demonstrates money's double edge, its complex relations with enslavement and liberation. The Parable duology will certainly repay close reading to further develop these themes. But this brief discussion is sufficient to raise the broader question of *how* we read speculative fiction in relation to economics. Speculative fiction is not a mirror held up to nature (or nature-culture), so much as a complex crystal prism. Darko Suvin's "cognitive estrangement" is one influential theorization of this principle. For Suvin, science fiction makes familiar things appear strange (money, labor, and so on), but in ways that are rigorously rooted in the normally concealed possibilities of those familiar things, and thus in ways that generate knowledge (the "estrangement" is "cognitive"). Writing in a Marxist tradition, Suvin also intends "cognitive estrangement" to be a kind of aporetic or contradictory term, one reflective of real social antagonisms. That is, it's only a small exaggeration to say that Suvin's cognitive estrangement is *not really meant* to make sense, since it is meant to continually poke you into recognizing that the world around you – the capitalist world – does not make sense.[23]

More recently, Seo-Young Chu has suggested that "to differentiate between science fiction and realism ... is misleading," and that "all representation is to some degree science-fictional because all reality is to some degree cognitively estranging." Instead, Chu theorizes science fiction as "a high-intensity variety of realism" that is especially suited to representing cognitively estranging referents. Chu argues that some things – "Fuji apples, pennies, maple leaves, toothbrushes, basketballs, and pencils" – spring quite comfortably into expression, affect, and comprehension.[24] But other things – globalization, cyberspace, artificial intelligence, trauma, the multigenerational legacy of collective trauma – tend to elude our capacity to talk, feel, and know about them. This is especially interesting for us here, since economics is filled with phenomena that Chu might count as cognitively estranging referents: business cycles, stock markets, networked supply chains, ecosystems managed through computer modelling, policies or institutions incorporating perverse incentives, opaque decision-making. Economics has a long tradition – traceable back at least as far as Bernard de Mandeville's maxim of private vices making public virtues – of foregrounding the epistemological limitations of the individual actor, especially in relation to the emergent systems-level implications of the individual action. It is speculative fiction that, in Chu's view, can "perform the massively complex representational and epistemological work necessary to render cognitively estranging referents available both for representation and for understanding."[25]

There are significant differences in Suvin's and Chu's approaches, which should not be elided. But they share a sense that speculative fiction provides access to ways of life that are *neither* our own, *nor* those of the characters that a text describes, but constitute other possibilities. This implies it is not only in utopias that we may garner significant crots, nuggets, mechanics, and sparks of post-capitalist economic systems, but also in all kinds of speculative fiction – even dystopias like Octavia Butler's Parable duology. Utopias may also become engines or catalysts of quite *different* utopian visions from the ones they more obviously present. Doctorow's *Walkaway* firmly rejects the algorithmic management of economic activity, in its polemic against gamification, and its embrace of the informal gift economy. Yet it's intriguing that (in a plot strand ostensibly unconnected with political economy) the novel also stages the computational modelling of a system of extraordinary complexity: the human brain and mind. These episodes are about a quite familiar problem: how do you foresee and avoid a crash?

This chapter opened by quoting Mark Fisher. A related maxim is that it is "easier to imagine the end of the world than the end of capitalism." In one sense, speculative fiction clearly does imagine both.[26] Yet to take the maxim seriously, we must remember that it emerges from a strong sense of the adaptability of capitalism (or really, of whatever is signified by that word in its most ruthlessly critical sense), and from a broadly Marxist conviction about the rootedness of language and thought in the material conditions of existence, and thus the limitations of our own perception, reasoning, and affect. What this maxim may be telling us, then, is that when we *think* we are imagining the end of capitalism – say, by reading and writing speculative fiction about it – we are probably not. Was capitalism ever "imagined"? Can it be imagined now? If this radical tradition of self-questioning often finds itself at odds with radical antiracist, feminist, and queer mobilizations of lived experience for critique and praxis, this might be interpreted as capital's cunning in deflecting and defusing the dynamics that oppose it. Furthermore, this chapter has mostly assumed that being able to *imagine* something is a step toward making it happen. We produce images as an interim step to producing changes based on them. But sometimes imagining things can make them less likely to happen. Things may be imagined *instead* of being done.

Finally, of course, much of what speculative fiction "imagines" as post-capitalism is already happening. Kim Stanley Robinson's *The Ministry for the Future* (2020) challenges kneejerk suspicion of blueprints for a better society, advocating for what the novel refers to as "Plan B," while making it clear that one source of blueprints is things that have already been built, and are already being done:

> The Zurich plan, the Mondragón system, Albert and Hahnel's participatory economics, communism, the Public Trust plan, the What's Good Is What's Good for the Land plan, the various post-capitalisms, and so on and so forth; there are lots of versions of a Plan B, but they all share basic features. It's not rocket science. The necessities are not for sale and not for profit.[27]

Speculative fiction asks to be read in the context of the more-than-capitalist practices around us.[28] This does not necessarily indicate a lack of insight from speculative fiction writers (although it might) so much as the plenitudinous variety of economic life. In gathering the rudiments of post-capitalism, we should not neglect the diverse economies that already exist all around us, flourishing in capitalism's wide cracks.

Notes

1 Mark Fisher, *Capitalist Realism: Is There No Alternative?* (Winchester: Zero Books, 2009), 2; emphasis in original.
2 As its protagonist Shevek explains: "The network of administration and management is called PDC, Production and Distribution Coordination. They are a coordinating system for all syndicates, federatives, and individuals who do productive work. They do not govern persons; they administer production" (Ursula K. Le Guin, *The Dispossessed* [1974; London: Gollancz, 2002], 65).

3 Edward Bellamy, *Looking Backward: 2000–1887*, edited by Matthew Beaumont (1888; Oxford: Oxford University Press, 2007), 53.

4 E.g. Fredric Jameson, *Archaeologies of the Future: The Desire Called Utopia and Other Science Fictions* (2005; London: Verso, 2007), 43. See also Tom Moylan *Demand the Impossible: Science Fiction and the Utopian Imagination* (New York: Methuen, 1986); Ruth Levitas, *The Concept of Utopia* (London: Philip Allan, 1990).

5 Heather J. Hicks, *The Culture of Soft Work: Labor, Gender, and Race in Postmodern American Narrative* (New York: Palgrave MacMillan, 2009).

6 Joanna Russ, *The Female Man* (1975; London: Gollancz, 2010), 51.

7 Ibid., 1, 55.

8 Ibid.

9 Murray Bookchin, *Post-Scarcity Anarchism*, 2nd ed. (Montreal and Buffalo, NY: Black Rose Books, 1986), 187.

10 Kenneth M. Roemer, *The Obsolete Necessity: America in Utopian Writings, 1888–1900* (Kent, OH: Kent State University Press, 1976).

11 Ruth Levitas, *Utopia as Method: The Imaginary Reconstitution of Society* (Basingstoke: Palgrave Macmillan, 2013), 10.

12 Samuel R. Delany, *Starboard Wine: More Notes on the Language of Science Fiction* (1984; Middletown, CT: Wesleyan University Press, 2012), 10; emphases in original.

13 Fredric Jameson, *Archaeologies of the Future*, 162.

14 Cory Doctorow, *Walkaway*, Kindle ed. (London: Head of Zeus, 2017), locations 1621–1626.

15 See also Cory Doctorow, "Wealth Inequality is Even Worse in Reputation Economies," *Locus Mag*, 3 March 2016, www.locusmag.com/2016/03/cory-doctorow-wealth-inequality-is-even-worse-in-reputation-economies/.

16 Brian Merchant, "Fully Automated Luxury Communism," *Guardian*, March 18, 2015, www.theguardian.com/sustainable-business/2015/mar/18/fully-automated-luxury-communism-robots-employment.

17 Occasionally the word "scarce" is treated as a synonym for "finite," which tends to lead to the slightly boring observation that true post-scarcity is impossible because a world where everything is infinite is incoherent. A better understanding of "scarce" is as a synonym for "not enough," which raises fruitful questions like, "Enough for what? And how much is enough?"

18 Although speculative fiction can also explore swarms, hive minds, and distributed consciousness in more complex and sympathetic ways, as the Majatt of C. J. Cherryh's *Serpent's Reach* (1980) or the Ancillaries in Ann Leckie's *Ancillary Justice* (2015) show us.

19 Jameson, *Archaeologies of the Future*, 296.

20 In *The Parable of the Talents*, Canadian dollars usurp US dollars as "hard currency."

21 In this sense, while the Duology doesn't explicitly address the theme of Basic Income, it can justly be classed alongside works such as Zoë Fairbairns's *Benefits* (1979), as well as a wave of recent work such as Tim Maughan's

"Flyover Country" (2016), William Squirrell's "They Built the New Jerusalem on the Ruins of the Old" (2018), and E. Lily Yu's "The Doing and Undoing of Jacob E. Mwangi" (2019), as speculative fiction concerned to explore Basic Income discourse while resisting any dogmatism about its actual social consequences. For older works touching on Basic Income, see Adeline Knapp's *One Thousand Dollars a Day: Studies in Practical Economics* (1894), Robert Heinlein's *For Us, The Living: A Comedy of Customs* (written in 1938, though published in 2003), and Philip José Farmer's *Riders of the Purple Wage* (1967).

22 Octavia Butler, *The Parable of the Talents* (1998; London: Headline, 2014), 185.

23 This is a point lost in Carl Freedman's version, which downgrades "cognition" to a "cognition effect," an *impression* of acquiring knowledge. Freedman's reworking of Suvin is otherwise extremely illuminating, linking his work to critical theory from Kant to the Frankfurt School. See Carl Freedman, *Critical Theory and Science Fiction* (Middletown, CT: Wesleyan University Press, 2000), 1, 56.

24 Seo-Young Chu, *Do Metaphors Dream of Literal Sleep? A Science-Fictional Theory of Representation* (Cambridge, MA: Harvard University Press, 2011), 7, 245.

25 Ibid., 7.

26 The wording is associated with Fredric Jameson and Slavoj Žižek. See Fredric Jameson, "Future City," *New Left Review* 21 (2005), 65–79; 76.

27 Kim Stanley Robinson, *The Ministry for the Future* (London: Orbit, 2020), 430–431.

28 J. K. Gibson-Graham, *A Post-Capitalist Politics* (Minneapolis: University of Minnesota Press, 2006).

PART III

Interdisciplinary Exchanges

CHAPTER 15

The Keynesian Theory of Jamesonian Utopia: Interdisciplinarity in Economics

Matt Seybold

In a special issue of *Boston Review* published in 2019, three economists from elite US universities take up the topic "Economics after Neoliberalism." The economists admit they are "on the defensive," having recently discovered that many colleagues in other disciplines believe "the culprits behind rising inequalities ... seem to be rooted in conventional economic doctrines" and "consequently, many people view [economists] with outright hostility."[1]

Their proposal of an economics after neoliberalism is potentially regarded as a contradiction in terms. If "neoliberalism appears to be just another name for economics," the world after neoliberalism is likely a world without economists.[2] In the five essays and eleven responses published alongside them, "Economics after Neoliberalism" is indeed often made to seem ridiculous. Yet those respondents – both in the specifics of what they say and their decisions to dignify the project by their participation – refrain from rejecting collaboration with economists wholesale.

Among the respondents is a cohort that describes itself as made up of "Complexity Economists." They rightly observe that "Economics after Neoliberalism" must be judged as much on what the economists seek to preserve as on what they propose reforming: "The vision they paint is still focused on the discipline of economics and anchored in the core ideas of neoclassical theory."[3] The conditioning of the contemporary economist, who is three times more likely to identify as male (six times more likely if he has tenure), is to place his expertise at the center of all inquiry, his department at the center of the academy, and himself in the center of the public square.[4] The Complexity collective writes, "Economics has yet to grapple with the harder question of how to integrate heterogeneity into its theoretical core and into the models used by policymakers."[5] Economics has, at present, no discernible commitment to pluralism, the definition of *interdisciplinarity* traditionally accepted in literary studies.[6]

In this chapter I will be treating speculative fiction as a model for imagining heterogeneous approaches to political-economic policymaking, particularly crossing what sometimes seems an impassable crux separating applied economics, climate science, and critical theory. What does it mean to integrate theories of narrative, rhetoric, media, and culture into the work of interdisciplinary economic collectives? This is yet another challenge that "Economics after Neoliberalism" poses. The Complexity Economists describe themselves by saying, "Our backgrounds are in economics, political science, psychology, anthropology, physics, computer science, evolutionary theory, and complex systems theory."[7] Readers of this companion will recognize a stark absence. Even in an academic collective considering a radical transdisciplinary approach to economics, there are no humanists.

The Polymathy of Political Economy before Neoliberalism

This was not always the case. Any advocacy for taking economics seriously, despite the guile of its Post45 canon, must begin in the history of economic thought, where one can find ample pluralism, including engagement with the humanities. By one account, the modern canon of economic thought begins with the publication of a satiric verse fable in 1705.

Bernard Mandeville's "The Grumbling Hive" would later be appended to his philosophical treatise, *The Fable of the Bees* (1714), which Adam Smith alludes to in *The Wealth of Nations* (1776), establishing a pattern that persisted well into the twentieth century. Commentary on Mandeville's work appears in many of the most-canonized works of economic thought, including Thomas Malthus's *Essay on the Principle of Population* (1826), Karl Marx's *Capital* (1867), and John Maynard Keynes's *The General Theory of Employment, Interest, and Money* (1936). Part of what made Mandeville scandalous was his insistence that "private vice" was a "public virtue." That is, behaviors discouraged by Christian morality – especially prodigality – were, though dangerous to the individual, beneficial to society in aggregate. This is the root logic of what we now know as Keynesian stimulus – public policies aimed at inducing individuals to consume during periods of economic contraction. Keynes placed Mandeville at the head of a "brave army of heretics" who had the courage to challenge orthodoxy that was equal parts religion and politics.[8]

Disciplinary histories that posit Mandeville as an originary figure for economics implicitly acknowledge a debt to literary studies. "The Grumbling Hive" was, after all, part of a distinct poetic tradition. It also reveals economic thought as interdisciplinary at its foundation. Mandeville was a physician by trade who dabbled in poetry, psychology, law, and philosophy. Thus, economics emerged as an epistemological mechanism for synthesizing diverse bodies of knowledge. In highlighting the proto-interdisciplinarity of Mandeville and Keynes, I am proposing but one disciplinary history that is an alternative to the methodological homogeneity, hyper-specialization, and insularity economists have overwhelming endorsed in the past half-century.

Readers will also recognize in the Mandevillian history of economic thought that ideological commitments to classical liberalism are interpolated into methodological practice, such that the collision of disciplines is something that happens to the economist in isolation. Keynes, though evidencing a selective partiality to communes and collectives in his social life and philanthropic work, embodies the professional mythos of the economic polymath. He is most often treated as a generational genius whose unique talent forced a paradigm shift. Though it was Keynes who famously cautioned economists to covet the humility and practicality of dentists rather than the attention of tyrants, he made ample time to counsel plenipotentiaries. His antagonists, notably of the Geneva and Chicago Schools, focused on formalizing pedagogy, organizing institutions, and synthesizing principles and praxis into the orthodoxy that has since proven resiliently resistant to reform.[9] Keynes was an aggressive advocate for multilateralism as a diplomat and public intellectual, but as an economist he was a maverick. That the economic orthodoxy that came to be called Keynesianism discarded much of what he claimed was essential is an indictment of his failure to make a leap from polymath to pluralism, from idiosyncratic to interdisciplinary.

The Post45 economics built upon neoclassical economic foundations, sometimes misleadingly described as "the Keynesian synthesis," provided the epistemological and rhetorical scaffolding for the political projects of regulatory capture, dismantling the welfare state, deunionization (aka, deindustrialization), downward redistribution of risk, trickle-up taxation, corporate immunity from rule of law, privatization of public goods, judicial arbitrage, and Klepto-Keynesianism (destabilizing democratic governments through economic crises ignited by financial malfeasance until oligopolists literally seize sovereignty). According to the great man theory of history that has often prevailed in economics, Keynes's failure to inspire collectives may be regarded as nothing short of catastrophic.[10] Even Michel Foucault, in his much-cited "Birth of Biopolitics" lectures, asserts that it is, foremost, opposition to their "main doctrinal adversary, Keynes, the common enemy" that unites the European and American schools of neoliberalism, a union essential to the political projects listed above.[11] Of course, to lay all the ills of neoliberalism at Keynes's feet would be naïve, but the attention paid to Keynes and Keynesianism even by Marxian theorists like David Harvey and Geoff Mann demonstrates how his work, policy based upon his work, rejection of his work, and the dismantling of policy based upon his work are all integral to narrating how we arrived at our dystopian present.[12]

Regressing toward Apocalypse

The Post45 failure of the Keynesian synthesis that became neoliberalism is characterized by the political projects mentioned in the preceding paragraph, as well as related ones like mass incarceration and mass surveillance. It is also characterized by secular eschatology. Over the course of the long downturn, apocalypticism became the most popular political literary form in the United States, and, as it has rapidly migrated into film, television, and other modes of US cultural imperialism, it has become reasonable to argue that apocalypticism is now the most globally accessible narrative form.[13] As Anna Kornbluh puts it, "Disaster porn [is] the house style of capitalist realism."[14]

While the apocalyptic imaginary still has plenty of room for the dominant eschatology of Keynes's final days – mutually assured destruction by atomic weapons – it has also, particularly since the end of the Cold War, made room for apocalypses extraterrestrial, viral, evolutionary, astrological, technological, and ecological. Ecological apocalypticism, buoyed first by accelerating investments in climate science and then by the politicization of the discoveries generated by climate scientists, is now a thriving subgenre, known as climate fiction (CliFi). Few instantiations of the political novel have had a more unified directive: depicting the terror of the near future so that readers might be motivated to change their lifestyles and loyalties.

Like midcentury nuclear war narratives, the secular eschatology of CliFi is made more persuasive by the mass media environment in which it is embedded. Coverage of natural disasters, new scientific findings, eco-friendly technologies, environmentalist protests, fraught diplomatic initiatives, and climate denialist controversies make it seem inevitable that the sensational events represented in CliFi will cross over to our cable news networks and social media feeds, if not our physical communities.

In a podcast episode released on November 30, 2020, Ezra Klein said of the new novel by one of CliFi's most recognizable voices, Kim Stanley Robinson, "God, it is imagining a future which felt realer than our present to me. It's a future where we don't stop climate change until tens of millions die. But it's also a future in which those deaths do spur a global response."[15] It is unclear whether Klein is more surprised at the verisimilitude of the heat wave depicted in the opening chapters of Robinson's book, a heat wave that kills 20 million residents of India, or more surprised that he was induced to believe that after such a crisis something might actually change.

Many of the early reviewers of the novel, including Klein, have been quick to point out that Robinson's *The Ministry for the Future* (2020) is a direct answer to the challenge made by Fredric Jameson, to whom the book is dedicated, with the oft-recycled and possibly misattributed aphorism: "It is easier to imagine an end to the world than an end to capitalism."[16] Robinson's novel does verge on doing both. One of the two protagonists, Frank May, is the sole survivor from a village wiped out by the heat wave. He vacillates between militant activism and regarding global apocalypse as appropriate cosmic vengeance on those responsible for the atrocity he witnessed. The other protagonist, Mary Murphy, who heads the titular Ministry, manages to catalyze the reorganization of the global economic system in a manner that not only reverses the carbon clock, but reduces economic inequality, attains universal adherence to multilateral agreements, eliminates tax avoidance and shadow banking, repairs social safety nets, and inspires social democratic movements.

But while the economic system depicted at the end of the novel does seem remarkably different from neoliberalism or what Jameson calls "late capitalism," it still allows for private property and private ownership of means of production. There are still multinational corporations. Banking and financial services still sit at its center, intertwined with governments and private industry. Rent-seekers have been neither guillotined nor euthanized. In fact, Robinson narrates neither the end of the world nor the end of capitalism, but more accurately the revival and apotheosis of what John Kenneth Galbraith calls "the planning system."[17]

In his conversation with Klein, Robinson acknowledges that the novel has long been regarded as a literary genre aligned with capitalism, potentially even, as Sarah Comyn has argued, a form inextricable from the orthodox economic model of human nature.[18] Robinson worries that *Ministry for the Future* might thus prove an exercise in futility, but he draws hope for his project from two competing traditions: Science Fiction,

which habitually shows communities overcoming harsh planetary environments; and the socialist miscellany novel (Robinson specifically mentions
John Dos Passos's *U.S.A.* trilogy), which depicts large casts of characters
caught in thick streams of history.

The documents that Robinson uses to imitate Dos Passos are polyph-
onous transcripts of interviews, staff meetings, public hearings, and private
negotiations. These documents show people with disparate training trying,
and usually failing, to persuade each another effectively. Often there are
basic, superficially comic miscommunications, but because of the
Ministry's mission, we are perpetually aware that this tedious trial and
error process is happening with lives in the balance. The effect of many of
these chapters is to show the intimidating difficulty of interdisciplinary
work, but also to show its urgency.

At the first staff meeting depicted, the resident "nat cat" (natural
catastrophe) ecologist, Bob Wharton, enraged by a discussion of climate
change's impact on the insurance industry, seethes, "We can't adapt to
some things we are now failing to mitigate. Need to clarify which is which.
Mainly need to tell adaptation advocates they're full of shit. Bunch of
economists, humanities professors, they have no idea what [they're] talking
about. Adaptation just a fantasy."[19] Wharton's "rant" stops just short of
stating the foundational challenge of climate activism, which also becomes
the core mission of the Ministry (though at this point in Murphy has not
recognized it as such) and thus the motive force of the novel: if humankind
does not become collectively committed to the reduction of carbon
emissions, humanity itself will become susceptible to the mass extinction
event that is already underway.

Setting aside the eschatological shock of Wharton's denigration of social
adaptation theory, there is an ancillary jarring in the dismissive spite
directed at "economists" and "humanities professors." This is particularly
jarring, I expect, for humanities professors, not accustomed to being
acknowledged by their STEM colleagues as agents of anything, much less
apocalypse, nor of being paired with economists as mutual advocates of, if
not climate denialism, at least climate gradualism destined to fail. But in
Robinson's novel, the success of the Ministry rides upon the triangulation
of these three fields of knowledge production: environmental science,
political economy, and the humanities, especially critical theory.[20]

Robinson manages to introduce and interweave the often exclusionary
disciplinary vocabularies of these fields. Quantitative easing, Gini coeffi-
cients, Jevons paradoxes, Modern Monetary Theory (MMT), and feebates
are made to coexist with – sometimes even correlated to – migration

corridors, wet-bulb temperatures, subglacial meltwater viscosity, and atmospheric carbon counts. But, Robinson makes clear, the Ministry's proposals cannot succeed without its technocrats also becoming conversant in theories like Raymond Williams's "structures of feeling," Sigmund Freud's "return of the repressed," Bruno Latour's "actor networks," and, of course, the epistemological escape from late capitalism theorized by Jameson.

The economists and humanities professors derided by Wharton are thereafter presented, primarily through Murphy, as necessary converts to the cause of carbon reduction, whose skills are integral for what Jameson (citing Stuart Hall) calls the "discursive struggle" with government agents, corporate executives, and the general public.[21] For transdisciplinary collectives, Robinson's heartening estimation of our importance is chastened by firsthand knowledge of how difficult it is for economists, critical theorists, scientists, and engineers to think through things together. Minutes from the Ministry meetings, particularly early in the novel, reproduce the crosstalk of faculty town halls and college committee meetings, in which the assembled fail to agree upon a common parlance or a set of priors, much less strategic action.

The first meeting ends with Murphy cutting through the cacophony of conflicting proposals to proclaim, "Stop. We need to lever change, and fast. However we can. By whatever means necessary."[22] This ambiguous charge is taken by some team members as permission to pursue their personal priorities, precluding collaboration, diffusing limited resources, diluting desired effects, and inflaming counterproductive competition. Heterogenous policymaking appears initially – as opponents of planned economy presume it be – atrophic and profligate.

The Odd Coupling of Fredric Jameson and John Maynard Keynes

The way Robinson describes Jameson in his interview with Klein is telling: "He's an unusually modest great philosopher in that there isn't so much a Jamesonian system as him always using everything at hand to build a flexible and creative Marxism."[23] Jameson's capacity implies a kind of interdisciplinarity, a reflexive disregard for the often arbitrary categorical distinctions between corpuses of knowledge and modes of inquiry. Interdisciplinarity is often, as Julie Klein argues, part of broader resistance to the epistemology of "boundary consciousness."[24] Preference for rigid prescriptions between how one studies economy and culture is homologically interdependent with overdetermined conceptions of national borders, racialization, and other prejudices informed by overreliance on the cognitive habit of categorization. Our need to overcome boundary consciousness in order to prevent catastrophes caused by climate change is part of what justifies the counterintuitive pairing of Jameson and Keynes that Robinson centers in *Ministry for the Future*. Keynes's polymathy proved an impediment to the multilateral and multigenerational strategic planning he envisioned, yet Robinson, channeling Jameson, turns polymathy into a synecdoche of and a necessary precondition for building global coalitions.

Other Marxian critical theorists – notably Mark Fisher, author of *Capitalist Realism* (2009), and Joshua Clover, author of *Riot Strike Riot* (2016), both of whose work Robinson also alludes to – have theorized escape from capitalism, but in texts that are dismissive of the entire canon of economic thought, even and sometimes especially Keynes. Robinson does not deny the possibility that those inculcated in economics can work towards the escape from capitalism. In *Ministry for the Future*, Jameson's critical theory infused with Keynes's political economy is the formula for surviving Climate Leviathan.[25]

For Jameson, across a series of texts, including *The Political Unconscious* (1981), *Postmodernism, or, The Cultural Logic of Late Capitalism* (1991), and *Archaeologies of the Future* (2005), Utopia became a category that absorbs SciFi, CliFi, and other subgenres of speculative fiction. Utopia also became a genre of critical theory, one that he argues should replace political theory because the latter "constitutes an ontology which is necessarily obliged to work within the limits of being and of reality as it currently exists," while the former "aims at a radical transformation of the present and its system."[26] *Ministry* is a novel that deploys and sometimes interrogates Jameson's evolving theory of Utopia. In this chapter I draw primarily upon one text: "An American Utopia" (2016). This is partially for the sake of concision, but has three other advantages. The essay reiterates and often crystallizes major points from Jameson's previous books. Also, Robinson clearly read "An American Utopia" in relative proximity to his composition of *Ministry*. His response is included alongside Jameson's essay in the 2016 Verso collection, *An American Utopia: Dual Power and The Universal Army*. Finally, Jameson characterizes "An American Utopia" as a "thought experiment," itself a work of speculative fiction imagining potential paths to a radically different future. Thus, it shares a method not only with Robinson's novel, but also with Keynes's essay, "Economic Possibilities For Our Grandchildren" (1930). The unexpected sympathies that Robinson reveals between Jameson and Keynes help to justify the novel's advocacy for interdisciplinarity.

Jamesonian interdisciplinarity is, of course, dialectical in its insistence upon collaborations bracketed by competition. "Jameson does not wish to abandon a commitment to pluralism," Roland Boer writes, but characterizes Jameson's specific brand as "conflictual pluralism of the battlefield and marketplace."[27] Boer's metaphors turn for inspiration to exactly that which Jameson wishes us to escape, but in their inappropriateness is precisely the problem the Ministry faces, a problem that seems at first insurmountable. It is the express problem of "An American Utopia": for our increasingly urgent project of escaping late capitalism and the militarized nationalism upon which it depends, we have only the tools of war and finance at our disposal. Judging twentieth-century instantiations of socialism irreversibly failed, Jameson goes looking for potential institutions of "dual power" that comfortably coexist with hegemonic power, but which might provide space for imagining something else. After considering several, he settles, paradoxically, on the armed forces. This epiphany is reproduced several times in Robinson's *Ministry*, as Murphy and her staff recognize that military drones, counterintelligence agencies, central banks, and cryptocurrencies, all things which they presumed were innately irreconcilable with a just and verdant future, can be deployed as transformative tools on its behalf. The same is true of economics.

Economics for Possibility

Robinson rightly credits Keynes with hypothesizing politically ameliorative effects from the adoption of a global standard currency. What Robinson refers to as "the Chen paper" inspires the novel's "carbon coin," a cryptocurrency created by a syndicate of central banks and pegged to carbon sequestration. It allows oil companies and petro-states temporarily to substitute *not* burning carbon reserves they control for burning them, thus replacing revenue during a precarious period of redeployment and reinvestment in clean energy and geoengineering.[28]

Chen et al. make no mention of Keynes, but Robinson flushes out the precedent, and by doing so recapitulates the novel's foremost historical analogy. If there is a crisis from which we can learn how to combat climate change, it is the eschatological crisis of atomic proliferation in the immediate aftermath of World War II. At Bretton Woods, Keynes, no longer the helpless bystander he had been at Versailles, embarked upon an aggressive program of international lobbying for a global central bank with the power to create its own currency. While elements of Keynes's proposal were integrated into the International Monetary Fund (IMF), the Bretton

Woods agreement established no multilateral economic regulator or trade
peacekeeper, as Keynes had insisted, who could stabilize debtor nations
and therefore preclude the revival of nationalist resentments in a nuclear
age. To the contrary, the international institutions that the treaty created
have since stoked those resentments by becoming tools for economic
imperialism. The European Troika is a direct descendent of Bretton
Woods, and Robinson cites its gutting of Greece during the 2010s as an
omen of catastrophes to come."[29]

Keynes's project was itself a speculative fiction. He attributed to the
International Clearing Union many of the same powers that converge in
Robinson's Ministry for the Future, and he presented it as an institution
that would work specifically on behalf of his "grandchildren," as he had
imagined them in his 1930 essay, "Economic Possibilities For Our
Grandchildren," a thesis statement for Keynes's political economy
throughout the remainder of his life. Just as the Ministry is mandated to
represent the interests of future generations, Keynes hoped that the
Clearing Union would manage, or at least monitor, three factors that he
claimed would contribute most to "the *pace* at which we can reach our
destination of economic bliss": the rates of population growth, the scale of
political violence, and "our willingness to entrust to science the direction
of those matters which are properly the concern of science."[30]

As Murphy's Ministry arrives, slowly, at a program of action, the factors
Keynes identified are all among their considerations, as is what Keynes
idiosyncratically called "the rate of accumulation as fixed by the margin
between our production and our consumption," more commonly known
today as wealth disparity or income inequality.[31] Keynes wrongly dismissed the equitable distribution of capital as something that would "easily
look after itself" given the management of the three primary factors.[32]
Murphy recognizes that, to the contrary, distribution of capital is the
political lever that makes possible demilitarization, open borders, and the
depoliticization of science. This is not so much a contradiction as a logical
extension of Keynes's political economy. Keynes's explicit goal from
1930 forward is to place economics in service of something else, to have
political priorities set independent of economic models, such that the
models are forced to conform to expressions of political will, not the other
way around.

Jameson and Keynes agree that the means to Utopia lie in existing
powers – armies and banks – that are in many respects reprehensible, but
whose infrastructures provide a necessary basis for mass adaptation: the
"map intact beneath a wholly different topology," as Jameson phrases it.[33]

The second Keynesian concept that Robinson explains in detail is, like the Clearing Union, a spectacularly failed project. Keynes forecasts "the euthanasia of the rentier, and, consequently, the euthanasia of the cumulative oppressive power of the capitalist."[34] Rentiers, whom he also dubs "functionless investors," exploit – and in some cases create scarcities of – land, subsistence goods, and other capital for the purpose of personal accumulation, which does harm to "the struggle for subsistence."[35] Keynes predicts that these scarcities will be regulated, legislated, and incentivized out of existence as part of a prolonged period of shrinking class disparities created by technocratic management of the productive abundances and distributive efficiencies emanating from technological advancement and globalization.

Critics have justly wondered how the author of *The Economic Consequences of the Peace* (1919) could so naively underestimate the capacity for avarice and cruelty among an entrenched ruling class. But for understanding Robinson's invocation of the euthanasia metaphor, what's most important is that Keynes explicitly offers it, contra-Marx, as a process that will "need no revolution."[36] Keynes defines as one of the purposes of economics the arbitraging of violence, even and especially righteous violence. For Keynes, violent revolutions, no matter how justified by conditions of oppression, can never escape the reproduction of their means independent of just ends. Prior to Keynes, the rare economists who were willing to talk about political violence treated it as either the unfortunate side effect of the natural and desirable cycle of capitalism (for instance, Schumpeter) or, like Marx, as a temporary, chaotic phase necessary for transition to a better system.

For Keynes, violence is something to be proactively economized. There is no room for violence in the world he imagines for his grandchildren, and so the proactive reduction of violence is the method for bringing us closer to that world. Strategies for realizing Keynes's Utopia must insist upon strict thrift in terms of death-dealing, even the dealing of death *to* the sadistic capitalist class who are disproportionately the agents of political violence. The logic of retributive justice which prevailed at Versailles and again, to a lesser extent, at Bretton Woods was, in Keynes's mind, sacrificing durable peace in favor of an impossible dream: the righting of past injustices. The urge to balance the moral or geopolitical scales is a death drive, because the only way to achieve true equilibrium is mutually-assured destruction.[37] The dual protagonists of *Ministry for the Future* – Murphy and May – are frequently seduced by the logic of retributive justice. May attempts to join a covert organization dedicated to attacking reckless carbon emitters. Murphy tacitly endorses the Ministry's black ops division. Thus, the novel does not full-throatedly accept the liberal refusal to stand in mortal judgment of the rentier class. But it does reject the spirit of vengeance, which inevitably reproduces itself across time and territory. As Keynes theorized was necessary in all matters of political economy, violence has to be economized in accordance with a speculative vision of future flourishing, not a ledger of past sins. This future-orientation is what most directly brings Jameson and Keynes together, seeking "the substitution of utopian thinking for politics and political theory."[38]

During the opening chapters of Robinson's novel, the Ministry for the Future seems primed to become like the Ministries of the paradigmatic Post45 speculative novel, George Orwell's *1984* (1949). Just as "The Ministry of Peace concerns itself with war" in George Orwell's novel, the Ministry for the Future seems to have been founded as an attempt to rewrite history, to assuage the Global North's collective guilt in the aftermath of the Indian heat wave by making the catastrophe appear an anachronism, born of problems already solved by doing nothing.[39] The Ministry begins the novel with limited authority to fulfill even its modest mission of enforcing the Paris Climate Agreement.

But the difference between Orwell's mature dystopia and Robinson's unrealized Utopia is contained in a prepositional choice. Whereas Winston Smith is employed by a Ministry *of,* Mary Murphy runs a Ministry *for.* Just as Keynes's "Economic Possibilities For Our Grandchildren" implies not the inevitable progress of laissez-faire capitalism, but economic equality achieved by collective sacrifice on behalf of progeny *for* whom we feel responsible, the Ministry's effectiveness increases when they decide to take seriously the future as a political constituency.

This "end of temporality" is another correspondence that Robinson finds between Jameson and Keynes. All treat past, present, and future as simultaneous and interpolated happenings. A presentism unburdened by careless parents and precarious grandchildren is what Keynes wishes for his descendants. He imagines himself as a proto-Minister, whose efforts may result in a society where living in the moment is the reward for escaping history, rather than a method of coping with the imminence of atrocity. "But beware!," Keynes exclaims, "The time for all this is not yet."[40] Utopia only exists at present in our duty to create it.

Like "American Utopia," written from a position of accepting the obsolescence of politics with which Jameson spent a lifetime in sympathy, Keynes's "Economic Possibilities" is Utopian thinking from the precipice of epochal crisis. Keynes had been a horrorstruck, but largely helpless, witness to the twin cruelties of postwar austerity and the extinction burst of European colonialism. He knew these were producing the conditions for fascist conquest. And when it was no longer reasonable for him to hope that the cataclysms emanating from worldwide mass unemployment and militarized nationalist resentment might be defused, he set about imagining a future on the other side of what he considered certain atrocity. This future became more important to Keynes than anything that had happened or was happening. It not only existed – it was more real to him than his present.[41] Determined not to revert to the futile logics of equilibrium and retribution, the speculative future was, for Keynes, as for Jameson, not escapist, but the only defensible motive for political action.

Analogously, *Ministry for the Future* offers no escape from the pandemic, insurrections, and economic crises unfolding in the year following its publication. While the central plot has a temporal arc from roughly the Indian heat wave of 2025 to the Mary Murphy's retirement around 2050 the novel's chapters sometimes flashback to the twentieth century, and often leave no clue of their temporal position. Its atrocities are already and inevitably upon us.

It is only when Mary Murphy embraces Keynes's position, considering her Ministry as the sole instrument of a global citizenry owed the possibility of something more than bare life, that her calculations change from navigating a path of survival for herself and her staff to overcoming long odds at great risk. Predictably, it is a traumatized revolutionary, Frank May, who shames Murphy into recognizing her complicity in Climate Leviathan. Unpredictably, it is an economist who reorients her praxis. Dick Bosworth, the Ministry's house economist, explains that the economic models relied on by banks, governments, and corporations take for granted the discount rate, a presumption that all future utility, life included, should be devalued by comparison to present utility. "The assumption is that future people will be richer and more powerful than we are, so they'll deal with any problems we create for them," Bosworth explains. "But now that's not true," Murphy protests. To which he replies, "Not even close to true."[42] He then alludes to three Keynes protégés.

Frank Ramsey called the discount rate an "ethically indefensible" assumption, which "arises merely from a weakness of imagination."[43] Ramsey's paper was published in the journal Keynes edited, and he called it "one of the most remarkable contributions to mathematical economics ever made."[44] One of Keynes's most trusted colleagues, Roy Harrod, called the discount rate "a polite expression for rapacity and the conquest of reason by passion."[45] And Robert Solow, part of the first generation of

American Keynesians, used his keynote lecture for the American Economic Association to warn that specifically because of environmental threats economists should abandon their absurd assumption of an "inexhaustible resource base" and set the discount rate to zero, which he called a "policy decision" directed at "intergenerational equity."[46] By having the Ministry's in-house economist allude to Ramsey, Harrod, and Solow in a conversation with his increasingly radicalized boss, Robinson establishes that the orthodox economic preference for the present over the future, perhaps more accurately phrased as discrimination against those who have the misfortune of being children, has long been disputed by not only the Marxian heterodoxy, but also by the Keynesian.

The Moral Art of Economic Science

In a 1938 letter to Harrod, Keynes categorizes economics as "a moral science" and defines it as "a science of thinking in terms of models joined to the art of choosing models which are relevant to the contemporary world."[47] As Robinson argues in *Ministry*, every macroeconomic model is "a speculative fiction." Economic models are "so filled with assumptions that each estimate [is] revealed to be an ideological statement of the viewer's priorities and values."[48] What makes Keynes's theory different is that rather than having to interpret the ideological assumptions of neoliberal models – which are often so steeped in scientism and indoctrination that economists are, like the authors of "Economics After Neoliberalism," appalled when others reveal their own politics to them – Keynes's theory begins with a statement of Utopia.

"The art of choosing models which are relevant to the contemporary world" begins with Keynes conceiving of his "contemporary world" not simply as present conditions (Carthaginian Peace) and recent disruptions (Great War), but also as catastrophic tomorrow (Depression and World War) *and* Utopian future (Guaranteed Income and Elective Labor). Only with Utopia in mind did he move forward with the art and science of economics. The perpetual failure to predict the future accurately, a disciplinary shortcoming that remains the source of much enmity directed at economics, results from the mistaken belief that the future is something that can be deduced from disinterested measurements rather than something that must be created by political action. Not *of*, but *for*.

Unless economists are satisfied with being robotic shills for an unexamined status quo, the practice of economics must begin with compelling speculative fiction. An economics that is not demanding from its practitioners the tenacious pursuit of the horizons of their intelligence *and* imagination is a terrifying solipsism autotrading the transhistorical suffering of millions for the marginal prolonging of a mildly gratifying livelihood for members of the cult.

Notes

1 Suresh Naidu, Dani Rodrik, and Gabriel Zucman, "Economics after Neoliberalism," in *Economics after Neoliberalism*, edited by Joshua Cohen, *Boston Review* 44.3(2019), 9–29; 13.
2 Ibid., 13.
3 Complexity Economists, "A Transdisciplinary Approach," in *Economics after Neoliberalism*, ed. Cohen, 64–69; 64.
4 Amanda Bayer and Cecilia Elena Rouse, "Diversity in the Economics Profession: A New Attack on an Old Problem," *Journal of Economic Perspectives* 30.4 (2016), 221–242.
5 Complexity Economists, "A Transdisciplinary Approach," 67.
6 Julie Thompson Klein, *Interdisciplinarity: History, Theory, and Practice* (Detroit, MI: Wayne State University Press, 1990), 30–32.
7 Complexity Economists, "Transdisciplinary Approach," 64–65.
8 John Maynard Keynes, *The General Theory of Employment, Interest, and Money* (1936; London: Macmillan St. Martin's Press, 1973), 371.
9 See Michel Foucault, *The Birth of Biopolitics*, edited by Michel Senellart, translated by Graham Burchell (New York: Palgrave Macmillan, 2008); Philip Mirowski, Robert Van Horn, and Thomas A. Stapleford, eds., *Building Chicago Economics: New Perspectives on the History of America's Most Powerful Economics Program* (Cambridge: Cambridge University Press, 2011); Quinn Slobodian, *Globalists: The End of Empire and the Birth of Neoliberalism* (Cambridge, MA: Harvard University Press, 2018).
10 See Richard A. Posner, *The Crisis of Capitalist Democracy* (Cambridge, MA: Harvard University Press, 2010); Robert Skidelsky, *Keynes: The Return of the Master* (New York: PublicAffairs, 2009).
11 Foucault, *Birth of Biopolitics*, 79.
12 See David Harvey, *The Enigma of Capital* (Oxford: Oxford University Press, 2010); Geoff Mann, *In the Long Run We Are All Dead: Keynesianism, Political Economy, and Revolution* (London: Verso, 2017).
13 See Dan Sinykin, *American Literature and the Long Downturn: Neoliberal Apocalypse* (Oxford: Oxford University Press, 2020).
14 Anna Kornbluh, "Climate Realism, Capitalist and Otherwise," *Meditations* 33.1 (2019), 99–118; 101.
15 Ezra Klein, "The Most Important Book I've Read This Year," *Vox Conversations*, November 30, 2020, www.vox.com/2020/11/30/21726563/kim-stanley-robinson-the-ezra-klein-show-climate-change.

16 Jameson deploys the aphorism with the qualifier "someone once said" in "Future City," *New Left Review* 21.3 (2003), 65–79; 76. He recycles it, qualifier included, in Fredric Jameson, "An American Utopia," in *An American Utopia: Dual Power and the Universal Army*, edited by Slavoj Žižek (London: Verso, 2016), 1–96; 3. Mark Fisher also famously uses the aphorism to title the opening chapter of *Capitalist Realism: Is There No Alternative?* (Winchester: Zero Books, 2009). Fisher acknowledges the attribution dilemma by splitting credit between Jameson and Žižek (2).

17 I prefer Galbraith's term here, rather than *interventionism, state capitalism*, or *Third Way capitalism*, because it does not assume persistent prioritization of national sovereignty. Durable multilateralism and the ability to sanction even the most powerful member nations are key ingredients of the future Robinson imagines. See John Kenneth Galbraith, *Economics and the Public Purpose* (Boston: Houghton Mifflin, 1973).

18 Sarah Comyn, *Political Economy and the Novel: A Literary History of "Homo Economicus"* (Basingstoke: Palgrave Macmillan, 2018).

19 Kim Stanley Robinson, *The Ministry for the Future* (New York: Orbit, 2020), 55.

20 By *critical theory*, I mean the study of rhetoric and representation, their political appropriations and ideological assumptions, by methods catholic, but practitioners concentrated in philosophy, history, language and literature, and cultural studies.

21 Jameson, "An American Utopia," 6.

22 Robinson, *Ministry for the Future*, 56.

23 Klein, "Most Important Book."

24 Julie Thompson Klein, *Humanities, Culture, and Interdisciplinarity: The Changing American Academy* (Albany: State University of New York Press, 2005), 174.

25 I use "Climate Leviathan" to describe the accelerating deterioration of civil society as a result of increasing climate-driven crises. While Robinson does not deploy the term himself, it clearly fits his plot. I draw the term from Geoff Mann and Joel Wainwright, *Climate Leviathan: A Political Theory of Our Planetary Future* (London: Verso, 2018).

26 Jameson, "American Utopia," 22.

27 Roland Boer, "A Level Playing Field? Metacommentary and Marxism," in *On Jameson: From Postmodernism to Globalization*, edited by Caren Irr and Ian Buchanan (Albany: State University of New York Press, 2006), 51–70; 65.

28 Delton B. Chen, Joel van der Beek, and Jonathan Cloud, "Hypothesis for a Risk Cost of Carbon: Revising the Externalities and Ethics of Climate Change," in *Understanding Risks and Uncertainties in Energy and Climate Policy*, edited by Haris Doukas, Alexandros Flamos, and Jenny Lieu (New York: Springer, 2019), 183–222.

29 While he never names Yanis Varoufakis, the heterodox economist who briefly and controversially served as Greece's Finance Minister, Robinson's descriptions of the Greek debt crisis resemble Varoufakis's account in *And The Weak*

Suffer What They Must? Europe's Crisis and America's Economic Future (New York: Nation, 2016) and *Adults in the Room: My Battle with the European and American Deep Establishment* (New York: Farrar, Straus, & Giroux, 2017).

30 John Maynard Keynes, "Economic Possibilities for Our Grandchildren," in *Essays in Persuasion* (London: Macmillan St. Martin's Press, 1972), 321–332; 331; emphasis in original.

31 Ibid., 331.

32 Ibid., 328–331.

33 Jameson, "American Utopia," 24.

34 Keynes, *General Theory*, 376.

35 Keynes, "Economic Possibilities," 326.

36 Keynes, *General Theory*, 376.

37 For fuller examination of Keynes's eschatology see Mann, *Long Run;* Matt Seybold, "The End of Economics," *Los Angeles Review of Books*, July 3, 2017, https://lareviewofbooks.org/article/the-end-of-economics/; Matt Seybold, "Keynes and Keynesianism," in *The Routledge Companion to Literature and Economics*, edited by Matt Seybold and Michelle Chihara (New York: Routledge, 2018), 272–282.

38 Jameson, "American Utopia," 26.

39 George Orwell, *1984* (1949; Boston: Houghton Mifflin, 1983), 206.

40 Keynes, "Economic Possibilities," 331.

41 My account of strategic presentism owes much to Jeffrey Insko, *History, Abolition, and the Ever-Present Now in Antebellum American Writing* (Oxford: Oxford University Press, 2019) and several works by Anna Kornbluh, notably "Present Tense Futures of the Past," *Victorian Studies* 59.1 (2016), 98–101.

42 Robinson, *Ministry for the Future*, 131.

43 Frank Ramsey, "A Mathematical Theory of Saving," *Economic Journal* 152 (1928), 543–559; 543.

44 John Maynard Keynes, "F. P. Ramsey," *Economic Journal* 157 (1930), 153–154; 153.

45 Roy Harrod, *Towards A Dynamic Economics* (London: Macmillan & Co., 1948), 40.

46 Robert Solow, "The Economics of Resources or the Resources of Economics," *American Economic Review* 64.2 (1974), 1–14; 4, 10.

47 John Maynard Keynes, *The General Theory and After, Part II: Defense and Development* (London: Macmillan St. Martin's Press, 1973), 296–297.

48 Robinson, *Ministry for the Future*, 344.

CHAPTER 16

Reading beyond Behavioral Economics

Gary Saul Morson and Morton Schapiro

In *Cents and Sensibility: What Economics Can Learn from the Humanities* (2017), we argue that while economics is more important than ever, its glaring deficiencies are unnecessary.[1] Its analytical rigor, focus on tradeoffs and efficiency, and ability to suggest beneficial policies make it unusually influential. In an age of fake facts, the statistical tools of economics counter empty political rhetoric.

But its hubris is astonishing. Fewer than half of academic economists believe they can learn from other fields. While 79 percent of psychology professors and 73 percent of sociologists think that interdisciplinary approaches make sense, only 42 percent of economists agree.[2]

But don't economists regularly look to other disciplines for topics of study? Sure. But citation and similar data indicate that economists rarely engage seriously with those fields.[3] Most economic models of behavior disregard psychology while studies of the cycle of poverty ignore sociology. It's as if other disciplines pose questions, but economics, which alone is rigorous, has all the answers. Economists view their discipline as the only true social *science*.

One might suppose that a history of accurate predictions and effective policies justifies such arrogance. Quite the contrary, but disappointments apparently occasion no caution. After failing to anticipate the dot com bubble, the Great Recession, the long-term slowdown in labor productivity growth, the sluggish nature of the last decade's recovery, the surging US stock market following President Trump's election, and the increase in UK employment after the Brexit vote, one might suppose that economists have been chastened. Not that we can see. Like characters in a Jane Austen novel, economists let their "pride and prejudice" obscure counter-evidence.

And this is odd indeed. A sign of a real science is falsifiability. Indeed, any serious discipline is open to contrary evidence.

Often enough, disciplines with deep insights are tempted to claim an unjustifiable status as a hard science and so become pseudo-sciences. Why was Freud not satisfied with saying that *some* errors arise from an unconscious intention to err and instead insisted, from *The Psychopathology of Everyday Life* (1901) on, that *all* errors are intentional in this way? Absolutely "nothing in the mind is arbitrary and undetermined."[4] Nothing at all: "Every change in the clothing usually worn, every small sign of carelessness – such as an unfastened button – ... is intended to express something which the wearer of the clothes does not want to say straight out and which for the most part he is unaware of."[5] In his late work *Civilization and Its Discontents* (1930), Freud again maintains: "in mental life nothing which has once been formed can perish"; "everything is somehow preserved and ... in suitable circumstances ... can once more be brought to light."[6] The reason Freud insisted that absolutely all errors are intentional is that he thought of psychoanalysis as a science like physics, and physical laws do not work only some of the time.

Economists, too, should recognize that some serious nonscientific disciplines offer genuine wisdom. If they thought of themselves this way, they could preserve the best of economics while making it less insular and more effective. One way would be to incorporate ideas from great literature.

Human lives do not unfold predictably, the way Mars orbits the sun. Life displays "narrativeness": some things must be explained by *stories*. The best appreciation of narrative comes from reading the most significant realist novels, which should be considered not just a literary form, but also a distinct way of understanding the social world. Although the events that novels describe are fictional, their shape, sequence, and ramifications often offer the subtlest account of *how* lives unfold. What's more, there is no better source of ethical insight than the novels of Tolstoy, Dostoevsky, George Eliot, Jane Austen, and the other major realists. Their stories convey the complexity of ethical questions that no overarching theory could begin to accommodate – questions calling for good *judgment*, which cannot be formalized.

Moreover, the very process of reading literature involves identifying with characters, an activity offering extensive practice in *empathy*. When you read a great novel, you sense from within what it is like to be someone else. You see the world from the perspective of a different social class, gender, religion, moral understanding, or many other categories differentiating human life. You experience how cultural norms and individual psychology shape each other. Living a character's life vicariously, you not only feel some of what she feels but also reflect on those feelings, consider the nature of the actions they engender, and, with practice, acquire the wisdom to appreciate actual people in all their complexity.

Understanding real people is as important in economics as in other disciplines. If you don't understand what motivates human beings, how can you predict how they will act or know what will benefit them? Sure, you can simply assume individuals act rationally in their own self-interest, and presume that standards of rationality are the same for everyone, and for always. But the founder of modern economics, Adam Smith, rejected the idea that people always act either rationally or in their own self-interest.[7] To fully understand *The Wealth of Nations* (1776), one must read his complementary volume, *The Theory of Moral Sentiments* (1759), which argues that care for others is an "original passion," irreducible to selfish concerns.

To appreciate people, one must develop sensitivity to fine shadings of feeling and motivation. "We are all of us born in moral stupidity, taking the world as an udder to feed our supreme self," observes George Eliot in a chapter of *Middlemarch* (1871–1872) describing how newly married Dorothea unwittingly hurts her husband by not seeing his life from his point of view.[8] She wants to help, but understands his situation as she would experience it, not as he experiences it. To use Smith's distinction, she has put herself in his "position" but not in his "person and character."[9] Her help turns out to be what most wounds him. Eliot continues

> Dorothea had early begun to emerge from that stupidity, but yet it had been easier to her to imagine how she would devote herself to Mr. Casaubon ... than to conceive with that distinctness which is no longer reflection but feeling – an idea wrought back to the directness of sense, like the solidity of objects – that he had an equivalent center of self, whence the light and shadows must always fall with a certain difference.[10]

Here Eliot voices the moral not only of *Middlemarch* but of realist novels generally, which enable us to discern how light and shadow are never the same for any two individuals. It is not enough to realize abstractly that each person has a self like our own. Novels want us to experience that equivalent center of self "with that distinctness which is no longer reflection but feeling."[11] That idea must seem palpable, like the solidity of objects.

Economists have resisted analyzing culture and individual psychology because one cannot mathematicise them, as (in their view) a hard science should. With a choice between incorporating insights about real people or maintaining a claim to scientific status, they chose the latter. If they made the other choice, none of the central economic theories would have to go. They would still stand or fall on the evidence. What would change are the claims made for them and the idea that nothing the humanities offers could matter.

But if literature is so valuable, why is its study in decline?[12] Why is literature lost?[13]

Literature Lost

Oddly enough, literature professors themselves have lost faith in its importance. The idea that great literature is a repository of wisdom has become positively quaint, if not politically suspect. Indeed, the very concept of "great literature" is associated with old fogeys who regard aesthetic value as objective or intrinsic, rather than as a play of ever-changing power interests. But if there is no such thing as great literature, why should anyone study it? If even literature professors deny that such masterpieces exist, it is unsurprising that students don't bother with them. What we like to call "negative fundamentalism" reigns.[14]

Mikhail Bulgakov's novel *The Master and Margarita* (published posthumously in 1966–1967) opens with the devil, who in the guise of a foreign professor visits officially atheist Soviet Russia, intruding on a conversation between an editor, Berlioz, and a poet, Bezdomny. Bezdomny has written a poem insulting Jesus, which might seem to accord with official ideology, but, as Berlioz explains, does not. For the poem presumes that Jesus actually existed, whereas he was a myth. The devil finds this denial amusing because he actually witnessed – and describes – Jesus's interview with Pontius Pilate. The devil is still more delighted when Berlioz and Bezdomny also deny the existence of God and, at last, the devil himself. "'Well, now, this is really getting interesting,' cried the professor, shaking with laughter. 'What is it with you? Whatever comes up you say doesn't exist!'"[15] In a similar spirit of negation, modern "theory and criticism" has for decades favored a rhetoric of denial. Arguably, the discipline's defining move has been assertions of nonexistence. There is no value, just evaluation, and no art, just what is called art.

This way of thinking was pioneered by those denying the very existence of "the author." In his classic essay "The Death of the Author" (1967), Roland Barthes describes authorship as an emptiness: "the author is never more than the instance writing, just as *I* is nothing other than the instance saying *I*: language knows a 'subject' not a 'person,' and this subject, empty outside of the very enunciation which defines it, suffices to make language 'hold together,' suffices, that is to say, to exhaust it." [16] It is not the author who creates but "language." The modern author is a mere "scriptor ... born simultaneously with the text ... in no way equipped with a being preceding or exceeding the writing."[17] Consequently, meaningfulness, too, disappears, as "writing ceaselessly posits meaning ceaselessly to evaporate it."[18]

As it became imperative to infuse criticism with "historical" (political) content, the writer's scriptoriness rendered her a mere recording tool for prevalent ideologies. Fast forward to the field of "cultural studies" and discover the same rhetoric of denial. The widely used *Norton Anthology of Theory and Criticism* explains this new field:

> Literary texts, like other artworks, are neither more nor less important than any other cultural artifact or practice. Keeping the emphasis on how cultural meanings are produced, circulated, and consumed, the investigator will focus on art or literature insofar as such works connect with broader social factors, not because they possess some intrinsic interest or special aesthetic values.[19]

Art contains no "aesthetic values." Neither does it exhibit any "intrinsic interest" making it more important than "any other cultural artifact or practice." Artifact, practice, production, circulation, consumption: the language here demystifies literature and art (or "literature" and "art") by reducing them to commodities. Strangely enough, then, literary theorists find as little wisdom in literature as economists do. Both could learn from the deep understanding of people, cultures, and ethics that great literature – which surely does exist – conveys.

Humanism and Behavioral Economics

We often hear that behavioral economics is already studying actual human beings. In fact, behavioral economists could also use insights from literature. Behavioral economists have shown that sometimes people behave irrationally, that is, differently from the way standard rational choice models predict.

For a humanist, this might seem like an improvement. In some respects, it is. But by and large behavioral economics repeats shortcomings of rational choice models. Whatever else it might do, behavioral economics does not humanize mainstream economics. Behavioral economics properly distinguishes between how people should behave (according to rationality models) and how they do behave – or, to use Richard Thaler's terms, between "Econs" and "Humans" (as determined by laboratory experiments).[20] Unfortunately, these "humans" bear little resemblance to actual people.

At their best, mainstream economists follow Milton Friedman's advice and offer their view of choice as a useful fiction justified by the predictions it enables.[21] They neither endorse nor reject the view that people actually make their choices rationally. Behavioral economists offer no such qualification.[22] They claim to describe how agents actually behave. Therefore, the objection that their view of people is shallow has real bite, as it would not for a mainstream economist following Friedman's advice. Only if you claim to do something can you be faulted for failing. We see at least three objections to these ideas. They concern the neglect of culture, the thin sense of a person, and the existence of genuine irrationalities.

The Neglect of Culture

Most strikingly, behavioral economists take no more account of culture than mainstream economists. Their portraits of decision-making show how people – any people – make biased decisions. To explain such irrationalities, they leap over culture to evolutionary psychology or neurobiology. Isn't this odd? Since we are dealing with people, rather than organisms, why go first to the organic? If one was trying to understand why Swedes or Saudis marry or divorce, and if one was unsatisfied by explanations offered by the economics of the family, one might first examine differences between Swedish and Saudi culture, before one invoked neurons and evolution. But behavioral economics does nothing of the kind. The model of a decision-maker remains just as acultural. And people remain just as predictable, as they would not be if something as complex as culture were considered. A humanist might identify a common fallacy, which we call the fallacy of abstraction. The mistaken idea is that because cultures vary, nothing cultural can be essentially human, and so one can best understand the human by *abstracting* everything merely cultural.

But it does not follow that because a model can abstract culture from humanness that the essentially human is precultural. One might as well argue that because languages vary, the essentially human is prelingual like a chimp. Cultures differ, but all people belong to *some* culture. To think away language and culture is not to arrive at, but to bypass, the human. The more novels we read the less likely we are to commit this fallacy, as behavioral economists do.

The Thin Sense of a Person

A humanist is often moved to say, "You mean, you had to prove that?" We are told of discoveries like these:

Sunk costs matter. If a person bought an expensive theatre ticket, but on the evening of the play would rather do something else, she might "irrationally" choose not to "waste" her purchase.

People use reference points to determine what is a good purchase, so establishing a different reference point may affect the decision. It is concluded that since only one of these decisions can be rational, the others must be irrational.

It matters how you frame a decision: if you want to charge two different prices (say, one for a cash purchase and another for a charge), you will encounter less resistance by calling the lower price a discount than by calling the higher price a surcharge.

People are more likely to expend a given amount of effort to save money on a small purchase than to save the same money on a large purchase. A person who would travel fifteen minutes to save $10 on a $25 coffeemaker will not travel the same distance to save $10 on a $30,000 car. But since it is the same effort for the same number of dollars, that (according to the behavioral economist) is irrational. Such a person "is not valuing time consistently."[23]

None of these insights seems remarkable, a humanist might think, to anyone with introspection. Indeed, they are unsurprising to shoppers. Everyone knows that marketers call prices markdowns whenever possible. And who has not noticed that merchants price products at $19.99 rather than $20, as if that penny made a bigger difference than a penny off $19.50? If marketers and their customers are aware of these facts, where's the discovery? Colleges realize that a $10,000 discount off the sticker price often has a larger enrollment impact if labeled "merit aid" rather than "need-based aid." Surprised? We doubt it.

Behavioral economics notwithstanding, these reactions may not be irrational. Imagine a novelist describing someone buying a car. The person has a specific story that, let us say, has led to reluctance to spend large sums. She has gone through a day, described at length, in which she quarreled with her spouse, endured indigestion, was trapped in traffic and then sped to make up for lost time, and, shortly before entering the showroom, heard distressing news on the radio. She is no expert on automobiles and knows she is at a disadvantage in negotiations. Would it really be wise for her to worry about $10 as she would when buying a toaster? After all, attention is a limited resource, and it would be foolish to spend it on something so small in proportion to the purchase. One risks overlooking something much more significant. Indeed, a salesman might try to distract a potential buyer from important issues by raising minor ones. Mainstream economics can handle the idea that husbanding attention is wise with a model accepting attention, like time, as a limited resource.

For the same reason, it is sometimes rational, not predictably irrational, to make a habit of trusting habits and a rule of following rules, even though on particular occasions the result is suboptimal outcomes. We are often aware that such outcomes happen and, even when clearly recognized, may choose to follow the rule so as not to establish the need to think through future choices. You can't just follow a rule, you have to make a rule of doing so, as any dieter knows. The standard behavioral economics examples of irrationality overlook rational accommodations to human limitations.

Culture, as well as human nature, may also shape how and whether one can properly negotiate, how much one should value money saved, and other aspects of a transaction. More is involved in an exchange than the exchange itself. We are always monitoring our self-image, which is shaped by cultural values. And what is irrational in one culture may be rational in another. Consider the issue that Richard Thaler calls "the gift paradox": "Lee's wife gives him an expensive cashmere sweater for Christmas. He had seen the sweater in the store and decided that it was too big of an indulgence to feel good about buying it. He is nevertheless delighted with the gift. Lee and his wife pool all their financial assets; neither has any separate source of money." Thaler regards this as economically irrational because "Lee feels better about spending family resources on an expensive sweater if his wife made the decision, though the sweater was no cheaper."[24]

It seems decidedly odd that any discipline studying people would be puzzled by the difference a gift makes. It is hardly surprising that in the history of anthropology, gifts, and their complex meanings in different cultures, have figured prominently, at least since Bronislaw Malinowski's *Argonauts of the Western Pacific* (1922) and Marcel Mauss's *The Gift* (1925).[25] It turns out that the market system belongs to a larger category of exchange types, involving different concepts of honor, and various expectations of reciprocity. Malinowski shows how "the economic standpoint" fails to capture what is involved in Trobriand Island gift giving, "since there is no enhancement of mutual utility through the exchange." For example, "it is quite a usual thing in the Trobriands for a type of transaction to take place in which A gives twenty baskets of yams to B, receiving for it a small polished blade, only to have the whole transaction reversed in a few weeks' time."[26] For that matter, gifts, which we all distinguish from purchases, play a prominent role in our own culture.

If Lee's feeling better requires explanation, then so do Christmas stockings, birthday and anniversary presents, gift certificates, and countless other behaviors that comprise daily lives. Indeed, we might regard someone not understanding gifts as deficient and wonder apprehensively what else to expect from him.

Thaler notes that "economic man" would be "perplexed by the very idea of gifts" because he would know that cash is the best possible gift "since it allows the recipient to buy whatever is optimal."[27] Then why do close friends not routinely give cash, and why do many regard such a gift as insensitive? To see what this perspective omits, one does not need to turn to the psychology of perception, neurobiology, or the "misbehaviors" studied by behavioral economists. One needs to understand one's culture, which one cannot grasp by inspecting the brain. One might instead turn to literature, beginning with the gifts Raskolnikov receives from his mother in *Crime and Punishment* (1866), or even the useless but immensely valuable gifts in O. Henry's sentimental tale "The Gift of the Magi" (1905).

Lee might appreciate the gift not because he uses a different mental accounting for gifts (as a behavioral economist might explain), but precisely because it came from his wife. She thought enough to anticipate what he might like. The main currency here is not money but *care*, which is why the fact that they share a bank account does not matter. Indeed, gifts often have no economic value at all. One might cherish an inept drawing done when one's son was eight precisely because at age eight he thought enough to make and give it. It's not available on eBay. Where's the puzzle?

Behavioral economists might reply to the query "you mean, you had to prove this?" by explaining that what is obvious to a humanist is not to an economist. And if that were all that behavioral economists were claiming, who would object? But it is not. If they were only reasserting a truism that everyone but mainstream economists knows, why seek support in laboratory experiments? One does not prove that the sexes are attracted to each other, that people are capable of aggression, or that taste in art differs by doing fMRIs. On the contrary, one would sooner suspect the usefulness of fMRIs if they showed anything else. And if they were only supplying economists with truisms, why claim to be remaking the social sciences generally, offer suggestions on public policy, or give advice to people about their social lives?

The Existence of Genuine Irrationalities

The "irrationalities" and "misbehaviors" cited by behavioral economics are not the irrationalities that occur to humanists. They are simply a sort of cognitive equivalent to optical illusions. These illusions and biases exist, of course. But there are other irrationalities. Sometimes we seem to act according to a will not our own. The military uses this tendency to bind soldiers in a group they would die for. Politicians at mass rallies exploit it, too. People get swept up and do what they would not otherwise do and wonder at later. It happens at football games. In the Middle Ages, this was thought of as possession because it seemed as if an alien will were in control. Social psychologists do not, of course, invoke the devil, but they do consider the fact that people are by nature members of groups, and that sometimes their "hive switch" is activated.[28] In his classic 1841 study, *Extraordinary Popular Delusions and the Madness of Crowds*, Charles MacKay traces a variety of phenomena, from the South Sea and Tulip Bubbles to witch manias, where people succumb to frenzies they later recognize as madness.[29] For a while, a person's will apparently ceases to be his own and is shaped by "the madness of crowds." The will becomes double, partly the person's own, partly that of the crowd acting within him. Afterward, these people can't fathom why they behaved that way or, as we say, "what possessed them." This vulnerability is entailed by our essentially social nature.

No less interesting, we sometimes deliberately act against our self-interest precisely to show that we can be unpredictable. That is the theme of Dostoevsky's *Notes from Underground* (1864). One may even take pride in one's own degradation, a phenomenon Dostoevsky calls "lacerations." In such cases, rational choice economics has met its match.

Human intentions are much more complex than behavioral economics allows. For example, it is commonly supposed that before one can do something, one must have chosen to do it (whether rationally or irrationally). In fact, we often do things without deciding at all. One might, for instance, enter a dream state or a sort of long-term trance, stupor, or other debilitating mood. Or one might keep options open by living in "hypothetical" time. In *Crime and Punishment*, Raskolnikov does both and winds up killing the old pawnbroker without ever having decided to do so. What's more, people deceive themselves about their wishes. Self-deception by its very nature involves double intentionality. It is also very hard to explain from any rationalist perspective: if you know you are trying to deceive yourself, why wouldn't you automatically detect the deception? And yet it happens all the time. Psychological novelists have detailed the processes by which self-deception takes place.

If we begin with mainstream economics, we can describe much human behavior. After all, people often do act rationally. Even when individuals don't, market forces may produce in the aggregate what rational individuals would have chosen. For all practical purposes, that may amount to the same thing. Mainstream economists, when careful, can avoid the accusation of psychological naiveté by adhering to Friedman's rule: claim not to be describing real people but only constructing a useful fiction to be judged by the accuracy of its predictions. This stance makes the objections raised by behavioral economists against mainstream economics – namely, that real individuals behave irrationally – largely beside the point. By contrast, behavioral economists rarely adhere to the Friedman rule. Based on their experiments, they make claims about individual psychology. In so doing they invite objections that they are not doing a good job at it. Omitting culture becomes a major problem. Making claims a Friedman-inspired mainstream economist would avoid, they have gone further from, not closer to, a humanist perspective.

But behavioral economists are not bound to this error. They too could observe the Friedman rule. In that case, the insights they derive would be offered not as adequate descriptions of individuals, but as prompts for predictions on the same scale (but different from) those of mainstream economists.[30] Their only claim would be that those predictions are superior. That is just what Raj Chetty does in his article "Behavioral Economics and Public Policy: A Pragmatic Perspective" (2015). Chetty's pragmatic approach avoids arguing that behavioral economics is theoretically superior or a better description of individual behavior. Instead, it "starts from a policy question ... and incorporates behavioral factors to the extent that they improve empirical predictions. ... This approach follows the widely applied methodology of positive economics advocated by Friedman, who argued that it is more useful to evaluate economic models on the accuracy of their empirical predictions than on their assumptions." So viewed, behavioral economics is not an assault on but a "natural progression" from mainstream economists, "part of all economists' toolkit."[31]

After offering several examples, Chetty concludes that "the applications reviewed in this paper show that an updated reading of the 'as if' approach to economic modeling advocated by Friedman ... calls for incorporating behavioral economics" insofar as it "can offer more accurate and robust predictions for optimal policy."[32] Viewed in this way, behavioral and mainstream economics stand together so far as claims are concerned. If either is understood as Friedman proposed, then it may, when appropriate, be usefully supplemented or corrected by insights from the humanities, both psychological (for descriptive accuracy) and moral (since policy recommendations are never of strictly economic concern).

The Future

If behavioral economics is unlikely to redeem the discipline, is it realistic that taking literature seriously will? Of course not. But we believe that learning from literature, philosophy, and the other humanities, along with history, sociology, anthropology, psychology, and political science, may lead economists to develop more realistic models of human behavior, recognize that they should not be so sure, and derive more effective and just policies. After all, what do we have to lose? As Andrew Haldane, Chief Economist of the Bank of England, put it when considering forecasts of a recession made by a wide variety of economic experts following the Brexit vote, as opposed to the employment and investment growth that actually took place, "Out of this crisis, there could be a rebirth of economics."[33] Perhaps that rebirth will begin in the library.[34]

Notes

1 Gary Saul Morson and Morton Schapiro, *Cents and Sensibility: What Economics Can Learn from the Humanities* (Princeton, NJ: Princeton University Press, 2017). We extend that discussion in *Minds Wide Shut: How the New Fundamentalisms Divide Us* (Princeton, NJ: Princeton University Press, 2021). This chapter draws on both.

2 We first learned of the survey from which these numbers are drawn, and of a fascinating talk by the Bank of England's Chief Economist, Andrew G. Haldane ("The Dappled World," G. L. S. Shackle Biennial Memorial Lecture, November 10, 2016) from John Lanchester, "On Money," *New York Times Magazine*, February 12, 2017. The survey, done by Neil Gross and Solon Simmons, "The Social and Political Views of American Professors," is discussed in detail, along with related analyses, in an illuminating paper by Marion Fourcade, Etienne Ollion, and Yann Algan, "The Superiority of Economists," *Journal of Economic Perspectives* 29.1 (2015), 89–114.

3 See Fourcade, Ollion, and Algan, "Superiority of Economists." According to their analysis of citations in top economic journals, there *is* a discipline economists increasingly embrace: not sociology or political science, but finance – not exactly a subject far removed from economics!

4 Sigmund Freud, *The Psychopathology of Everyday Life*, Standard Edition of the Complete Psychological Works of Sigmund Freud, Vol. VI, edited and translated by James Strachey in collaboration with Anna Freud, assisted by Alix Strachey and Alan Tyson (1901; London: Hogarth Press, 1960), 242.

5 Ibid., 194. See John Farrell, *Freud's Paranoid Quest: Psychoanalysis and Modern Suspicion* (New York: New York University Press, 1996), 47.

6 Sigmund Freud, *Civilization and Its Discontents*, edited and translated by James Strachey (1930; New York: Norton, 1961), 16–17.

7   Deirdre McCloskey presents an intriguing look at Adam Smith as well as other influential economists in "Adam Smith Did Humanomics: So Should We," a talk given at the Eastern Economic Association meetings, February 25, 2016.

8   George Eliot, *Middlemarch* (1871–1872; New York: Modern Library, 1984), 205.

9   Smith argues that care for others is not just another form of selfishness. Some say that when I sympathize with another (say, for the loss of a son), I am simply imaging what I would feel like in such circumstances and so am being entirely selfish. On the contrary, says Smith, when I enter your grief "I do not consider what I, a person of such a character and profession, should suffer, if I had a son." Rather, "I not only change circumstances with you, but I change persons and characters. My grief, therefore, is entirely upon your account, and not in the least upon my own" (Adam Smith, *The Theory of Moral Sentiments*, edited by D. D. Raphael and A. L. Macfie [1759; Indianapolis, IN: Liberty, 1982], 317).

10 Eliot, *Middlemarch*, 205.

11 Ibid.

12 See, for example, Colleen Flaherty, "Withering Humanities Jobs: Full-Time Jobs in English and Languages Continue to Decline, Reaching a New Low, Says Preliminary Annual Jobs Report from the Modern Language Association," *Inside Higher Ed*, November 21, 2017, www.insidehighered .com/news/2017/11/21/full-time-jobs-english-and-languages-reach-new-low-mla-report-finds. Moreover, the long-standing trend continues of having non-tenure-line positions growing more rapidly than tenure-track ones, with contingent faculty often working under difficult conditions: see Scott Jaschik, "The Shrinking Humanities Job Market: New Analysis Finds the Number of Doctorates Awarded Keeps Rising, Even as Number of Job Openings Drops," *Inside Higher Ed*, August 28, 2017, www.insidehighered .com/news/2017/08/28/more-humanities-phds-are-awarded-job-openings-are-disappearing; and Colleen Flaherty, "GAO Report on Non-Tenure-Track Faculty," *Inside Higher Ed*, November 21, 2017, www.insidehighered.com/ quicktakes/2017/11/21/gao-report-non-tenure-track-faculty. Kevin Carey, "The Bleak Job Landscape of Adjunctopia for PhDs," *New York Times*, March 6, 2020, www.nytimes.com/2020/03/05/upshot/academic-job-crisis-phd.html, concludes: "The humanities labor market is in crisis. Higher education industry trade publications are full of essays by young PhDs who despair of ever finding a steady job ... The number of new jobs for English professors has fallen every year since 2012, by a total of 33 percent."

13 We borrow this phrase from John M. Ellis, *Literature Lost: Social Agendas and the Corruption of the Humanities* (New Haven, CT: Yale University Press, 1997).

14 For more on how humanists sow the seeds of their own destruction, see: Charlie Tyson, "The Rise of Reassurance Lit," *Chronicle of Higher Education*, February 28, 2020, www.chronicle.com/article/the-rise-of-reassurance-lit/;

Karen E. Spierling, "The Humanities Must Go on the Offensive," *Chronicle of Higher Education*, December 8, 2019, www.chronicle.com/article/the-human ities-must-go-on-the-offensive/; Eric Adler, "When Humanists Undermine the Humanities," *Chronicle Review*, May 14, 2017, www.chronicle.com/arti cle/when-humanists-undermine-the-humanities/; Timothy Brennan, "The Digital-Humanities Bust," *Chronicle Review*, October 20, 2017, www .chronicle.com/article/the-digital-humanities-bust/; and Scott Jaschik, "Hoax with Multiple Targets: Fake Article Is Published, Calling for the Penis to be Seen Conceptually, Not as a Body Organ. Debates Take Off about Gender Studies and Open-Access Journals," *Inside Higher Ed*, May 22, 2017, www .insidehighered.com/news/2017/05/22/faux-scholarly-article-sets-criticism- gender-studies-and-open-access-publishing. Not that changing student tastes are completely blameless: see Colleen Flaherty, "Liberal Arts College Students Are Getting Less Artsy: At Colleges Proud of Attracting Students Who Want a Broad-Based, Non-Vocational Education, Numbers of Majors in Arts and Humanities Are Falling," *Inside Higher Ed*, February 21, 2017, www .insidehighered.com/news/2017/02/21/liberal-arts-students-fears-about-job- market-upon-graduation-are-increasingly.

15 Mikhail Bulgakov, *The Master and Margarita*, translated by Diana Burgin and Katherine Tiernan O'Connor (1966–1967; New York: Random House, 1995), 35.

16 Roland Barthes, "The Death of the Author," translated by Stephen Heath, in *The Norton Anthology of Theory and Criticism*, 2nd ed., edited by Vincent B. Leitch (New York: Norton, 2011), 1322–1326; 1323.

17 Ibid., 1324.

18 Ibid., 1325.

19 *Norton Anthology*, 2478.

20 Richard Thaler, *Misbehaving: The Making of Behavioral Economics* (New York: Norton, 2015). For a superb review of the field, see Raj Chetty, "Behavioral Economics and Public Policy: A Pragmatic Perspective," Richard T. Ely Lecture, *American Economic Review: Papers and Proceedings 2015*, 1–33.

21 In his celebrated 1953 essay, "The Methodology of Positive Economics," Friedman conceded that the rational choice model might be based on implau- sible psychology, but that would not matter if the model led to good pre- dictions. Milton Friedman, "The Methodology of Positive Economics," in *Essays in Positive Economics* (Chicago: University of Chicago Press, 1953), 3–43, reprinted in *The Methodology of Positive Economics*, edited by Uskali Maki (Cambridge: Cambridge University Press, 2009), 3–42.

22 An important exception is Chetty, cited above and discussed subsequently.

23 Thaler, *Misbehaving*, 21

24 Ibid., 20–21.

25 Bronislaw Malinowski, *Argonauts of the Western Pacific: An Account of Native Enterprise and Adventure in the Archipelagoes of Melanesian New Guinea* (1922; New York: Dutton, 1961), and Marcel Mauss, *Essai sur le don: Form et raison de l'echange dans les societies archaiques*, translated as *The Gift: The Form and*

Reason for Exchange in Archaic Societies, translated by W. D. Halls (1925; London: Routledge, 1990).

26 Malinowski, *Argonauts*, 175.

27 Thaler, *Misbehaving*, 6.

28 See, for example, Jonathan Haidt, *The Righteous Mind: Why Good People Are Divided by Politics and Religion* (New York: Pantheon, 2012), 221–245.

29 Charles MacKay, *Extraordinary Popular Delusions and the Madness of Crowds* (1841; Radford, VA: Wilder Publications, 2008).

30 In *Thinking Fast and Slow* (New York: Farrar, Straus, & Giroux, 2011), Daniel Kahneman stresses that when he and Amos Tversky were developing ideas leading to behavioral economics, they relied heavily on introspection.

31 Chetty, "Behavioral Economics," 1, 29.

32 Ibid., 29.

33 See Phillip Inman, "Chief Economist of Bank of England Admits Errors in Brexit Forecasting," *Guardian*, January 5, 2017, www.theguardian.com/business/2017/jan/05/chief-economist-of-bank-of-england-admits-errors.

34 We hold out hope. On January 7, 2017, just a few months after Haldane's provocative lecture challenging economists to look at economic systems through a cross-disciplinary lens, Robert Shiller gave his presidential address to the American Economic Association. Entitled "Narrative Economics" (published in the *American Economic Review* 107.4 [2017], 967–1004), it argued that economists ignore stories at their peril, since "stories motivate and connect activities to deeply felt values and needs" (967). See also Shiller's subsequent book *Narrative Economics: How Stories Go Viral and Drive Major Economic Events* (Princeton, NJ: Princeton University Press, 2019). A recent article, Josh Angrist, Pierre Azoulay, Glenn Ellison, Ryan Hill, and Susan Feng Lu, "Inside Job or Deep Impact? Extramural Citations and the Influence of Economic Scholarship," *Journal of Economic Literature* 58.1 (2020), 3–52, argues that economists are becoming less insular: "We document a clear rise in the extramural influence of economic research, while also showing that economics is increasingly likely to reference other social sciences" (3). It's a start.

CHAPTER 17

Fictional Expectations and Imagination in Economics

Jens Beckert and Richard Bronk

This chapter demonstrates how economics can learn lessons and draw useful analogies from literature and literary theory. These lessons apply at two levels: they help illuminate the everyday behavior and belief systems of economic agents, and they also have implications for the nature of economics as an academic discipline.[1]

We argue that, to understand behavior and the formation of expectations in modern economies, it is necessary to examine the role of imagined states of the world in helping people construct and navigate the uncertain future. Modern capitalism is a quintessentially creative and imaginative system: it is driven as much by dreams, emotions, and dystopias as by calculation; it is structured by language and narratives; and it has novelty and radical uncertainty at its heart. This has implications at a meta level for the nature of economics: economists need to engage in metaphorical thinking – the imaginative transfer of concepts from one domain to another – to shine new light on the dynamism and innovation that are central to economic activity but poorly explained by current economic models. They must take seriously the role of imagined futures and other forms of fiction in guiding the expectations and behavior of economic actors. Indeed, we argue for a new form of "narrative economics" and the use of analytical imagination to help "read" and "interpret" the stories, imagined futures, social frames, and calculative practices that structure economic decision-making.

Suggesting a central role for fiction and imagination jars with the conception that most economists have of their discipline as the most precise and empirically grounded of the social sciences: they focus on using mathematical models to analyze and predict the market behavior of economic agents. These models are frequently sophisticated and incorporate vast data sets of relevant factors. But at their core is a simple assumption that economic actors rationally optimize their utility within given constraints in the light of "rational expectations" (or informed predictions of the future) with the result that economic outcomes tend to a predictable equilibrium. Since markets are fiercely competitive, economists assume that anyone behaving irrationally would tend to lose out to those who internalize the correct model of how the economy works and have a firm grasp of objective probability functions. From their perspective, it would be retrograde to assume that market participants in practice *imagine* the future and attempt to convince others of their fictions. Why would it make sense to replace (or complement) the dominant "rational expectations" hypothesis with one of "fictional expectations?"[2]

Our theory of fictional expectations is founded on two pillars: firstly, empirical observation of actual economic decision-making; and secondly, epistemological theory about the problems of knowledge facing economic actors, especially in relation to the future.

There is now a growing body of empirical studies demonstrating the large role played by narratives in structuring behavior and guiding expectations in the economy. Robert Boyer has detailed how successive phases of recent capitalist history characterized by increasing levels of uncertainty have been structured around a series of beguiling "grand narratives" (or overarching stories) – such as "*Japan number one, the new economy*, and the omniscience of financial markets" – each of which has served for a time to coordinate investment and increase confidence.[3] David Tuckett has likewise shown that stock-market investors rely on investment *stories* to give them the necessary conviction to act.[4] At a policy level, Douglas Holmes has demonstrated how far central banks rely on rhetoric and communication to achieve the goals of policy: a central bank's public statements seek to persuade market participants to internalize policy goals as their own expectations. So, for example, when Mario Draghi said in 2012 that the European Central Bank would do "whatever it takes" to rescue the euro, these three words did more than anything else to calm market expectations and solve the euro crisis.[5] At the level of consumption, we are frequently influenced by imaginaries of future pleasure that we project onto the next generation of new goods, under the influence of a constant stream of marketing images and narratives.[6]

To understand why narratives and imagined futures seem to have such a significant effect in structuring expectations and behavior, we need to understand the problems that economic actors face in knowing enough to make the sort of rational calculations that economic models assume are possible. In all walks of life, human beings face barriers to knowledge and struggle to make sense of multifaceted reality. But economic actors face an additional problem: a large part of the economic activity typical of modern capitalism is geared to the future. People save for a retirement that may never happen; they invest in new products or processes that they expect will deliver useful service in the future; or they buy assets in the hope they will rise in value. But, crucially, the future envisaged is not – as is commonly assumed by economists – a straightforward statistical shadow of the past: it is neither predictable according to well-understood laws of motion like the future of planetary orbits; nor, for the most part, is it predictable in objective probability terms (like the incidence of road deaths) on the basis of past data and observed factors. To use Frank Knight's terminology, the future is often a matter of radical *uncertainty* rather than calculable *risk*.[7]

There are several reasons for this: first, global markets and financial networks have many of the classic properties of complex adaptive systems – with non-linear reactions and threshold effects – so that small changes in initial conditions can snowball into radically novel outcomes.[8] Second, market capitalism is frequently subject to counter-movements of social and political protest and the unpredictable policy changes these imply.[9] Most importantly of all, the economic future is to a significant extent the contingent creation of a dynamic series of collective and individual attempts to *reimagine* and refashion the economy. In other words, the economic future is not "out there" waiting to be discovered; rather, as James Buchanan and Viktor Vanberg put it, it is unknowable in advance because it has "yet to be created" by how we and others imagine, choose, and *will* it to be.[10]

This has enormous implications for the nature of economic behavior: first, economic actors frequently become disoriented and anxious when faced with what Zygmunt Bauman calls "liquid modernity" and the growing realization that uncertainty is "*the only* certainty"; and, as David Tuckett argues, they consequently rely on "conviction narratives" to "manage anticipations of gain and loss" and "support action emotionally."[11] Second, it can no longer be assumed that market prices reflect the best available facts about the future, nor that expectations are guided largely by calculations of objective probability functions. Instead, as George Shackle put it: "Valuation is expectation and expectation is imagination."[12] Economic actors have no choice but to imagine the unknowable future; and the contingent imaginaries (and attendant emotional states) that structure their expectations and motivate action help determine market prices and construct the future. Imagined futures or fictional expectations matter to economic decision-making as much as data about past regularities.

Once this insight is acknowledged, it puts a whole new complexion on the nature of economics as a discipline: economic models themselves can be seen as simplifying fictions designed to encapsulate causal mechanisms and help us spot emerging patterns and diagnose persistent tendencies; and, in many cases, it is these modelling fictions that structure market expectations and behavior and thereby influence (or "perform") the future. At the same time, economists must learn to interpret the particular fictions (whether in the form of models or narratives) that motivate economic actors in different situations if they wish to explain outcomes or have any hope of predicting uncertain futures.

Uncertainty and Imagination in Modern Capitalism

To underline the importance of fictional expectations in the economy, it is worth explaining further why uncertainty is such a central feature of modern capitalism and how the human capacity to imagine new futures and create different types of fiction relates to that uncertainty.

Joseph Schumpeter first pointed out that the competition that counts in markets comes "from the new commodity, the new technology ... the new type of organization." The consequent "process of industrial muta-tion," he argued, "incessantly revolutionizes the economic structure *from within*"; and this "process of Creative Destruction is the essential fact about capitalism."[13] In other words, the economic system is itself a source of constant novelty, which disrupts the predictable links between past and future and makes the future inherently uncertain. It is the capacity of entrepreneurs to imagine new ways of doing business, new products, or simply new symbolic significance for existing items that is responsible both for the dynamism of capitalist economies and for the radical uncertainty at their heart. The economist George Shackle noted that "our own original ungoverned novelties of imagination" are responsible for "injecting, in some respect *ex nihilo*, the unforeknowable arrangement of elements."[14] It is this imaginative capacity to invent new ideas and novel fictions (or counterfactuals) – and to react creatively to the innovations of others – that makes it impossible for economic agents to assume that the future will closely resemble the past or behave in accordance with existing models. The limitless ability of the human mind to make new connections across synapses in the brain (and between existing ideas) and then, as William Wordsworth put it, to "build up greatest things / From least suggestions" is sufficient to ensure that our socioeconomic future is indeterminate and unpredictable.[15]

If the human imagination is deeply "subversive of established order" and one of the main causes of uncertainty, it is also our principal tool for navigating uncertain futures.[16] It facilitates choice by allowing us to play with different scenarios and visualize a variety of counterfactuals and possible options. It can also furnish us with the confidence and motivation to act *despite* uncertainty by providing us with working fictions detailing how the future might unfold – fictions that go well beyond existing information. Actors act *as if* the future will unfold in a certain way, even though they cannot know. In this sense, fictional expectations take the role of "placeholders," compensating for the impossibility of knowing for sure. As the essayist William Hazlitt pointed out, even the basic utilitarian notion central to economics that individuals pursue their own self-interest should be recognized as essentially an imaginative enterprise: because the future is "undetermined" and even our identities and preferences change over time, we must imagine the interest that our imagined future selves would feel for an imagined future, and it is this imaginary that excites in us a current "emotion of interest" sufficient to motivate us to act.[17] This link between imaginaries and emotions is crucial. As John Stuart Mill noted, "the imaginative emotion which an idea when vividly conceived excites in us, is not an illusion but a fact, as real as any of the other qualities of objects."[18]

Decisions made in conditions of economic uncertainty are then based on fictional expectations – on contingent imaginaries and interpretations of what the future may hold. But these fictions and interpretations are not solely individually formed or internalized. Indeed, most fictions are strongly influenced by the social norms and institutional settings in which they operate. At key points, narrative entrepreneurs and opinion formers seek to challenge prevailing orthodoxies, refashion the social context in which we form expectations, and make their images of the future count; but, to be socially influential, these new images must in turn become shared – what Kenneth Boulding calls "public images" that structure beliefs and action beyond an individual.[19]

The socially constructed nature of expectations may reduce the uncertainty that individuals face by constraining the likely range of their fellow citizens' reactions to novel situations. But, crucially, this can have knock-on effects that actually increase uncertainty in the economic system: since interpretations of the uncertain future are always prone to error, the social formation of fictional expectations and the prevalence of widely shared narratives (for example, homogenous scripts of what constitutes best practice) can lead to herd behavior and the sort of highly correlated errors that can destabilize markets and lead to disruptive and indeterminate outcomes.[20]

Fictional expectations are not, of course, formed without recourse to rational calculation. Indeed, as William Hazlitt argued, we need a "reasoning imagination" that adapts our imaginaries to emerging patterns and evidence of hard constraints.[21] Just because the future is uncertain does not mean that we have no clue about the future. Economic activity is largely structured by the "often fraught co-production of expectations" by imagination, information, and calculative devices. Calculative instruments and models act as instruments of – and props to – the economic imagination.[22]

Four Types of Working Fiction

Before we explore some of the resemblances between fictional expectations and literary fictions, and outline a new form of narrative economics, it is important to distinguish between fiction and fantasy and to uncover the layers of fiction at work in economic decision-making.

The prospectuses and narratives peddled by the "projectors" in eighteenth-century Europe were often little different from the fantasies found in novels, except they were designed to persuade the gullible to invest.[23] Today, for the most part, the fictional expectations of market participants are not willful fantasies designed to deceive themselves or others; instead, they include a story of what will constitute the actors' own best interests, in which (as Martin Giraudeau argues) imaginative foresight is "under strict knowledge oversight."[24] Economic actors create fictions about the future that are heavily laced with, and structured by, the output of analytical procedures and models designed to diagnose emerging patterns and analyze relevant information. Their expectations nevertheless remain fictional – the product of imagination – to the extent that it is impossible to overcome barriers to knowledge. In particular, statements regarding uncertain futures (and how to reach or avoid such futures) necessarily entail assumptions that cannot be based solely on observable truths. Intentionally rational decisions must be based on how we imagine the future – on the kind of "*as if*" thinking central to fictional texts.

The fictional element envisaged here is complementary to – and more radical than – the constructive fictions that Hans Vaihinger and others argue are necessarily a feature of our attempts to make sense of brute reality.[25] We all act *as if* the world-as-it-appears-to-us when constructed according to contingent categories and linguistic frames our minds supply resembles the world-as-it-really-is. As Wordsworth put it: "In weakness we create distinctions, then / Believe that all our puny boundaries are things / Which we perceive and not which we have made."[26] In other words, all rational analysis – indeed all perception – is to some extent fictional in the sense of being a necessarily contingent construction of reality-as-it-appears-to-us. The English Romantic poets were among the first to recognize the significance of this. Samuel Taylor Coleridge saw the mind as a "lantern" directing our attention to some aspects of reality; while for Wordsworth, the mind is a "creator and receiver both" and half-creates what we perceive.[27] As M. H. Abrams wrote in *The Mirror and the Lamp* (1953), facts (as the derivation of the word from the Latin *facta* implies) came to be seen as "things made as much as things found, and made in part by the analogies through which we look at the world as through a lens."[28]

To this primary element of *constructive fiction* in all human understanding of the world, we can add a second type of working fiction found in any *social* interaction. When individuals try to make sense of societies or economies, they are interpreting a social reality that is *preinterpreted* by the actors enacting it. This means that citizens and social scientists alike must interpret the fictional constructions that others place on their own predicament because these fictions help structure social reality by influencing perceptions and behavior. All social analysis (whether practical or academic) is then a sort of *reflexive fiction* – a simplifying (often narrative-based) construction and interpretation of the fictions guiding the behavior of others.

In addition to these constructive and reflexive forms of working fiction used by human beings in all societies, there is a third found in capitalist economies characterized by widespread policy and product innovation and the emergence of novel outcomes in complex systems. When dealing with indeterminate and uncertain futures, our everyday expectations are fictional in a more radical sense: it is not only that – epistemologically speaking – we are always deprived of unmediated access both to the world-as-it-really-is and to the contingent and socially performative interpretations of others; it is also that in an ontological sense there is no socio-economic future-as-it-really-*will*-be "out there" ahead of its creation by the interdependent decisions, choices, and innovations as yet unmade. Our *fictional expectations* can have no anchor in – or uniquely rational relation to – underlying future reality for the simple reason that the future does not yet exist.

There is a fourth and final working fiction relevant to economics: economists create models to represent the workings of the economy. As

Deirdre McCloskey argues, these models are fictions comparable to literary texts, and – as Mary Morgan points out – stories are central to their construction and use.[29] Game theory, for example, is heavily grounded in a story of the prisoners' dilemma that both structures the model and defines its relevance to analysis. Many models embed metaphors deep in their mathematical structure – those of standard economics drawing heavily on analogies from nineteenth-century physics and its structuring assumptions of a system-tendency to equilibrium.[30] General equilibrium theory, in particular, is a metaphorical system of great imaginative as well as mathematical power – where the economy as a whole is modelled as a closed system tending to a general equilibrium, thanks to complete futures markets and complete information. As Kurt Heinzelman argues, the economist is "a poet, a maker of fictions."[31] These fictions are hopefully useful as diagnostic tools for teasing out such systematic tendencies as do exist in economies, but they can also distort analysis as a result of the simplifying assumptions and misleading metaphors embedded within them. What is more, as Michael Power points out, the "fictional ideas" dreamt up in academic departments often end up constituting the "rationalities" and regulating the practices of financial markets. Fiction blends seamlessly into social reality – by structuring everyday beliefs, norms, and practices.[32]

Fictional Expectations and Narrative

The act of naming the expectations of economic actors "fictional" draws attention to their literary features and implies that lessons can be learned from literary theory about the nature and function of the imaginaries involved. In particular, fictional expectations generally adopt a narrative form that helps make sense of the world and generates the required conviction and social legitimacy for action.[33] Such narratives combine due-diligence assessments of known constraints and causal mechanisms with imaginaries of how the future might look that go well beyond observable facts. They may take the form of "new era" stories, promised fortunes, or dystopias that must be avoided. They may be influential in their own right or become embedded in the assumptions of algorithms or other calculative technologies. As Harro van Lente and Arie Rip demonstrate in empirical studies of innovation processes, narratives assign roles to economic actors and technological objects and develop a "plot" – a storyline of how an imagined future may unfold.[34] Such stories motivate by delineating an emotionally charged vision of the future. They provide a road map that helps counter anxiety in the face of uncertainty by simulating possible outcomes and making them feel tangible. In short, narratives provide a logic of action and populate the present with imagined futures that seem worth investing in. Aptly, David Tuckett speaks of "conviction narratives."[35]

One of the main reasons that fictional expectations adopt a narrative form is to ensure that an imagined future can be conveyed to others. In so doing, they ape literary texts by following social conventions of language and narrative structure but also by occasionally departing from these conventions in original and enlightening ways, thereby casting a new and unexpected light on current reality and economic possibilities. For example, the fictional expectations of economic actors may use surprising metaphors to illuminate novel possibilities or express abstract ideas, and they often experiment with different counterfactual images of reality. Whenever fictional expectations are promulgated to others, their originators – like the authors of literary texts – also rely on various rhetorical devices such as plot consistency and verisimilitude to render their imaginaries credible and secure the authority needed to convince their audience.

In a further parallel with the concerns of literary theory, there is often a significant gap between the meaning of an economic story intended by its author and that read into it by other actors. The fictions created by (and motivating) any one actor become – in the act of being told to others – open to reinterpretation according to what the literary theorist Jonathan Culler calls the "horizon of expectations" of the reader.[36] This essential process of reading and interpreting the narratives and expectations of others (the better to know how to act) is partly a creative act of imaginative empathy – and, as such, is itself a source of indeterminacy in the economy. Social and linguistic context play an important but not necessarily deterministic role in structuring interpretations.

The fictional expectations motivating *individual* behavior are, of course, themselves partially dependent on *social* narratives and the social context of institutions, networks, and power structures. The stories we tell and the expectations we have are influenced by key opinion formers, as well as the grand narratives and shared calculative devices that structure the field of expectations. The formation of expectations in the economy is – like the writing of literature – a combination of individual creative thinking and social construction. It is impossible to understand the expectations of particular economic actors or the credibility of their narratives without considering the conceptual and linguistic context in which they are formed, and without being alive to their resonance with the dominant social narratives and economic structures of the day. So, for example, the fictional expectations of most of those operating in derivative markets ahead of the financial crisis of 2007–2008 were inextricably bound up with what Michael Power has called the "grand narrative of risk management" and a series of related risk practices, models, and manuals that ensured a widespread and ultimately fatal confusion between radical uncertainty and forms of risk amenable to objective probabilities.[37] As Elena Esposito argues, these financial models were – like all fictions – "extremely controlled constructions"; but since they were not accurate representations of future reality, they ended up "reproducing" the very uncertainty they claimed to control.[38]

Performative Fictions and Power

Fictional expectations and the stories, mathematical models, and calculative devices embedded in them matter to economic outcomes (and to the discipline of economics) because they structure beliefs and help actors decide how to act *despite* the uncertainty they face. When widely shared, economic stories and models help coordinate the actions of multiple actors. Indeed, expectations can be said to have the sort of "performative" effects in markets that Donald MacKenzie noted in relation to the models derived from finance theory.[39] They tend to structure the future at least partially in their own image or – in the case of dystopias – in sharp reaction against the vision implied. And, since economic narratives and theories (like finance models) tend – if internalized by sufficient numbers – to influence outcomes, they inevitably become instruments of political or market power. The future is shaped by political battles to establish the dominance of particular narratives.

A straightforward economic example of these battles is the use by central banks of "forward guidance" to cajole expectations in the desired direction. As Douglas Holmes puts it, communication has become for central banks the "decisive means to achieve" the goals of policy; or, in the words of Ben Bernanke, the former chair of the US Federal Reserve, "monetary policy is 98 percent talk and only two percent action."[40] The direction of capitalist economies is increasingly the outcome of a struggle between different state and market actors to establish their narratives and visions of the future as the most credible.

One performative effect of economic narratives and models is more indirect than this simple notion of steering the expectations of others implies, namely that they influence how other actors frame evidence, construct data, and define their own interests. As Michel Foucault argued in his analysis of the relationship between knowledge and power, power depends on the "production of truth," and knowledge is partly a product of contingent power relations. Indeed, power – together with the discourses and related practices associated with it – "produces reality; it produces domains of objects and rituals of truth."[41]

Jenny Andersson gives a topical example of this point in an analysis of the Arctic as a political and economic realm. Rival claims over the region are partly established with the help of predictive technologies that, through a "highly selective *sorting* of available images of the future," seek to establish a dominant narrative about the future that suits particular interests. Yet crucially, since "future opportunities do not by definition yet exist," the interests that the different actors pursue are partly defined by a "repertoire of future-making," ranging from quantitative forecasts to "highly narrative genres of nation branding" and images of pristine wilderness or natural resources under threat.[42] Political and economic power belongs to those who make their narratives, imaginaries, and models count as those that will frame evidence, define interests, and structure behavior.

Narrative Economics and Analytical Imagination

Empirical evidence of the role played by narratives in structuring expectations and coordinating behavior – together with theoretical and psychological understanding of the importance of narratives in enabling people to make sense of their predicament and have the confidence to act *despite* uncertainty – has led to high-profile calls for the establishment of a new form of "narrative economics." For example, in his book, *Narrative Economics* (2019), the Nobel-Prize-winning economist, Robert Shiller, takes seriously the role of narratives in explaining key inflection points in the economy and examines the usefulness of epidemiological models in capturing the *contagion* dynamics underlying the diffusion of influential stories.[43] The ex-Governor of the Bank of England, Mervyn King, agrees that narratives "play a big part in decisions taken under conditions of radical uncertainty" and argues that sudden "narrative revisions" underlie many of the abrupt changes in perceptions of the future that cause market and political instability.[44]

If such narrative economics is to reach its full potential, though, its methods of research need to be improved by better analytical techniques for uncovering how economic narratives, models, and shared calculative devices are successfully transmitted between individuals and come to structure market expectations. For this, a prime source of insight is literature and literary theory – in conjunction with the methods of economic sociology, anthropology, political economy, economic history, and science and technology studies.

In particular, economists should engage in more *discourse analysis* – close reading of the contingent narratives and models structuring fictional expectations. This may involve deconstruction of the hidden ideologies, social power structures, rhetorical devices, and linguistic frames determining both the meaning and ease of transmission of narratives or models for the actors whose expectations they guide. As Charles Taylor and others have argued, social scientists can only fully explain patterns of behavior if they read and carefully interpret the significance and meanings that discourse and actions have for the actors concerned. Such a reading involves grasping the relevant nexus of culture, language, and practice – the "web of intersubjective meanings" – and entering into the actors' way of life "if only in imagination."[45] In the study of economic history, too, an investigation of the narratives and imaginaries that people have used and projected to give themselves and others the necessary conviction to act provides a fascinating lens to explain the course of historical events.[46]

Economic actors, economists, and economic historians alike must interpret a pre-interpreted world – in particular, the contingent ways in which various actors visualize and imagine uncertain futures. This puts a premium on what cofounder of the London School of Economics, Beatrice Webb, called *analytical imagination*: the ability to project yourself into the specific mindset of others and understand how they see the world. As F. R. Leavis pointed out, Webb believed that such analytical imagination – or intellectual sympathy with those different from ourselves – is best acquired by engaging in the study of literature, which can consequently be considered highly "relevant to the essential qualifications" of social scientists.[47]

Economists also need a firmer grasp of how far their own discipline is structured by fictions and language. For example, as McCloskey argues, economists should acknowledge the "metaphorical saturation of economic theories" and the extent to which metaphors (for example, those derived from physics or games) unconsciously structure and distort the assumptions made, while determining the mathematical logic of models and framing the way data is collected.[48] Such understanding of the role of metaphor may then allow for open-minded experimentation with different structuring metaphors and fictional assumptions to yield complementary insights and alternative perspectives on economic conditions and behavior.[49]

Finally, the prevalence of radical uncertainty in capitalist economies underscores the need for economic actors and the social scientists studying them to treat their expectations, interpretations, and explanations as provisional. In other words, they must learn to combine the conviction necessary for action or analysis with what the poet John Keats calls *"negative capability,"* the capacity to live with "uncertainties, mysteries, doubts, without any irritable reaching after fact and reason."[50] We can only hope to interpret events, spot emerging patterns, and create new solutions if we are imaginatively receptive to new pointers and flexible in the fictions we use to make sense of the world and construct a better future.

Notes

1 For the key distinction between economic behavior and the discipline of economics, and the relevance of literature and literary studies to understanding both these "object" and "meta" levels, see Richard Bronk, *The Romantic Economist: Imagination in Economics* (Cambridge: Cambridge University Press, 2009); and Doris Pichler, "The Inter- and Transdisciplinary Potential of Literary Studies: Law, Economics, & Literature – Reflections on a Possible Liaison," in *Literaturwissenschaft heute: Gegenstand, Positionen, Relevanz*, edited by Susanne Knaller and Doris Pichler (Goettingen: V&R Unipress, 2013), 232.

2 For a canonical expression of the "rational expectations hypothesis" central to standard economics, see John F. Muth, "Rational Expectations and the Theory of Price Movements," *Econometrica* 29.3 (1961), 315–335; and for the theory of "fictional expectations," see Jens Beckert, *Imagined Futures: Fictional Expectations and Capitalist Dynamics* (Cambridge, MA: Harvard University Press, 2016).

3 Robert Boyer, "Expectations, Narratives, and Socio-Economic Regimes," in *Uncertain Futures: Imaginaries, Narratives, and Calculation in the Economy*, edited by Jens Beckert and Richard Bronk (Oxford: Oxford University Press, 2018), 39–61; 41.

4 David Tuckett, *Minding the Markets: An Emotional Finance View of Financial Instability* (London: Palgrave Macmillan, 2011).

5 Douglas Holmes, *Economy of Words: Communicative Imperatives in Central Banks* (Chicago: University of Chicago Press, 2014).

6 See Colin Campbell, *The Romantic Ethic and the Spirit of Capitalism* (Oxford: Blackwell, 1987).

7 Frank H. Knight, *Risk, Uncertainty, and Profit* (Boston: Houghton Mifflin, 1921).

8 See W. Brian Arthur, *Complexity and the Economy* (New York: Oxford University Press, 2015).

9 See Karl Polanyi, *The Great Transformation: The Political and Economic Origins of Our Time* (Boston: Beacon Press, 1957).

10 James M. Buchanan and Viktor J. Vanberg, "The Market as Creative Process," *Economics and Philosophy* 7.2 (1991), 167–186.

11 Zygmunt Bauman, *Liquid Modernity*, 2nd ed. (Cambridge: Polity, 2012), viii; emphasis in original; David Tuckett, "Conviction Narrative Theory and Understanding Decision-Making in Economics and Finance," in *Uncertain Futures*, ed. Beckert and Bronk, 62–82; 74.

12 George Shackle, *Epistemics and Economics: A Critique of Economic Doctrines* (New Brunswick: Transaction, 1992), 8.

13 Joseph Schumpeter, *Capitalism, Socialism, and Democracy* (London: Routledge, 1992), 83–84; emphasis in original.

14 George Shackle, *Imagination and the Nature of Choice* (Edinburgh: Edinburgh University Press, 1979), 52–53.

15 To understand the nature and power of the human imagination, there is no better source than the writings of the Romantic poets and philosophers. The quotation here is from William Wordsworth, *The Prelude*, edited by E. de Selincourt (1805; Oxford: Oxford University Press, 1960), Book XIII, 231, ll. 98–99.

16 Bronk, *Romantic Economist*, 201.

17 William Hazlitt, *An Essay on the Principles of Human Action* (1805), reprinted in *The Selected Writings of William Hazlitt, Vol. 1*, edited by Duncan Wu (London: Pickering & Chatto, 1998).

18 John Stuart Mill, *Autobiography* (1873; London: Penguin 1989), 123.

19 Kenneth E. Boulding, *The Image: Knowledge in Life and Society* (Ann Arbor: University of Michigan Press, 1961).

20 See Richard Bronk and Wade Jacoby, "Uncertainty and the Dangers of Monocultures in Regulation, Analysis, and Practice," MPIfG Discussion Paper 16/6 (Cologne: Max Planck Institute for the Study of Societies, 2016).

21 Hazlitt, *Principles of Human Action*, 19, 21.

22 See Jens Beckert and Richard Bronk, "An Introduction to *Uncertain Futures*," in *Uncertain Futures*, ed. Beckert and Bronk, 1–37; 4, 10, 13–15.

23 See Martin Giraudeau, "Performing Physiocracy: Pierre Samuel du Pont de Nemours and the Limits of Political Engineering," *Journal of Cultural Economy* 3.2 (2010), 225–242; Valerie Hamilton and Martin Parker, *Daniel Defoe and the Bank of England: The Dark Arts of Projectors* (Winchester: Zero Books, 2016).

24 Martin Giraudeau, "Processing the Future: Venture Project Evaluation at American Research and Development Corporation (1946–73)," in *Uncertain Futures*, ed. Beckert and Bronk, 259–277; 275.

25 Hans Vaihinger, *The Philosophy of "As-If": A System of the Theoretical, Practical, and Religious Fictions of Mankind* (London: Routledge & Kegan Paul, 1924).

26 William Wordsworth, "Fragment," dated by E. de Selincourt to 1798–1800, reproduced in Bronk, *Romantic Economist*, 285.

27 Wordsworth, *Prelude*, Book II, 27, l. 273; and Samuel Taylor Coleridge, *Table Talk*, 21 September 1830, reprinted in *The Oxford Authors Samuel Taylor Coleridge*, edited by H. J. Jackson (Oxford: Oxford University Press, 1985), 596.

28 M. H. Abrams, *The Mirror and the Lamp: Romantic Theory and the Critical Tradition* (Oxford: Oxford University Press, 1953), 31.

29 Deirdre N. McCloskey, *The Rhetoric of Economics*, 2nd ed. (Madison: University of Wisconsin Press, 1998); Mary S. Morgan, "Models, Stories, and the Economic World," in *Fact and Fiction in Economics: Models, Realism and Social Construction*, edited by Uskali Mäki (Cambridge: Cambridge University Press, 2002), 178–201.

30 See Philip Mirowski, *More Heat than Light: Economics as Social Physics, Physics as Nature's Economics* (Cambridge: Cambridge University Press, 1989).

31 Kurt Heinzelman, *The Economics of the Imagination* (Amherst: University of Massachusetts Press, 1980), 50.

32 Michael Power, *Organized Uncertainty: Designing a World of Risk Management* (Oxford: Oxford University Press, 2007), 183–184.

33 See Beckert, *Imagined Futures*, 61–94.

34 Harro van Lente and Arie Rip, "Expectations in Technological Developments: An Example of Prospective Structures to Be Filled in by Agency," in *Getting New Technologies Together: Studies in Making Sociotechnical Order*, edited by Cornelis Disco and Barend van der Meulen (Berlin: de Gruyter, 1998), 203–229.

35 David Tuckett, "Conviction Narrative Theory."

36 Jonathan Culler, *Literary Theory: A Very Short Introduction* (Oxford: Oxford University Press, 1997), 64.

37 Power, *Organized Uncertainty*, viii.

38 Elena Esposito, "Predicted Uncertainty: Volatility Calculus and the Indeterminacy of the Future," in *Uncertain Futures*, ed. Beckert and Bronk, 219–235; 228, 233.

39 Donald MacKenzie, *An Engine, Not a Camera: How Financial Models Shape Markets* (Cambridge, MA: Massachusetts Institute of Technology Press, 2006).

40 Douglas R. Holmes, "A Tractable Future: Central Banks in Conversation with Their Publics," in *Uncertain Futures*, ed. Beckert and Bronk, 173–193; 178; Ben Bernanke, "Inaugurating a New Blog," Brookings Institute, March 30, 2015, www.brookings.edu/blog/ben-bernanke/2015/03/30/inaugurating-a-new-blog/.

41 Michel Foucault, *Power/Knowledge: Selected Interviews and Other Writings 1972–1977* (London: Harvester Press, 1980), 93; and *Discipline and Punish: The Birth of the Prison* (London: Allen Lane, 1977), 194.

42 Jenny Andersson, "Arctic Futures: Expectations, Interests, Claims, and the Making of Arctic Territory," in *Uncertain Futures*, ed. Beckert and Bronk, 83–103; 85–86; emphasis in original.

43 Robert J. Shiller, *Narrative Economics: How Stories Go Viral and Drive Major Economic Events* (Princeton, NJ: Princeton University Press, 2019).

44 Mervyn King, *The End of Alchemy: Money, Banking, and the Future of the Global Economy* (London: Abacus, 2017), 136, 332.

45 Charles Taylor, "Interpretation and the Sciences of Man," *Review of Metaphysics* 25.1 (1971), 3–51; reproduced in *Readings in the Philosophy of Social Sciences*, edited by Michael Martin and Lee C. McIntyre (Cambridge. MA: Massachusetts Institute of Technology Press, 1994), 181–211.

46 See Jonathan Levy, "Capital as Process and the History of Capitalism," *Business History Review* 91.3 (2017), 483–510.

47 Beatrice Webb, *My Apprenticeship* (1883), extracts quoted and discussed in F. R. Leavis, "Introduction," *Mill on Bentham and Coleridge* (London: Chatto & Windus, 1958), 24–26. See also the American pragmatist George Herbert Mead and his notion of "taking the role of the other": George Herbert Mead, *Mind, Self, and Society: From the Standpoint of a Social Behaviorist* (Chicago: University of Chicago Press, 1934).

48 McCloskey, *Rhetoric of Economics*, 40.

49 See Bronk, *Romantic Economist*, 4–5, 22–25, 273–276.

50 John Keats, "Letter to George and Tom Keats," December 21, 1817, extract reprinted in *Romanticism: An Anthology*, edited by Duncan Wu (Oxford: Blackwell, 1998), 1019.

Further Reading

GENERAL SOURCES

Akdere, Çınla and Christine Baron, eds., *Economics and Literature: A Comparative and Interdisciplinary Approach* (London: Routledge, 2017).

Balfour, Robert, ed., *Culture, Capital, and Representation* (Basingstoke: Palgrave Macmillan, 2010).

Crosthwaite, Paul, Peter Knight, and Nicky Marsh, "The Economic Humanities and the History of Financial Advice," *American Literary History,* 31.4 (2019), 661–686.

"Economic Criticism," *Year's Work in Critical and Cultural Theory* 23 (2015), 108–133; 24 (2016), 151–173; 25 (2017), 104–124; 26 (2018), 44–64.

Poovey, Mary, *Genres of the Credit Economy: Mediating Value in Eighteenth- and Nineteenth-Century Britain* (Chicago: University of Chicago Press, 2008).

Seybold, Matt and Michelle Chihara, eds., *The Routledge Companion to Literature and Economics* (New York: Routledge, 2019).

Shell, Marc, *The Economy of Literature* (Baltimore: Johns Hopkins University Press, 1978).

Money, Language, and Thought: Literary and Philosophic Economies from the Medieval to the Modern Era (Baltimore: John Hopkins University Press, 1982).

Vogl, Joseph, *The Specter of Capital,* translated by Joachim Redner and Robert Savage (2010; Stanford, CA: Stanford University Press, 2014).

Woodmansee, Martha and Mark Osteen, eds., *The New Economic Criticism: Studies at the Intersection of Literature and Economics* (London: Routledge, 1999).

CHAPTER 1

Abu-Lughod, Janet, *Before European Hegemony: The World System A. D. 1250–1350* (Oxford: Oxford University Press, 1989).

Bertolet, Craig E., (2013). *Chaucer, Gower, Hoccleve, and the Commercial Practices of Late Fourteenth-Century London* (Farnham: Ashgate, 2013).

"Tales of Two Transactions: The Franklin, the Shipman, Feudalism, and the Fourteenth-Century World System," in *Later Middle English Literature, Materiality, and Culture: Essays in Honor of James M. Dean,* edited by B.

Gastle and E. Keleman (Newark: University of Delaware Press, 2018), 167–188.

Bertolet, Craig E. and Robert Epstein, eds., *Money, Commerce, and Economics in Late Medieval English Literature* (New York: Palgrave Macmillan, 2018).

Bolton, J. L., *Money in the Medieval English Economy: 973–1489* (Manchester: Manchester University Press, 2012).

Campbell, Bruce M. S., *The Great Transition: Climate, Disease, and Society in the Late-Medieval World* (Cambridge: Cambridge University Press, 2016).

Dyer, Christopher, *An Age of Transition? Economy and Society in England in the Later Middle Ages* (Oxford: Oxford University Press, 2005).

Epstein, Robert, *Chaucer's Gifts: Exchange and Value in the Canterbury Tales* (Cardiff: University of Wales Press, 2018).

Faith, Rosamond, *The Moral Economy of the Countryside: Anglo-Saxon to Anglo-Norman England* (Cambridge: Cambridge University Press, 2020).

Newhauser, Richard, "Historicity and Complaint in Song of the Husbandman," in *Studies in the Harley Manuscript: The Scribes, Contents, and Social Contexts of British Library MS Harley 2253,* edited by Susanna Fein (Kalamazoo, MI: Medieval Institute Publications, 2000), 203–217.

Nightingale, Pamela, *A Medieval Mercantile Community: The Grocers' Company and the Politics and Trade of London, 1000–1485* (New Haven, CT: Yale University Press, 1995).

CHAPTER 2

Appleby, Joyce Oldham, *Economic Thought and Ideology in Seventeenth-Century England* (Princeton, NJ: Princeton University Press, 1978).

Bailey, Amanda, *Of Bondage: Debt, Property, and Personhood in Early Modern England* (Philadelphia: University of Pennsylvania Press, 2013).

Baker, David J., *On Demand: Writing for the Market in Early Modern England* (Stanford, CA: Stanford University Press, 2010).

Bates, Catherine, *On Not Defending Poetry: Defence and Indefensibility in Sidney's Defence of Poesy* (Oxford: Oxford University Press, 2017).

Correll, Barbara, "Terms of 'Indearment': Lyric and General Economy in Shakespeare and Donne," *ELH* 75.2 (2008), 241–262.

Forman, Valerie, *Tragicomic Redemptions: Global Economics and the Early Modern English Stage* (Philadelphia: University of Pennsylvania Press, 2011).

Halpern, Richard, *The Poetics of Primitive Accumulation: English Renaissance Culture and the Genealogy of Capital* (Ithaca: Cornell University Press, 1991).

Harris, Jonathan Gil, *Sick Economies: Drama, Mercantilism, and Disease in Shakespeare's England* (Philadelphia: University of Pennsylvania Press, 2004).

Hawkes, David, *The Culture of Usury in Renaissance England* (New York: Palgrave Macmillan, 2010).

Shakespeare and Economic Theory (London: Bloomsbury, 2015).

Korda, Natasha, *Shakespeare's Domestic Economies: Gender and Property in Early Modern England* (Philadelphia: University of Pennsylvania Press, 2002).

Leinwand, Theodore, *Theatre, Finance, and Society in Early Modern England* (Cambridge: Cambridge University Press, 1999).

Muldrew, Craig, *The Economy of Obligation: The Culture of Credit and Social Relations in Early Modern England* (New York: Palgrave, 1998).

Vilches, Elvira, *New World Gold: Cultural Anxiety and Monetary Disorder in Early Modern Spain* (Chicago: University of Chicago Press, 2010).

Wrightson, Keith, ed., *A Social History of England: 1500–1750* (Cambridge: Cambridge University Press, 2017).

CHAPTER 3

Batchelor, Jennie, *Women's Work: Labour, Gender, Authorship, 1750–1830* (Manchester: Manchester University Press, 2010).

Brantlinger, Patrick, *Fictions of State: Culture and Credit in Britain, 1684–1994* (Ithaca, NY: Cornell University Press, 1996).

Brown, Laura, *Fables of Modernity: Literature and Culture in the English Eighteenth Century* (Ithaca, NY: Cornell University Press, 2001).

Clery, E. J., *Eighteen Hundred and Eleven: Poetry, Protest, and Economic Crisis* (Cambridge: Cambridge University Press, 2017).

  The Rise of Supernatural Fiction (Cambridge: Cambridge University Press, 1995).

Copeland, Edward, *Women Writing about Money: Women's Fiction in England, 1790–1820* (Cambridge: Cambridge University Press, 1995).

Davis, Lennard J., *Factual Fictions: The Origins of the English Novel* (New York: Columbia University Press, 1983).

Grapard, Ulla, and Gillian Hewitson, eds., *Robinson Crusoe's Economic Man: A Construction and Deconstruction* (London: Routledge, 2011).

Ingrassia, Catherine, *Authorship, Commerce, and Gender in Early Eighteenth-Century England: A Culture of Paper Credit* (Cambridge: Cambridge University Press, 1998).

Lynch, Deidre, *The Economy of Character: Novels, Market Culture, and the Business of Inner Meaning* (Chicago: University of Chicago Press, 1998).

Nicholson, Colin, *Writing and the Rise of Finance: Capital Satires of the Early Eighteenth Century* (Cambridge: Cambridge University Press, 1994).

Novak, Maximillian E., *Economics and the Fiction of Daniel Defoe* (Berkeley, CA: University of California Press, 1962).

Rostek, Joanna, *Women's Economic Thought in the Romantic Age: Towards a Transdisciplinary Herstory of Economic Thought* (Abingdon: Routledge, 2021).

Sherman, Sandra, *Finance and Fictionality in the Early Eighteenth Century: Accounting for Defoe* (Cambridge: Cambridge University Press, 1996)

Thompson, James, *Models of Value: Eighteenth-Century Political Economy and the Novel* (Durham, NC: Duke University Press, 1996).

CHAPTER 4

Bigelow, Gordon, *Fiction, Famine, and the Rise of Economics in Victorian Britain and Ireland* (Cambridge: Cambridge University Press, 2003).

Brantlinger, Patrick, *Fictions of State: Culture and Credit in Britain, 1694–1994* (Ithaca, NY: Cornell University Press, 1996).

Comyn, Sarah, *Political Economy and the Novel: A Literary History of "Homo Economicus"* (Basingstoke: Palgrave Macmillan, 2018).

Finn, Margot C., *The Character of Credit: Personal Debt in English Culture, 1740–1914* (Cambridge: Cambridge University Press, 2003).

Gagnier, Regenia, *The Insatiability of Human Wants: Economics and Aesthetics in Market Society* (Chicago: University of Chicago Press, 2000).

Gallagher, Catherine, *The Body Economic: Life, Death, and Sensation in Political Economy and the Victorian Novel* (Princeton, NJ: Princeton University Press, 2006).

Houston, Gail Turley, *From Dickens to Dracula: Gothic, Economics, and Victorian Fiction* (Cambridge: Cambridge University Press, 2005).

Klaver, Claudia C., *A/Moral Economics: Classical Political Economy and Cultural Authority in Nineteenth-Century England* (Columbus, OH: Ohio State University Press, 2003).

Kornbluh, Anna, *Realizing Capital: Financial and Psychic Economies in Victorian Form* (New York: Fordham University Press, 2014).

Lysack, Krista, *Come Buy, Come Buy: Shopping and the Culture of Consumption in Victorian Women's Writing* (Athens, OH: Ohio University Press, 2008).

Poovey, Mary, *Genres of the Credit Economy: Mediating Value in Eighteenth- and Nineteenth-Century Britain* (Chicago: University of Chicago Press, 2008).

CHAPTER 5

Bataille, Georges, *The Accursed Share, Vol. 1: An Essay on General Economy.* London: Zone Books, 1991).

Bowlby, Rachel, *Just Looking: Consumer Culture in Dreiser, Gissing, and Zola* (London: Routledge, 1985).

Brantlinger, Patrick, *Fictions of State: Culture and Credit in Britain, 1694–1994* (Ithaca, NY: Cornell University Press, 1996).

Colesworthy, Rebecca, *Returning the Gift: Modernism and the Thought of Exchange* (Oxford: Oxford University Press, 2018).

Esty, Jed, *A Shrinking Island: Modernism and National Culture in England* (Princeton, NJ: Princeton University Press, 2003).

Huyssen, Andreas, *After the Great Divide: Modernism, Mass Culture, Postmodernism* (Bloomington, IN: Indiana University Press, 1986).

Karl, Alissa G. *Modernism and the Marketplace: Literary Culture and Consumer Capitalism in Rhys, Woolf, Stein, and Nella Larsen* (New York: Routledge, 2009).

Marsh, Alec. *Money and Modernity: Pound, Williams, and the Spirit of Jefferson* (Tuscaloosa, AL: University of Alabama Press, 1998).

Mauss, Marcel, *The Gift: The Form and Reason for Exchange in Archaic Societies,* translated by W. D. Halls (New York: W. W. Norton, 2000).

Michaels, Walter Benn, *The Gold Standard and the Logic of Naturalism: American Literature at the Turn of the Century* (Berkeley, CA: University of California Press, 1987).

Mini, Piero V., *Keynes, Bloomsbury, and* The General Theory (London: MacMillan, 1991).

Rainey, Lawrence, *Institutions of Modernism: Literary Elites and Public Culture* (New Haven, CT: Yale University Press, 1998).

Szalay, Michael, *New Deal Modernism: American Literature and the Invention of the Welfare State* (Durham, NC: Duke University Press, 2005).

Tratner, Michael, *Deficits and Desires: Economics and Sexuality in Twentieth-Century Literature* (Stanford, CA: Stanford University Press, 2010).

CHAPTER 6

Bambara, Toni Cade, *Deep Sightings and Rescue Missions,* edited by Toni Morrison (New York: Random House, 2008).

Bayor, Ronald H., *Race and the Shaping of Twentieth-Century Atlanta* (Chapel Hill, NC: University of North Carolina Press, 2000).

Bone, Martyn, "Capitalist Abstraction and the Body Politics of Place in Toni Cade Bambara's *Those Bones Are Not My Child,*" *Journal of American Studies* 37.2 (2003), 229–246.

Davis, Mike, "Urban Renaissance and the Spirit of Postmodernism," *New Left Review* 151.1 (1985), 106–113.

Dubey, Madhu, *Signs and Cities: Black Literary Postmodernism* (Chicago: University of Chicago Press, 2014).

Hanhardt, Christina B., *Safe Space: Gay Neighborhood History and the Politics of Violence* (Durham, NC: Duke University Press, 2013).

Jameson, Fredric, *Postmodernism, or, the Cultural Logic of Late Capitalism* (London: Verso, 2019).

Keating, Larry, *Atlanta: Race, Class, and Urban Expansion* (Philadelphia: Temple University Press, 2010).

Kruse, Kevin Michael, *White Flight: Atlanta and the Making of Modern Conservatism* (Princeton, NJ: Princeton University Press, 2007).

Limón, José Eduardo, *Dancing with the Devil: Society and Cultural Poetics in Mexican-American South Texas* (Madison: University of Wisconsin Press, 1994).

Melamed, Jodi, *Represent and Destroy: Rationalizing Violence in the New Racial Capitalism* (Minneapolis, MN: University of Minnesota Press, 2011).

Rutheiser, Charles, *Imagineering Atlanta: The Politics of Place in the City of Dreams* (London: Verso, 1996).

Smith, Neil, *The New Urban Frontier: Gentrification and the Revanchist City* (London: Routledge, 1996).

Taylor, Carole Anne, "Postmodern Disconnection and the Archive of Bones: Toni Cade Bambara's Last Work," *Novel* 35.2–3 (2002), 258–280.

CHAPTER 7

Amin, Samir, *Theory Is History* (New York: Springer, 2014).

Bhattacharyya, Gargi, *Rethinking Racial Capitalism: Questions of Reproduction and Survival* (London: Rowman and Littlefield, 2018).

Brouillette, Sarah, *Postcolonial Writers in the Global Literary Marketplace* (London: Palgrave Macmillan, 2007).

Chibber, Vivek, *Postcolonial Theory and the Specter of Capital* (London: Verso, 2013).

Huggan, Graham, *The Postcolonial Exotic: Marketing the Margins* (London: Routledge, 2001).

Mezzadra, Sandro, "How Many Histories of Labour? Toward a Theory of Postcolonial Capitalism," *Postcolonial Studies* 14.2 (2011), 151–170.

Naruse, Cheryl Narumi, Sunny Xiang, and Shashi Thandra, eds. "Literature and Postcolonial Capitalism," special issue of *ARIEL: A Review of International English Literature* 49.4 (2018).

Ong, Aihwa, *Neoliberalism as Exception: Mutations in Citizenship and Sovereignty* (Durham, NC: Duke University Press, 2006).

Sanyal, Kalyan, *Rethinking Capitalist Development: Primitive Accumulation, Governmentality, and Post-Colonial Capitalism* (London: Routledge, 2013).

Venn, Couze, *After Capital* (London: Sage, 2018).

CHAPTER 8

Appadurai, Arjun, *Banking on Words: The Failure of Language in the Age of Derivative Finance* (Chicago: University of Chicago Press, 2016).

Bahng, Aimee, *Migrant Futures: Decolonizing Speculation in Financial Times* (Durham, NC: Duke University Press, 2018).

Barrett, Lindon, *Blackness and Value: Seeing Double* (Cambridge: Cambridge University Press, 1999).

Clymer, Jeffory A., "Family Money: Race and Economic Rights in Antebellum US Law and Fiction," *American Literary History* 21.2 (2009), 211–238.

Fisher, Mark, *Capitalist Realism: Is There No Alternative?* (Winchester: Zero Books, 2009).

Germana, Michael, *Standards of Value: Money, Race, and Literature in America* (Iowa City, IA: University of Iowa Press, 2009).

Goux, Jean-Joseph, *Symbolic Economies: After Marx and Freud*, translated by Jennifer Curtiss Gage (Ithaca, NY: Cornell University Press, 1990).

Heinzelman, Kurt, *The Economics of the Imagination* (Amherst, MA: University of Massachusetts Press, 1980).

La Berge, Leigh Claire, *Scandals and Abstraction: Financial Fiction of the Long 1980s* (Oxford: Oxford University Press, 2015).

McClanahan, Annie, *Dead Pledges: Debt, Crisis, and Twenty-First-Century Culture* (Stanford, CA: Stanford University Press, 2017).

McCloskey, Deirdre N., *The Rhetoric of Economics* (Madison, WI: University of Wisconsin Press, 1985).

Shell, Marc, *Money, Language, and Thought: Literary and Philosophic Economies from the Medieval to the Modern Era* (Baltimore, MD: Johns Hopkins University Press, 1993).

Shonkwiler, Alison, *The Financial Imaginary: Economic Mystification and the Limits of Realist Fiction* (Minneapolis, MN: University of Minnesota Press, 2017).

Shonkwiler, Alison, and Leigh Claire La Berge, eds., *Reading Capitalist Realism* (Iowa City, IA: University of Iowa Press, 2014).

Woodmansee, Martha, and Mark Osteen, eds., *The New Economic Criticism: Studies at the Intersection of Literature and Economics* (London: Routledge, 1999).

CHAPTER 9

Clare, Ralph, *Fictions Inc.: The Corporation in Postmodern Fiction, Film, and Popular Culture* (New Brunswick, NJ: Rutgers University Press, 2014).

Hardack, Richard, "New and Improved: The Zero-Sum Game of Corporate Personhood," *Biography* 37.1 (2014), 36–68.

Jaros, Peter, "A Double Life: Personifying the Corporation from *Dartmouth College* to Poe," *Poe Studies* 47.1 (2014), 4–35.

Michaels, Walter Benn, *The Gold Standard and the Logic of Naturalism: American Literature at the Turn of the Century* (Berkeley, CA: University of California Press, 1987).

Mrozowski, Daniel J., "How to Kill a Corporation: Frank Norris's *The Octopus* and the Embodiment of American Business," *Studies in American Naturalism* 6.2 (2011), 161–184.

Mueller, Stefanie, "The Silence of the Soulless Corporation: Corporate Agency in James Fenimore Cooper's *The Bravo*," *Law & Literature* (2020), https://doi.org/10.1080/1535685X.2020.1754022.

O'Brien, John, *Literature Incorporated: The Cultural Unconscious of the Business Corporation, 1650–1850* (Chicago: University of Chicago Press, 2015).

Rajski, Brian. "Corporate Fictions: Cameron Hawley and the Institutions of Postwar Capitalism," *Textual Practice* 25.6 (2011), 1015–1031.

Siraganian, Lisa, *Modernism and the Meaning of Corporate Persons* (Oxford: Oxford University Press, 2020).

Thomas, Brook, *American Literary Realism and the Failed Promise of Contract* (Berkeley, CA: University of California Press, 1997).

CHAPTER 10

Alderson, David, *Sex, Needs, and Queer Culture: From Liberation to the Postgay* (London: Zed Books, 2016).

Barrett, Michèle, and Mary McIntosh, *The Anti-Social Family*, 2nd ed. (London: Verso, 1991).

Becker, Gary S., *A Treatise on the Family*, enlarged ed. (Cambridge, MA: Harvard University Press, 1991).

Claeys, Gregory, *Mill and Paternalism* (Cambridge: Cambridge University Press, 2013).

Cooper, Melinda, *Family Values: Between Neoliberalism and the New Social Conservatism* (New York: Zone Books, 2017).

Edelman, Lee, *No Future: Queer Theory and the Death Drive* (Durham, NC: Duke University Press, 2004).

Eribon, Didier, *Insult and the Making of the Gay Self,* translated by Michael Lucey (Durham, NC: Duke University Press, 2004).

  Returning to Reims, translated by Michael Lucey (Los Angeles, CA: Semiotext (e), 2013).

Greenberg, Jonathan, and Nathan Waddell, eds., *Brave New World: Contexts and Legacies* (London: Palgrave Macmillan, 2016).

Marcuse, Herbert, *Eros and Civilization: A Philosophical Investigation Into Freud* (Abingdon: Routledge, 1987).

  One-Dimensional Man: Studies in the Ideology of Advanced Industrial Society (London: Routledge, 2002).

Mitchell, Kaye, *Writing Shame: Gender, Contemporary Literature, and Negative Affect* (Edinburgh: Edinburgh University Press, 2021).

Piketty, Thomas, *Capital in the Twenty-First Century,* translated by Arthur Goldhammer (Cambridge, MA: Belknap Press of Harvard University Press, 2014).

Poster, Mark, *Critical Theory of the Family* (London: Pluto Press, 1978).

CHAPTER 11

Aubry, Timothy, *Reading as Therapy: What Contemporary Fiction Does for Middle-Class Americans* (Iowa City: University of Iowa Press, 2011).

Bourdieu, Pierre, *The Rules of Art: Genesis and Structure of the Literary Field,* translated by Susan Emanuel (Cambridge: Polity, 1996).

Brouillette, Sarah, *Literature and the Creative Economy* (Stanford: Stanford University Press, 2014).

Brown, Nicholas, *Autonomy: The Social Ontology of Art under Capitalism* (Durham, NC: Duke University Press, 2019).

Crosthwaite, Paul, *The Market Logics of Contemporary Fiction* (Cambridge: Cambridge University Press, 2019).

Davies, William, *The Limits of Neoliberalism: Authority, Sovereignty, and the Logic of Competition* (London: Sage, 2014).

Huang, Betsy, *Contesting Genres in Contemporary Asian American Literature* (New York: Palgrave Macmillan, 2010).

Jacques, Juliet, "Forms of Resistance: Uses of Memoir, Theory, and Fiction in Trans Life Writing," *Life Writing* 14.3 (2017), 357–370.

Konstantinou, Lee, and Dan Sinykin, eds., "Publishing American Literature, 1945–2020," special issue of *American Literary History* 33.2 (2021).

Mirowski, Philip, *Never Let a Serious Crisis Go to Waste: How Neoliberalism Survived the Financial Meltdown* (London: Verso, 2013).

Rosen, Jeremy, *Minor Characters Have Their Day: Genre and the Contemporary Literary Marketplace* (New York: Columbia University Press, 2016).

Sinykin, Dan N., "The Conglomerate Era: Publishing, Authorship, and Literary Form, 1965–2007," *Contemporary Literature* 58.4 (2017), 462–491.

So, Richard Jean, *Redlining Culture: A Data History of Racial Inequality and Postwar Fiction* (New York: Columbia University Press, 2020).

Thompson, John B., *Merchants of Culture: The Publishing Business in the Twenty-First Century*, 2nd ed. (Cambridge: Polity, 2012).

Young, John K., *Black Writers, White Publishers: Marketplace Politics in Twentieth-Century African American Literature* (Jackson, MI: University Press of Mississippi, 2006).

CHAPTER 12

Chase-Dunn, Christopher, *Global Formation: Structures of the World-Economy* (London: Basil Blackwell, 1989).

Dunaway, Wilma A., "The Double Register of History: Situating the Forgotten Woman and Her Household in Capitalist Commodity Chains," *Journal of World-Systems Research* 7 (2001), 2–29.

Goldfrank, Walter L., "Paradigm Regained? The Rules of Wallerstein's World-System Method," *Journal of World-Systems Research* 6 (2000), 150–195.

Shannon, Thomas R., *An Introduction to the World-System Perspective* (Boulder, CO: Westview Press, 1992).

Shapiro, Stephen, and Philip Barnard, *Pentecostal Modernism: Lovecraft, Los Angeles, and World-Systems Culture* (London: Bloomsbury, 2017).

Wallerstein, Immanuel, *The Modern World-System IV: Centrist Liberalism Triumphant, 1789–1914* (Berkeley, CA: University of California Press, 2011)
The Capitalist World-Economy (Cambridge: Cambridge University Press, 1979).
Historical Capitalism (London: Verso, 1983).
The Politics of the World-Economy: The States, the Movements, and the Civilizations (Cambridge: Cambridge University Press, 1984).
Geopolitics and Geoculture: Essays on the Changing World-System (Cambridge: Cambridge University Press, 1991).
After Liberalism (New York: The New Press, 1995).

Wallerstein, Immanuel, and Terence K. Hopkins, *World-Systems Analysis: Theory and Methodology* (Beverly Hills, CA: Sage, 1982).

WReC (Warwick Research Collective), *Combined and Uneven Development: Towards a New Theory of World-Literature* (Liverpool: Liverpool University Press, 2015).

CHAPTER 13

Arendt, Hannah, *The Human Condition*, 2nd ed. (Chicago: University of Chicago Press, 1998).
Brouillette, Sarah, *Literature and the Creative Economy* (Stanford: Stanford University Press, 2014).
Clare, Ralph, *Fictions Inc.: The Corporation in Postmodern Fiction, Film, and Popular Culture* (New Brunswick, NJ: Rutgers University Press, 2014).
Connell, Liam, *Precarious Labour and the Contemporary Novel* (London: Palgrave Macmillan, 2017).
Elliott, Jane, *The Microeconomic Mode: Political Subjectivity in Contemporary Popular Aesthetics* (New York: Columbia University Press, 2018).
Federici, Silvia, *Revolution at Point Zero: Housework, Reproduction, and Feminist Struggle* (Oakland, CA: PM Press, 2012).
Lukács, Georg, "Realism in the Balance," in *Aesthetics and Politics,* edited by Ronald Taylor (1977; London: Verso, 1980), 28–59.
McClanahan, Annie, *Dead Pledges: Debt, Crisis, and Twenty-First-Century Culture* (Stanford, CA: Stanford University Press, 2017).
Shaw, Katy, *Crunch Lit* (London: Bloomsbury, 2015).
Weeks, Kathi, *The Problem with Work: Feminism, Marxism, Antiwork Politics, and Postwork Imaginaries* (Durham, NC: Duke University Press, 2011).

CHAPTER 14

Bookchin, Murray, *Post-Scarcity Anarchism* (Montreal: Black Rose Books, 1986).
Davies, William, ed., *Economic Science Fictions* (London: Goldsmiths Press, 2018).
Fisher, Mark, *Capitalist Realism: Is There No Alternative?* (Winchester: Zero Books, 2009).
Gibson-Graham, J. K., *A Postcapitalist Politics* (Minneapolis, MN: University of Minnesota Press, 2006).
Hicks, Heather J., *The Culture of Soft Work: Labor, Gender, and Race in Postmodern American Narrative* (New York: Palgrave Macmillan, 2009).
Jameson, Fredric, *Archaeologies of the Future: The Desire Called Utopia and Other Science Fictions* (London: Verso, 2007).
Levitas, Ruth, *The Concept of Utopia* (Syracuse, NY: Syracuse University Press, 1991).
Moylan, Tom, *Demand the Impossible: Science Fiction and the Utopian Imagination* (New York: Methuen, 1986).
Roemer, Kenneth M., *The Obsolete Necessity: America in Utopian Writings, 1888–1900* (Kent, OH: Kent State University Press, 1976).

Seo, Young Chu, *Do Metaphors Dream of Literal Sleep? A Science-Fictional Theory of Representation* (Cambridge, MA: Harvard University Press, 2011).

CHAPTER 15

Cohen, Joshua, ed., *Economics After Neoliberalism, Boston Review* 44.3 (2019), http://bostonreview.net/forum/suresh-naidu-dani-rodrik-gabriel-zucman-economics-after-neoliberalism.

Comyn, Sarah, *Political Economy and the Novel: A Literary History of "Homo Economicus"* (Basingstoke: Palgrave Macmillan, 2018).

Foucault, Michel, *The Birth of Biopolitics,* edited by Michel Senellart, translated by Graham Burchell (New York: Palgrave Macmillan, 2008).

Jameson, Fredric, "Future City," *New Left Review* 21.3 (2003), 65–79.

"An American Utopia," in *An American Utopia: Dual Power and the Universal Army,* edited by Slavoj Žižek (London: Verso, 2016), 1–96.

Keynes, John Maynard, "Economic Possibilities For Our Grandchildren," in *Essays in Persuasion* (London: Macmillan St. Martin's Press, 1973), 321–332.

The General Theory of Employment, Interest, and Money (London: Macmillan St. Martin's Press, 1973).

Klein, Julie Thompson, *Interdisciplinarity: History, Theory, and Practice (Detroit*: Wayne State University Press, 1990), 30–32.

Humanities, Culture, and Interdisciplinarity: The Changing American Academy (Albany, NY: SUNY Press, 2005).

Mann, Geoff, *In The Long Run We Are All Dead: Keynesianism, Political Economy, and Revolution* (London: Verso, 2017).

Mirowski, Philip, Robert Van Horn, and Thomas A. Stapleford, eds., *Building Chicago Economics: New Perspectives on the History of America's Most Powerful Economics Program* (Cambridge: Cambridge University Press, 2011).

Seybold, Matt, "Keynes and Keynesianism," *in The Routledge Companion to Literature and Economics,* edited by Matt Seybold and Michelle Chihara (New York: Routledge, 2018), 272–282.

"The End of Economics," *Los Angeles Review of Books*, July 3 2017, https://lareviewofbooks.org/article/the-end-of-economics/.

Sinykin, Dan, *American Literature and the Long Downturn: Neoliberal Apocalypse* (Oxford: Oxford University Press, 2020).

Slobodian, Quinn, *Globalists: The End of Empire and the Birth of Neoliberalism* (Cambridge, MA: Harvard University Press, 2018).

CHAPTER 16

Bakhtin, Mikhail, *Problems of Dostoevsky's Poetics,* translated by Caryl Emerson (Minneapolis: University of Minnesota Press, 1984).

Ellis, John M., *Literature Lost: Social Agendas and the Corruption of the Humanities* (New Haven, CT: Yale University Press, 1997).

Farrell, John, *Freud's Paranoid Quest: Psychoanalysis and Modern Suspicion* (New York: New York University Press, 1996).

Haidt, Jonathan, *The Righteous Mind: Why Good People Are Divided by Politics and Religion* (New York: Pantheon, 2012).

Malinowski, Bronislaw, *Argonauts of the Western Pacific: An Account of Native Enterprise and Adventure in the Archipelagoes of Melanesian New Guinea* (New York: Dutton, 1961).

Morson, Gary Saul, and Morton Schapiro, *Cents and Sensibility: What Economics Can Learn from the Humanities* (Princeton, NJ: Princeton University Press, 2017).

Minds Wide Shut: How the New Fundamentalisms Divide Us (Princeton, NJ: Princeton University Press, 2021).

Shiller, Robert, *Narrative Economics: How Stories Go Viral and Drive Major Economic Events* (Princeton, NJ: Princeton University Press, 2019).

Smith, Adam, *The Theory of Moral Sentiments*, edited by D. D. Raphael and A .L. Macfie (Indianapolis, IN: Liberty, 1982).

Thaler, Richard, *Misbehaving: The Making of Behavioral Economics* (New York: Norton, 2015).

CHAPTER 17

Beckert, Jens, *Imagined Futures: Fictional Expectations and Capitalist Dynamics* (Cambridge, MA: Harvard University Press, 2016).

Beckert, Jens, and Richard Bronk, eds., *Uncertain Futures: Imaginaries, Narratives, and Calculation in the Economy* (Oxford: Oxford University Press, 2018).

Bronk, Richard, *The Romantic Economist: Imagination in Economics* (Cambridge: Cambridge University Press, 2009).

Buchanan, James M., and Viktor J. Vanberg, "The Market as Creative Process," *Economics and Philosophy* 7.2 (1991), 167–186.

Holmes, Douglas, *Economy of Words: Communicative Imperatives in Central Banks* (Chicago: University of Chicago Press, 2014).

Jasanoff, Sheila, and Sang-Hyun Kim, *Dreamscapes of Modernity: Sociotechnical Imaginaries and the Fabrication of Power* (Chicago: University of Chicago Press, 2015).

King, Mervyn, *The End of Alchemy: Money, Banking, and the Future of the Global Economy* (London: Abacus, 2017).

Knight, Frank H., *Risk, Uncertainty, and Profit* (Boston: Houghton Mifflin, 1921).

Mackenzie, Donald, *An Engine, Not a Camera: How Financial Models Shape Markets* (Cambridge, MA: MIT Press, 2006).

McCloskey, Deirdre N., *The Rhetoric of Economics*, 2nd ed. (Madison, WI: University of Wisconsin Press, 1998).

Morgan, Mary S., *The World in a Model: How Economists Work and Think* (Cambridge: Cambridge University Press, 2012).

Shackle, George, *Epistemics and Economics: A Critique of Economic Doctrines* (New Brunswick: Transaction, 1992).

Shiller, Robert J., *Narrative Economics: How Stories Go Viral and Drive Major Economic Events* (Princeton, NJ: Princeton University Press, 2019).

Sugden, Robert, "Credible Worlds: The Status of Theoretical Models in Economics," *Journal of Economic Methodology* 7.1 (2000), 1–31.

Tuckett, David, *Minding the Markets: An Emotional Finance View of Financial Instability* (London: Palgrave Macmillan, 2011).

Index

Cambridge Companions To ...

AUTHORS

For EU product safety concerns, contact us at Calle de José Abascal, 56–1°, 28003 Madrid, Spain or eugpsr@cambridge.org.

www.ingramcontent.com/pod-product-compliance
Ingram Content Group UK Ltd.
Pitfield, Milton Keynes, MK11 3LW, UK
UKHW042149130625
459647UK00011B/1249

* 9 7 8 1 0 0 9 0 1 2 9 9 7 *